Advance Praise for *Catch Up*

'For far too long, the world economic history has been told almost exclusively from the point of view of the rich countries. Nayyar's book tells it from 'the other side', tracing the fall and then the rise of Asia, particularly China and India, and other developing countries over centuries. It is an essential reading for anyone who wants to get a balanced understanding of the history of the world economy. The book's narrative is literary and engaging, accessible to everyone, but its content is based on rigorous analyses. Its attention to detail is meticulous. Yet, it offers a breath-taking historical sweep. A masterpiece.'

HA-JOON CHANG, University of Cambridge, author of *Kicking Away the Ladder* and *23 Things They Don't Tell You About Capitalism*

'This book is a brilliant overview of the role of the developing countries in the world economy as it has evolved over the centuries, focusing first on the Great Divergence and Great Specialization from about 1820 to 1950, and then in much greater detail on the period from 1950 to the present. Nayyar skillfully blends a fascinating narrative of the "Catch Up" process with sharp analytical interpretation and incisive policy critiques to provide a unique assessment of this momentous process in global history and its possible future trajectory. It will be a major reference for both general readers interested in development and globalization as well as specialists in international trade, economic development and economic history, who will all appreciate the wider context into which this book will place their individual research.'

RONALD FINDLAY, Professor of Economics, Columbia University, New York

'Deepak Nayyar's ambitious and exciting book spans global economic developments over the last two centuries. He shows how the Great Divergence between North and South, resulting from the nineteenth century industrial revolution, was gradually reversed from 1950 as developing country growth rates accelerated. Although the catch-up is uneven across countries and between people, this perceptive and forward looking book offers the alluring prospect of a multi-polar world in the twenty-first century, with power and economic wealth far more evenly distributed across the globe.'

FRANCES STEWART, Emeritus Professor of Development Economics, University of Oxford

'Almost unnoticed, we are in the midst of a Great Transformation—from a world in which a disproportionate part of global income accrued to Europe, the US, and a few other countries dotted around the world, to one in which billions of those in the rest are "catching up": to a large extent, a restoration of the world as it was in 1820, when Asia had more than 50 per cent of the world's GDP, before the industrial revolution and colonialism created the imbalanced world that we have come to take for granted. Nayyar analyzes lucidly the ongoing change and discusses forcefully the prospects for this great transformation, how it will be brought about, and what it will imply for the world order which will emerge.'

JOSEPH STIGLITZ, University Professor, Columbia University, New York, and Nobel Laureate in Economics

'Deepak Nayyar's succinct and insightful analysis of development experience in the world economy ranges over wide swathes of time and space. Developing countries fell well behind the now industrialized world from the early 19th century until halfway through the 20th. Thereafter, a vanguard began to catch up. Nayyar discusses the reasons why in terms of international engagement, industrialization, and distribution. The key question for the 21st century is whether the rest of the developing world will follow the vanguard, or fall back? The book closes with an acute analysis of the possibilities for truly inclusive growth.'

LANCE TAYLOR, Arnhold Professor Emeritus, New School for Social Research, New York

'Beginning on a historical note, this book considers the world economy on the cusp of colonialism. The pre-eminence of Asia was then replaced by the advance of the West, often ascribed to its colonization of Asia, Africa, and Latin America. The core of the book addresses the question of whether and how the developing world will catch up with the West, which makes a significant contribution to our understanding of the process. Deepak Nayyar's strikingly lucid, lively, and insightful discussion of this question will stimulate thinking not only among economists and historians but also among other social scientists and concerned general readers.'

ROMILA THAPAR, Professor Emeritus, Jawaharlal Nehru University, New Delhi

Catch Up

Developing Countries in the World Economy

Deepak Nayyar

OXFORD
UNIVERSITY PRESS

OXFORD

UNIVERSITY PRESS

Great Clarendon Street, Oxford, OX2 6DP,
United Kingdom

Oxford University Press is a department of the University of Oxford.
It furthers the University's objective of excellence in research, scholarship,
and education by publishing worldwide. Oxford is a registered trade mark of
Oxford University Press in the UK and in certain other countries

© Deepak Nayyar 2013

The moral rights of the author have been asserted

First Edition published in 2013
Impression: 1

Published in the United States of America by Oxford University Press
198 Madison Avenue, New York, NY 10016, United States of America

British Library Cataloguing in Publication Data
Data available

Library of Congress Control Number: 2013942023

ISBN 978–0–19–965298–3

Printed in and bound by
CPI Group (UK) Ltd, Croydon, CR0 4YY

For Rohini

Contents

Contents

Preface

The object of this book is to analyse the evolution, situated in a long-term historical perspective, of developing countries in the world economy from the onset of the second millennium, but with a focus on the second half of the 20th and the first decade of the 21st centuries. It is perhaps among the first to address this theme on such a wide spectrum that spans both time and space. This book is about the big picture that is sketched with bold strokes on a wide canvas. And it is not about joining the little dots. It outlines an untold story about the overwhelming significance until the late eighteenth century of the countries and continents now described as the developing world, followed by their economic decline during the period from 1820 to 1950. It analyses the extent, nature, and distribution of catch up, in terms of output, income, industrialization, and trade, driven by rapid economic growth in the developing world since 1950, which gathered further momentum in the three decades from 1980 to 2010. This unfolding story about the developing world is important as it is beginning to change the balance of power in the world economy and it could reshape the future.

The endeavour began life on a modest note when I delivered the WIDER Annual Lecture at Helsinki in February 2009, which led me to reflect further on this theme and think about the unanswered questions. The idea of writing a book on the subject surfaced some time later. And the intersection of economics with history seemed an exciting prospect. Yet it seemed an ambitious, if not daunting, task to write a book that spanned centuries in time and continents in space and to engage with so many contemporary debates in economics about development. Even so, I decided to take the plunge two years ago. The research turned out to be a journey in exploration and discovery. This book is the outcome.

Such academic pursuits are always associated with an accumulation of intellectual debts to professional colleagues. For perceptive questions, helpful comments, and constructive suggestions, I am deeply indebted to Ha-Joon Chang and Lance Taylor who read the entire manuscript from beginning to end as it was being written. For engaging questions and valuable comments, I am similarly indebted to Romila Thapar, who found the time and made the effort to read the whole manuscript. José Antonio Ocampo read most of the chapters to provide incisive comments and helpful suggestions. Duncan Foley, Padmanabha Gopinath, Rolph van der Hoeven, and Will Milberg read one or more chapters that were of interest to them, to provide helpful comments.

There were many who helped me in the research process. Ananya Ghosh-Dastidar assisted with the work on historical statistics. She also read several chapters and made useful suggestions. Mariangela Parra at the United Nations in New York and Shyam Upadhyaya at UNIDO in Vienna helped in my search for information. I would specially like to thank my research assistant over the past two years, Jessica Singer, who was conscientious, meticulous, and efficient. In the earlier stages of work, Jonas Shaende, my teaching assistant at the time, provided valuable research assistance. Nicole Hunt at the United Nations in New York was most helpful in assistance with UN statistical databases.

For constructive criticisms and valuable suggestions at the earlier stages of my work, I would like to thank Amit Bhaduri, Ronald Findlay, and Joseph Stiglitz. I would also like to thank the late Alice Amsden and the late Angus Maddison, who did some pioneering work in this domain, for perceptive comments and engaging conversations. Some parts of the work in progress were the basis of public lectures at the New School for Social Research, New York, and at the Celso Furtado International Congress in Rio de Janeiro, where listeners came up with stimulating questions. I also recall comments from researchers and students at several seminar presentations at universities in many countries.

This book is the product of research in the academic sense of the word. But it is not written as a conventional academic monograph for specialists. It is accessible to a much wider readership. I am convinced that economics is, and should be, comprehensible to concerned readers who have an interest in the subject. Economics may be difficult, but it is not occult. However, matters are sometimes made worse by the jargon of economists that mystifies non-specialist readers. But it is possible to explain complex things in a simple manner. It is perhaps even more important to avoid setting out simple things in a complex manner! In writing this book I have attempted to simplify, to explain, and reach out to the reader. It should be of interest to economists irrespective of their specialization. I also sincerely hope that it would interest scholars across disciplines in the social sciences, just as I hope that it might engage the policy practitioner and the concerned citizen.

In the quest to be reader-friendly, there are no copious footnotes about nuances or esoteric academic debates and even the endnotes are few, while references are noted in parentheses in the text. The tables and graphs, often relating to long periods of time, are based on research from many primary sources. But the citation at the bottom of tables or graphs is short and simple. For research scholars, the details on statistical sources and notes on the compilation methods are set out in an Appendix. In the text, there is an occasional overload of information or a blizzard of numbers because the facts are important and are not widely known. Readers could, if they wish, be selective about statistics. But the text is self-sufficient. And it is possible to read the book without studying the tables. The graphs, however, are worthy of attention for they sketch a picture or tell a story.

Much of the research and writing for this book was done over the past two years at the New School for Social Research, New York, and some of the work was done while I was at Jawaharlal Nehru University, New Delhi. I would like to thank my colleagues in the Department of Economics at both places for providing me with an intellectual home. I would also like to thank Allen House in New York for providing me with the comfort of a home away from home, as I carved out the solitude to write the book in the hustle and bustle of Manhattan.

The enormous support from my family throughout was invaluable. I recall many conversations with my elder son, Dhiraj, a reputed journalist, about how to connect with readers who have an interest in, but are intimidated by, economics. My younger son, Gaurav, a promising economist, read the entire manuscript as it was being written, to ask perceptive questions and make valuable suggestions. My wife, Rohini, provided the moral and intellectual support. She has been a sounding board for ideas. She has been a patient listener. She has been a perceptive reader. She has been sagacious in advice. And she has been an incredible source of strength in the hours of frustration and moments of despair that are an integral part of the lives of authors. This book, which she wanted me to write, is dedicated to her.

Deepak Nayyar

New York
November 2012

List of Figures

List of Tables

List of Tables

Prologue

1

An Untold Story

The world has changed. Sixty years ago, *c*.1950, soon after the end of the Second World War and at the beginning of the post-colonial era, there were two sharp divides in the world: the East-West divide between communist and capitalist countries and the North-South divide between rich and poor countries. The distinction between East and West vanished with the collapse of communism in the USSR and Eastern Europe in 1990, as capitalism emerged triumphant. The world of competing political ideologies was replaced by a world with a single dominant political ideology. The distinction between the North and the South has also become more diffused with the passage of time, as the reality has changed during the past three decades. The financial crisis of late 2008, which led to the Great Recession, turned out to be the deepest crisis in capitalism since the Great Depression more than 75 years ago. The recovery is fragile and the prospects are uncertain. This has eroded the triumph of capitalism. But it has also reinforced the shift in the balance of economic power somewhat more towards the South. This process began some time ago but is now more discernible. Even so, perceptions have changed slowly. There are oversimplified pictures of one billion people in rich countries and six billion people in poor countries, although there are poor people in rich countries and rich people in poor countries. It is time for a dispassionate analysis of how much this reality has changed.

At the outset, it is important to recognize that the term used to describe countries in Asia, Africa and Latin America changed often in a relatively short span of time. In the beginning, it was 'poor' or 'underdeveloped' countries. During the Cold War, when there was a sharp divide between East and West, it was the 'Third World'. Later, it was 'less developed' countries. For a while now, it has been 'developing countries'. These descriptions have kept changing, either with fashions of the time in usage or with perceptions about what is politically correct, but the different descriptions continue to be used in an interchangeable manner. It needs to be said that the term used throughout this book is 'developing countries', or 'the developing world'; made up of Africa, Asia excluding Japan, and Latin America including the Caribbean.

The object of this book is to analyse the evolution of developing countries in the world economy situated in a long-term historical perspective, from the onset of the second millennium, but with a focus on the second half of the twentieth century and the first decade of the twenty-first century. It is perhaps among the first to address this theme on such a wide canvas that spans both time and space. It poses and endeavours to answer some unexplored or neglected questions.

The first set of questions is about the distant past. Does the distinction between rich and poor countries go back a long time? If not, when did the countries or continents now described as the developing world, begin their decline and fall? What was their significance in the world economy, in terms of shares of world population and world output, a thousand years ago, five hundred years ago, or two hundred years ago? How did they compare with other parts of the world in levels of per capita income through the second millennium? What was their share of manufacturing output in the world economy two centuries earlier and how did it change during the colonial era? Did their interaction with the world economy since the mid-19th century, through international trade and international migration, exercise any influence on the nature of their participation in the division of labour between countries?

The second set of questions is about the more recent past, the period from 1950 to 2010, which is also the primary focus of the book. To what extent did the rapid economic growth in developing countries since 1950, which gathered further momentum in 1980, lead to a recovery in their share of world output? Did the divergence in their per capita incomes, relative to the rest of the world, come to an end and did convergence begin? How did the growth in their national income and per capita income compare with that in industrialized countries? Were there any significant changes in the degree or nature of their engagement with the world economy through international trade, international investment, and international migration? What was the extent of catch up in industrialization?

The third set of questions is also about the recent past, since 1950, which disaggregate the whole into its parts. How was the catch up, in terms of aggregate output, per capita income and industrial production, distributed among the three constituent regions of the developing world? And was this distribution uneven or unequal between countries within regions? What were the differences between the leaders and the laggards in industrialization? Did the process of catch up reduce inequalities between countries and among people in the world? Did it lead to convergence or divergence between countries in the developing world? Was rapid economic growth associated with a decrease or an increase in poverty and inequality within countries?

There is another question that arises from the three sets of questions. Is there something to learn from this experience of the past six decades, and from the earlier past, about the future of developing countries in the world economy?

The structure of the book is simple. Following this prologue, which serves as an introduction, it is divided into two parts. The first part sets the stage before the play begins. It outlines a mostly untold story about the overwhelming significance in the world economy of three continents, Asia, Africa, and South America, until the middle of the second millennium, followed by three centuries that witnessed the beginnings of change, to focus on their falling behind during the period from 1820 to 1950. The second part is the primary objective and the essential focus of the book. It analyses the extent and nature of the catch up on the part of developing countries in the world economy during the period from 1950 to 2010. In doing so, it considers the changes in their share of aggregate output, level of per capita income, engagement with the world economy, and catching up in industrialization, to highlight the uneven distribution of this process between regions and within countries in the developing world. The contours of change that emerge from this analysis are also a largely untold story.

The first part is made up of two chapters. Chapter 2 provides the narrative. It traces the share of these three continents in world population and world income through the second millennium to highlight the dramatic transformation of the world economy that began around 1820 to create an enormous divide between rich and poor countries by 1950. It also considers the outcome of this process, over a short span of 130 years, for Asia, Africa, and Latin America, reflected in the divergence in per capita incomes, the collapse in manufacturing production and the unequal terms of engagement with the world economy. Chapter 3 provides the analysis. It considers the developments in Europe starting c.1500 that shaped the evolution of the world economy over the next three centuries, compares the economies of Europe and Asia in the mid-18th century, discusses why the Industrial Revolution occurred in Britain rather than elsewhere in Europe or Asia, and examines the consequences of this occurrence for Europe, Asia and the world economy. The separation of the narrative from the analysis, it is hoped, would make it easier for the reader to follow the essential contours of the story through a maze of facts and the complexity of the underlying factors through a simplified analysis.

The second part begins with Chapter 4, an overview, which analyses changes in developing countries' share of world income and their levels of per capita income, compared with industrialized countries, during the six decades from 1950 to 2010, with a disaggregated analysis for Asia, Africa, and Latin America, to highlight the underlying differences in growth rates of GDP and GDP per capita between country-groups and regions. In the light of this experience, it also discusses the hypotheses about convergence in unconventional economic history and orthodox economic theory, to provide a critical evaluation.

Chapter 5 considers the engagement of developing countries with the world economy since 1950, to make comparisons with the past. It examines the participation of developing countries in world trade to trace the contours of change, draws a distinction between trade in goods and services, and highlights the significant differences between regions. It discusses international investment, in different forms, to focus on the relative importance of developing countries and asymmetries between their constituent regions. It analyses international migration to underline the significance of developing countries and stress its implications for the world economy.

Chapter 6 explores whether developing countries met with success in their quest for industrialization during the period 1950–2010, disaggregated by regions wherever possible. It considers structural changes in the composition of output and employment. It examines changes in developing countries' share of world manufacturing production. It discusses how these changes shaped trade patterns for developing countries including their share in world exports of manufactures. It seeks to focus on industrialization with reference to openness and intervention, which are critical issues in the debate about policies and strategies, to analyse the underlying factors.

Chapter 7 extends the analysis beyond regions to consider how this catch up in industrialization was distributed among countries in the developing world. It shows that there was a high degree of concentration in just fourteen countries, which are described in this book as the 'Next-14', and examines the enormous diversity within this small group. It analyses the common factors underlying success at industrialization in these few countries and the differences that set them apart from other countries in the developing world, to highlight the lessons that can be drawn from the experience of countries that have led the process of catch up so far, for the next set of latecomers that might follow.

Chapter 8 is about emerging divergences that are discernible in the world economy. It analyses international inequality in terms of the wide gap between rich and poor countries and the unequal income distribution between rich and poor people in the world. It considers the exclusion of countries, in particular the least developed countries, and regions within countries, to highlight divergences that are beginning to surface within the developing world. It asks whether rapid economic growth, underlying the catch up in terms of aggregate income, improved the well-being of ordinary people, focusing on poverty and inequality within countries.

The epilogue, Chapter 9, concludes. It outlines the contours of change experienced by developing countries in the world economy, situated in historical perspective, which provide answers to the questions posed at the start of this prologue, to recapitulate the essentials of an untold story. It considers prospects, in terms of possibilities and constraints, for countries that have led this process of catch up during the six decades from 1950 to 2010 and for countries that might follow in their footsteps. It also contemplates the future of developing countries in the world economy, which is obviously uncertain and unpredictable, to speculate how this catch up might reshape, or be influenced by, the international context.

Part One
Falling Behind

2

The Great Divergence
and The Great Specialization

The division of the world into industrialized and developing countries is more recent than is widely believed. It does not go back far in time. This chapter seeks to focus on the emergence of developing countries in the world economy. In doing so, it considers the changes in the economic importance of Asia, Africa, and Latin America (now described as the developing world), as compared with Western Europe, Eastern Europe, North America, Japan, and Oceania (now described as the industrialized world), in the world economy, situated in a long-term historical perspective. The focus of this chapter is on the narrative, to outline an untold story. The analysis of the underlying factors follows in the next chapter. The structure of the discussion is as follows. Section 1 examines the shares of these two groups of countries in world population and world income. Section 2 compares levels of per capita income between country groups and their constituent regions in the world economy, to trace the emergence of differences over time. Section 3 sets out the changes in the shares of these two country groups in industrial production or manufacturing output in the world economy. Section 4 traces the engagement of Asia, Africa, and Latin America with the world economy, through international trade, international investment and international migration, but with a focus on the period since the late 19th century.

1. Shares in Population and Income of the World

Changes in the significance of countries or regions in the world economy, over time, are reflected in changes in their shares of world population and world income. However, if the period under consideration spans centuries, this is easier said than done. The reason is simple. Population censuses and national income accounts began life in most countries during the 20th century. In fact, systematic time series data are available for most countries beginning 1950 or even later, although such data are available for rich countries beginning 1900 or even earlier. But there are studies by Angus Maddison (1995, 2001, 2003, and 2007) that provide estimates of long-term changes in world population and world income for selected benchmark years. For a cross-country comparison of GDP levels and aggregate estimates of regional and world totals, it is necessary to convert national currencies into a common unit, or a numeraire, which reflects differences in purchasing power across countries over time. International comparisons of income, based on Purchasing Power Parity (PPP), which are often binary and relate to shorter time periods, are associated with methodological problems. These limitations are discussed in Chapter 4, which considers the period from 1950 to 2010, to present trends in income not only in PPP terms but also at market exchange rates. However, the latter is simply not an option for the historical analysis in this chapter because there were no national income accounts in most countries of the world until the 20th century. The Maddison estimates of GDP are in 1990 international (Geary-Khamis) dollars, in PPP terms, which are used to evaluate output. These calculations are based on a specific method of defining international prices so as to facilitate cross-country comparisons over time.[1] It needs to be said that the Maddison estimates of population and income are subject to criticism in the academic literature on economic history (Clark, 2009). Even so, this is about the only comprehensive source of historical statistics. Hence it is widely used. In the analysis, it is important to recognize its limitations and use other sources wherever possible to provide confirmation.

In a long-term historical perspective, beginning with the onset of the second millennium, it is worth making a distinction between three periods. From 1000 to 1500, the significance of Asia, Africa, and South America (it was not Latin then), taken together, in the world economy was overwhelming. From 1500 to 1820, beginnings of change were discernible. From 1820 to 1950, the significance of these three continents experienced a decline. It is also worth noting that in the period before the 19th century, divides in the world were defined primarily by geography, whereas in the period since the 19th century, divides in the world came to be defined largely by economics.

Table 2.1, based on the Maddison estimates, presents evidence on the distribution of population and income in the world economy for selected years from 1000 to 1820. The first group is made up of Asia, Africa, and South America, while the second group is made up of Western Europe, Western Offshoots (United States, Canada, Australia, and New Zealand), Eastern Europe, the former USSR, and Japan. For 1000, 1500, 1600 and 1700, the statistics on population and income in these regions are based on estimates for twenty major countries with residual estimates for other countries in each of the regions. For 1820, the figures are based on estimates for a larger number

Table 2.1. Distribution of Population and Income in the World Economy: 1000–1820
(in percentages)

World Population					
	1000	1500	1600	1700	1820
Group I					
Asia *of which*	65.5	61.2	64.7	62.1	65.2
China	22.1	23.5	28.8	22.9	36.6
India	28.1	25.1	24.3	27.3	20.1
Africa	12.1	10.6	9.9	10.1	7.1
South America	4.3	4.0	1.5	2.0	2.1
Group Total	*81.8*	*75.8*	*76.2*	*74.2*	*74.4*
Group II					
Western Europe	9.6	13.1	13.3	13.5	12.8
Western Offshoots	0.7	0.6	0.4	0.3	1.1
Eastern Europe	2.4	3.1	3.0	3.1	3.5
Former USSR	2.7	3.9	3.7	4.4	5.3
Japan	2.8	3.5	3.3	4.5	3.0
Group Total	*18.2*	*24.2*	*23.8*	*25.8*	*25.6*
TOTAL	100	100	100	100	100
World GDP					
	1000	1500	1600	1700	1820
Group I					
Asia *of which*	68.2	61.9	62.6	57.7	56.5
China	22.7	24.9	29.0	22.3	33.0
India	27.8	24.4	22.4	24.5	16.1
Africa	11.3	7.8	7.0	6.9	4.5
South America	3.8	2.9	1.1	1.7	2.2
Group Total	*83.3*	*72.6*	*70.8*	*66.4*	*63.1*
Group II					
Western Europe	9.0	17.8	19.8	21.8	22.9
Western Offshoots	0.6	0.5	0.3	0.2	1.9
Eastern Europe	2.1	2.7	2.8	3.1	3.6
Former USSR	2.3	3.4	3.4	4.4	5.4
Japan	2.6	3.1	2.9	4.1	3.0
Group Total	*16.7*	*27.4*	*29.2*	*33.6*	*36.9*
TOTAL	100	100	100	100	100

Source: Author's calculations from Maddison Online Database, see Appendix.

of countries. Obviously, these estimates, which are put together from a wide range of sources, are indicative numbers rather than precise statistics. Even so, the figures do highlight the relative importance of different regions and outline the broad contours of change in the world economy.

Overwhelming Significance: 1000 to 1500

The proportions are striking. In the year 1000, Asia, Africa, and South America, taken together, accounted for 82 per cent of world population and 83 per cent of world income. In fact, this overwhelming importance of Asia, Africa, and

13

South America continued in the second millennium for some time to come. Even 500 years ago, in 1500, they accounted for about 75 per cent of both world population and world income. This dominant share in world population and world income was attributable in large part to Asia, which was in turn attributable to just two countries, India and China. During the period 1000 to 1500, India and China, taken together, accounted for around 50 per cent of world population and 50 per cent of world income. It is just as clear that Western Europe, Western Offshoots, Eastern Europe, the former USSR, and Japan, even taken together, were far less important in the world economy. Their share in world population increased from less than one-fifth in 1000 to about one-fourth in 1500. Over the same period, their share in world income rose from one-sixth in 1000 to more than one-fourth in 1500, which represented an increase of 10 percentage points. Of this increase, almost 9 percentage points was attributable to Western Europe. This was at the expense of Africa (almost 4 percentage points) and Asia (6 percentage points) but there was no change in the share of China and India taken together. It would seem that the first half of the second millennium witnessed signs of change in the economic significance of Western Europe.

Beginnings of Change: 1500–1820

This change became clearer over the next three centuries. Between 1500 and 1820, the share of Asia, Africa, and Latin America in world population remained unchanged at three-fourths but their share in world income declined from 73 per cent to 63 per cent. Over the same period, the share of Western Europe, Western Offshoots, Eastern Europe, the former USSR, and Japan, taken together, in world income increased from 27.4 per cent to 36.9 per cent, although their share in world population remained in the range of one-fourth. The increased income share was attributable to Western Europe (5 percentage points), Eastern Europe with former USSR (3 percentage points), and Western Offshoots (1.5 percentage points). This was mostly at the expense of Africa (3.3 per cent) and Asia (5.4 per cent), but there was no change in the share of China and India taken together. In this context, it must be recognized that, until the end of the eighteenth century, distinctions between countries or regions were more geographical or political rather than economic. The clear division of the world into industrialized and developing economies, or rich and poor countries, came later.

Decline and fall: 1820 to 1950

It is somewhat difficult to find a turning point in time for this division of the world economy. The process began around 1820, its outcome was discernible by 1870, and it continued until 1950. Table 2.2 presents evidence on the share of two sets of countries and regions in world population and world GDP for selected benchmark years from 1820 to 1950. The first set, described as 'The West', is made up of Western Europe, Western Offshoots, Eastern Europe, the former USSR, and Japan. The second set, described as 'The Rest', is made up of Asia, Africa, and Latin America. The Maddison data on GDP from which this table is derived are, once again, in 1990 international (Geary-Khamis) dollars, in PPP, which facilitates inter-country comparisons over time. It needs to be said that these estimates starting 1820 are far more robust, in terms of their statistical foundations, than the corresponding estimates for the earlier years. Even so, Tables 2.1 and 2.2 are roughly comparable. Group I in Table 2.1 corresponds to 'The Rest' in Table 2.2, while Group II in Table 2.1 corresponds to 'The West' in Table 2.2.

Table 2.2. Shares of the West and the Rest in World Population and World GDP: 1820–1950

(in percentages)

World Population						
	1820	1870	1900	1913	1940	1950
THE WEST	*25.6*	*32.2*	*35.8*	*36.8*	*35.2*	*33.0*
Western Europe	12.8	14.7	14.9	14.6	12.8	12.1
Western Offshoots	1.1	3.6	5.5	6.2	6.7	7.0
Eastern Europe	3.5	4.2	4.5	4.4	4.1	3.5
Former USSR	5.3	7.0	8.0	8.7	8.5	7.1
Japan	3.0	2.7	2.8	2.9	3.2	3.3
THE REST	*74.4*	*67.8*	*64.2*	*63.2*	*64.8*	*67.0*
Asia *of which*	65.2	57.6	53.0	51.7	50.7	51.5
China	36.6	28.1	25.6	24.4	22.6	21.6
India	20.1	19.8	18.2	16.9	16.8	14.2
Africa	7.1	7.1	7.0	7.0	8.4	9.0
Latin America	2.1	3.2	4.1	4.5	5.7	6.5

World GDP						
	1820	1870	1900	1913	1940	1950
THE WEST	*36.9*	*57.4*	*67.4*	*70.4*	*71.0*	*72.9*
Western Europe	22.9	33.0	34.2	33.0	29.7	26.2
Western Offshoots	1.9	10.0	17.6	21.3	23.2	30.7
Eastern Europe	3.6	4.5	5.2	4.9	4.1	3.5
Former USSR	5.4	7.5	7.8	8.5	9.3	9.6
Japan	3.0	2.3	2.6	2.6	4.7	3.0
THE REST	*63.1*	*42.6*	*32.6*	*29.6*	*29.0*	*27.1*
Asia *of which*	56.5	36.1	25.6	22.3	19.9	15.6
China	33.0	17.1	11.1	8.8	6.4	4.6
India	16.1	12.2	8.6	7.5	5.9	4.2
Africa	4.5	4.1	3.4	2.9	3.5	3.8
Latin America	2.2	2.5	3.6	4.4	5.6	7.8

Source: Author's calculations from Maddison Online Database, see Appendix.

There was a dramatic change in the situation during the 19th century and the first half of the 20th. Between 1820 and 1950, the share of 'The West' in world population rose from one-fourth to one-third, while their share in world income almost doubled from 37 per cent to 73 per cent. Over the same period, from 1820 to 1950, the share of 'The Rest' in world population declined from three-fourths to two-thirds, but their share in world income witnessed a much more pronounced decline from 63 per cent to 27 per cent. This transformation of the world economy occurred in just 130 years, a short span of time in history. But a new international economic order was clearly discernible at the end of the first fifty years. By 1870, the share of 'The West' in world population had already increased to one-third while that of 'The Rest' had already decreased to two-thirds. And, by 1870, the share of 'The West' in world income had risen to 57 per cent while that of 'The Rest' had fallen to 43 per cent. For the world economy, the significance of 1870 is clear. The international division of labour had changed. The beginning of a divide between what are now described as industrialized countries and developing countries in the world economy was visible.

These dramatic changes in shares of world income are broadly consistent with evidence from other sources. Bairoch (1981 and 1983) estimates GNP in selected benchmark years from 1750 to 1950 for two country-groups in the world economy: Asia, Africa, and Latin America; and Europe, North America, and Japan. These estimates are in 1960 US dollars and prices, in PPP terms, adjusted for differences in the purchasing power of currencies. The share of Asia, Africa, and Latin America in world GNP was 69.1 per cent in 1830 and 57.4 per cent in 1860 (somewhat higher than the Maddison estimates of 63.1 per cent in 1820 and 42.6 per cent in 1870). This share dropped sharply to 38.3 per cent in 1900 and 33.5 per cent in 1913 (closer to the Maddison estimates of 32.6 per cent in 1900 and 29.6 per cent in 1913). It was 30.2 per cent in 1928 and 27.5 per cent in 1950 (almost the same as the Maddison estimates of 29 per cent in 1940 and 27.1 per cent in 1950).

It would seem that the Bairoch estimates of these shares in world income are higher than the corresponding Maddison estimates, particularly during the 19th century. But the decline of 'The Rest' and the rise of 'The West' are just as clear. It is no surprise that, between 1820 and 1950, there was a sharp increase in the asymmetries between the two sets of countries in world population and world income. These asymmetries are clearly illustrated in Figure 2.1.

It may, however, be misleading to consider 'The Rest' as an aggregate. Some disaggregation is necessary because there were significant differences between the three constituent regions. This is visible from the evidence in Table 2.2. The increase in the asymmetry was particularly pronounced in Asia. Between 1820 and 1950, its share in world population diminished from 65 per cent to 52 per cent but its share in world income dropped from 57 per cent to 16 per cent.

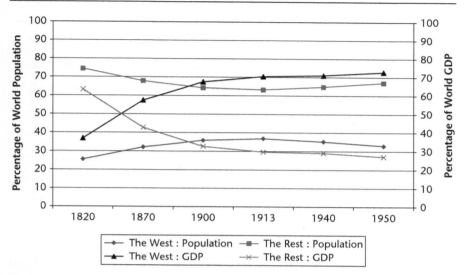

Figure 2.1. Asymmetrical Trends in Changing Shares of World Population and World GDP: 'The West' and 'The Rest': 1820–1950
Source: Table 2.2.

Much of this was attributable to the decline and fall of China and India. Taken together, between 1820 and 1950, their share in world population dropped from 57 per cent to 36 per cent, while their share in world income plummeted from 49 per cent to 9 per cent. This reflected and shaped the asymmetry for 'The Rest' as a group. For Africa, the shares in world population and world income were relatively stable, although the latter was consistently lower. For Latin America, the shares in world population and world income were symmetrical throughout the period from 1820 to 1950. What is more, both proportions rose significantly during the period under consideration. And, in 1950, Latin America's share in world income was higher than in world population. These asymmetrical trends for Asia and symmetrical trends for Latin America, as also Africa, emerge even more clearly from Figure 2.2. It is clear that Latin America was the exception among 'The Rest'. There was a slight increase, rather than a decline, in Latin America's share of world GDP from 1820 to 1870. The period thereafter witnessed the rise of Latin America as its share in world GDP more than trebled from 2.5 per cent in 1870 to 7.8 per cent in 1950. Indeed, it would seem that Latin America was the success story among 'The Rest' during the period from 1870 to 1950. In sharp contrast, Asia was the disaster. The economic decline of Asia, which began in 1820, continued apace thereafter as its share in world GDP dropped by more than half from 36 per cent in 1870 to 16 per cent in 1950. Of course, much of this decline was attributable to China and India.

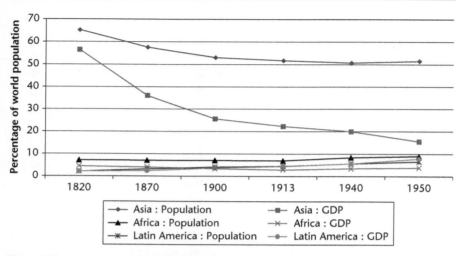

Figure 2.2. Asymmetries and Symmetries in Shares of World Population and World GDP: Asia, Africa and Latin America: 1820–1950
Source: Table 2.2.

Similarly, it may be misleading to consider 'The West' as an aggregate. To start with, the asymmetry was pronounced for Western Europe. Between 1820 and 1870, its share in world population increased just a little from 13 per cent to 15 per cent, while its share in world GDP rose from 23 per cent to 33 per cent. These shares stayed around the same levels until 1913 but declined thereafter. However, the asymmetry was far more pronounced for the Western Offshoots, particularly after 1870. Their share in world population was about 4 per cent in 1870 and 7 per cent in 1950, while their share in world GDP was 10 per cent in 1870 and 31 per cent in 1950. This was attributable to Western Offshoots, primarily the United States, that surpassed Western Europe and the United Kingdom by 1914. It would seem that the rise of 'The West' was about Western Europe until 1870 and about the United States after 1870. Eastern Europe, former USSR and Japan were not quite part of this story, but constitute an intermediate group, which is included in 'The West' because it was not part of 'The Rest'. Even so, for Eastern Europe and former USSR, shares in world population and world GDP were roughly symmetrical during the period from 1820 to 1950, and both shares registered an increase for the former USSR. For Japan, the shares were symmetrical and stable throughout. Following the Meiji Restoration in 1868, it was the exception in Asia. This was reflected in its economic and political rise during the first half of the 20th century. It was clearly not a part of 'The Rest'.

2. Incomes per Capita: Levels and Divergence

It is most difficult to compare levels of income per capita across countries and regions in the world economy at the start and middle of the second millennium because estimates of population and income are at best rough approximations. Even so, it is worth considering the Maddison estimates of GDP per capita, in 1990 international (Geary-Khamis) dollars, for the years 1000, 1500, 1600, 1700, and 1820, which are presented in Table 2.3. The country-groups and regions are the same as in Table 2.1. This evidence shows that a thousand years ago, levels of income per capita were about the same across the world and not significantly different even 500 years ago. It is no surprise then, that shares in world population and world income were roughly symmetrical for regions and country-groups. But this situation changed in the centuries that followed. The ratio of income per capita in Group I countries (Asia, Africa, and Latin America) to income per capita in Group II countries (Western Europe, Western Offshoots, Eastern Europe, former USSR, and Japan) was 1.10 in 1000, 0.84 in 1500, 0.76 in 1600, 0.69 in 1700, and 0.59 in 1820. Of course, the comparison often made is that between Western Europe and Asia. The Maddison statistics show that the ratio of income per capita in Asia as compared to Western Europe was 1.11 in 1000, 0.74 in 1500, 0.65 in 1600, 0.58 in 1700, and 0.47 in 1820.

Table 2.3. Levels of GDP per capita in the World Economy: 1000–1820
(in 1990 international Geary-Khamis dollars)

	Group I				
	1000	1500	1600	1700	1820
Asia *of which*	472	572	576	572	577
China	466	600	600	600	600
India	450	550	550	550	533
Africa	425	414	422	421	420
South America	400	416	438	527	691
Group Average	461	542	553	550	565

	Group II				
	1000	1500	1600	1700	1820
Western Europe	427	771	888	993	1234
Western Offshoots	400	400	400	476	1194
Eastern Europe	400	496	548	606	1202
Former USSR	400	499	552	610	688
Japan	425	500	520	570	669
Group Average	418	643	732	802	959
WORLD AVERAGE	453	566	596	615	666

Source: Author's calculations from Maddison Online Database, see Appendix.

This proposition is a subject of debate in the literature on the subject. There are two contesting views. Landes (1969) argues that Western Europe was already rich in comparison with other parts of the world even before the Industrial Revolution, which was attributable to centuries of slow accumulation, the appropriation of resources outside Europe and substantial technological progress. Kuznets (1971) endorsed this conclusion, indirectly, by suggesting that per capita product levels in less developed parts of the world in 1965 were much lower than in Western Europe before industrialization. Such analysis is the basis of the view that, c.1750, income per capita in Western Europe was roughly twice that in Asia. In contrast, Bairoch (1981) shows that, in 1750, the average standard of living, as measured by GNP per capita, in the now industrialized countries was slightly lower than that in countries he describes as the Third World. Maddison (1983) studied these contrasting perspectives to conclude that the evidence supported Landes more than Bairoch, although there are contradictory elements in the evidence. The Maddison figures in Table 2.3 are consistent with his conclusion.

It is almost impossible to resolve this debate one way or another, because, given the gap in per capita income between industrialized countries and developing countries in 1965, the conclusion depends almost entirely on the adjustment factor used for the level of per capita income in developing countries at market exchange rates for a PPP comparison with per capita income in industrialized countries, c.1965, and the assumption made about the growth in per capita income in Asia, Africa, and Latin America over the period from 1750 to 1965. Different adjustment factors and different assumptions about growth rates can produce very different results. There is, however, research beyond statistics on income per capita. It suggests that in the mid-18th century levels of development in Europe and Asia were broadly similar and not vastly different (Pomeranz, 2000 and Parthasarathi, 2011). However, it was not long before the Industrial Revolution in Britain, which spread to Europe, led to a dramatic transformation.

During the period from 1820 to 1950, changes in the shares of 'The West' and 'The Rest' in world population and world income were not only far-reaching but also characterized by sharp asymmetries. These asymmetries were most pronounced for Asia among 'The Rest' and for Western Europe and Western Offshoots among 'The West'. Therefore, Table 2.4 compares GDP per capita in Western Europe and Western Offshoots, taken together, with GDP per capita in other regions or countries of the world. It reveals an enormous divergence, which has been described as the 'Great Divergence'. Between 1820 and 1950, as a percentage of GDP per capita in Western Europe and Western Offshoots, GDP per capita in Latin America dropped from three-fifths to two-fifths, in Africa from one-third to one-seventh and in Asia from one-half to one-tenth. What happened in Asia reflected the collapse of its two

Table 2.4. Divergence in GDP per capita between Western Europe-Western Offshoots and Rest of the World: 1820–1950

	GDP per capita ratios					
	1820	1870	1900	1913	1940	1950
Western Europe and Western Offshoots	*100*	*100*	*100*	*100*	*100*	*100*
Eastern Europe	57.2	45.8	45.1	42.5	36.9	33.6
Former USSR	57.6	46.1	38.8	37.3	40.2	45.2
Japan	56.0	36.1	37.0	34.8	53.9	30.5
Asia[a] *of which*	48.3	26.6	19.1	16.5	14.4	10.1
China	50.2	25.9	17.1	13.8	10.5[b]	7.1
India	44.6	26.1	18.8	16.9	12.9	9.8
Africa	35.1	24.5	18.8	16.0	15.2	14.1
Latin America	57.8	33.1	34.9	37.5	36.2	39.9

[a] Asia excludes Japan but includes China and India; [b] For China, this figure relates to 1938.

Source: Author's calculations from Maddison Online Database, see Appendix.

giant economies, as the same proportions dropped from 50 per cent to 7 per cent in China and from 45 per cent to 10 per cent in India. Clearly, the divergence was modest in Latin America, massive in Asia and somewhere in the middle for Africa. It is worth noting that this divergence was not confined to what is now described as the developing world. Over the same period, from 1820 to 1950, the corresponding proportion dropped from 58 per cent to 45 per cent in former USSR, from 57 per cent to 34 per cent in Eastern Europe and from 56 per cent to 31 per cent in Japan. It would seem that, in a short span of 130 years, Western Europe and Western Offshoots (primarily the United States) shot ahead leaving the rest of the world behind. The Great Divergence from Asia is widely recognized, but there was also a substantial divergence from other regions, and a little divergence within Europe as its northwest pulled away from its south and east (Bairoch and Kozul-Wright, 1996 and Williamson, 1996).

There are significant differences between the Maddison estimates and the Bairoch estimates of per capita income in terms of levels. Yet both suggest that there was a sharp divergence. Bairoch (1981) estimates GNP per capita in 1960 US dollars and prices, PPP adjusted, in selected benchmark years from 1750 to 1950 for two country groups in the world economy. These estimates show that per capita income in Asia, Africa and Latin America as a proportion of that in Europe, North America and Japan was 95 per cent in 1800 and 77 per cent in 1830. But this proportion dropped sharply thereafter to 54 per cent in 1860, 32 per cent in 1900, 29 per cent in 1913, 25 per cent in 1928, 24 per cent in 1938 and 18 per cent in 1950. It must be said that these proportions are not comparable with the proportions in Table 2.4, not only because the levels of per capita income differ but also because the country-groups are different.[2] Even so, the two sets of estimates reveal a striking divergence in per capita incomes between the West and the rest of the world during the period from the early 19th century to the mid-20th.

It is no surprise that this divergence is mirrored in differences between regions of the world economy in growth rates of income per capita over time. Table 2.5 presents evidence on growth rates in GDP and GDP per capita for the periods 1820–1870, 1870–1913 and 1913–1950. These growth rates are based on the Maddison estimates of GDP and GDP per capita, in 1990 international (Geary-Khamis) dollars, for the specified regions, country groups or countries, in the selected benchmark years. The divergence in incomes per capita that emerged over time is clearly reflected in growth rates of GDP per capita. For Western Europe, these were in the range of 0.8–1.4 per cent per annum and for Western Offshoots in the range of 1.4–1.8 per cent per annum, which were modest by contemporary standards. It is just that these growth

Table 2.5. Growth Rates in the World Economy by Regions: 1820–1950 (percent per annum)

	GDP		
	1820–1870	1870–1913	1913–1950
THE WEST			
Western Europe	1.68	2.12	1.19
Western Offshoots	4.31	3.92	2.83
Eastern Europe	1.41	2.33	0.86
Former USSR	1.61	2.40	2.15
Japan	0.41	2.44	2.21
THE REST			
Asia *of which*	0.04	0.98	0.84
China	−0.37	0.56	0.04
India	0.38	0.97	0.23
Africa	0.75	1.32	2.56
Latin America	1.22	3.52	3.39
	GDP per capita		
	1820–1870	1870–1913	1913–1950
THE WEST			
Western Europe	0.99	1.34	0.76
Western Offshoots	1.41	1.81	1.56
Eastern Europe	0.63	1.39	0.60
Former USSR	0.63	1.06	1.76
Japan	0.19	1.48	0.88
THE REST			
Asia *of which*	−0.11	0.43	−0.08
China	−0.25	0.10	−0.56
India	0.00	0.54	−0.22
Africa	0.35	0.57	0.90
Latin America	−0.04	1.86	1.41

Source: Author's calculations from Maddison Online Database, see Appendix.

rates were significantly lower elsewhere during the period 1820–1870. However, during the periods 1870–1913 and 1913–1950, GDP per capita growth rates were higher in Latin America, comparable in the former USSR and Japan, only slightly lower in Eastern Europe, and distinctly lower in Africa. It was Asia that was the disaster story with GDP per capita growth rates that were negative over long periods, 1820–1870 as also 1913–1950, and barely positive at less than 0.5 per cent per annum during 1870–1913 which was a period of prosperity for the world economy when these growth rates were much higher almost everywhere. China and India fared even worse. It was the power of compound growth rates over a span of 130 years that led to the striking divergence in incomes per capita.

It is a matter of arithmetic that differences in growth rates of GDP per capita were shaped by differences in growth rates of GDP and population, which, in turn, also determined changes in the shares of regions or countries in world GDP and world population. Even so, it is worth noting that the differences in GDP growth rates between 'The West' and 'The Rest', set out in Table 2.5, underlie the changing shares of these country-groups in world GDP over time.

For Western Europe, its GDP growth rate compared with others accounts for the increase in its share of world GDP during 1820–1870, the stability in its share during 1870–1913, and a decrease in its share during 1913–1950. For the Western Offshoots, much higher GDP growth rates than elsewhere in the world account for the continuous increase in their share of world GDP throughout the period 1820–1950. Eastern Europe and the former USSR managed to retain their share in world GDP from 1870 to 1950 on account of GDP growth rates that were broadly comparable with others and conformed to the world average. Japan also managed to retain, and for a period increase, its share of world GDP because its GDP growth rates were comparable with or higher than growth rates elsewhere.

In parallel, the dramatic decline in the share of Asia in world income from 1820 to 1950 was attributable to its much slower GDP growth as compared with every other part of the world. This problem was even more acute for China and India. In contrast, the rise in the share of Latin America in world income from 1870 to 1950 was attributable to its fast GDP growth rates that matched the Western Offshoots and were higher than in Western Europe. The share of Africa in world GDP was maintained during 1820–1870, dipped in 1870–1913, and recovered during 1913–1950, on account of its respectable GDP growth in the first and third periods. In this limited sense, growth performance accounts for, even though it cannot explain, the past.

It needs to be said that per capita income is simply an arithmetic mean, often used as a proxy for average living standards, so that it does not measure the well-being of people. Social indicators such as life expectancy and literacy rates or demographic indicators such as birth, death or infant mortality rates, are thus helpful complements. However, there is little in terms of historical statistics on such indicators. But available evidence on life expectancy does provide some confirmation on the narrative so far. In 1000, life expectation at birth was 24 years, about the same everywhere in the world (Maddison, 2001). In 1750, life expectancy and birth rates were both similar in Western Europe and Asia (Pomeranz, 2000, pp.36–41). The situation changed thereafter. In Western Europe, Western Offshoots and Japan, average life expectancy increased to 36 years in 1820, 46 years in 1900 and 66 years in 1950, while in Asia, Africa, and Latin America, average life expectancy remained significantly lower at 24 years in 1820 and 26 years in 1900 although it rose to 44 years in 1950 (Maddison, 2001, p.31). It would seem that the divergence in incomes was associated with a divergence in the well-being of people, so that the divide between rich and poor countries was sharp and clear by 1950.

3. Industrialization and De-Industrialization

It is clear that, until 1500, the continents now described as the developing world had overwhelmingly large shares in world population and world income. This was attributable mostly to Asia. These shares diminished over the next 300 years, but were still substantial at the beginning of the 19th century. Even in the sphere of manufacturing capacities in the world economy, the significance of Asia was overwhelming, although Africa and South America produced primary commodities. Indeed, during the 17th and 18th centuries, the world economy was characterized by a flow of manufactured goods from Asia to Europe that was balanced by a flow of silver from Europe to Asia (Findlay and O'Rourke, 2007). This was not simply trade in spices. Cotton textiles from India and porcelains or silks from China were much sought after. And some of the most dynamic sectors in 18th century Europe were those that were seeking to imitate and compete against goods from Asia (Parthasarathi, 2011). The Industrial Revolution in Britain transformed this reality during the 19th century.

In a study of industrialization levels across the world since 1750, Bairoch (1982) provides estimates of manufacturing production for selected countries and country-groups. Table 2.6, based on these estimates, outlines the changes in the distribution of manufacturing production in the world economy over two centuries from 1750 to 1953. It makes a distinction between two country-groups: the first is made up of Asia, Africa, and Latin America, described by Bairoch as the 'Third World', while the second is made up of Europe, North America, and Japan, described by Bairoch as 'Developed Economies'. Manufacturing production covers the entire range of output without differentiating between technology levels or organizational structures. Thus, it includes both

Table 2.6. Distribution of Manufacturing Production in the World
Economy: 1750–1953

(in percentages)

Year	Europe, North America and Japan	Latin America, Africa and Asia	World
1750	27.0	73.0	100
1800	32.3	67.7	100
1830	39.5	60.5	100
1860	63.4	36.6	100
1880	79.1	20.9	100
1900	89.0	11.0	100
1913	92.5	7.5	100
1928	92.8	7.2	100
1938	92.8	7.2	100
1953	93.5	6.5	100

Source: Bairoch (1982).

the traditional sector with production by craftsmen and modern industry with production in factories. The figures are based on triennial or quinquennial annual averages to eliminate the impact of short-term fluctuations. The evidence presented in this table mirrors the story about changes in shares of world income over the same period. It shows that Asia, Africa, and Latin America, taken together, accounted for almost three-fourths of world industrial output in 1750. At that time much of it was in Asia. This proportion remained high even if it was lower at two-thirds in 1800 and three-fifths in 1830. But it plummeted from 60.5 per cent in 1830 to 20.9 per cent in 1880 and just 7.5 per cent in 1913. It stayed at roughly that level during the next forty years. On the other hand, the share of Europe, North America and Japan in world industrial output rose from 39.5 per cent in 1830 to 79.1 per cent in 1880 and 92.5 per cent in 1913. In fact, the proportional contribution of the two country groups to world manufacturing production was almost reversed in just thirty years between 1830 and 1860. Yet, in 1860, China ranked second and India third, just below the United Kingdom ranked first, but above France fourth, United States fifth, and Germany sixth, in the world in terms of total manufacturing output (Bairoch, 1982, p.284). Surprisingly, China and India remained among the top ten countries in total manufacturing output even in 1913 and 1953 essentially because of their size.

It would be interesting to explore how productivity per worker in manufacturing changed over time in these two parts of the world. But that is not possible because there is no evidence of the number of persons employed in the industrial sector. Thus, Bairoch studied levels of industrialization in terms of volume of manufacturing production per capita. The results of this exercise are just as striking. The ratio of manufacturing production per capita in Asia,

Africa, and Latin America to that in Europe, North America, and Japan dropped from 7:8 in 1750 and 3:4 in 1800 to 1:4 in 1860, 1:8 in 1880, 1:17.5 in 1900 and 1:27.5 in 1913 (Bairoch, 1993, p.91). But China and India were not even among the top twenty countries in the world, in terms of per capita manufacturing output, in 1860 let alone in 1913 or 1953 (Bairoch, 1982, p.286).

Until the late 18th century, pre-capitalist industrial production everywhere was decentralized though artisans, craftsmen and guilds. It would be reasonable therefore to infer that the dominance of Asia in the world industrial economy was bound to diminish, just as the importance of Western Europe was bound to increase with the advent and spread of the Industrial Revolution, as capitalist forms of organization of production in factories employing industrial workers raised productivity through division of labour and new technologies. This presumption is partly correct but not entirely so. The transformation of industrial production was a gradual process. In 1830, the share of new technology industries in world manufacturing production was in the range of 5 per cent and, in 1860, almost a century after they began life, this share was in the range of 20 per cent. Even in what are now the industrialized countries, in 1860, new technology industries that were born with the Industrial Revolution contributed about one-third of manufacturing output, although this share was much higher, probably close to two-thirds, in the United Kingdom (Bairoch, 1982, p.288). There can be little doubt, however, that the de-industrialization of Asia, particularly in India and China but also elsewhere, was largely attributable to the industrialization of the West. The story of Africa is similar to that of Asia, albeit on a smaller scale. The story of Latin America is different, especially after 1870. But it is clear that the industrialization of Europe and the de-industrialization of Asia, during the 19th century, were two sides of the same coin.

4. Integration with the World Economy

Asia and Africa have been engaged with the world economy for a long time. So has South America since the discovery of the New World. The nature and degree of this engagement may have changed over time through different epochs of globalization. It would be interesting to see how it changed through their phases of significance, decline and fall in the world economy. But it is difficult to find statistical evidence for the period before the late 19th century. Hence, the discussion in this section seeks to focus on the period from 1870 to 1950, for which some evidence is available on their integration with the world economy, through international trade, international investment and international migration, even if it is partial and incomplete.

International Trade

Table 2.7 presents evidence on exports from, and imports into Asia, Africa, and Latin America, in current prices at market exchange rates, for selected years during the period 1900 to 1948. The statistics are not exhaustive but do provide a reasonably accurate picture.[3] It shows that exports from what is now described as the developing world increased from $1.7 billion in 1900 to $7.9 billion in 1928 and $15.4 billion in 1948, while imports increased from $1.5 billion to $6.5 billion and $14.9 billion respectively. Their share in world exports rose from 17 per cent in 1900 to 24 per cent in 1928 and 27 per cent in 1948, while their share in world imports, somewhat lower, also rose from 15 per cent to 20 per cent and 26 per cent respectively. Evidence from a different source suggests that their share in world exports was 16 per cent in 1870.[4] It would seem that the integration of Asia, Africa and Latin America with the world economy through international trade experienced a significant increase during the period from 1870 to 1928 and stabilized thereafter.

Some believe that this expansion in international trade was attributable to trade liberalization. It was in part, but not wholly. In fact, free trade was imposed on Asia, Africa, and Latin America as imperialism prised open markets through gunboat diplomacy or colonial dominance. In 1842, China signed a treaty with Britain which opened its markets to trade and capped tariffs at 5 per cent. In the 1840s, free trade was imposed on India by Britain and on Indonesia by the Netherlands. In 1858, Japan signed the Shimoda-Harris treaties, persuaded by the American gunboats of Commodore Perry to switch from autarchy to free trade. Korea followed the same path through its market integration with Japan (Williamson, 2002 and Nayyar, 2006).

Latin America was the exception. The unequal treaties signed at the beginning of the 19th century before independence, expired in the 1870s, after

Table 2.7. Exports from, and Imports into, Asia, Africa and Latin America in the context of World Trade: 1900–1948

(in US $million)

Year	Exports from Latin America, Africa and Asia	Imports into Latin America, Africa and Asia	Percentage Share in World Trade	
			Exports	Imports
1900	1694	1490	16.9	14.9
1913	3899	3310	19.9	16.9
1928	7894	6450	24.1	19.7
1935	4495	3660	23.4	19.1
1938	5219	4640	22.9	20.4
1948	15,421	14,890	26.9	26.0

Source: Author's calculations from United Nations statistics, see Appendix.

which tariff levels in Latin America were among the highest in the world, leading to explosive growth with industrialization, whereas tariff levels in Asia were among the lowest in the world, which led to a dismal performance with de-industrialization (Clemens and Williamson, 2002). In the late 19th and early 20th centuries, India, China, and Indonesia practiced free trade as much as Britain and the Netherlands, where average tariff levels were close to negligible in the range 3–5 per cent (Nayyar, 2006). In contrast, tariff levels in Germany, Japan and France were significantly higher at around 12–14 per cent, whereas tariff levels in the United States were very much higher at 33 per cent (Bairoch, 1993 and Maddison, 1989).

During the period 1870 to 1914, a large proportion of this international trade consisted of inter-sectoral trade, in which primary commodities were exchanged for manufactured goods. The leading trading nation in this era, Britain, exported manufactures to, and imported primary commodities from Asia, Africa, and Latin America (Foreman-Peck, 1983). Much the same was true for northwest Europe. North America exported primary commodities for some time but rapid industrialization there also turned the United States into a net exporter of manufactures by 1914 (Findlay and O'Rourke, 2007). The international division of labour implicit in this pattern of trade, termed the 'Great Specialization' (Robertson, 1938), was simply a corollary of the process of industrialization and de-industrialization.

International Investment

The gross value of the stock of foreign capital in Asia, Africa, and Latin America, at current prices, increased from $5.3 billion in 1870 to $11.3 billion in 1900, $22.7 billion in 1914 and $24.7 billion in 1928 (Maddison, 1989, p.30). This was the equivalent of 32 per cent of the GDP of 15 selected countries in Asia and Latin America in 1900, which were the major destinations for investment from abroad.[5] It has also been estimated that in 1914 total foreign investment in the world economy was $44 billion, of which $30 billion was portfolio investment while $14 billion was direct investment (Dunning, 1983). In terms of destination, it was distributed as follows: $14 billion in Europe (32 per cent), $10.5 billion in the United States (24 per cent), $8.5 billion in Latin America (19 per cent) and $11 billion in Asia and Africa (25 per cent); (UNCTAD, 1994, p.158). In terms of origin, it was far more concentrated: $19 billion from the United Kingdom (43 per cent), $9 billion from France (21 per cent), $6 billion from Germany (13.5 per cent), $5.5 billion from Belgium (12.5 per cent), and $4.5 billion from the United States (10 per cent).

Thus, in 1914, 44 per cent of foreign investment in the world was in Asia, Africa, and Latin America, but 90 per cent of it came from Europe. In 1913, the primary sector accounted for 55 per cent of long-term foreign investment in the world, transport, trade and distribution accounted for 30 per cent, while manufacturing accounted for only 10 per cent and much of that was concentrated in the United States or Europe (Dunning, 1983). During the period 1870–1914, such capital flows were a means of transferring investible resources to *de jure* or *de facto* colonies and newly industrializing countries with the most attractive growth opportunities. The object of these flows was to find avenues for long-term investment in search of profit. Banks were the only financial intermediaries between lenders and borrowers while the financial instruments were bonds with very long maturities. The debt was mostly securitized, with sovereign guarantees provided by imperial powers in Europe or governments in borrowing countries (Nayyar, 2006). It would seem that during the late 19th and early 20th centuries, Asia, Africa, and Latin America as sources of primary commodities were integrated into the world economy through international investment in mines and plantations, or in connectivity from the hinterland to ports, in an international division of labour shaped by imperialism and trade.

International Migration

International migration goes back a long time. Indeed, the migration of people is as old as humankind. And migration across borders and oceans is at least as old as nation states. There were, of course, invaders and conquerors. There were also adventurers and merchants. Migration, however, is different, for it is associated with the movement from countries where there is a labour surplus to countries where there is a labour shortage. Even such movements started centuries ago.

It began with slavery. The European slave trade is often the focus because it is written about, in part because its consequences are embedded in a past that is discernible in the present. Of course, the market for, and trade in, slaves began life in ancient Greece and Rome. There was also an Islamic slave trade, which started earlier and lasted longer than its European counterpart but is not written about as much. It began in the 7th century and ended in the late 19th. Over this period, it is estimated that around 15 million people were transported from sub-Saharan Africa to the Muslim world, of which about 8 million were moved as slaves in the period from 1500 to 1890 (Bairoch, 1993). The European slave trade started in the mid-16th century. The market for slaves developed along the African coastline from Senegal in the north to Angola in the south. This trade in slaves continued until the early 19th century when it was brought to an end. It is believed that over two centuries, more than 15 million people were taken from Africa to Europe, North America, the Caribbean, and Brazil, to work in households or on plantations

(Nayyar, 2002). The slave trade was the largest, enforced, mass migration in history. Slavery was ultimately abolished in the British Empire in 1833 and in the United States of America in 1865. The slave trade came to an end. But slavery did not. For example, slavery continued in Brazil and Cuba where it was abolished only in the late 1880s.

The abolition of slavery in the British Empire was followed by the movement of indentured labour which was yet another form of servitude. Starting around the mid-1830s, for a period of fifty years, about 50 million people left India and China to work as indentured labour in mines, plantations and construction in the Americas, the Caribbean, southern Africa, Southeast Asia, and other distant lands (Tinker, 1974 and Lewis, 1978). This was probably close to 10 per cent of the total population of India and China c.1880 (Nayyar, 2002). The destinations were mostly British, Dutch, French, and German colonies. But the United States was another important destination, where indentured labour also came from Japan.

There was some movement of people from Europe during these periods of slavery and indentured labour. English convicts were transported to Australia. People from Portugal and Spain moved to Mexico, Central America, and the Spanish Caribbean, while people from England, Holland, and France moved to North America. Some were adventurers, some refugees. Many of them, however, were migrants. Later, between 1870 and 1914, more than 50 million people left Europe, of whom two-thirds went to the United States while the remaining one-third went to Canada, Australia, New Zealand, South Africa, and Argentina (Lewis, 1978). There was also some migration from Europe and Japan to Brazil. These people were essentially displaced labour from the agricultural sector that could not find industrial employment. The migration was, in effect, driven by the push of land-scarce Europe and the pull of land-abundant Americas, as also other new lands with temperate climates that attracted white settlers (Nayyar, 2008). Colonized Africa, needing agricultural entrepreneurs, also attracted European settlers. This mass emigration from Europe amounted to one-eighth of its population in 1900. For some countries, Britain, Italy, Spain, and Portugal, such migration constituted as much as 20 to 40 per cent of their population (Massey, 1988 and Stalker, 1994).

International migration on this massive scale came to an end with World War I. From 1919 to 1939, migration continued at much lower levels, as immigration laws were put in place and passports came to be needed. The Great Depression of the 1930s further dampened these flows as unemployment levels rose sharply everywhere. The end of World War II led to a massive movement of people within Europe, an estimated 15 million, most of whom were refugees seeking to settle. But the aftermath of the war also witnessed emigration on a significant scale from Europe to the United States and Latin America.

The migration of people from India and China as indentured labour for mines and plantations, together with the movement of capital from European countries, sought to exploit natural resources or climatic conditions in Southeast Asia, southern Africa, and the Caribbean. In this process, contrary to the dominant construct in orthodox trade theory, international movements of capital and labour were complements not substitutes (Nayyar, 1998). It also shaped the international division of labour in the age of imperialism, which led to industrialization in some and de-industrialization in other parts of the world. The subsequent migration of people from Europe to the United States, Canada, Australia, and New Zealand, described as Western Offshoots, provided the foundations for the development of industrial capitalism in the new worlds. In either case, international migration was critical in the evolution of the world economy during the 19th century.

In retrospect, it is clear that the second half of the 19th century and the first half of the 20th witnessed a progressive integration of Asia, Africa, and Latin America into the world economy. This process may have gathered momentum in the 'Age of Empire' from 1870 to 1914 (Hobsbawm, 1987), but it evolved throughout the 19th century and spanned more than one hundred years (Findlay and O'Rourke, 2007). It was driven by the economic and political interests of Western Europe further reinforced by the emergence of the United States. This coincided in time with the rise of the West. It also coincided in time with the decline and fall of Asia. Africa was left behind. Latin America fared much better but for the divergence in incomes.

Conclusion

This chapter considered the evolution of the world economy in a long-term historical perspective to set the stage. It is worth recapitulating the essential contours of change, to connect with the analysis of catch up which is the focus of this book. The striking reality to emerge is that the present distinction between industrialized and developing economies, or rich and poor countries, is relatively recent in the span of history. In fact, one thousand years ago, Asia, Africa, and South America, taken together, accounted for more than 80 per cent of world population and world income. The beginnings of change were discernible from the early 16th century to the early 19th. Yet, in 1820, less than 200 years ago, these three continents still accounted for almost three-fourths of world population and around two-thirds of world income. This was attributable in large part to Asia, where just two countries, China and India, accounted for approximately 50 per cent of world population and world income through the centuries from 1000 to 1820. The dramatic transformation of the world economy, however, began around 1820. Slowly but surely, the geographical divides in the world turned into economic divides. The divide rapidly became a wide chasm. The economic significance of Asia, Africa, and Latin America witnessed a precipitous decline such that, by 1950 there was a pronounced asymmetry between their share in world population at two-thirds and their share in world income at about one-fourth. In sharp contrast, between 1820 and 1950, Europe, North America, and Japan increased their share in world population from one-fourth to one-third and in world income from more than one-third to almost three-fourths. The rise of 'The West' was concentrated in Western Europe and North America. The decline and fall of 'The Rest' was concentrated in Asia, much of it attributable to China and India, while Latin America was the exception as its shares in world population and income were not only symmetrical throughout but also rose over time.

The Great Divergence in per capita incomes was, nevertheless, the reality. In a short span of 130 years, from 1820 to 1950, as a percentage of GDP per capita in Western Europe and Western Offshoots, GDP per capita in Latin America dropped from three-fifths to two-fifths, in Africa from one-third to one-seventh and in Asia from one-half to one-tenth. But that was not all. Between 1830 and 1913, the share of Asia, Africa, and Latin America in world manufacturing production, attributable mostly to Asia, in particular China and India, collapsed from 60 per cent to 7.5 per cent, while the share of Europe, North America, and Japan rose from 40 per cent to 92.5 per cent, to stay at these levels until 1950. The industrialization of Western Europe and the de-industrialization of Asia during the 19th century were two sides of the same coin. It led to the Great Specialization, which meant that Western Europe, followed by the United States, produced manufactured goods while Asia, Africa and Latin America produced primary commodities. The century from 1850 to 1950 witnessed a progressive integration of Asia, Africa and Latin America into the world economy, through international trade, international investment and international migration, which created and embedded a division of labour between countries that was unequal in its consequences for development. The outcome of this process was the decline and fall of Asia and a retrogression of Africa, even if Latin America fared better except for the divergence in incomes, so that, by 1950, the divide between rich industrialized countries and poor underdeveloped countries was enormous.

This narrative about the three continents, which began with their overwhelming significance in the world economy and traced the contours of their decline, is followed in the next chapter by an analysis of the underlying factors. The rest of the book, however, is about the period from 1950 to 2010. It seeks to analyse catch up on the part of developing countries, reflected in their share of world output, levels of per capita income, and pursuit of industrialization, situated in the wider context of their engagement with the world economy.

3

Underlying Questions and Answers

The first half of the second millennium witnessed the beginnings of change in the world economy, which became discernible in terms of outcomes during the period from the early 16th to the late 18th century. This set the stage for a dramatic transformation of the world economy which gathered momentum through the 19th century to create an enormous economic divide between rich and poor countries that reached its zenith in the mid-20th century. The underlying factors were manifold and complex. It is no surprise that there is a vast academic literature on the subject that seeks to analyse this process of change. Much of it is in the domain of history. Some of it is economic history. And some of it is history in which geography plays a critical role.

It needs to be said that this book is about economics and not about geography in which history matters. It seeks to provide a long-term historical perspective essentially to set the stage for an analysis of the process of change in the world economy since 1950. Even so, it is necessary to outline the factors underlying the profound changes in the world economy during the preceding two hundred years. In doing so, this chapter draws upon the existing literature. But it remains a digression that cannot do justice to an extensive literature, which is rich in both range and depth, let alone touch upon the substance, or nuances, of its debates and controversies.

The chapter asks four questions to provide skeleton answers. First, what were the developments starting c.1500, or earlier, particularly in Europe, which shaped the evolution of the world economy? Second, how did the economies of Europe and Asia compare with each other in the mid-18th century? Third, why did the Industrial Revolution occur in Britain, rather than elsewhere in Europe or in Asia? Fourth, what were the implications and consequences of this occurrence for Europe, Asia, and the world economy, and how did the political context, manifest in colonialism and imperialism, influence outcomes?

1. Europe from 1500 to 1780

It has been argued (Landes, 1999) that late medieval Europe was among the most inventive societies in history, as division of labour and widening of the market provided a stimulus to technological innovation. Some examples cited are the water wheel, eyeglasses, the mechanical clock, printing and gunpowder, although the water wheel existed in Roman times while both printing and gunpowder came from China. Innovation was supposedly rewarded by the free market and institutionalized property rights, so that success led to imitation or emulation. Yet, in 1500, most Europeans lived in backward economies where three-fourths of the population was in agriculture, so that productivity and incomes were low (Allen, 2009). Commerce and manufacturing were concentrated in the Mediterranean, mostly in the Italian city-states, or in the Iberian Peninsula, Portugal and Spain, with a small offshoot in Bruges and Antwerp.

The voyages of discovery in the late 15th century, led by the Iberian states, were perhaps a major turning point (Findlay and O'Rourke, 2007). The Europeans were trying to bypass the Arabs, who had monopolized the Asian maritime trade. Hence, there was a need to find a direct sea route to India, which could also lead further east. The first milestone was attained in 1488 when Bartolomeu Dias found the southern tip of Africa that was aptly named as the Cape of Good Hope. Christopher Columbus, a native of Genoa, peddled his idea of sailing west across the Atlantic to many European states, and was ultimately supported by the Spanish monarchs of Aragon and Castile. Columbus sailed from Cadiz to his momentous discovery in 1492, with just ninety men in three ships, 'even if he rarely knew where he was, let alone where he was going' (Morris, 2010, p.16).[1] Vasco da Gama left Lisbon in 1497, with two ships and a support vessel, to reach Calicut on the Malabar Coast of India in May 1498. The voyages of Columbus to the Caribbean were followed by several Spanish expeditions. The exploratory flotilla, led by Hernan Cortes, of 11 ships, 100 sailors, and 500 soldiers, touched the Mexican coast in Yucatan and landed at Vera Cruz in April 1519. Just two years later, the mighty Aztec Empire was destroyed. These voyages were brought to completion by Magellan's circumnavigation of the globe in 1521.

This sequence of discoveries led to the first phase of European colonial expansion in the early 16th century. It began with Spain and Portugal. The slave trade from Africa, the search for silver in the New World, and the colonization of the Americas were a part of this process which unleashed a somewhat different dynamic in the formation of the world economy. It was the age of mercantilism in Europe. The acquisition of colonies was associated with a mercantile expansion of trade. Old World trade and New World silver turned out to be powerful complements in stimulating trade flows, as Europe paid for its imports of textiles, spices, porcelains and silks from Asia by exports of silver obtained from the Americas. The New World provided Europe with a source of primary commodities such as sugar, tobacco, cotton and timber, apart from the windfall ecological gains through access to indigenous plants like maize and potatoes, just as these colonies provided export markets for manufactured goods from Europe (Maddison, 2007). The slaves from Africa provided the labour for plantations, mines and agriculture (although the indigenous people in Spanish America were also a source of labour in mines), while the migrants from Europe provided entrepreneurs in the New World. At the same time, profits from the slave trade generated resources.[2]

The growing network of world trade laid the foundations for a specialization in production between continents the benefits of which accrued to Europe. It is no surprise that there was a struggle for hegemony in the emerging world economy. In the late sixteenth century, Portugal and Spain were displaced by Holland, a merchant oligarchy, as the Dutch rose to primacy in world trade. Their dominance continued into the eighteenth century before it was lost to the British. In this world, where 'guns and sails' were critical, power provided for plenty (Findlay and O'Rourke, 2007). This power was obviously sustained by economy and technology. Geopolitics shaped possibilities. Economic primacy was about state power and naval power which provided protection for economic interests in distant lands and merchant ships in distant waters.

By the mid-18th century, northwest Europe occupied the economic centre-stage even though France and Austria were major military powers. Between 1500 and 1800, the structural transformation of England was striking as the proportion of the population in agriculture dropped from 75 per cent to 35 per cent. This proportion also declined significantly in the Netherlands and Belgium, modestly in France, Germany, and Austria but there was little change in Italy and Spain (Allen, 2009). Structural change meant an increase in urbanization and manufacturing. But England also experienced an agricultural revolution and a growing rural industrialization, so that productivity and income levels rose.

Institutional, social, and cultural changes were conducive for the transition (Allen, 2009 and Landes, 1999). The end of serfdom, the reduced influence of religion (partly attributable to diminishing Roman Catholic dominance with the rise of Protestantism), and the decline of superstition were part of this process. So was the creation of universities and the progress in science from Copernicus through Galileo to Newton and Halley. The printing revolution led to a sharp drop in the price of books, spreading literacy and numeracy. The expansion of international commerce and increasing urbanization led to increased literacy and the emergence of more participatory political institutions (Hill, 1966, Brenner, 1993, and Acemoglu, Johnson, and Robinson, 2005).

35

In sum, the initial conditions for capitalist development had been created, which provided the roots for the industrial revolution that surfaced in the late 18th century.

2. Europe and Asia c.1750

The existing literature compares levels of development in Europe and Asia during the mid-18th century. It reveals two schools of thought with sharply contrasting perspectives. There is one that stresses differences to suggest that Europe had a distinct edge over Asia. There is another that stresses similarities to suggest that Europe and Asia were roughly comparable in terms of development.

The intellectual origins and foundations of the view that seeks to focus on differences can be traced to the writings of two of the most influential thinkers in the social sciences: Karl Marx and Max Weber. Ironically enough, their thinking was embedded in polar opposite worldviews. And it is no surprise that those who follow in their respective footsteps invoke different reasons or arguments for coming to the same conclusion. For Marx, the 'Asiatic Mode of Production' was a characterization of non-Western societies where 'Oriental Despots' exercised absolute power over their populations, which constrained individual initiative and did not allow representative institutions. The essential perception was that these were static societies without evolution or change. Indeed, Hegel argued that the concept of the State was simply absent in India. In such a world, it was not possible for capitalism to emerge so that colonialism in India and Western intrusion into China were perceived as paths to future progress. Weber believed that instrumental rationality, which had its origins in the Protestant ethic, was unique to Europe and provided the foundations for culture, politics and economics that were conducive to the development of capitalism. Thus, even if societies in India and China had the capacity to reason, it was constrained by the dominance of religion and the existence of institutions such as caste or clan, which curbed individual freedom and limited reason to adaptive behaviour that could not question social norms or practice. The similarities between Marx and Weber in their perspective on Asia are striking insofar as individual initiative and instrumental rationality are ultimately the same idea. Edward Said (1978) was perhaps among the first to question this influential belief system. It led social scientists to question, contest, and reject the idea that Europe was superior to Asia, or that Asia was essentially different from Europe.

Even so, the influence of Weberian thinking persists. Landes (1999) argues that Europe had a decisive edge over Asia in terms of knowledge, science, technology, culture, politics, and institutions. The argument, which runs as follows, is easily translated into neo-classical economics. Europe at that time had an efficient market system, which protected property rights so that the allocation and utilization of resources, whether land, labour or capital, was much better than in Asia. Some Marxian thinking also argues that the agricultural revolution in England, which raised productivity, was possible only because of efficient markets and strong property rights (Brenner, 1985). This belief is contested. Historical research shows that in the mid-18th century both China and India had markets that functioned efficiently and property rights systems that were secure (Pomeranz, 2000 and Parthasarathi, 2011).

There is another argument, Malthusian in conception, that demographic factors, marriage age, or fertility rates, enabled Europe to find a much better balance between people and resources than Asian countries with large populations where famines and disasters restored the balance. The inference drawn is that Europe could attain higher savings rates that were supportive of capital accumulation. This belief is also contestable. Indeed, it is has been argued, rightly, that Malthusian demographics were common to both east and west in the Eurasian landmass, so that the large populations of China and India were a sign of their success and not of failure (Findlay and O'Rourke, 2007).

The competing school of thought sketches a picture that is very different. It highlights the similarities between Europe and Asia at the time. Pomeranz (2000) compares Western Europe and China to show that fertility rates and life expectancy were similar. Capital stock in Western Europe was not significantly larger and the embodied technology was not superior. Markets for land and labour in China were characterized by efficiency ánd freedom that were about the same. Indeed, there were surprising resemblances between the two worlds in terms of the markets and commercialization, manifest in the commodification of land, labour and goods, as also in terms of luxury consumption and capital accumulation. Parthasarathi (2011) compares Britain and Western Europe with India to show that markets for goods and credit were at similar levels of development. Agrarian property rights were well defined so that substantial populations outside agriculture were fed while food was also exported. Merchants ran vast empires that straddled continents, which meant that their property was secure. Living standards were roughly comparable.

Findlay and O'Rourke (2007) also compare Western Europe not only with China and India but also with other regions in Eurasia, to show that there was significant economic and political change everywhere so that demography, technology and institutions were not stable anywhere but were broadly comparable. Developed systems of bookkeeping and accounting were not unique to Western Europe but existed in China, India, and elsewhere. So did scientific knowledge and technological learning. Cotton textiles from India and silks and porcelain from China were the leading manufactured exports in the world economy until the late 18th century. Merchants from India, using both its coasts, plied the Indian Ocean for more than one thousand years and competed on equal terms with European trading companies during the 19th century. The political institutions and empires or dynasties in Asian countries were sophisticated and formidable in terms of strong military, productive agriculture and vibrant commerce.[3] Some scholars go much further to argue that Asia was, if anything, more developed than Western Europe during this period and better placed to have an industrial revolution (Frank, 1998 and Hobson, 2004). And some historians suggest that there was a proto-industrialization in pre-colonial India (Perlin, 1983). In sum, it would seem that the similarities between Western Europe and Asia in the mid-18th century were far more significant than the differences. It is not quite plausible, therefore, to sustain the claim that Western Europe had a distinct edge over Asia in terms of technology, productivity, or incomes at the time. The period from 1500 to 1750 did witness a growing economic significance of Western Europe in the world economy, but the share of the Asian giants, China and India, in world output remained unchanged at about 50 per cent through this era.

3. Industrial Revolution in Britain: Why not Europe or Asia?

The Industrial Revolution happened in Britain during the late 18th century. This occurrence has spawned an extensive literature on the questions of where, when and why. There are speculative hypotheses and competing explanations. Any meaningful analysis would require a large digression. This section simply outlines some bare essentials. The literature suggests proximate causes that span a wide range: the Scientific Revolution, the Enlightenment, efficient markets, property rights, agricultural productivity, technological inventions, laissez-faire policies, political institutions, natural resource endowments such as coal and iron ore, capital accumulation due to high savings or low interest rates, and so on. However, it serves little purpose to enumerate factors. Many of these attributes existed in other countries too. And the nature of causation is important. Thus, the brief discussion that follows is selective in its focus on a few plausible hypotheses. It cannot pretend to be systematic, let alone exhaustive.

Pomeranz (2000), who sets out to explain the great divergence in incomes between Europe and Asia, with a focus on China, during the 19th century, argues that the Industrial Revolution in Britain was attributable to the fortunate location of coal in abundance, which substituted for timber in a time of dwindling forests, and trade with the Americas that allowed Britain the option of growth along resource-intensive and labour-saving paths, while Asia hit a cul-de-sac where growth slowed down as it was forced into labour-intensive and resource-saving paths because of ecological constraints. Allen (2009), who seeks to analyse the British Industrial Revolution in global perspective, suggests that it was a successful response to the world economy of the times. And Britain's international expansion in the preceding decades made a decisive contribution. During the 18th century in Britain, high wages combined with cheap capital and cheap energy, as compared with Asia, as also other countries in Europe, meant that the famous technologies of the Industrial Revolution, whether the steam engine, the spinning jenny and the cotton mill, or coke smelting, were profitable to invent and to use in Britain, while the substitution of coal for wood as a source of energy made an enormous difference to everything. Parthasarathi (2011), who addresses the question of why Europe grew rich and Asia did not, with a focus on India, argues that two factors were critical. The search for new technologies might have been driven by competition from Asian manufactures, whether cotton textiles from India or silks and porcelains from China, while the search for coal was obviously driven by shortages of wood that followed deforestation at home.

These pressures exercised a strong influence. But state actions also shaped outcomes. In 18th century Britain the state provided patronage for science and technology and helped to promote the mining and adoption of coal. Most important, perhaps, trade policies that protected domestic industry performed a critical role (Bairoch, 1993 and Chang, 2002). In the wider historical context, Findlay and O'Rourke (2007), who study how international trade shaped the world economy during the second millennium, emphasize that Britain's military success overseas and its mercantilist dominance during the era from 1688 to 1780 played a vital role. The extension of empire, later in the 19th century, which provided markets for manufactures and sources of raw materials overseas, was driven by this mercantilist urge to use power in order to secure plenty. Hence the origins of the Industrial Revolution were closely connected with the state-driven international trade and overseas expansion in the preceding era.

There is also a literature on the companion question of why the Industrial Revolution did not occur elsewhere in Europe, say France or the Netherlands, or in Asia, say China, India, or Japan (Frank, 1998, Landes, 1999, Pomeranz, 2000, Findlay and O'Rourke, 2007, Allen, 2009, Morris, 2010, and Parthasarathi, 2011). An industrial transformation was possible in these economies, which had productive agricultures, commerce networks, handicrafts industries and sufficient populations. Some potential, more or less, existed everywhere because there were structural similarities in levels of development. Yet, processes and outcomes were shaped by the context in space and the conjuncture in time, which had economic, political and social aspects. Indeed, in both Europe and Asia, events were influenced by a complex mix of economic, social and political factors in the national context (Kindleberger, 1996). Thus generalizations are difficult. Counterfactuals make it even more difficult. Even so,

there are explanations in the literature that are suggestive but cannot be definitive. It would mean too much of a digression to enter into a discussion here.
Instead, it is worth reiterating three conclusions drawn by Findlay and O'R-
ourke (2007) that are eminently sensible. First, the search for a single explanation, which seeks to exclude, or to deny, competing explanations is futile, as
there might be some truth in several hypotheses. Second, it is necessary to make
a clear distinction between necessary and sufficient conditions, because there
were characteristics and attributes that Britain had in common with some
countries in Western Europe and Asia at the time. Third, there must be multiple
answers to the question why the Industrial Revolution did not take place
elsewhere, as the explanations for countries in regions as diverse as Europe,
the Muslim world, or Asia cannot be the same but have to be country specific.

4. Implications and Consequences for the World Economy

The Industrial Revolution in Britain had far reaching implications and
consequences not only for Europe but also for Asia and the world economy.
Its beginnings, the steam engine, cheap iron, and the spinning jenny with
the cotton mill, turned out to be transformative (Allen, 2009). The cotton
mill pioneered the mechanization of industrial production. The steam
engine produced energy through technology by using water and burning
coal. The cheap iron came from coal that made it possible to substitute coke
for charcoal in smelting. Taken together, these developments helped create
an engineering industry that could produce machinery to unleash large
productivity increases. The process was reinforced by improved technologies that reduced coal consumption for a more fuel-efficient steam engine.
This led to an industrial and geographical spread in the use of the new
technologies, even if it was a gradual process as noted in Chapter 2. More was
to come later, in the mid-19th century, from the same beginnings. The idea of
railways began life much earlier, to haul coal in mines and from mines to
rivers. It was iron rails and steam locomotives that made it into a means of
surface transport on land when roads did not exist or were not suitable for
the purpose. The substitution of steam for sails and of iron for wooden hulls
in ships led to a revolution in shipping. Both led to an enormous reduction
in the time needed, as also the cost incurred, in traversing geographical
distances.

This shaped the context in which the 19th century witnessed the evolution
of an international economic order that led to a profound change in the
balance of economic and political power in the world. It was attributable to
three developments. The first was the Industrial Revolution in Britain in the
late 18th century which spread to Western Europe, even if slowly, during the

first half of the 19th century. The second was the emergence of a newer, somewhat different, form of colonialism in the early 19th century which culminated in the advent of imperialism that gathered momentum through that century. The third was the revolution in transport and communication in the mid-19th century, manifest in the railway, the steamship, and the telegraph, which dismantled geographical barriers of distance and time to shrink the world (O'Rourke and Williamson, 1999 and Nayyar, 2006). These three developments, which overlapped and partly coincided in time, transformed the world economy by creating patterns of specialization in production associated with a division of labour through trade reinforced by the politics of imperialism.

The revolutionary change in methods of manufacturing, which were developed in Britain in the late 18th century and spread to countries in Western Europe through the early 19th, meant profound changes in the economic life of Europe. Innovation, followed by continuous improvements in technologies, yielded sharp increases in productivity, output and incomes. The rapid diffusion of the new technologies, combined with their geographical spread, brought about rapid industrialization in Britain, Belgium, the Netherlands, France and Germany. This industrialization in Western Europe, associated with scale economies that sharply reduced the prices of manufactured goods, led to the demise of traditional industries in Asia, particularly India and China, so that the outcome was de-industrialization elsewhere (Bairoch, 1981, Pomeranz, 2000, Nayyar, 2006, Findlay and O'Rourke, 2007, Maddison, 2007, and Parthasarathi, 2011). Consequently, the knowledge and skills that had been developed in Asia over centuries were slowly but surely eroded and diminished. Thus the 19th century witnessed a divergence not just in incomes but also in labour productivity, skill levels and technological capabilities. Path dependence and cumulative causation meant long-term consequences for development.

The proximate, almost obvious, cause of this deindustrialization in Asia was the much greater competitiveness of industry in Britain and Western Europe. But that was not all. The transport revolution of the 19th century dismantled the natural protection, provided by the distance and time implicit in geographical barriers to handicrafts or manufacturing industries in countries such as India and China (Nayyar, 2006, and Findlay and O'Rourke, 2007). The advent of the steamship reduced ocean freight by two-thirds between 1870 and 1900 (Lewis, 1978). The opening of the Suez Canal halved the distance from London to Bombay, bringing about a sharp reduction in the cost of freight which was just as dramatic on shipping routes passing through the Black Sea and Egyptian ports (Williamson, 2002). The spread of the railways, everywhere, brought the hinterland of countries into the world economy, not only to source raw materials but also to sell manufactured goods (Nayyar,

41

2006). It would have required high tariffs, possibly even an exclusion of imports through prohibitive protection, for India and China, or countries in Asia, to neutralize the impact of the revolutions in industry and transport on the prices of manufactures imported from Britain or Western Europe. Of course, colonialism and imperialism meant that countries in Asia did not have the freedom to use tariffs to protect domestic industries. The mix of gunboat diplomacy and colonial dominance, noted in the preceding chapter, imposed free trade on China, India, Indonesia, Japan, and Korea. Europe also imposed free trade on the Ottoman Empire. There was sustained productivity growth with industrialization in Western Europe and a steady productivity decline with de-industrialization in Asia. This widening productivity gap was the essential factor underlying the divergence in per capita incomes between Western Europe and Asia.

The economic growth of Britain was, in important part, attributable to the organization of production in the capitalist system, based on a division of labour associated with capital accumulation and technical progress, strongly supported by State policies. Countries in Western Europe followed a similar path a little later. The process of industrialization in Britain and northwest Europe led to an increase in the share of the manufacturing sector and a decrease in the share of the agricultural sector in both output and employment. Over time, the outcome was a structural transformation in the composition of output and employment (Kuznets, 1971), which resulted in much higher rates of growth of output. International migration, which moved people from land-scarce Europe to land-abundant America, as also to Australia and Africa, supported the process (Nayyar, 2002 and 2008). The movement of labour from employment in agriculture to employment in manufacturing, led, in turn, to sustained increases in productivity. This process of industrialization was also supported by State intervention through tariff protection and industrial policies in countries such as France, Germany and the United States that were latecomers following in the footsteps of Britain (Bairoch, 1993 and Chang, 2002). The consequent increases in GDP growth rates, even if modest by present standards, were responsible for the rising shares of Western Europe and Western Offshoots (mostly the United States) in world GDP during the 19th and 20th centuries respectively.

The rise of 'The West' was associated with a decline of 'The Rest' in the world economy and, among the latter, the fall of Asia, particularly India and China. There are competing explanations for this outcome in Asia and Africa although Latin America fared somewhat better. Some emphasize economic factors to argue that an industrial revolution was dependent on a prior or simultaneous agricultural revolution (Lewis, 1978). Some emphasize political factors to argue that imperial powers did not allow industrialization in their colonies (Baran, 1957). Some emphasize a mix of economic and political factors to argue that the economics of colonialism and the politics of imperialism together created this unequal international economic order (Furtado, 1970 and Frank, 1971).

The space constraint does not allow discussion of these competing explanations. Suffice it to say that the outcome was unambiguous. The world economy was divided into countries (mostly with temperate climates) that industrialized and exported manufactures, and countries (mostly with tropical climates) that did not industrialize and exported primary commodities. The 'Great Divergence' in incomes between countries was closely related to the 'Great Specialization' in division of labour between countries. Consequently, there was almost no change in the structural composition of output and employment in Asia, Africa, and Latin America, as the share of the primary sector remained dominant (Bairoch, 1975 and 1993) constraining both productivity increase and output growth. Slowly but surely these countries became dependent on the industrializing countries in Western Europe, not simply for markets and finance but also as their engine of growth (Lewis, 1978). This led to de-industrialization and underdevelopment in what became the developing world, just as it led to industrialization and development in what became the industrialized world. Both outcomes were an integral part of the development of capitalism in the world economy.

The Industrial Revolution in Britain, which spread to Western Europe, combined with the revolution in transport and communication, created huge asymmetries and inequalities in the world economy that provide an important part of the explanation for observed outcomes in the 19th century and this process was strongly reinforced by colonialism and imperialism. The changed political context in the world made an enormous difference. It established the geopolitical dominance of Britain, along with France, followed by some smaller countries in Western Europe, over Asia and Africa. The characteristics of British, French, and Dutch colonialisms, as well as Spanish and Portuguese colonialisms that began life in an earlier phase, differed but there were basic similarities (Maddison, 2007), particularly in terms of consequences for the colonized. However, it is worth noting that during the early 19th century, when countries in Asia and Africa were being colonized, countries in Latin America were beginning to attain independence. This process of independence from colonial rule in Latin America started in 1810 but was consolidated only in the 1820s. For this reason, perhaps, there was a slight increase, rather than a decline, in Latin America's share of world GDP during the period 1820–1870. Beginning in the 1870s, as noted earlier, Latin American countries invoked their autonomy to use tariffs to promote industrialization in their resource-abundant economies. This did lead to rapid growth and some industrialization, which explains the substantial increase in Latin America's share in world GDP during the period 1870–1950.[4] Yet the mix of

43

technological, economic, and political forces in those times was such that Latin America remained locked into the 'Great Specialization', exporting primary commodities to, and importing manufactured goods from, Western Europe (Findlay and O'Rourke, 2007). Even so, political independence did increase degrees of freedom enabling Latin America to treble its share of world GDP between 1870 and 1950, although it was not enough to reverse the divergence in per capita incomes.

The evolution of the world economy during this era was shaped by two sets of factors. The first, which exercised a strong influence over the period 1820–1870, was made up of the Industrial Revolution in Britain, which spread to Western Europe, the emergence of the next phase of colonialism which spread to Asia and Africa, and the revolution in transport and communication which shrank the world. The second set, which exercised a strong influence over the period 1870–1914, was made up of the politics of imperialism and the economics of globalization, which created winners and losers (Hobsbawm, 1987, Rodrik, 1997, Williamson, 2002, and Nayyar, 2006). The influence of these factors possibly waned over the period 1914–1950, interspersed as it was by two World Wars and the Great Depression, but the inherent logic and the essential characteristics of industrial capitalism meant that uneven development for unequal partners persisted in the world economy.

Conclusion

At the risk of a digression, it is worth noting that the rise of the West and the fall of the Rest, analysed in this chapter, have spawned a growing literature on why some countries succeed while other countries fail in their quest for power and prosperity. Simply put, there are three perspectives, each with a different focus, respectively on culture, geography, and institutions. And they claim to be mutually exclusive.

The first perspective stresses the critical importance of culture. Its origins can be traced to the writings of Marx and Weber that emphasized the cultural differences between Europe and Asia. Their thinking, of course, was much wider. Marx used history to project the absence of a historical dialectic in his concept of the Asiatic mode of production, while Weber brought in religion to emphasize the absence of the Protestant ethic and instrumental rationality that were essential to the evolution of capitalism. Said (1978) questioned this influential belief system. So did some historians. It led social scientists to contest and reject the idea that Europe was superior to Asia. Even so, in the contemporary literature on economic history, Landes (1999) and Clark (2007), among others, seek to explain the Industrial Revolution in Britain, as also the economic and social transformation of Western Europe over the next two centuries, in terms of cultural characteristics. The corollary is that the decline and fall of Asia over the same period was also attributable to cultural characteristics. The discussion in this chapter shows that such a hypothesis is not tenable.[5]

The focus of the second perspective is on geography. In his seminal book, Diamond (1997) assigns geography a critical role in the history of human societies to explain why some countries succeeded and others did not. For one, there are differences between temperate countries and tropical countries, attributable to a mix of geography and biology, which make the incidence of disease much higher in tropical climates and the potential for increasing agricultural productivity much greater in temperate climates. For another, access to the ocean or to navigable rivers makes an enormous difference to the economic potential of countries so that landlocked countries face difficult hurdles. Diamond recognizes the importance of technology and history. But the basic argument is that the wealth and poverty of nations are shaped by geographical factors. In the same tradition, Morris (2010) provides a long-term view, spanning five millennia, of human history in the world. He seeks to explain why and how the West came to rule the world. The essential argument is that biology (life sciences) and sociology (social sciences) together explain the shape of history in terms of social progress for humanity as a whole; human beings may be very different as individuals but are very similar as a collective of humankind even if progress or regression are uneven over time. Yet, Morris believes that geography alone explains why people in one part of the world fare so much better than people in other parts. It is reasonable to suggest that geography matters, but it is far-fetched to claim that it provides a complete, or sole, explanation for the difference between the prosperity and poverty of countries.

The third perspective emphasizes institutions. Its origins are attributable to North (1990), who analysed the significance of institutions in change and development. In a similar worldview, Acemoglu and Robinson (2012) argue that economic institutions determine whether a country is rich or poor while political institutions shape its economic institutions. Countries that succeed have inclusive economic institutions that allow people to participate in economic activities to make the best use of their talents, created by political institutions that distribute power across a broad coalition of groups. Countries that fail have extractive political institutions that force people to work largely for the benefit of ruling elites or dictators, the outcome of absolutist political institutions that concentrate power in narrow groups. This hypothesis is not convincing because, in the cited book, the authors seek its validation by 'just-so' stories from the history of countries to conclude that the story explains why nations succeeded or failed. The benefit of hindsight makes this storytelling easier. The fundamental question is why some countries have inclusive

45

institutions while other countries have extractive institutions. It is no surprise that rich countries have good and poor countries have bad institutions. It could well be that good or inclusive institutions are a consequence rather than cause of progress.

Clearly, the difference between success and failure or prosperity and poverty of countries is not attributable to culture. Geography and institutions matter but cannot provide complete explanations and must not be claimed as mono-causal explanations. The real danger is that these generalized hypotheses, over time and across space, fail to recognize the obvious reality that outcomes are shaped by a complex mix of economic, social and political factors in the national context where history matters.

It is time to return to the questions posed at the beginning of the chapter, if only to provide short answers. First, the developments in Europe c.1500 that exercised a profound influence on the shape of things to come in the world economy were the voyages of discovery and the colonization of the Americas. The mercantile expansion of trade, supported by state power and naval power, led to an expansion of commerce and an increase in urbanization, conducive to the social, political, and institutional change that created the initial conditions for capitalist development. Second, in the mid-18th century, the similarities between Europe and Asia were far more significant than the differences. Life expectancy and fertility rates, scientific knowledge and technological learning, markets and property rights, commerce and trade were not very different. Indeed, demography, technology and institutions were broadly comparable. Third, there was a wide range of factors underlying the occurrence of the Industrial Revolution in Britain, so that single explanations are futile. High wages combined with cheap capital and cheap energy made it profitable to invent and use the new technologies, while the substitution of coal for wood as a source of energy made an enormous difference. But the search for new technologies was also driven by competition from Asian manufactures and shortages of wood that followed deforestation. International and overseas expansion in the preceding era laid the foundations, while state action in the form of trade policies that protected domestic industry or patronage for science and technology performed a critical role. Fourth, these revolutionary changes in methods of manufacturing transformed economic life, as industrialization spread to Europe yielding sharp increases in productivity, output and incomes. It also led to the demise of traditional industries in Asia, particularly China and India, which reduced their skill levels and technological capabilities over time. This process was reinforced by the politics of imperialism that imposed free trade and the economics of the transport revolution that dismantled the natural protection provided by geography implicit in distance and time, to hasten the process of de-industrialization in Asia with a devastating impact on China and India.

Part Two
Catching Up

4

End of Divergence:
Beginnings of Convergence?

The preceding chapters situated the theme of this book in its wider historical context, to highlight the overwhelming significance of Asia, Africa and Latin America in the world economy until the mid-18th century, followed by their rapid decline through the 19th, culminating in a fall that was almost complete by the mid-20th century. This chapter traces the changes in the significance of developing countries in the world economy, in terms of population and income, during the second half of the 20th century and the first decade of the 21st century. In doing so, it provides a global perspective with a focus on the share of developing countries in world income and their incomes per capita as compared with the industrialized countries. Given the diversity and differences within the developing world, it also attempts to disaggregate the analysis for Asia, Africa, and Latin America, but this does not extend beyond regions to countries.

The structure of the chapter is as follows. Section 1 considers the changes in the share of developing countries in world GDP and levels of per capita income relative to the industrialized countries, in terms of the Maddison PPP statistics, to highlight the catch up in aggregate output and make comparisons with the past. Section 2 analyses the changes in the shares and levels of income in developing countries, at market exchange rates based on national accounts statistics, to focus on the differences between regions and the asymmetries between changes in shares and levels of income when compared with the industrialized countries. Section 3 examines the evidence on growth rates of GDP and GDP per capita, underlying the changing shares of country-groups or regions in world GDP and the convergence or divergence in GDP per capita. Section 4 discusses the main hypotheses about convergence in economic history and economic theory, to provide a critical evaluation and relate it to the theme of this chapter.

1. Catch up in Output and Comparisons with the Past

For developing countries in the world economy, 1950 was perhaps an important turning point. It was the beginning of the post-colonial era as newly independent countries, to begin with in Asia and somewhat later in Africa, sought to catch up in terms of industrialization and development. Table 4.1 presents evidence on the share of developing countries, with their constituent regions, industrialized countries and transition economies of Eastern Europe including the former USSR, in world population and world GDP, for selected benchmark years during the period from 1950 to 2008.[1] The Maddison data on GDP in terms of PPP, from which this table is derived, are in 1990 international (Geary-Khamis) dollars. This serves an important purpose insofar as it enables comparisons with the past. But it also has a significant limitation that the purchasing power parity method developed for international comparisons of real income between individuals at a micro-level is not quite appropriate for aggregates at a macro-level. Hence, the next section considers changes in the share and level of income in developing countries at market exchange rates.

The data in Table 4.1 suggest that two phases are distinguishable: 1950 to 1980 and 1980 to 2008. It is worth noting that 2008 is the latest year for which

Table 4.1. The Share of Developing Countries, Industrialized Countries and Eastern Europe-former USSR in World Population and World GDP: 1950–2008

(in percentages)

	1950	1962	1973	1980	1990	2001	2008
	World Population						
Asia	51.5	52.2	54.6	55.5	56.6	57.3	57.4
Africa	9.0	9.5	10.1	10.8	12.0	13.5	14.6
Latin America	6.5	7.3	7.8	8.1	8.4	8.6	8.7
Developing Countries	*67.0*	*69.1*	*72.5*	*74.4*	*77.0*	*79.4*	*80.7*
Industrialized Countries	*22.4*	*20.7*	*18.3*	*17.0*	*15.2*	*14.0*	*13.3*
Eastern Europe and former USSR	*10.6*	*10.3*	*9.2*	*8.6*	*7.8*	*6.6*	*6.0*
TOTAL	*100*	*100*	*100*	*100*	*100*	*100*	*100*
	World GDP						
Asia	15.6	14.9	16.3	18.3	23.3	31.0	38.0
Africa	3.8	3.5	3.4	3.6	3.3	3.2	3.4
Latin America	7.8	8.1	8.7	9.8	8.3	8.2	7.9
Developing Countries	*27.1*	*26.6*	*28.4*	*31.7*	*34.9*	*42.5*	*49.4*
Industrialized Countries	*59.8*	*59.8*	*58.7*	*56.4*	*55.4*	*51.9*	*44.2*
Eastern Europe and former USSR	*13.0*	*13.6*	*12.9*	*11.9*	*9.8*	*5.6*	*6.4*
TOTAL	*100*	*100*	*100*	*100*	*100*	*100*	*100*

Note: The percentages have been calculated from data on population in millions and data on GDP in millions of 1990 international (Geary-Khamis PPP) dollars.

Source: Author's calculations from Maddison Online Database, see Appendix.

the Maddison statistics are available. But it is also appropriate as the terminal year for a study of long-term trends because the financial crisis, which surfaced in late 2008, was transformed into the Great Recession that has persisted since then.

Between 1950 and 1980, the share of developing countries in world population rose from 67 per cent to 74 per cent, while their share in world GDP stopped its decline and rose from 27 per cent to 32 per cent. The share of industrialized countries, made up of North America, Western Europe, Japan, and Oceania, in world population fell from 22 per cent to 17 per cent, while their share in world GDP fell from 60 per cent to 56 per cent. Much of the increase in the share of developing countries was at the expense of industrialized countries. The rest of the increase was at the expense of the erstwhile centrally-planned economies in Eastern Europe and the USSR, which witnessed a modest decline in their share of world population and GDP. It is important to recognize that this period coincided broadly with the golden age of capitalism in the industrialized countries, associated with rapid economic growth (Marglin and Schor, 1990) and the era of economic success in the socialist countries, also associated with rapid economic growth. But economic growth was even faster in the developing countries.

This was a clear reversal of the trends in growth during the period from 1820 to 1950 when 'The West' fared so much better than 'The Rest'. The share of Asia in world population increased by 4 percentage points but its share in world GDP also increased by almost 3 percentage points. The share of Latin America in world population increased by 1.6 percentage points but its share in world GDP increased by 2 percentage points, and the latter was consistently higher than the former. Africa was the exception, as its share in world population rose by almost 3 percentage points but its share in world GDP was almost unchanged. It would seem that, for developing countries taken together, the divergence in growth of output, characteristic of the preceding 130 years, came to a stop.

Given the asymmetrical distribution of output and population in the world, it is no surprise that this profound change did not stop the divergence in per capita incomes, which continued even if not at the same pace as in the past. Table 4.2 compares GDP per capita in industrialized countries taken together, with GDP per capita in Eastern Europe, the former USSR and developing countries with their constituent regions.[2] Between 1950 and 1980, as a percentage of GDP per capita in the industrialized countries, GDP per capita in Latin America dropped from 45 per cent to 36 per cent, in Africa from 16 per cent to 10 per cent and in Asia from 11 per cent to 10 per cent. The rapid growth in population in the developing world meant that divergence in per capita income increased everywhere. In proportionate terms, it was considerable in Latin America and Africa, while it was somewhat less in Asia, possibly

51

Table 4.2. Comparing GDP per capita between Industrialized Countries, Eastern Europe-former USSR and the Developing World: 1950–2008

	Per Capita GDP Ratios						
	1950	1962	1973	1980	1990	2001	2008
Industrialized Countries	*100*	*100*	*100*	*100*	*100*	*100*	*100*
Eastern Europe	*37.4*	*38.5*	*38.2*	*38.7*	*28.9*	*27.0*	*33.9*
Former USSR	*50.4*	*49.1*	*46.4*	*43.0*	*36.8*	*20.9*	*31.3*
Developing Countries	*15.1*	*13.3*	*12.2*	*12.9*	*12.4*	*14.4*	*18.4*
Asia	11.3	9.9	9.3	10.0	11.3	14.6	19.9
Africa	15.8	12.7	10.6	10.1	7.6	6.5	7.0
Latin America	44.5	38.4	34.6	36.4	27.0	25.7	27.6

Note: GDP per capita is measured in millions of 1990 international (Geary-Khamis PPP) dollars.
Source: Author's calculations from Maddison Online Database, see Appendix.

because the divergence was already so large. Interestingly enough, during this period, the centrally planned economies fared better. There was no divergence in GDP per capita for Eastern Europe and modest divergence in GDP per capita for the USSR, when compared with the industrialized countries.

The trends were more pronounced and the transformation more significant during the period that followed. Between 1980 and 2008, the share of developing countries in world population registered a similar increase from 74 per cent to 81 per cent, but their share in world GDP increased far more from 32 per cent to 49 per cent. Over the same period, the share of industrialized countries in world population fell from 17 per cent to 13 per cent, while their share in world GDP fell from 56 per cent to 44 per cent. As much as two-thirds of the increase in the share of developing countries in world GDP was at the expense of industrialized countries, while the remaining one-third was at the expense of Eastern Europe and former USSR where economic performance turned out to be distinctly worse after the collapse of communism, as there was a sharp contraction in output during the earlier years of transition. It would seem that, for developing countries as a group in the world economy, the trend that was reversed *c*.1980 gathered momentum thereafter.

But the story was very different across regions. Asia was the exception, as its share in world population increased by less than 2 percentage points whereas its share in world GDP jumped by almost 20 percentage points. The share of Latin America in world population increased by half a percentage point, while its share in world GDP decreased by 2 percentage points. Africa fared worse, as its share in world population rose by about 4 percentage points but its share in world GDP remained unchanged. Eastern Europe and former USSR also fared badly, as their share in world population dropped by 3 percentage points whereas their share in world GDP dropped by 6 percentage points. In this context, it is important to recognize that the 1980s were the worst times for

Latin America and Africa while the 1990s were the worst times for Eastern Europe and former USSR. These were indeed lost decades.

How did these trends influence the divergence in per capita incomes? Table 4.2 shows that between 1980 and 2008, as a percentage of GDP per capita in the industrialized countries, GDP per capita in Latin America dropped from 36 per cent to 28 per cent and in Africa from 10 per cent to 7 per cent, whereas in Asia it rose from 10 per cent to almost 20 per cent. The divergence was clearly the biggest in Eastern Europe and the former USSR, which experienced a sharp economic retrogression in the decade that followed the collapse of communism with some recovery in the 2000s.

Tables 4.1 and 4.2 provide data on selected benchmark years to keep the statistics within manageable proportions. The picture that emerges from a study of these tables is complemented and completed by time series data set out in graphs.

Figure 4.1 outlines the trends in shares of the three country-groups in world population and world GDP during the period from 1950 to 2008. It confirms that there was a turning point around 1980. It also shows there were significant asymmetries between shares in world population and world GDP, for industrialized countries that had a much higher share in world GDP and for developing countries that had a much higher share in world population. But these shares were broadly symmetrical for Eastern Europe and former

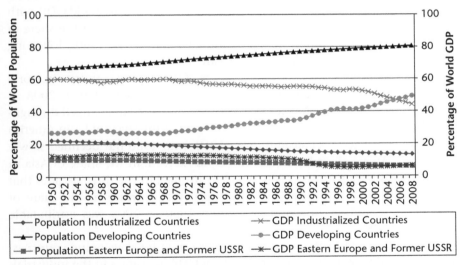

Figure 4.1. Trends in Shares of Country-Groups in World Population and World GDP: 1950–2008

Note: Population in millions and GDP in millions of 1990 international (Geary-Khamis PPP) dollars.

Source: Author's calculations from Maddison Online Database, see Appendix.

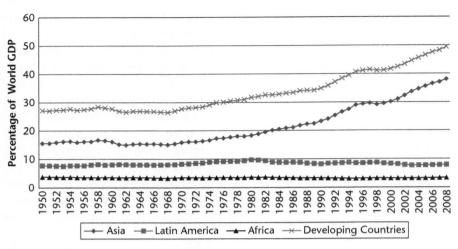

Figure 4.2. Trends in Share of Developing Countries, disaggregated by Regions, in World GDP: 1950–2008

Note: GDP in millions of 1990 international (Geary-Khamis PPP) dollars.
Source: Author's calculations from Maddison Online Database, see Appendix.

USSR. Most important, perhaps, the figure highlights the rapid increase in the share of developing countries in world GDP, beginning *c.*1980, and the corresponding decline in the share of industrialized countries in world GDP, with the former overtaking the latter in 2006. The sharp decline in the share of Eastern Europe and former USSR in world GDP during the 1990s, following the collapse of communism, is just as clear.

Figure 4.2 outlines the trends in the share of developing countries in world GDP, disaggregated by regions, during the period from 1950 to 2008. It confirms that the share of Africa in world GDP remained unchanged throughout the period of almost six decades. It shows that the share of Latin America in world GDP increased steadily from 1950 until 1980 but declined slowly thereafter. Above all, it highlights the rapid increase in the share of Asia in world GDP starting around 1980, which continued in the three decades that followed. Indeed, it is clear that the substantial increase in the share of developing countries in world GDP from 1980 to 2008 was attributable entirely to Asia.

Figure 4.3 sets out the trends in GDP per capita for developing countries, disaggregated by regions, as a percentage of GDP per capita in the industrialized countries, during the period from 1970 to 2008. It confirms that, for developing countries as a group, the great divergence in per capita income as compared with industrialized countries, which began in 1820 and continued for 150 years, came to an end in the early 1970s. And, starting in 1980, the

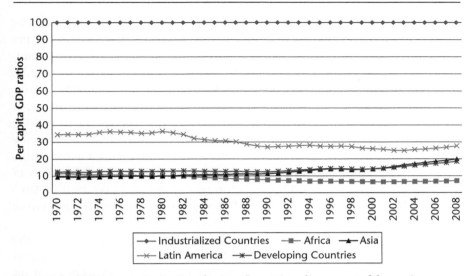

Figure 4.3. GDP per capita in Developing Countries, disaggregated by regions, as a percentage of GDP per capita in Industrialized Countries: 1970–2008

Note: GDP per capita in 1990 international (Geary-Khamis PPP) dollars.
Source: Author's calculations from Maddison Online Database, see Appendix.

modest beginnings of a convergence are discernible. However, the picture that emerges from a disaggregated analysis is somewhat different. It would seem that for Africa, the divergence persisted. In Latin America, where the widening of the income gap with industrialized countries stopped in the 1970s, divergence returned and continued until the end of the century but despite the recovery in the 2000s, the income gap in 2008 was greater than it was in the 1970s. The convergence, beginning around 1980, which gathered momentum from 1990, was confined to Asia. In fact, it drove the convergence for developing countries as a group. It is worth noting that the income gap for Asia, which was wider than that for developing countries through the 1970s and the 1980s, was progressively reduced in the 1990s and became narrower than that for developing countries in the 2000s. For developing countries, taken together, there was a broader-based modest convergence during the 2000s.

The use of Maddison statistics for the period since 1950 makes comparisons with the past possible and consistent, particularly for income shares and levels, as the GDP estimates for the period from 1820 to 1950, indeed even earlier, used for the analysis in Chapter 2 are also in 1990 international (Geary-Khamis) dollars. Table 4.1 and Figure 4.1 both suggest that the share of developing countries in world GDP reached its lowest level in the early 1960s and was less than 27 per cent in 1962. This share reached 49 per cent of world GDP in 2008. In comparison, the share of developing countries in world GDP was 43 per cent in 1870 and 63 per cent in 1820 (Table 2.2). The story is not quite so impressive in terms of per capita income levels. GDP per capita in developing countries as a proportion of that in industrialized countries reached its lowest level in the early 1970s and was 12 per cent in 1973. This proportion rose to 18 per cent in 2008. In comparison, the same proportion was 18 per cent in 1913 and 20 per cent in 1900 but significantly higher at 27 per cent in 1870 (Chapter 2, note 2). Therefore, it would seem that in 2008 the share of developing countries in world GDP returned to its level of the mid-19th century, whereas their per capita income relative to that in industrialized countries returned to the proportion of the early 20th century. The share of developing countries in world population was lowest at 63 per cent in 1913 (Table 2.2). It was 67 per cent in 1950. This share reached almost 81 per cent in 2008, which was close to its level of 82 per cent in 1000 (Table 2.1).

The preceding discussion on the significance of developing countries in the world economy since 1950, in terms of population, income and per capita income, is based on estimates made by Maddison. The focus has been on percentage shares in world population or world income and on proportional divergence or convergence in per capita income. The percentages or proportions, in turn, are derived from data on income in 1990 international (Geary-Khamis) dollars, which are PPP, but better than usual PPP estimates, that facilitate inter-country comparisons over time. For an analysis of trends in GDP and GDP per capita since 1950, it is also essential to have some sense of absolute magnitudes. More important, perhaps, it is both necessary and appropriate to make international comparisons at market exchange rates. The reason is simple. Computation of GDP per capita in terms of PPP may be helpful for international comparisons of relative living standards for individuals at a micro-level. Even such comparisons are not without problems. Consider the example of a barber in Mumbai who works at the Taj Hotel and returns to live at home in Dharavi, as compared with a barber in New York who works at a salon on Fifth Avenue in Manhattan and returns to live at home in Queens. Their incomes might be similar in PPP terms, but the living standards of the barber in Mumbai are likely to be lower than his or her counterpart in New York. However, it is not quite appropriate or correct, even if it is fashionable, to add up GDP in terms of PPP across countries, to estimate shares in world GDP in terms of PPP, because these estimates are based on an artificial upward adjustment in the price of non-traded goods and services in developing countries.[3] This leads to an upward bias in PPP-GDP estimates for developing countries, which are thus not comparable with other macroeconomic variables such as foreign trade, international investment, or industrial production, valued at market prices and market exchange rates.

For this reason, the next section presents evidence on GDP and GDP per capita in developing countries, in the context of the world economy, with absolute magnitudes, in market prices and at market exchange rates. Even so, it needs to be said that the Maddison statistics for the period before 1950, which are used in the analysis in Chapter 2, serve a most valuable purpose in providing a long-term historical perspective, especially as there is no other source that provides such a complete database. The use of Maddison statistics for the period after 1950 in this section also serves a valuable purpose because it allows for comparisons with the past, which would not be possible otherwise, and because national accounts statistics compiled by the United Nations are available only from 1970. For the period since 1970, there is, of course, evidence on international comparisons of GDP and GDP per capita at market prices and market exchange rates considered below, which can be easily compared with the Maddison statistics.

2. Asymmetries between Regions in Income Shares and Levels

It is worth beginning with a perspective on changes in population, particularly during the second half of the 20th century and the first decade of the 21st, which also requires some reference to absolute size. And it is worth using census data from countries compiled together by the United Nations. Table 4.3 presents evidence on the size of population in developing countries and the world, at five-year intervals, during the period from 1950 to 2010. It shows that the size of the population in the developing world, made up of Asia, Africa, and Latin America, increased from 1.7 billion in 1950 to 3.4 billion in 1980 and 5.7 billion in 2010. In large part this was attributable to demographic factors. As death rates dropped because of improvements in

Table 4.3. Size of Population in Developing Countries and the World: 1950–2010

	Population (in billions)		
Year	World	Developing Countries	*Percentage Share of Developing Countries*
1950	2.5	1.7	*68.0*
1955	2.8	1.9	*68.9*
1960	3.0	2.1	*69.9*
1965	3.3	2.4	*71.1*
1970	3.7	2.7	*72.8*
1975	4.1	3.0	*74.3*
1980	4.5	3.4	*75.7*
1985	4.9	3.7	*77.0*
1990	5.3	4.1	*78.3*
1995	5.7	4.5	*79.4*
2000	6.1	4.9	*80.5*
2005	6.6	5.3	*81.3*
2010	6.9	5.7	*82.1*

Source: United Nations, Population Division, UNDATA.

public health systems that eliminated epidemic diseases, birth rates did not because poverty and illiteracy persisted. Such increases in population growth rates for a time are characteristic of demographic transitions. It also shows that the share of developing countries in world population increased from two-thirds in 1950 to three-fourths in 1980 and more than four-fifths in 2010. This was attributable to rapid population growth in developing countries and stable or declining populations in industrialized countries.

It would seem that the share of developing countries in world population in 1980 returned to its level during the period from 1500 to 1820. And, by 2010, this share returned to its level in 1000. In the developing world, this population growth was concentrated in Asia and Africa. As in the past, China and India were once again home to a large proportion of the world population, but there were several other countries in Asia and Africa with large and rapidly growing populations. It is worth noting that in 2010, China and India together accounted for about 36 per cent of world population as compared with a share that was much larger, in the range of 50 per cent between 1000 and 1700 and even higher at 57 per cent in 1820 (Nayyar, 2010).

It is even more important, indeed essential, to consider trends in output or income of developing countries in terms of absolute magnitudes valued at market prices. Table 4.4 presents evidence in current prices and at market exchange rates, on GDP for developing countries and the world economy, and GDP per capita for developing and industrialized countries, at five-year intervals, during the period from 1970 to 2010. It shows that the GDP of developing countries increased from $0.5 trillion in 1970 to $3.9 trillion in 1990 and $20.4 trillion in 2010, while, as a proportion of world GDP, it

Table 4.4. GDP and GDP per capita in Developing Countries and the World Economy: 1970–2010

(in current prices and at market exchange rates)

Year	Developing Countries GDP (US $billion)	World GDP (US $billion)	GDP of Developing Countries as percentage of World GDP	Developing Countries GDP per capita (US $)	Industrialized Countries GDP per capita (US $)	Developing Countries GDP per capita as percentage of Industrialized Countries GDP per capita
1970	549	3283	16.7	209	2873	7.3
1975	1228	6410	19.2	416	5387	7.7
1980	2540	11865	21.4	772	9710	8.0
1985	2552	12993	19.6	697	10761	6.5
1990	3851	22206	17.3	947	19303	4.9
1995	5896	29928	19.7	1324	24898	5.3
2000	6973	32244	21.6	1444	25711	5.6
2005	10789	45722	23.6	2081	33977	6.1
2010	20362	63151	32.2	3715	39723	9.4

Source: United Nations, National Account Statistics, see Appendix.

increased from 16.7 per cent in 1970 to 17.3 per cent in 1990 and 32.2 per cent in 2010. But these trends were not smooth or continuous. There was an increase in this share in 1975 and 1980 because of the increase in oil prices and the boom in commodity prices, just as there was a decrease in this share in 1985 and 1990 because of the lost decade in Latin America and the economic crises in Africa. Even so, it is clear that the share of developing countries in world GDP, at market exchange rates, doubled from one-sixth in 1970 to one-third in 2010.

The story is very different for per capita income. GDP per capita in developing countries increased from $209 in 1970 to $947 in 1990 and $3715 in 2010, while, as a proportion of GDP per capita in industrialized countries, it fell from 7.3 per cent in 1970 to 4.9 per cent in 1990 but rose to 9.4 per cent in 2010. Once again, the trend is uneven, as this proportion increased in 1975 and 1980 but decreased in 1985 and 1990, for the reasons mentioned above. In four decades, GDP per capita in developing countries as a ratio of that in industrialized countries, recorded a modest increase from 1:13.6 in 1970 to 1:10.6 in 2010. The asymmetrical increase in the two sets of proportions was obviously attributable to the rising denominator in the latter, as the population of the developing world more than doubled from 2.7 billion in 1970 to 5.7 billion in 2010.

The picture for developing countries as a group might conceal significant differences between regions. Table 4.5 outlines trends in the share of developing countries in world GDP and in GDP per capita in developing countries as a percentage of that in industrialized countries, disaggregated by regions, at five-year intervals, during the period from 1970 to 2010. It reveals that the trends

Table 4.5. GDP and GDP per capita in Regions of Developing World as proportion of World GDP and GDP per capita in Industrialized Countries: 1970–2010
(in percentages)

Year	GDP as a percentage of World GDP			GDP per capita as a percentage of that in Industrialized Countries		
	Asia	Africa	Latin America	Asia	Africa	Latin America
1970	8.7	2.7	5.3	5.1	8.4	21.2
1975	9.9	3.2	6.0	5.3	9.0	22.3
1980	11.3	3.7	6.3	5.7	9.3	21.6
1985	10.9	3.0	5.7	4.9	6.6	17.2
1990	10.0	2.2	5.0	3.9	4.0	13.2
1995	11.8	1.8	6.1	4.4	3.0	15.4
2000	13.1	1.8	6.6	4.7	2.9	16.0
2005	15.5	2.2	5.9	5.6	3.2	14.4
2010	21.8	2.6	7.8	8.9	4.2	21.5

Note: The percentages have been calculated from data on GDP (in US $million) and GDP per capita (in US $) in current prices and at market exchange rates.
Source: United Nations, National Accounts Statistics, see Appendix.

were most uneven across regions. The share of Africa in world GDP registered an increase between 1970 and 1980, declined thereafter until 2000, which was followed by some recovery, but this share was about the same in 1970 and in 2010 at a little over 2.5 per cent. The share of Latin America in world GDP remained in the range of 5–6 per cent between 1980 and 2005, but rose to almost 8 per cent in 2010. It is no surprise that Asia was the exception, as its share in world GDP increased steadily between 1970 and 1980, fluctuated around that level until 1995, but rose sharply thereafter, so that, at market exchange rates, this share more than doubled from less than 9 per cent in 1970 to almost 22 per cent in 2010.

The story of three continents in terms of per capita income reflects these trends although their initial levels were very different. The ratio of GDP per capita in Africa to that in industrialized countries was about 1:12 from 1970 to 1980, dropped continuously thereafter to 1:35 in 2000, and recovered a little to about 1:24 in 2010. The ratio of GDP per capita in Latin America to that in industrialized countries was more than 1:5 from 1970 to 1980, dropped to the range of 1:6 to 1:7 until 2005, but recovered to its initial level of more than 1:5 in 2010. The ratio of GDP per capita in Asia to that in the industrialized countries was about 1:20 from 1970 to 1980, somewhat lower until 2000, but rose rapidly thereafter to reach 1:11 in 2010.

Tables 4.4 and 4.5 provide data at five-year intervals to keep the statistics within manageable proportions. The picture that emerges from a study of these tables is complemented by time series data set out in graphs.

Figure 4.4 outlines the trends in shares of industrialized countries, developing countries and, to complete the picture, Eastern Europe including the former USSR, in world GDP at current prices and market exchange rates, during the period from 1970 to 2010. The decline in the share of Eastern Europe and former USSR in world GDP is striking. It started in 1970 but gathered momentum around 1980 and turned into a rapid decline during the lost decade of the 1990s. The modest recovery that followed in the 2000s was at best partial, as their share in 2010 was about one-third what it was in 1970. The share of industrialized countries in world GDP was dominant in the range of 70 per cent through the 1970s. It rose sharply to about 80 per cent in the mid-1980s and stayed in that range until the turn of the century. This increase in their share was mostly at the expense of Eastern Europe and former USSR. In small part, it was also at the expense of developing countries during the 1980s. But the industrialized countries experienced a substantial decline in their share of world GDP during the first decade of the 21st century, from almost four-fifths to roughly two-thirds. This was mostly attributable to the rising share of developing countries, and partly due to some recovery in the share of Eastern Europe and former USSR, although the financial crisis and economic recession in the industrialized countries must have also contributed

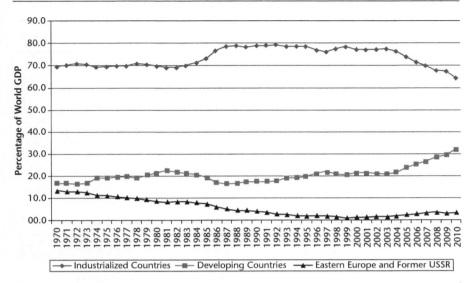

Figure 4.4. Distribution of GDP in the World Economy: 1970–2010 (as a percentage of World GDP)

Note: GDP in US $million in current prices at market exchange rates.
Source: United Nations, National Accounts Statistics, see Appendix.

to this decline in the closing years of the decade. The share of developing countries in world GDP increased through the 1970s. It was probably driven by the sharp increases in oil prices and partly by the boom in commodity prices. But this share declined in the 1980s. The debt crises in Latin America and sub-Saharan Africa, which led to stabilization and adjustment programmes with strong contractionary effects, were almost certainly the underlying factors in this lost decade. However, the share of developing countries in world GDP increased steadily in the 1990s and rapidly in the 2000s. The latter was mostly at the expense of industrialized countries.

Figure 4.5 outlines the trends in the share of developing countries in world GDP in current prices and market exchange rates, disaggregated by regions, during the period from 1970 to 2010. It confirms that the share of Africa in world GDP increased slowly in the 1970s, declined in the 1980s and 1990s, recovered in the 2000s, but its level was about the same in 1970 as in 2010. It shows that the share of Latin America in world GDP increased steadily through the 1970s but declined through the 1980s to recover and increase in the 1990s, followed by a short dip in the early 2000s, to rise thereafter. It reveals that the share of Asia in world GDP increased from 1970 to the mid-1980s, stabilized at a slightly lower level for a short period, increased steadily through the 1990s and rapidly in the 2000s. It is clear that the substantial

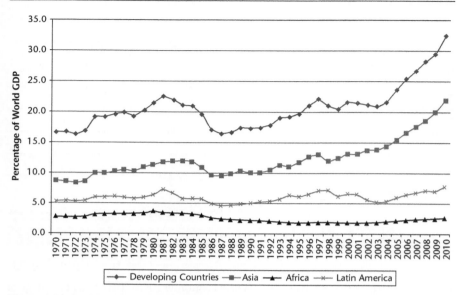

Figure 4.5. Distribution of GDP in the Developing World: 1970–2010 (as a percentage of World GDP)

Note: GDP in US $million in current prices at market exchange rates.
Source: United Nations, National Accounts Statistics, see Appendix.

increase in the share of developing countries in world GDP from 1990 to 2010 was attributable mostly to Asia.

Figure 4.6 sets out the trends in GDP per capita for developing countries as a percentage of GDP per capita in the industrialized countries, in current prices and market exchange rates, disaggregated by regions, for the period from 1970 to 2010. GDP per capita in developing countries as a percentage of that in industrialized countries increased slowly in the 1970s, declined in the 1980s, recovered partly through the 1990s, and rose significantly in the 2000s. It would seem that divergence came to an end earlier but convergence, even if modest, started during the 2000s. GDP per capita in Africa as a percentage of that in industrialized countries rose modestly in the 1970s but fell rapidly through the 1980s and 1990s, to recover just a little in the 2000s. GDP per capita in Latin America as a percentage of that in industrialized countries increased modestly in the 1970s, fell rapidly in the 1980s, with a partial recovery through the 1990s and another decline around the turn of the century, followed by a recovery and rise from the early 2000s. GDP per capita in Asia as proportion of that in industrialized countries was broadly stable around a level of 5 per cent from 1970 to 2000 to increase rapidly thereafter. In sum, over this span of four decades, Africa experienced a significant divergence and became the poorest continent, Latin America witnessed more

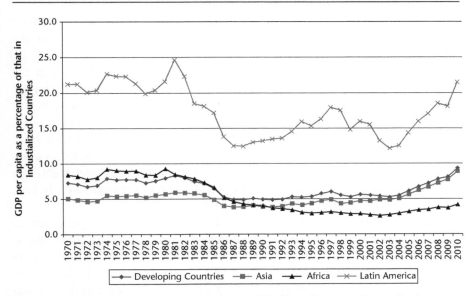

Figure 4.6. GDP per capita in the Developing World and its constituent Regions as a proportion of that in Industrialized Countries: 1970–2010

Note: GDP per capita in US dollars in current prices at market exchange rates.
Source: United Nations, National Accounts Statistics, see Appendix.

divergence than convergence to stay roughly where it was but remained the richest continent, while Asia brought an end to the divergence, no longer the poorest continent, and saw the modest beginnings of a slight convergence.

It would be natural to ask whether national accounts statistics in current prices at market exchange rates sketch a picture that is different from the Maddison PPP statistics in 1990 international (Geary-Khamis) dollars. Interestingly enough, the broad contours of the story turn out to be similar on the three essential questions: the distribution of world output or income between country-groups, the distribution of output or income between regions in the developing world, and the divergence in per capita income between industrialized countries and developing countries.

First, a comparison of Figures 4.1 and 4.4, which plot the changes in the shares of industrialized countries, developing countries, and Eastern Europe including former USSR, in world GDP for the period from 1970 to 2008 and 2010 respectively, show a decrease in the share of industrialized countries starting 1990 which gathered momentum in 2000, and an almost matching increase in the share of developing countries, with a continuous decline in the share of Eastern Europe and former USSR. There are only two differences. For one, the Maddison PPP statistics understate the share of industrialized countries and overstate the share of developing countries as well as Eastern Europe and former USSR, as compared with national accounts statistics at market exchange rates, and *vice-versa*. For another, the former smoothes out the fluctuations more than the latter.

Second, a comparison of Figures 4.2 and 4.5, which plot changes in the share of developing countries in world GDP, disaggregated by regions, for the period from 1970 to 2008 and 2010 respectively, shows amazing similarities in trends, with relatively small changes for Africa and Latin America, but a significant increase for Asia starting around 1990 that gathered pace from 2000. The differences, once again, are that the Maddison PPP statistics overstate the share of developing countries and make for smoother trends, as compared with national accounts statistics at market exchange rates. In fact, but for scale, the images are almost the same.

Third, a comparison of Figures 4.3 and 4.6, which plot GDP per capita in developing countries as a percentage of that in industrialized countries, disaggregated by regions, for the period 1970 to 2008 and 2010 respectively, shows considerable similarities in terms of inter-regional differences with a steady decline for Africa, fluctuations around a slightly declining trend for Latin America, and a rising trend for Asia starting around 1990 that gathered pace from 2000 which almost coincides with the trend for developing countries as a group from 1990 to 2008 and 2010 respectively. The substantive difference, yet again, lies in the scale, as Maddison PPP statistics overstate the proportion to suggest a significant convergence for Asia, during the period from 1990 to 2010, whereas national accounts statistics at market exchange rates understate the proportion to suggest the beginnings of a modest convergence for Asia, although the stories for Africa and Latin America are similar.

3. Underlying Growth Rates

The changes in the significance of any subset of countries in the world over time depend upon their economic performance as compared with the rest of the world. It is obvious that differences in GDP growth rates, in real terms, underlie the changing shares of country-groups in world GDP. It is simple arithmetic that differences in growth rates of GDP and population determine differences in growth rates of GDP per capita, which in turn shape divergence or convergence in per capita incomes between countries. Therefore, it is worth considering evidence on economic growth, in terms of GDP and GDP per capita, for developing countries and industrialized countries during the period from 1950 to 2010. However, time series data on GDP and GDP per capita for the entire period are not available from a single source. The Maddison database provides a time series on GDP and GDP per capita in 1990 international (Geary-Khamis) dollars in PPP terms for the period 1950–2008. But United

Nations national accounts statistics at market exchange rates only provide a time series on GDP and GDP per capita in constant 1990 US dollars starting from 1970.

Table 4.6 sets out growth rates in GDP and GDP per capita for regions within the developing world, the developing countries, the industrialized countries, and the world economy during the periods 1951–1980 and 1981–2008. The choice of periods is determined by the evidence available which suggests that 1980 was the turning point in terms of economic growth when there was a discernible break in the trend almost everywhere in the world economy (Nayyar, 2008b). It is also influenced by the fact that, up to 2008, evidence is available from both sources, and long term growth rates might be distorted by the impact of the financial crisis and economic downturn that affected growth performance everywhere in 2009 and 2010. These two sources are not strictly comparable. However, it is possible to resolve the problem, as data are available from both sources for the period 1981–2000. To facilitate a comparison, Table 4.6 also presents figures on growth rates calculated separately from Maddison and from UN data. A comparison of the two sets of growth rates during the period 1981–2000, from the two sources, shows that the numbers correspond closely. Thus, it is reasonable to infer that growth rates for 1951–1980 and 1981–2008, even if calculated from different sources, are comparable.

Table 4.6. Growth Rates in the World Economy by Regions and Country Groups: 1951–1980 and 1981–2008

(percent per annum)

	Maddison Data		UN Data	
	1951–1980	1981–2000	1981–2000	1981–2008
GDP				
Asia	5.08	5.77	5.84	6.16
Africa	4.33	2.44	2.37	3.28
Latin America	5.31	2.25	2.20	2.61
Developing Countries	*4.97*	*4.31*	*4.10*	*4.63*
Industrialized Countries	*4.30*	*2.73*	*2.73*	*2.50*
World	*4.54*	*3.38*	*3.01*	*2.99*
GDP per capita				
Asia	2.87	3.97	3.95	4.42
Africa	1.79	−0.23	−0.33	0.66
Latin America	2.59	0.37	0.29	0.87
Developing Countries	*2.70*	*2.42*	*2.14*	*2.79*
Industrialized Countries	*3.30*	*2.09*	*1.90*	*1.69*
World	*2.55*	*1.70*	*1.25*	*1.34*

Note: GDP and GDP per capita are measured in 1990 international (Geary-Khamis PPP) dollars in the Maddison data and in US dollars in current prices at market exchange rates in the UN data.

Source: Author's calculations from Maddison online database and United Nations, National Accounts Statistics, see Appendix.

A study of the evidence presented in Table 4.6 confirms that differences in GDP growth rates underlie the changing shares of developing countries and industrialized countries in world GDP during the second half of the 20th century and the first decade of the 21st. The arrest of the decline in the relative importance of developing countries in the world economy, during the period 1951–1980, is easily explained in terms of their GDP growth of 5 per cent per annum that was somewhat higher than the 4.3 per cent per annum in indus-trialized countries. In fact, GDP growth rates in each of the three regions of the developing world over these three decades were higher than that in the industrialized world. This was in sharp contrast with their growth per-formance during the period 1820–1950 that witnessed a dramatic decline in their share of world GDP. Similarly, the significant increase in the relative importance of developing countries in the world economy, during the period 1981–2008, is clearly attributable to their GDP growth rate of 4.6 per cent per annum that was much higher than the 2.5 per cent per annum in industrial-ized countries. But in this period there were marked differences in GDP growth rates between the three regions of the developing world. The significant increase in the share of Asia in world GDP was on account of its much higher GDP growth rate at 6 per cent per annum over three decades. It is no surprise that Africa, with a GDP growth rate of 3.3 per cent per annum, and Latin America, with a GDP growth rate of 2.6 per cent per annum, experienced slight declines in their shares of world GDP during 1981–2008. It was Asia that increased its share in world GDP at the expense of industrialized countries.

The story was not the same for per capita incomes. Table 4.6 shows that although GDP growth rates in the developing world and in each of its three continents were higher than in industrialized countries in both periods, GDP per capita growth rates were significantly lower because population growth rates remained at high levels as death rates declined but birth rates did not. This difference was substantial during the period 1951–1980, when growth in GDP per capita in developing countries was 2.7 per cent per annum compared with 3.3 per cent per annum in industrialized countries. It is no surprise that the divergence continued, albeit at a much slower rate than in 1820–1950. In proportionate terms, given the disparities in GDP per capita growth rates, it was the smallest in Asia and the largest in Africa with Latin America in the middle. During the period 1981–2008, despite the economic slowdown, growth in GDP per capita in the industrialized countries was 1.7 per cent per annum as compared with 2.8 per cent per annum for developing countries. But the latter aggregate is deceptive. Asia was the exception. Its GDP per capita growth was 4.4 per cent per annum as compared with 0.7 per cent per annum in Africa and 0.9 per cent per annum in Latin America. The outcome was the end of divergence and the beginnings of a modest convergence in Asia, while

Africa experienced a significant divergence, and Latin America saw ups and downs to stay almost where it was.

The preceding discussion is complemented by Table 4.7, which presents evidence on growth rates in GDP and GDP per capita for developing countries, with their constituent regions, industrialized countries and the world economy, using both Maddison PPP and UN national accounts statistics at market exchange rates, which is also disaggregated in time for the periods 1971–1980, 1981–1990, 1991–2000, and 2001–2008. It confirms that the two sets of data, which are not comparable in absolute figures, yield remarkably similar growth rates for each of the country-groups or regions even for shorter periods of a decade. The further disaggregation in terms of time periods is also valuable because it provides more information on the decades that witnessed an important transformation in income shares, even if not levels, in the world economy. First, it shows that developing countries fared much better than industrialized countries in terms of growth in both GDP and GDP per capita during the periods 1971–1980 and 2001–2008 when there was some catch up in total output if not output per capita. Second, it highlights the rapid growth in GDP and GDP per capita in Asia, significantly higher than in the industrialized countries, particularly during the periods 1991–2000 and 2001–2008, when there was a substantial increase in Asia's share of world GDP and the beginnings of a convergence in GDP per capita. Third, for Africa, it reveals the slowdown in GDP growth and the stagnation or decline in GDP per capita, during the periods 1981–1990 and 1991–2000, the lost decades, which was responsible for a drop in the share of world GDP and a growing divergence in GDP per capita, just as it shows that things might have been worse without the rapid growth during 2001–2008. Fourth, for Latin America, it points to the consequences of the sharp contraction in GDP growth and the negative GDP per capita growth during 1981–1990, the lost decade, while the slowdown that persisted during 1991–2000 had implications for its share and level of income in relation to the world economy. Fifth, it establishes that, during 2001–2008, both GDP and GDP per capita growth rates in every region of the developing world were significantly higher than the corresponding growth rates in industrialized countries, which explains the rapid increase in the share of developing countries in world GDP and the more broad-based convergence in GDP per capita in the 2000s.

For a study of long-term trends, it is appropriate to focus on the period until 2008 as the global economic crisis led to a sharp slowdown in growth thereafter. Even so, to complete the picture, Table 4.8 presents evidence on growth rates in GDP and GDP per capita for the years 2008, 2009, 2010 and 2011, as compared with 2001–2008, in the same format as Table 4.7. It confirms that there was a sharp slowdown in growth in industrialized countries, while growth rates in Asia were almost the same and in Latin America somewhat

Table 4.7. Growth Rates in the World Economy by Regions, Countries and Decades: 1971–2008
(percent per annum)

	Maddison Data				UN Data			
	1971–1980	1981–1990	1991–2000	2001–2008	1971–1980	1981–1990	1991–2000	2001–2008
GDP								
Asia	5.31	5.60	5.76	7.26	5.88	5.54	6.15	6.94
Africa	4.01	2.22	2.67	5.01	4.22	2.15	2.59	5.60
Latin America	5.57	1.34	3.19	3.52	6.00	1.28	3.12	3.65
Developing Countries	5.23	4.07	4.93	6.41	5.67	3.54	4.67	5.94
Industrialized Countries	3.34	2.89	2.58	1.91	3.38	2.97	2.49	1.93
World	3.82	3.08	3.06	4.20	3.76	3.08	2.94	2.93
GDP per capita								
Asia	3.08	3.60	4.14	5.93	3.62	3.40	4.51	5.60
Africa	1.27	-0.61	0.16	2.62	4.22	2.15	2.59	3.17
Latin America	3.13	-0.71	1.52	2.13	3.50	-0.81	1.41	2.32
Developing Countries	2.91	1.95	3.15	4.89	3.34	1.36	2.92	4.44
Industrialized Countries	2.55	2.29	1.90	1.39	2.63	2.04	1.76	1.16
World	1.92	1.33	1.60	2.94	1.77	1.12	1.38	1.57

Note: GDP and GDP per capita are measured in 1990 international (Geary-Khamis PPP) dollars in the Maddison data and in US dollars in current prices at market exchange rates in the UN data.

Source: Author's calculations from Maddison online database and United Nations, National Accounts Statistics, see Appendix.

Table 4.8. Impact of the Global Economic Crisis on Growth Rates in the World Economy: 2001–2011

(percent per annum)

	2001–2008	2001–2008	2008	2009	2010	2011
	(1990 dollars)	(2005 dollars)	(2005 dollars)			
			GDP			
Asia	6.9	7.0	5.5	4.4	8.4	6.9
Africa	5.6	5.3	4.8	0.9	4.0	0.7
Latin America	3.7	3.6	3.9	−2.2	6.0	4.3
Developing Countries	5.9	5.8	5.1	2.5	7.5	5.8
Industrialized Countries	1.9	1.9	−0.1	−4.0	2.7	1.4
World	2.9	2.9	1.4	−2.3	4.0	2.7
			GDP per capita			
Asia	5.6	5.8	4.4	3.2	7.3	5.1
Africa	3.2	2.9	2.4	−1.4	1.6	−1.5
Latin America	2.3	2.2	2.7	−3.3	4.8	3.0
Developing Countries	4.4	4.4	3.7	1.2	6.1	4.0
Industrialized Countries	1.2	1.2	−0.7	−4.5	2.1	0.9
World	1.6	1.6	0.2	−3.5	2.9	1.2

Source: United Nations, National Accounts Statistics, see Appendix.

higher as compared with 2001–2008. Africa fared worse than in 2001–2008 but better than the industrialized countries. In the aftermath of the crisis, the growth performance of developing countries, taken together, was far better than that of industrialized countries.[4] This explains the sharp rise in the share of developing countries in world GDP and the continued convergence in GDP per capita, from 2008 to 2010, which is clearly visible in Figures 4.5 and 4.6.

4. Hypotheses About Convergence

The idea that latecomers to industrialization would, over time, catch up with countries that are leaders in the process of development does exist in the literature on the subject, but in two somewhat different strands. There is one school of thought in unconventional economic history and there is another school of thought in orthodox economic theory. It is worth considering these, even if briefly, because the notion of catch up, in the context of developing countries in the world economy since 1950, is also the analytical focus of this chapter.

In economic history, this idea of countries that are followers catching up with leaders can be traced back to Veblen (1915) in his writing about Germany following in the footsteps of England. For the latter, it was characterized as the 'penalty of taking the lead'. This notion was conceptualized further by

Gerschenkron (1962), as the 'advantages of relative economic backwardness', to consider the experience of Russia as a latecomer that was subsequently extended to include France, Italy, and Austria. The essential hypothesis can be summed up as follows. Economic backwardness, relative to others, creates a tension between the actual stagnation and the potential prosperity. The gap provides the economic incentive to catch up, while the political process drives institutional innovation. Wider gaps create stronger incentives to leap forward. State intervention then creates the missing initial conditions for growth, to compensate for the scarcities of capital, skilled labour, entrepreneurship and technological capabilities. Greater backwardness needs greater intervention. The mobilization of savings for investment is critical. In Russia, this was done by the State, whereas in Germany the same role was performed by the creation of a banking system that financed industrialization. The greater degree of backwardness in Russia required an emphasis on producer rather than consumer goods, larger rather than small firms, and capital- rather than labour-intensive technologies. There are benefits to be derived by learning from the mistakes of predecessors, so that economic growth for latecomers is characterized by spurts with periods of high, sometimes exceptional, growth rates. Obviously, the model has limitations, but its generalizations from history, particularly the industrialization experience in Russia, provide analytical insights into how a mix of ideology and institutions, or economics and politics, might foster success in countries that are latecomers to industrialization.

It is no surprise that the Gerschenkron mode of thinking influenced studies in the economic history of other countries, such as Japan (Okhawa and Rosovsky, 1973). It also led to a quantitative assessment of historical analysis across countries. Abramovitz (1986) tested the hypothesis that productivity growth rates are inversely related to productivity levels so that there is a tendency for convergence over time, to find that there was such a catch up in Western Europe to productivity levels in the United States during the quarter century that followed World War II. However, it is recognized that catching up is a function not only of technological opportunities but also of social capabilities, which have institutional dimensions that are slow to develop in economies, firms and individuals. Hence, every country may not be able to realize its potential for catching up since that depends on its social history and initial conditions. In the long term, convergence is, at best, a tendency that emerges from the average experience of a group of countries, which cannot be oversimplified into generalized outcomes. The central Gerschenkron idea was also formalized in several models. Nelson and Phelps (1966) suggested that the greater the technology gap between the follower and the leader the greater the rate of innovation in the former, which implies a relationship that is positive and linear. Thus, the gap reduces with catch up over time but is asymptotic towards a positive constant. Of course, this abstraction does not recognize that, for some countries, the technology gap could be so large that it rules out the essential conditions for even beginning to close the gap. Findlay (1976) examined the dynamics of catching up in relation to technological diffusion through direct foreign investment, while Gomulka (1970), explored the possibilities of trading conventional goods for embodied technology.

In economic theory, modern theorizing about growth in the neo-classical tradition has spawned a large literature on the idea of convergence. This draws inspiration largely from the original contribution of Solow (1956), where the prediction of convergence is at the core of the model. It makes a distinction between unconditional and conditional convergence. In the former, income differences between countries must wither away in the long run if there is no tendency for countries to have differences in technical progress, savings rates, population growth, and even capital depreciation. In this world, initial conditions do not matter. Indeed, neither does history. Countries converge to their steady states. And these steady states are the same everywhere. Available evidence provides no support for this notion of unconditional, or absolute, convergence (De Long, 1988). The weaker version of the hypothesis, conditional convergence, argues that countries converge to their own steady states but that these steady states can differ between countries, so that it is possible to control for differences in cross-country parameters such as differences in savings rates or population growth. The essential proposition remains the same. Convergence means a negative relationship between growth rates and initial levels of income per capita. The evidence on this latter formulation is less contrary but not sufficient to sustain any generalization. What is more, it provides no explanation about why the controlled parameters for which the statistical exercises make adjustments, in fact differ across countries. It would seem this orthodox literature reduces the complexity of the growth process to the simplicity of abstract models. It is no surprise that the notion is contradicted by stylized facts and unfolding realities about development.

What does experience during the second half of the 20th century suggest? There are studies that focus on the industrialized countries, the original 21 members of OECD, which show that countries with lower levels of GDP per capita in 1950 have typically recorded higher growth rates in GDP per capita until 2000. However, if this sample is enlarged beyond the OECD to 70 countries including countries from Asia and Africa, evidence for the period from 1960 to 2000 shows that there is no clear relationship between the level of GDP per capita in 1960 and the growth rate in GDP per capita until 2000 (Blanchard, 2011).

There are also attempts to support the convergence hypothesis by going back to the 19th century (Baumol, 1986) and forward to the 21st century (Lucas,

2000), both of which are characterized by the limitations stressed above. The Baumol (1986) study of sixteen countries, the richest in the present world, from 1870 to 1979, shows a negative relationship between the initial level of GDP per capita and the growth in GDP per capita over the period (Baumol, 1986). But another study for the same period from 1870 to 1979 that added just seven countries to this set of countries, all of which had higher levels of GDP per capita than Japan and Finland, which were at the bottom in the original sample of sixteen countries in 1870, reveals that the negative relationship between the initial level and growth of GDP per capita vanishes (De Long, 1988). It needs to be said that a selective focus on some rich countries that succeeded is an exercise that validates itself through its choice of countries because there were several others with higher levels of GDP per capita than Japan in 1870, which were not included possibly because that would have refuted the convergence hypothesis. These exercises could be described as almost tautological (De Long, 1988 and Pritchett, 1997). Clearly, studies in retrospect, when the facts about the present are known, should not be used to support generalizations that predict outcomes.

This belief in convergence as a generalizable or predictable outcome is not new. It is also stressed as a virtue of markets and openness during the epoch of globalization from 1870 to 1914. But it is worth noting that there was no convergence of growth, let alone incomes, across countries in the world economy during that era (Nayyar, 2006 and Williamson, 2002). The factor price convergence was confined to the Atlantic economies, which was also attributable to mass migration from Western Europe to the United States rather than to commodity price convergence. There was some convergence in real wages but this was confined to a few countries in Europe such as Denmark, Ireland, Norway, and Sweden. There was little in terms of catch up for Italy while Spain and Portugal witnessed a widening gap in wages. As noted earlier, much of Southern and Eastern Europe experienced a divergence in per capita incomes during this era.

It is clear that hypothesizing about observed outcomes is one thing but predicting future outcomes is quite another. In reality, there is nothing automatic about convergence, just as there is nothing automatic about growth. Convergence and divergence are often simultaneous. What is more, convergence is often uneven across space and over time. This may be reflected in differences between countries in rates of growth of GDP and GDP per capita but it is also important to analyse the underlying factors. Therefore, it would be reasonable to ask whether we can learn something about this issue of convergence from the experience of developing countries in the world economy during the period from 1950 to 2010 studied in this chapter. It does not quite validate the convergence hypothesis. Asia had the lowest initial level of GDP per capita and the highest rate of growth in GDP per capita. Latin America had the highest level of GDP per capita but its rate of growth of GDP per capita was somewhere in the middle among the three continents. Africa had an initial level of GDP per capita that was higher than in Asia and lower than in Latin America, but it had the lowest rate of growth of GDP per capita. Of course, it is difficult to generalize at the level of continents, while it is possible to draw conclusions about convergence or divergence with reference to particular countries. That will be done later. Even so, it is clear that there were the modest beginnings of convergence in Asia but growing divergence in Africa.

Conclusion

It is appropriate to return to the four issues posed at the outset. The changes in the significance of developing countries in the world economy during the period from 1950 to 2010 provide a sharp contrast when compared with the period from 1820 to 1950. In terms of Maddison PPP statistics, the share of developing countries in world GDP stopped its continuous decline in 1962, when it was one-fourth, to increase rapidly after 1980 so that it was almost one-half by 2008, which was close to their share c.1850. The divergence in GDP per capita also came to a stop in 1980 and was followed by a modest convergence thereafter, but as a proportion of GDP per capita in industrialized countries in 2008 it was somewhat less than one-fifth, which was about the same as in 1900. In current prices at market exchange rates, between 1970 and 2010, the share of developing countries in world GDP doubled from one-sixth to one-third, while their GDP per capita as a proportion of that in industrialized countries recorded a modest increase from one-fourteenth to one-eleventh. In terms of both PPP and market exchange rates, however, the significant rise in share of world output and modest convergence in per capita income were both attributable almost entirely to Asia, as Latin America witnessed neither, while Africa experienced a declining share and continuing divergence. During the 2000s, convergence was more discernible and broader based. Differences in GDP growth rates underlie the rising share of developing countries and falling share of industrialized countries in world GDP. But differences in GDP per capita growth rates were significantly smaller because of high population growth rates in developing countries so that convergence in per capita incomes was modest. The idea that latecomers to industrialization catch up with countries that are leaders, over time, exists in unconventional economic history and orthodox economic theory. In reality, there is nothing automatic about convergence, just as there is nothing automatic about growth. Convergence and divergence are often simultaneous. Convergence is often uneven across space and over time. This is borne out by the experience of developing countries in the world economy since 1950, which does not quite validate the convergence hypothesis.

5

Engagement with the World Economy

This chapter considers the nature and degree of interaction between developing countries and the world economy, to focus on changes during the second half of the 20th century and the first decade of the 21st. In doing so, it makes comparisons with the past. It also attempts to disaggregate the analysis for Asia, Africa, and Latin America, wherever possible, but this does not extend beyond regions to countries. The obvious channels of engagement are international trade, international investment, and international migration. Section 1 examines the participation of developing countries in world trade to trace the contours of change, draws a distinction between trade in goods and trade in services, and highlights the significant differences between regions. Section 2 considers the changes in stocks and the trends in flows of both inward and outward foreign direct investment, as also other forms of international investment, to focus on the relative importance of developing countries, asymmetries among their constituent regions, and similarities or differences with the past. Section 3 analyses international migration since 1950 from a global perspective, to explore changes over time, distinguish between different forms of cross-border movements of people, show the relative importance of developing countries, examine the implications for development, and highlight the differences between the past and the present, to explain why it is a significant form of interaction with the world economy.

1. International Trade

International trade is the most visible, perhaps critical, form of engagement with the world economy. During the period from the mid-19th to the mid-20th century, it was trade that locked developing countries into an international division of labour which was not conducive to industrialization or economic growth. Indeed, there was a causal connection between the Great Specialization and the Great Divergence. For that reason, perhaps, in the early stages of the post-colonial era, starting around 1950, most poor countries adopted strategies of development that provided a sharp contrast with the preceding hundred years. There was a conscious attempt to limit the degree of openness and of integration with the world economy because open economies of the colonial past were associated with de-industrialization and underdevelopment. Industrialization was seen as an imperative in catching up, which had to start with import substitution in the manufacturing sector. This approach also represented the development consensus at the time and exercised a profound influence on trade policies. The industrialization experience over the next three decades led to changes in both thinking and policies about trade beginning c.1980.[1] The spread of markets and the gathering momentum of globalization reinforced the process, which led to a marked increase in the degree of economic openness in developing countries. This began with trade, to be followed by investment and finance (Nayyar, 2006). It is no surprise that these shifts were reflected in the significance of international trade.

Table 5.1 sets out statistics on the value of exports and imports of developing countries in relation to world trade at five-year intervals from 1950 to 2010. It shows that total exports from developing countries increased from about $20 billion in 1950 to $600 billion in 1980 and almost $6400 billion in 2010, while total imports also registered a broadly similar increase. But these values are in current prices and at market exchange rates, which exaggerate

Table 5.1. Merchandise Exports from, and Imports into Developing Countries and the World: 1950–2010 (in US $billion)

Year	EXPORTS		IMPORTS		Percentage share of Developing Countries in World Trade	
	Developing Countries	World	Developing Countries	World	Exports	Imports
1950	21	62	19	64	34.0	29.6
1955	27	94	28	100	29.0	28.0
1960	32	130	35	137	24.4	25.3
1965	41	189	42	199	21.6	21.1
1970	60	317	61	330	19.0	18.5
1975	226	888	204	909	25.4	22.4
1980	600	2036	497	2078	29.5	23.9
1985	501	1973	470	2036	25.4	23.1
1990	842	3480	798	3589	24.2	22.2
1995	1435	5178	1500	5237	27.7	28.6
2000	2056	6449	1917	6659	31.9	28.8
2005	3796	10,494	3414	10,789	36.2	31.6
2010	6396	15,230	5931	15,262	42.0	38.9

Note: The data on exports and imports are in current prices and at market exchange rates.

Source: United Nations, UNCTADStat, based on UN International Trade Statistics.

the increase. Hence, it is necessary to consider these values as a proportion of world trade. The share of developing countries in world exports was 34 per cent in 1950, 30 per cent in 1980 and 42 per cent in 2010, while their share in world imports was 30 per cent, 24 per cent and 39 per cent respectively, but their shares in exports and imports were both lower than 20 per cent in 1970.

The trends are revealed more clearly by Figure 5.1, based on time series data, which plots these shares in world trade over the six decades. It shows that the share of developing countries in world exports, as well as imports, declined continuously from around one-third in the early 1950s to less than one-fifth in the early 1970s. This was attributable partly to trade policies in the developing world that reduced openness, but much more to the rapid expansion in trade between countries in the industrialized world during the golden age of capitalism. There was an increase in 1973 and 1979 which coincided with increases in oil prices, reflected more in exports than in imports, followed by a decrease through the first half of the 1980s as oil prices declined in real terms. These shares in world exports and imports rose almost in tandem from the mid-1980s to the mid-1990s, to climb more rapidly thereafter so that developing countries accounted for two-fifths of world trade in 2010. And, from the late 1990s, their share in world exports was continuously higher than their share in world imports. Much of the increase in these shares reflected the growing significance and an increasing engagement of developing countries with the world economy. Some of it was possibly a consequence of the rapid

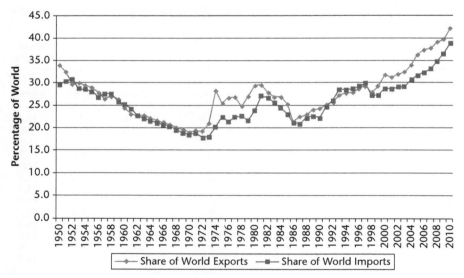

Figure 5.1. Share of Developing Countries in World Merchandise Trade: 1950–2010
Source: United Nations, UNCTADStat, based on UN International Trade Statistics.

internationalization of production associated with the rise of global value chains, which would have increased the import content and gross value of exports from developing countries. Of course, this phenomenon also increased the value of world exports, which is the denominator for calculating these shares. Even so, assembly operations and value chains run by large international firms probably did enlarge the share of developing countries in world trade. In this context, it is worth noting that, in 1970, the share of developing countries in world trade was just 2 percentage points higher than their share of world GDP but, by 2010, it was 10 percentage points higher than their share of world GDP.

It is important to recognize that this rapid expansion of international trade was most unevenly distributed among regions of the developing world. Table 5.2 presents evidence on exports from and imports into Asia, Africa and Latin America for the selected benchmark years from 1950 to 2010. The picture it reveals is striking. There was a massive increase in exports from Asia, in current prices and at market exchange rates, which rose from $9 billion in 1950 to $364 billion in 1980 and jumped to $5010 billion in 2010. There was, of course, an increase in the absolute value of total exports and imports for Africa and Latin America but it was relatively modest. The share of Africa in world exports and imports dropped continuously from more than 7 per cent in 1950 to about 3 per cent in 2010, and much of the drop had occurred by 1990. The share of Latin America in world trade halved between 1950 and 2010, from almost 12 per cent in exports and 10 per cent in imports to less than 6 per cent in both, and much of the decline had occurred by 1970. Between 1950 and 1970, Asia also witnessed a sharp decline in its share of world exports, by almost one-half, and of world imports, by about one-third. There was a dramatic reversal thereafter. In the 1970s, Asia recovered its lost share of world trade but this was largely attributable to the two rounds of oil price increases. The real change occurred between 1980 and 2010, when Asia's share of world exports and imports more than doubled, to account for almost one-third of world trade at the end of this period.

A comparison with the past is worthwhile. Table 2.7 showed that the share of developing countries in world exports at current prices and market exchange rates was 19.9 per cent in 1913, 24.1 per cent in 1928 and 26.9 per cent in 1948, while their share in world imports was 16.9 per cent, 19.7 per cent and 26 per cent respectively. Their share in world exports was lower at 15.9 per cent in 1870 and 16.9 per cent in 1900. These historical trade statistics are not strictly comparable with the more complete data in Table 5.1. Even so, it would seem that the significance of developing countries in world trade in 1970 was greater than it was in 1870 and about the same as it was in 1913, while in 2010 it was one-and-a-half times what it was in 1948. However, between the late 19th and 20th centuries, the change in the significance of

Catch Up

Table 5.2. Merchandise Trade for Asia, Africa, and Latin America and Shares in World Merchandise Trade: 1950–2010 (in US $billion)

Year	EXPORTS			Percentage share of Region in World Exports		
	Asia	Africa	Latin America	Asia	Africa	Latin America
1950	9	4	7	15.2	7.2	11.6
1955	12	6	9	12.6	6.6	9.7
1960	15	7	10	11.2	5.5	7.5
1965	18	10	12	9.7	5.3	6.5
1970	27	16	17	8.4	5.0	5.5
1975	135	44	45	15.2	5.0	5.1
1980	364	122	111	17.9	6.0	5.5
1985	306	84	109	15.5	4.3	5.5
1990	590	105	144	17.0	3.0	4.1
1995	1087	113	230	21.0	2.2	4.4
2000	1535	149	367	23.8	2.3	5.7
2005	2895	317	577	27.6	3.0	5.5
2010	5010	504	872	32.9	3.3	5.7

Year	IMPORTS			Percentage share of Region in World Imports		
	Asia	Africa	Latin America	Asia	Africa	Latin America
1950	8	5	6	12.5	7.1	9.9
1955	12	7	9	11.7	7.1	9.1
1960	16	8	10	11.6	6.2	7.4
1965	20	10	12	9.8	5.2	5.9
1970	28	14	18	8.4	4.4	5.5
1975	101	45	56	11.1	4.9	6.2
1980	273	97	124	13.1	4.7	5.9
1985	309	75	84	15.2	3.7	4.1
1990	571	94	127	15.9	2.6	3.6
1995	1120	124	250	21.4	2.4	4.8
2000	1389	130	392	20.9	2.0	5.9
2005	2612	258	534	24.2	2.4	5.0
2010	4577	449	891	30.0	2.9	5.8

Note: The data on exports and imports are in current prices and at market exchange rates.
Source: United Nations, UNCTADStat, based on UN International Trade Statistics.

international trade for developing countries, as also the world economy, was qualitative rather than quantitative (Nayyar, 2006). The real difference, set out in the next chapter, was in the composition of trade, as the overwhelming importance of primary commodities in their exports came to be replaced by an increasing significance of manufactured goods.

There was also a change in the channels of trade. Trade flows then were in the domain of large international firms. Transnational corporations also drive trade flows now. But the apparent similarity is deceptive. There are two important differences. First, the large trading firms of the 19th century, such as the East India Company and the Royal Africa Company, 'were like dinosaurs, large in bulk but small in brain, feeding on the lush vegetation of the new worlds' (Hymer, 1972). The forerunners of what are now described as transnational corporations were not these giant trading firms but the small workshops and entrepreneurial firms of the late 19th century. Second, in the late 20th century, an increasing proportion of international trade is intra-firm trade, across national boundaries but between affiliates of the same firm. In the early 1970s, such intra-firm trade accounted for about one-fifth of world trade, but by the early 1990s this proportion was one-third (UNCTAD, 1994, p.143) and, by the late 2000s, this proportion would have risen to at least two-fifths. Even more important, perhaps, is the changed composition of intra-firm trade, which also shifted from primary commodities to intermediate products and manufactured goods (Nayyar, 2006). Global value chains, considered in the next chapter, are an important part of this story.

The focus so far has been on merchandise trade, as exports and imports of goods were always the primary form of international trade. Of course, services such as shipping and insurance, which are intimately linked with merchandise trade, were always traded, and there was tourism. But the past three decades have witnessed real change in the possibilities of international trade in services (Nayyar, 1988). The technological revolution in transport and communications has made hitherto non-traded services tradable either by a dramatic reduction in the cost of transport, which increases the mobility of producers and consumers of services, or by developing a means of communication, such as satellite links or video transmission, which eliminates the need for physical proximity between producers and consumers of services. The phenomenal pace of technological change in the sphere of telecommunications and informatics has created an altogether new category of services such as information technology, particularly software, that enter into international trade. Such technological change has also substantively enhanced the possibility of trade in what have always been traded services. Financial services, such as banking and insurance, have become so much more tradable. And so have education or medical services. Hence, there has been a phenomenal expansion of international trade in services.

Table 5.3 outlines the dimensions of international trade in services in current prices and market exchange rates. It shows that between 1980 and 2010, world exports of services increased from about $400 billion to $3800 billion, while world imports of services increased from around $450 billion to $3600 billion. During this period, world trade in services, as a proportion of world merchandise trade, increased from 20 per cent to 25 per cent. For developing countries, exports of services increased more than fifteen-fold from $73 billion to $1134 billion, rising from 12 per cent to 18 per cent of their merchandise exports, while imports of services increased less than ten-fold from $140 billion to $1292 billion, falling from 28 per cent to 22 per cent of their merchandise imports. Consequently, between 1980 and 2010, the share of developing countries in

Table 5.3. International Trade in Services: 1980–2010 (in US $billion)

Year	Exports of Services			Imports of Services		
	Developing Countries	World	Percentage Share of Developing Countries in World	Developing Countries	World	Percentage Share of Developing Countries in World
1980	73.4	395.7	18.5	139.6	447.7	31.2
1985	80.5	411.2	19.6	129.2	443.7	29.1
1990	150.4	829.1	18.1	193.8	876.1	22.1
1995	273.0	1220.7	22.4	335.0	1235.4	27.1
2000	351.1	1518.2	23.1	415.3	1513.5	27.4
2005	629.3	2555.2	24.6	698.6	2448.9	28.5
2010	1133.5	3819.4	29.7	1292.0	3620.2	35.7

Source: United Nations, UNCTADStat, based on IMF *Balance of Payments Statistics*.

world exports of services rose from 19 per cent to 30 per cent, while their share in world imports of services increased from 31 per cent to 36 per cent.

The trends in these shares are brought out more clearly in Figure 5.2, which plots a time series from 1980 to 2010. It shows that the share of developing countries in world exports of services remained in the range of 20 per cent from 1980 to 1990, but increased steadily in the 1990s and rapidly in the 2000s, as their comparative advantage in information technology services evolved and surfaced. Their share in world imports of services fell in the 1980s, reflecting the slowdown in their growth, recovered partly in the 1990s and rose in the 2000s, which was attributable to a faster expansion in their imports rather than a slowdown in world imports. It is worth noting that, despite the rapid growth in exports, developing countries ran a modest deficit on account of international trade in services throughout this period, in contrast with their modest surplus on account of merchandise trade. Of course, there were probably surpluses in sub-sectors such as information technology services and deficits in sub-sectors such as financial services.

It would seem that the significance of developing countries in international trade diminished from 1950 to 1970 but revived in 1980 to gather momentum thereafter. Compared with the past, the share of developing countries in world trade even in 1970 was the same as it was in 1913, while in 2010 it was one-and-a-half times what it was in 1948. However, between the late 19th and 20th centuries, changes in the significance of international trade were qualitative rather than quantitative. The most important changes were in the composition and channels of trade. The real difference was the emergence of a flourishing international trade in services, an altogether new phenomenon, which gathered momentum in the first decade of the 21st century.

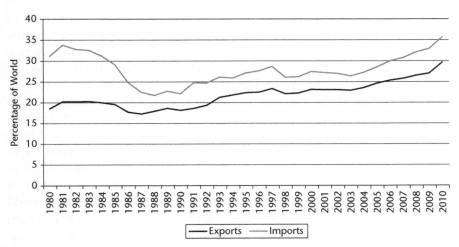

Figure 5.2. Share of Developing Countries in World Exports and Imports of Services
Source: United Nations, UNCTADStat, based on IMF *Balance of Payments Statistics*.

2. International Investment

The picture of international investment is more difficult to sketch and cannot go back as far in time. But it is much easier than constructing a profile of intra-firm trade which is driven by international investment. Table 5.4 sets out the magnitudes of the stock of foreign direct investment, inward and outward, in the world economy, industrialized countries, developing countries, and their constituent regions, at five-year intervals for 1990, 1995, 2000, 2005, and

Table 5.4. Stocks of Foreign Direct Investment in the World Economy: 1990–2010 (in US $billion)

	INWARD					OUTWARD				
	1990	1995	2000	2005	2010	1990	1995	2000	2005	2010
World	2081	3393	7446	11,539	19,141	2094	3616	7962	12,416	20,408
Industrialized Countries	1562	2534	5653	8563	12,502	1948	3281	7083	10,983	16,804
Developing Countries	517	848	1732	2701	5951	146	330	857	1281	3132
Asia	343	568	1073	1618	3663	68	210	608	879	2276
Africa	61	89	154	262	554	20	32	44	48	122
Latin America	111	187	502	817	1722	58	88	205	354	733
Share of Developing Countries in World Total (in percentages)	24.9	25.0	23.3	23.4	31.1	6.9	9.1	10.8	10.3	15.3

Source: UNCTAD Foreign Direct Investment Online Database.

2010. Table 5.5, in the same format, provides the magnitude of flows of foreign direct investment, inward and outward, with annual averages for the periods 1991–1995, 1996–2000, 2001–2005, and 2006–2010. Taken together, the two tables provide a complete picture. The basic reason for the choice of period is that increasing openness and deepening integration in the world economy led to a phenomenal expansion in foreign direct investment in the 1990s and 2000s. The data are also more complete in coverage for this period.

The stock of inward foreign direct investment in the world increased from $2 trillion in 1990 to $19 trillion in 2010. In this stock, the share of industrialized countries fell from 75 per cent to 65 per cent, while the share of developing countries rose from 25 per cent to 31 per cent, with the residual in transition economies. The inflows of foreign direct investment in the world increased from $228 million per annum during 1991–1995 to $1521 million per annum during 2006–2010. In these inflows, for the same periods, the share of industrialized countries fell from 65 per cent to 58 per cent, while the share of developing countries rose from 34 per cent to 36 per cent. It is clear that the relative importance of developing countries as a destination for foreign direct investment in the world economy increased during this period. The regional distribution was once again unequal. Of the inward stock in, as also inflows to, developing countries, Asia accounted for three-fifths to two-thirds, Africa for about one-tenth and Latin America for one-fourth to three-tenths.

The stock of outward foreign direct investment in the world increased from $2 trillion in 1990 to $20 trillion in 2010. In this stock, the share of industrialized countries was dominant even if it decreased from 93 per cent to 82 per cent, while the share of developing countries was small even if it increased from 7 per cent to 15 per cent, with the negligible residual attributable to transition economies. The outflows of foreign direct investment in the world increased from roughly $260 million per annum during 1991–1995 to almost $1600 million per annum during 2006–2010. In these outflows, the share of industrialized countries was dominant although it decreased from 86 per cent to 79 per cent, while the share of developing countries was modest even if it increased from 14 per cent to 18 per cent. It would seem that the significance of developing countries as an origin of foreign direct investment in the world economy did register an increase during this period, as they were no longer just recipients (UNCTAD, 2006). The regional distribution was inevitably unequal. Of the outward stock, as also outflows, from developing countries, Asia accounted for almost three-fourths, while Latin America accounted for about one-fourth, with just a negligible residual in Africa.

In recent times, cross-border mergers and acquisitions have emerged as a form of international investment. Table 5.6 sets out the value of such mergers and acquisitions through sales and purchases in the world economy,

Table 5.5. Flows of Foreign Direct Investment in the World Economy: 1990–2010 (in US $billion: annual averages)

	INWARD				OUTWARD			
	1991–1995	1996–2000	2001–2005	2006–2010	1991–1995	1996–2000	2001–2005	2006–2010
World	228	815	750	1521	259	776	735	1597
Industrialized Countries	148	604	490	891	222	696	641	1262
Developing Countries	78	203	240	549	36	78	84	286
Asia	52	111	144	333	28	52	57	211
Africa	5	10	23	60	2	2	0.5	8
Latin America	20	81	72	155	6	24	26	66
Share of Developing Countries in World Total (in percentages)	*34.1*	*24.9*	*32.0*	*36.1*	*13.8*	*10.0*	*11.5*	*17.9*

Source: UNCTAD Foreign Direct Investment Online Database.

Table 5.6. Cross-border Mergers and Acquisitions in the World Economy: 1991–2010 (in US $billion: annual averages)

	SALES				PURCHASES			
	1991–1995	1996–2000	2001–2005	2006–2010	1991–1995	1996–2001	2001–2006	2006–2010
World	63	453	310	589	63	453	310	589
Industrialized Countries	57	406	264	491	53	416	251	457
Developing Countries	7	45	43	83	6	22	34	107
Asia	2	17	25	56	4	18	23	81
Africa	0.3	0.7	6	11	0.6	0.6	4	8
Latin America	4	28	12	15	2	4	7	18
Share of Developing Countries in World Total (in percentages)	*10.4*	*10.0*	*13.7*	*14.1*	*10.2*	*4.8*	*10.9*	*18.2*

Source: UNCTAD cross-border M&A Database.

industrialized countries, developing countries and their constituent regions, in terms of annual averages, for the periods 1991–1995, 1996–2000, 2001–2005, and 2006–2010. Obviously, sales and purchases are exactly the same for the world economy but differ for country-groups or regions because sales and purchases are reported on a net basis. It is difficult to discern trends over time and that would not mean much either. For the entire period from 1991 to 2010, the total value of such cross-border mergers and acquisitions was $7 trillion or $350 billion per annum. During the same period, the total flows of foreign direct investment were about $16.5 trillion or $825 billion per annum. In these cross-border mergers and acquisitions, industrialized countries, which are the home for most transnational firms, were dominant, accounting for 86 per cent of sales and 83 per cent of purchases. However, developing countries, where some large domestic firms are in the process of becoming international firms, accounted for 12 per cent of both sales and purchases.

It is no surprise that the regional distribution in the developing world was unequal. Asia accounted for 59 per cent of sales and 74 per cent of purchases, Latin America for 32 per cent of sales and 18 per cent of purchases, while Africa accounted for less than 10 per cent of both sales and purchases. It would seem that firms from developing countries have also entered the world of cross-border mergers and acquisitions. The conventional literature argues that the internationalization of firms through mergers and acquisitions is driven by the oligopolistic or monopolistic power of these firms, which seek to source inputs or capture markets through ownership or control rather than trade. But firms from developing countries may use outward foreign direct investment not as a means of exploiting existing competitive advantage but as a means of realizing or augmenting potential competitive advantage. Hence, their motivation is mixed and diverse. In fact, the objectives range from sourcing raw materials in the sphere of primary commodities to market access for exports, horizontal or vertical integration, delivery of services, capture of international brand names, and access to technology in the world of manufactured goods (Nayyar, 2008a).

There is yet another form of international investment which has emerged in recent times with capital account liberalization and the internationalization of finance—portfolio investment. Unfortunately, it is exceedingly difficult to find evidence on distribution by countries of origin and destination or inflows and outflows. But there can be little doubt that it has grown in significance as mutual funds and pension funds from industrialized countries have searched worldwide for financial assets that would yield higher capital appreciation or higher returns on their investible resources. Much of this placement is still in industrialized countries but some countries in the developing world are also destinations for these footloose and volatile capital flows.

In these developing countries, portfolio investment (capital flows that can be withdrawn on demand) is, or was, a source of financing current account deficits in the balance of payments. An economy needs high interest rates together with a strong exchange rate to sustain portfolio investment in terms of profitability and confidence. This erodes the competitiveness of exports over time and enlarges the trade deficit. Larger trade deficits and current account deficits require larger portfolio investment flows, which, beyond a point, undermine confidence and create adverse expectations even if the government keeps the exchange rate pegged. But when a stifling of exports does ultimately force an exchange rate depreciation, confidence may simply collapse and lead to capital flight. This precipitates a currency crisis. The frequency and intensity of such crises have only increased with the passage of time. And it is no coincidence that the most advanced among developing countries, which are integrated into international financial markets, have been ravaged by such crises (Nayyar, 2003). Clearly, this form of engagement with the world economy is fraught with risk (Ocampo and Stiglitz, 2008).

Some comparisons with the past are interesting. In 1913, the stock of foreign investment in the world economy was the equivalent of 9 per cent of world output (UNCTAD, 1994). The stock of foreign direct investment in the world economy as a proportion of world GDP increased steadily from 6.1 per cent in 1980 to 8.9 per cent in 1990 and remained in the range of 9 per cent through the first half of the 1990s. This proportion surpassed its 1913 level only in the late 1990s (Nayyar, 2006). The significance of foreign investment in developing countries reveals a similar parallel. In 1914, foreign investment in developing countries, direct and portfolio together, was $179 billion at 1980 prices, which was almost double the stock of foreign direct investment in developing countries in 1980 at $96 billion in current (1980) prices. In real terms, it reached its 1914 level only in the mid-1990s (Nayyar, 2006). In 1900, foreign investment in developing countries, direct and portfolio together, was the equivalent of 32 per cent of the GDP of developing countries (Chapter 2, p. 28). A century later, foreign direct investment in developing countries, as a proportion of their GDP, was 25 per cent in 2000, while it was 29 per cent in 2010 (Tables 5.4 and 4.4). The two proportions are not exactly comparable because the former includes portfolio investment but is based on the estimated GDP of selected countries that probably accounted for a large proportion of GDP in the developing world, while the latter does not include portfolio investment but is based on national accounts statistics that includes the GDP of all developing countries. Yet, the broad orders of magnitude do suggest similarities between the past and the present.

It is also worth making some comparisons with the past on the geographical distribution and sectoral composition of foreign investment.[2] The stock of foreign investment in 1914 was distributed as follows: 55 per cent in the industrialized world and 45 per cent in the underdeveloped world. In 2009, the stock of foreign direct investment in the world economy was distributed in a more unequal manner: 69 per cent in industrialized countries and 27 per cent in developing countries with the residual in transition economies. Comparable data on flows of foreign direct investment a century apart are not available. But, during 2007–2009, of the total inward flows, industrialized countries absorbed 66 per cent whereas developing countries received 30 per cent with the residual in transition economies. In 1913, the primary sector accounted for 55 per cent of long-term foreign investment in the world, while transport, trade and distribution accounted for another 30 per cent. The manufacturing sector accounted for only 10 per cent and much of this was concentrated in North America and Europe. In 2009, the stock of inward foreign direct investment in the world economy was distributed as follows: the primary sector accounted for 7 per cent, the manufacturing sector for 28 per cent and the services sector accounted for 63 per cent, with an unspecified residual possibly in property.

In sum, it would be reasonable to infer that the significance of foreign investment for developing countries at the end of the 20th century was about the same as it was at the end of the 19th century. But there were differences. For one, the geographical distribution shifted towards industrialized countries and away from developing countries. For another, the sectoral distribution experienced a major shift with a sharp decline in the overwhelming importance of the primary sector, an expected increase in the share of the manufacturing sector, and a massive rise in the share of the services sector. The biggest difference, however, was qualitative rather than quantitative. In the first decade of the 21st century, developing countries became an increasingly significant source of foreign direct investment in the world economy and this is an altogether new phenomenon.

3. International Migration

International migration is, possibly, the most significant form of engagement with the world economy, particularly in the past but also in the present, although its importance differs across countries and has changed over time. Developing countries have always been, and continue to be, important countries-of-origin for international migration. This has important implications and consequences for their development, just as it does for countries-of-destination and for the world economy.[3]

During the second half of the 20th century, it is possible to discern two phases of international migration: from the late 1940s to the mid-1970s and from the mid-1970s to the late 1990s. The latter continued into the first decade of the 21st century.

In the first phase, from the late 1940s to the mid-1970s, there were two distinct streams of international migration. First, people migrated from Europe to the United States, Canada, Australia and New Zealand. This movement was driven by the search for economic opportunities on the part of migrants. It was also shaped by the nature of immigration laws in countries-of-destination, which, with the exception of the United States, restricted immigration largely to Europeans. In the period from 1951 to 1975, total immigration was 7.8 million into the United States, 3.8 million into Canada and 2.8 million into Australia (Nayyar, 1994). Second, people moved from developing countries in Asia, North Africa and the Caribbean to Western Europe where economic growth combined with full employment created labour shortages and led to labour imports. To begin with, this demand was met from the labour surplus countries in southern Europe and Italy was perhaps the most important source. But such sources were not sufficient for long. And, by the late 1950s the labour-scarce countries of Europe were searching elsewhere for labour, mostly unskilled or semi-skilled workers for employment in the manufacturing and services sectors. Britain imported workers from the Indian subcontinent and the Caribbean islands. France imported workers from North Africa. The Netherlands imported workers from Indonesia. Colonial ties and a common language were the underlying factors that shaped these flows.[4] Germany imported workers from Yugoslavia and Turkey. It is estimated that, in the period from 1951 to 1975, total immigration into Western Europe was about 10 million (Stalker, 1994).

During the second phase, beginning in the mid-1970s, migration from Europe to the United States and Canada continued, but migration to Europe slowed down for a while. It was the end of rapid economic growth combined with full employment. And immigration laws became restrictive almost everywhere in Western Europe. But this did not last long either. Migration to Europe revived in the 1980s, to gather momentum in the 1990s and 2000s. Some new destinations emerged as latecomers to the European Union began to import labour. The sources were also different, as a significant proportion of the migrants came from Eastern Europe to begin with and then from the former USSR. This process was reinforced in the 2000s as the European Union enlarged its membership to include some countries from Eastern Europe. There were, in addition, two different streams of migration. First, there was a permanent emigration of people to the United States not only from Europe but also from the developing world. These were mostly people with professional qualifications or technical skills. This was made possible, in part, by a change in immigration laws in the United States which meant that entry was related to skill-levels rather than country-of-origin, thereby providing more access to people from developing countries. And, in the period from 1976 to 2000, total immigration into the United States was 16.3 million, more than twice the level in the preceding quarter century, while total immigration into Canada at 4.2 million and into Australia at 2.4 million witnessed little change (Nayyar, 2008). Second, there was a temporary migration of people from labour-surplus developing countries, mostly unskilled, but also semi-skilled or skilled workers in manual or clerical occupations. There were three sets of destinations for the movement of such people. Some went to the industrialized countries. Some went to the high-income, labour-scarce, oil-exporting countries. Some went to the middle-income newly industrializing countries, which attained near full employment. The guest workers in Western Europe, the seasonal import of Mexican labour in the United States, the export of workers from South Asia, Southeast Asia and North Africa to oil-exporting countries of the Middle East, and the more recent import of temporary workers by labour-scarce countries in East Asia[5] are all components of these temporary cross-border labour movements.

It is clear that international migration in the period since 1950 was significant despite stringent immigration laws and restrictive consular practices. The database on international migration is slender on flows but better on stocks. But the flows cannot be inferred from changes in stocks because migration is a process that often stretches over time as a significant proportion change their different forms of temporary status into becoming residents and then citizens.

The available evidence on the stock of international migrants and its distribution across regions and country-groups in the world, during the period from 1960 to 2010, is presented in Table 5.7. For a study of the trends, it is both necessary and appropriate to exclude the former USSR. Its inclusion distorts the picture for comparisons over time, because its break-up into fifteen independent countries in 1991 instantly transformed internal migrants into international migrants. This table shows that the number of international migrants in the world, excluding the former USSR, rose from 74.2 million in 1960 to 188.5 million in 2010. Over this period, the share of developing countries in this stock of migrant population decreased from 58 per cent to 42 per cent while that of industrialized countries increased from 42 per cent to 58 per cent. The distribution of the migrant population within regions in these country-groups remained almost unchanged. Asia was home to two-thirds of the migrant population in developing countries, while more than 90 per cent of the migrant population in industrialized countries lived in North America and Europe, divided between the two regions in almost equal proportions.

Table 5.8 highlights the significance of this phenomenon for host countries by outlining the trends in the stock of international migrants as a proportion of the total population in the respective country-groups and regions during the period from 1960 to 2010. The proportion of international migrants in the

Table 5.7. International Migrants in the World: The Distribution of the Stock across Country-Groups and Regions: 1960–2010

(in millions)

	1960	1965	1970	1975	1980	1985	1990	1995	2000	2005	2010
Asia	27.8	27.5	27.4	27.5	31.2	37.1	41.8	40.1	43.9	47.1	53.4
Africa	9.2	9.5	10.0	10.7	13.8	14.1	16.0	17.9	17.1	17.7	19.3
Latin America-Caribbean	6.2	6.0	5.8	5.8	6.1	6.3	7.1	6.2	6.5	6.9	7.5
Developing Countries	*43.2*	*43.2*	*43.4*	*44.1*	*51.3*	*57.8*	*65.2*	*64.6*	*67.7*	*72.1*	*80.5*
North America	13.6	14.4	15.2	17.5	20.2	23.4	27.8	33.6	40.4	45.6	50.0
Europe	14.6	17.1	19.2	21.6	23.1	24.2	27.8	34.1	37.7	44.6	50.1
Oceania	2.0	2.4	2.9	3.2	3.4	3.6	4.1	4.4	4.7	5.2	5.7
Industrialized Countries	*30.9*	*34.6*	*38.0*	*43.0*	*47.4*	*52.1*	*60.7*	*73.5*	*84.5*	*97.4*	*108.0*
Total	**74.2**	**77.8**	**81.4**	**87.2**	**98.7**	**109.9**	**125.9**	**138.1**	**152.3**	**169.5**	**188.5**
Former USSR	2.9	3.0	3.1	3.2	3.3	3.3	29.6	27.9	26.2	25.8	25.4
World	77.1	80.8	84.5	90.4	102.0	113.2	155.5	166.0	178.5	195.2	213.9

Source: United Nations, Population Divison, Department of Economic and Social Affairs, *Trends in International Migrant Stock: The 2008 Revision.*

Table 5.8. Stock of International Migrants as a proportion of Total Population in Country-Groups and Regions: 1960–2010

(in percentages)

	1960	1965	1970	1975	1980	1985	1990	1995	2000	2005	2010
Asia	1.8	1.6	1.4	1.2	1.3	1.4	1.4	1.2	1.3	1.3	1.4
Africa	3.2	2.9	2.7	2.5	2.9	2.5	2.5	2.5	2.1	1.9	1.9
Latin America-Caribbean	2.8	2.4	2.0	1.8	1.7	1.6	1.6	1.3	1.2	1.2	1.3
Developing Countries	*2.1*	*1.9*	*1.6*	*1.5*	*1.6*	*1.6*	*1.6*	*1.4*	*1.4*	*1.4*	*1.4*
North America	6.7	6.6	6.6	7.2	7.9	8.8	9.9	11.4	12.9	13.8	14.5
Europe	3.7	4.2	4.5	4.9	5.2	5.3	6.0	7.3	8.0	9.3	10.2
Oceania	16.1	17.5	18.4	18.6	18.9	19.0	20.0	20.4	20.5	21.2	21.3
Industrialized Countries	*4.4*	*4.7*	*4.9*	*5.3*	*5.7*	*6.1*	*6.9*	*8.1*	*9.1*	*10.1*	*10.9*
Total	**2.5**	**2.4**	**2.3**	**2.2**	**2.3**	**2.3**	**2.9**	**2.9**	**2.9**	**3.0**	**3.1**
Former USSR	1.4	1.3	1.3	1.2	1.2	1.2	10.2	9.6	9.1	9.0	8.9

Source: United Nations, Population Division, Department of Economic and Social Affairs, *Trends in International Migrant Stock: The 2008 Revision.*

world population increased from 2.5 per cent in 1960 to 3.1 per cent in 2010. Over the same period, this proportion decreased in developing countries from 2.1 per cent to 1.4 per cent, whereas it rose significantly in industrialized countries from 4.4 per cent to 10.9 per cent. These proportions rose even more in some parts of the industrialized world. In North America, the number of international migrants per 1000 in the population increased from 67 in 1960 to 145 in 2010. In Europe, the number of international migrants per 1000 in the population increased from 37 in 1960 to 102 in 2010.

The aggregate statistics do not reveal changes in the nature of international migration. There are different forms of labour flows across national boundaries. Indeed, new distinctions can be drawn between voluntary and distress migration, permanent emigration and temporary migration, or legal and illegal migration. In the contemporary world, it is possible to distinguish between five categories of cross-border movements of people, of which two are old and three are new. The old categories are made up of emigrants and refugees. Emigrants are people who move to a country and settle there permanently. Most such people are admitted for their professional qualifications or for reunification of families. Refugees are people who leave their homes because of famine, ethnic strife, civil war, or political persecution, to seek a home or asylum to take up permanent residence in other countries. The new categories are guest workers, illegal immigrants and professionals. Guest workers are people who move to a country, on a temporary basis, for a specified purpose and a limited duration. Most of them are unskilled or semi-skilled. Illegal migrants are people who enter a country without a visa, take up employment on a tourist visa, or simply stay on after their visa has expired. Most of them are at low levels in the spectrum of skills. Professionals are people with high levels of education, experience, and qualifications whose skills are in demand everywhere and who move from country to country, temporarily or permanently, since immigration laws or consular practices are not restrictive for them. Developing countries are the primary source of guest workers and illegal immigrants in the industrialized world. Some countries in the developing world are also a significant source of professionals who move across borders.

It needs to be said that these categories are not mutually exclusive or exhaustive. Nor do they define a once-and-for-all status. After a time it is difficult to distinguish between emigrants and refugees in their countries of settlement. Guest workers who acquire a right-of-residence are, in effect, not very different from emigrants. Illegal immigrants who benefit from amnesties which come from time to time, acquire legal status. The distinction between professionals and emigrants is in any case somewhat diffused, for the former are often a subset of the latter in industrialized countries. Yet, these categories serve an analytical purpose insofar as the distinctions are clear at the time that the cross-border movement of people first takes place.

Starting around 1980, globalization has led to an expansion and diversification in the movement of people across national boundaries. In fact, globalization has set in motion forces that are creating a demand for labour mobility and is, at the same time, developing institutions on the supply side to meet this demand (Nayyar, 2008). The basic reason is simple. The factors which make it easier to move goods, services, capital, technology, and information across borders, but for explicit immigration laws and implicit consular practices that are barriers to entry, also make it easier to move people across borders. Clearly, globalization has increased labour mobility in the three new categories. The professionals, at the top of the ladder of skills, are almost as mobile as capital. Indeed, it is possible to think of them as globalized people who are employable almost anywhere in the world. Similarly, where it is not feasible or is less profitable to import goods or export capital as a substitute for labour imports, the use of guest workers is bound to increase. And, despite the political reality of immigration laws, conditions and institutions being created by globalization will sustain, perhaps even increase, illegal immigration, for markets are adept at circumventing regulations.

The most obvious positive short- or medium-term consequence of international migration for economic development is remittances from migrants. The importance of this phenomenon is widely recognized (Nayyar, 1994 and 2008, and Solimano, 2008). Table 5.9 presents available evidence on remittances in the world economy, as also their distribution across country-groups and regions, during the period from 1980 to 2010. It shows that remittances in the world economy grew from $43 billion in 1980 to $102 billion in 1995, and $444 billion in 2010. In the same years, remittances to developing countries increased rapidly from $20 billion to $55 billion, and $297 billion, while remittances to industrialized countries also increased but at a slower pace from $19 billion to $44 billion, and $116 billion respectively. Over the same period, as a proportion of total remittances in the world economy, the share of developing countries rose from 47 per cent to 67 per cent, whereas the share of industrialized countries fell from 44 per cent to 26 per cent. The residual represents remittances to the transition economies of Eastern Europe and the former USSR.

The distribution of remittances between regions in the developing world was unequal. Between 1980 and 2010, Asia's share of remittances in the world economy increased from 29 per cent to 44 per cent, while that of Latin America including the Caribbean increased from 4 per cent to 14 per cent, but that of Africa decreased from 14 per cent to 9 per cent. These changes in shares were a consequence of the fact that the value of remittances increased at a pace that was significantly different across these three regions. This is

Table 5.9. Remittances in the World Economy: 1980–2010. Distribution across Country-Groups and Regions

(in US $billion)

	1980	1985	1990	1995	2000	2005	2010
World	*43.2*	*39.5*	*79.6*	*102.0*	*134.6*	*275.4*	*443.6*
Developing Countries	*20.2*	*21.3*	*33.4*	*54.7*	*80.2*	*173.4*	*297.3*
Industrialized Countries	*18.9*	*15.1*	*36.8*	*43.6*	*48.1*	*85.2*	*116.0*
Developing Countries: Asia	12.4	12.7	18.5	30.3	47.7	98.3	196.0
Eastern Asia	0.8	0.8	1.2	2.1	6.4	26.3	55.4
Southern Asia	5.3	5.8	6.8	11.6	17.7	35.0	83.7
South-Eastern Asia	1.1	1.8	2.9	8.5	13.1	25.8	39.5
Western Asia	5.3	4.3	7.5	8.0	10.5	11.3	17.4
Developing Countries: Africa	5.8	5.9	9.0	10.2	11.3	22.4	39.7
Northern Africa	4.7	5.0	7.3	7.3	7.2	14.1	21.3
Western Africa	0.5	0.4	0.7	1.6	2.2	5.3	12.9
Developing Countries: Latin America	1.9	2.6	5.8	14.1	21.1	51.2	59.7
Caribbean	0.4	0.5	0.8	2.4	4.4	6.7	8.7
Central America	1.2	1.9	3.8	6.2	10.9	32.2	34.8
South America	0.3	0.2	1.3	5.5	5.8	12.3	16.1

Note: The figures on remittances are in current prices and at market exchange rates. The figures for developing and for industrialized countries do not add up to the total for the world economy on account of remittances to Eastern Europe and the former USSR which are not presented in the table.

Source: United Nations, UNCTADStat, based on IMF *Balance of Payments Statistics*, World Bank *Migration and Remittances*, Economist Intelligence Unit *Country Data*, and national sources.

brought out clearly in Figure 5.3, based on time series data, which plots the trends in remittances for developing countries and their constituent regions. It shows that remittances increased steadily at a broadly similar pace in the three regions during the 1980s but differences surfaced thereafter. Remittances to Africa continued to grow at the same modest pace. Remittances to Latin America started to grow rapidly in the 2000s. Remittances to Asia picked up pace in the 1990s and gathered momentum in the 2000s. Indeed, a large part of the increase in remittances to developing countries during the period from 1990 to 2010 was attributable to Asia. It is worth noting that after the financial crisis in 2008 that led to a slowdown in growth in industrialized countries, remittances declined everywhere except in Asia.

For developing countries taken together, during the period from 1980 to 2010, there was a discernible increase in the economic significance of remittances.[6] Remittances were the equivalent of about 1 per cent of their GDP from the early 1980s to the mid-1990s, but this proportion increased steadily thereafter to stabilize in the range of 1.8 per cent of GDP through the 2000s until the global economic crisis led to a drop but remittances were in the range of 1.5 per cent of GDP even in 2010. Of course, their significance varied across countries. More important, perhaps, remittances became the second largest source of external finance, less than foreign direct investment but more than official development assistance. As a proportion of net aid inflows to

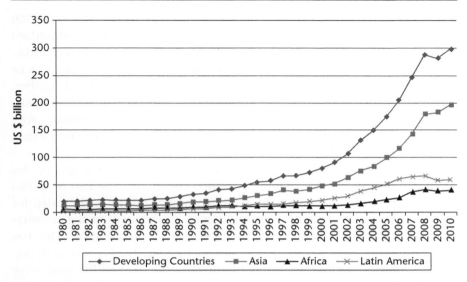

Figure 5.3. Trends in Remittances to Developing Countries Disaggregated by Regions: 1980–2010

Source: United Nations, UNCTADStat, based on IMF *Balance of Payments Statistics*, World Bank *Migration and Remittances*, Economist Intelligence Unit *Country Data*, and national sources.

developing countries, remittances increased from one-half through the 1980s to more than double through the 2000s. As a proportion of foreign direct investment flows to developing countries, however, remittances were in the range of 40 to 60 per cent through the 1990s and 2000s, as compared with equal or higher levels in the early 1980s.

The macroeconomic impact of remittances is significant (Nayyar, 1994 and 2008). In a situation where the departure of migrants does not reduce domestic output, remittances should increase national income. Alternatively, so long as the value of remittances exceeds income foregone as a consequence of migration, which is a plausible assumption, the migration of workers should lead to some increase in national income. The difference between the increase in income and the increase in consumption attributable to remittances would be saved. The use of such savings would influence not only the level but also the mix of investment. The consequent increase in investment may lead to a further increase in output and income through the multiplier effect. An increase in income attributable to remittances may also enable an economy to realize an excess of investment over savings, through a corresponding excess of imports over exports, with a smaller drain on external resources than would otherwise be the case.[7] Therefore, remittances from migrants can alleviate either the savings constraint or the foreign exchange constraint, thus enabling the economy to attain a higher rate of growth, which is somewhat akin to the role of aid in two-gap models (Chenery and Strout, 1966 and Taylor, 1994). In this context, it is also worth noting two important attributes of remittances. For one, remittances appear to be a more stable source of external finance, which is not characterized by the instability or volatility of foreign capital inflows such as portfolio investment. For another, remittances appear to be counter-cyclical with respect to growth in home countries. This is because remittances may increase during economic crises to support domestic consumption, or an economic downturn at home may induce migration and increase remittances.

The most obvious negative consequence of international migration for economic growth, in the long-term, is the brain drain. The loss of skilled persons represents income foregone for the home country and created for the host. The cost of training and education is incurred by the country-of-origin while the benefit accrues to the country-of-destination. This has been both recognized and emphasized for a long time. The brain drain represents an unrequited transfer of human capital, associated with a qualitative and quantitative depletion of the labour force, which is bound, for a number of reasons, to constrain growth. First, there is a loss of scarce skills that are not easy to replenish. Second, the education or training of professional or skilled workers absorbs scarce investible resources, but the returns to public investment in education do not accrue to society. Third, the training of workers to replace emigrants imposes additional costs in terms of both resources and time. Fourth, the migration of people at the higher end of the spectrum of incomes means revenue foregone for the government, particularly in the sphere of direct taxes. But that is not all. The brain drain may also be associated with negative externalities. New growth theory suggests that the knowledge embedded in a person has a positive effect on the productivity of another person whose knowledge, in turn, has a positive effect on the productivity of the first. Thus the emigration of highly educated workers is not simply a once-and-for-all knowledge loss to the home country. It also restrains the productivity of those left behind. Such negative externalities in productivity can only impede economic growth in the long-term. There is, however, a silver lining to this cloud that appeared not so long ago. The spread and momentum of globalization provides a stimulus to return migration that could reverse the brain drain and transform it into a brain gain. If so, it may create new opportunities for developing countries as it could, almost overnight, provide them with access to a workforce that is well educated and highly trained in the industrialized world.

Some reference to, and comparison with the past is essential. During the 19th century there were two enormous waves of international migration. The abolition of slavery in the British Empire in 1833 was followed by another form of servitude. For a period of fifty years, from the mid-1830s to the mid-1880s, about 50 million people left India and China to work as indentured labour on mines, plantations and construction in the Americas, the Caribbean, Southern Africa, Southeast Asia, and other distant lands. This was probably close to 10 per cent of the population of India and China $c.1880$. During the period from 1870 to 1914, more than 50 million people left Europe of whom two-thirds went to the United States while the remaining one-third went to Canada, Australia, New Zealand, South Africa, Argentina, and Brazil. This mass emigration from Europe amounted to one-eighth of its population in 1900. International migration was thus critical to the evolution of the world economy in the 19th century by shaping the international division of labour and providing foundations for the development of industrial capitalism in the New Worlds, driving industrialization in some countries and de-industrialization in others.

International migration was much easier in the past than it is at present. The explanation is simple enough. In the late 19th century, until 1914, there were no restrictions on the movement of people across national boundaries. Passports were seldom needed. Immigrants were granted citizenship with ease. And international labour migration was enormous. In sharp contrast, during the last quarter of the 20th century and the first decade of the 21st, the cross-border movement of people was closely regulated through immigration laws and consular practices. Yet, international migration was substantial and significant. The proportion of international migrants in world population increased from 2.5 per cent in 1960 to 3.1 per cent in 2010. Thus in 1960, 1 in every 40 persons in the world was an international migrant, while in 2010, this figure was 1 in every 32. A comparison with the early 20th century is revealing. It is estimated that in 1910, 33 million persons lived in countries other than their own and international migrants made up 2.1 per cent of the world population, so that 1 in every 48 persons in the world at that time was an international migrant (ILO, 1936).

In absolute numbers, also, the dimensions are revealing. The discussion in this section suggests that since 1950 the movement of people across borders has been significant in absolute terms, even if much less as a proportion of the total population when compared with the 19th century. Table 5.7 shows that, between 1960 and 2010, the stock of international migrants in the industrialized countries rose from 31 million to 108 million to increase by 77 million, of which as many as 72 million migrants were, in almost equal numbers, in North America and Europe. Table 5.8 shows that, in North America, 1 in every 7 persons was an international migrant in 2010 as compared with 1 in every 15 in 1960, while, in Europe, 1 in every 10 persons was an international migrant in 2010 as compared with 1 in every 27 in 1960.

There can be little doubt that the immigration into Western Europe from developing countries during the period from the late 1940s to the mid-1970s, the golden age of capitalism, was an important source of economic growth. Similarly, the immigration of educated people with professional talents or technical qualifications into the United States, from developing countries and Europe since 1950, has been an important factor underlying productivity increase and economic dynamism. In addition, illegal immigrants in the industrialized countries c.2000 were estimated to be in the range of 12 million (Nayyar, 2008). These immigrants are sought out by employers for work which residents or citizens are unwilling to do, while governments turn a blind eye to this reality. At the same time, the movement of guest workers from developing countries to oil-exporting countries in the Middle East, to industrialized countries, particularly the United States and Western Europe, and to newly industrializing countries in East Asia, provides scarce labour to support economic growth in host countries and remittances to support economic development in home countries. The cross-border movement of guest workers and professionals, indeed even illegal immigrants, is driven partly by markets and globalization. Guest workers and illegal immigrants in the industrialized world come primarily from developing countries, which are also a significant source of professionals who move across borders. It is clear that the cross-border movement of people is an important form of engagement with the world economy for developing countries, just as international migration continues to be significant in the contemporary world despite draconian immigration laws and restrictive consular practices.

It is interesting to juxtapose the past and the present in the interaction of developing countries with the world economy through international migration. There is a connection that is attributable to the diaspora from the past and to globalization in the present. The diaspora from India and China, beyond its traditional meaning of Jews in exile, has its historical origins in indentured labour. There is a significant presence of this diaspora from the two Asian giants across the world not only in industrialized but also in developing countries. This is associated with entrepreneurial capitalism, Indian and Chinese, across the world. Migrants from other developing countries are entrepreneurs too but, for historical reasons, the number of people whose origins lie in India or China is so much larger. The advent of globalization has also made it easier to move people across borders, whether guest workers or illegal immigrants, most of whom come from developing countries, many of them staying on in industrialized countries, often in an incarnation of small entrepreneurs. On a smaller scale, there is a movement of professionals from developing countries who can migrate permanently, live abroad temporarily, or stay at home and travel frequently, for business. These people are almost as mobile as capital. This phenomenon is associated with their rise as managers to the top echelons of the corporate world in the age of shareholder capitalism. The most striking example is the substantial presence of professionals from India in the United States and the United Kingdom. Of course, there are similar professionals from other developing countries, such as Brazil, Mexico, and South Korea, in the industrialized world.

Conclusion

To recapitulate, it would seem that the engagement of developing countries with the world economy witnessed a decline during the period from 1950 to 1980, particularly as compared with the past, but revived *c.*1980 to gather momentum thereafter. Their share in world merchandise trade, exports and imports, more than doubled from less than 20 per cent in 1970 to more than 40 per cent in 2010. In 1970, their share in world trade was just 2 percentage points higher than their share in world GDP but, by 2010, it was 10 percentage points higher than their share of world GDP. Between 1990 and 2010, their share of international trade in services, exports and imports alike, registered a substantial increase to reveal their comparative advantage in exports of services. But this rapid expansion in international trade was distributed most unevenly between regions, as much of it was attributable to Asia. During the 1990s and 2000s, the share of developing countries in the stock and flows of inward and outward foreign direct investment in the world economy increased at the expense of industrialized countries, although they were more important as countries-of-destination than as countries-of-origin. This distribution was less uneven between regions. International migration is possibly the most significant form of engagement. Developing countries are the home countries while industrialized countries are the host countries for international migrants. There are new forms of mobility, such as guest workers, illegal immigrants, and professional persons, driven by markets and globalization. And international migration has exercised an important influence on the world economy. It has been a major factor underlying productivity increase and economic dynamism in industrialized countries. It has created flows of remittances from migrants, which have witnessed a phenomenal increase since 1980, to provide a source of external finance and ease macroeconomic constraints on growth in developing countries. The obvious negative consequence for the developing world is the brain drain but return migration could transform this into a brain gain. The three channels of engagement are connected and interactive. There is an obvious complementarity between international trade and international investment through cumulative causation, of which intra-firm trade is only one dimension, that runs in both directions. But international migration, through the diaspora, also drives international trade and international investment. In fact, the whole is greater than the sum total of the parts.

6

Catch Up in Industrialization

In the post-colonial era, which began around 1950, most underdeveloped countries adopted strategies of development that provided a sharp contrast with their past during the second half of the nineteenth and the first half of the twentieth century. This change had three dimensions. There was a conscious attempt to limit the degree of openness and of integration with the world economy in pursuit of a more autonomous development. The state was assigned a strategic role in development because the market, by itself, was not seen as sufficient to meet the aspirations of latecomers to development. Industrialization was seen as an imperative in the catch up process, which had to start from import substitution in the manufacturing sector. These three essentials represented points of departure from the colonial era characterized by open economies and unregulated markets that had been associated with de-industrialization in the preceding one hundred years in much of the underdeveloped world. Sixty years later, it is worth exploring whether developing countries met with success in their quest for catch up in terms of industrialization. This chapter seeks to address the question. In doing so, it provides a global perspective and makes comparisons with the past. It also attempts, wherever possible, to disaggregate the evidence for Asia, Africa and Latin America, although reference to leading countries in this process is not made until the next chapter.

The discussion in the chapter is organized as follows. Section 1 examines structural changes in the composition of output and employment in developing countries to explore their relationship with industrialization and economic growth. Section 2 considers trends in industrial production, by compiling evidence on the distribution of manufacturing value added in the world economy during the five decades from 1960 to 2010, to highlight the dramatic change in the significance of developing countries, which suggests catch up in terms of manufacturing output. Section 3 discusses how this process of industrialization has shaped patterns of trade for developing countries in the world economy, reflected in their growing share of world exports of manufactures as also in the changing composition of their exports and imports. Section 4 seeks to focus on industrialization with reference to openness and intervention, which have been the critical issues in the debate about policies and strategies, to discuss the process of catch up since 1950 and to analyse the factors underlying the rapidly rising share of developing countries in industrial production and manufactured exports in the world economy since the early 1970s.

1. Structural Change

The process of industrialization is associated with a structural transformation of economies. In a long-term perspective, the most important dimension of such transformation is structural change in the composition of output and employment over time. To begin with, the share of the agricultural sector in both output and employment is overwhelmingly large. As industrialization proceeds, the share of the manufacturing sector in output and in employment rises, while that of the agricultural sector falls. Following industrialization, at an advanced stage of development, the share of the industrial sector in both output and employment declines while that of the services sector rises. This is the classical pattern, formulated by Fisher (1935), Clark (1940), Chenery (1960) and Kuznets (1966), from the experience of countries that industrialized during the second half of the 19th and the first half of the 20th century.

It is, then, possible to make an analytical distinction between three stages in the structural transformation of economies that succeeded at industrialization in the past (Nayyar, 1994a). In the first stage, there is absorption of surplus labour from the agricultural sector into industry at existing levels of real wages and productivity (Lewis, 1954). This is associated with a decline in the share of agriculture and a rise in the share of the industrial sector in output and in employment. The process can be described as labour absorption at the extensive margin. In the second stage, there is a transfer of labour from low productivity to high productivity occupations in manufacturing while, at the same time, there is an increase in the average productivity of labour in both sectors, so that real wages rise in both. There is a further increase in the share of industry and a further decrease in the share of agriculture, more pronounced in output than in employment. The process can be described as labour use at the intensive margin. In the third stage, the share of the agricultural sector continues to decline, even as the share of the industrial sector is maintained while that of the services sector rises, but after a stage, when labour is no longer available from agriculture or from domestic personal services, the share of the services sector increases at the expense of the industrial sector, more in employment than in output. This outcome in industrialized countries has also been described as de-industrialization (Rowthorn and Wells, 1987).

The focus of the conventional narrative is on economic growth in which structural change is an associated outcome. It is postulated that the income elasticity of demand for industrial goods is higher than that for agricultural goods, while the income elasticity of demand for services is even higher than that for industrial goods (Fisher, 1935). The expansion of markets creates new demands so that new production activities follow. And growing economies almost always follow the sequence of moving, in terms of relative importance, from the primary sector to the secondary sector and then to the tertiary sector. In this characterization, productivity growth in the services sector is slower than in the manufacturing sector because the scope for attaining it through capital accumulation, scale economies or technical progress is much less (Baumol, 1967). This provides an explanation for why the share of the services sector in total employment increases further (Rowthorn and Wells, 1987). At the same time, the increase in its share of total output is attributable mostly to an increase in the relative price of services (Baumol, 1967).

It is important to recognize that patterns of structural change are not simply an associated outcome of economic growth. Indeed, the causation runs in both directions. And the heterodox perspective stresses that structural change drives economic growth (Schumpeter, 1942, Hirschman, 1958, Chenery, 1960, and Ocampo, Rada and Taylor, 2009). This proposition was implicit in the Lewis (1954) model, where the transfer of surplus labour from the agricultural sector to the industrial sector, at a subsistence plus wage, increases the profits of capitalists, reinvestment of which is a source of capital accumulation and economic growth. The Kaldor (1966) model went much further in developing this causation to suggest that the manufacturing sector is the engine of growth in economies. This was set out in terms of three laws. First, there is a positive relationship between the growth of manufacturing output and the growth of GDP, which is explained partly by the absorption of surplus labour from the agricultural sector into the industrial sector. Second, growth of manufacturing output leads to growth of productivity in manufacturing, which is attributable to static and dynamic scale economies, where the former depend upon plant size or output levels at any point in time while the latter derive from learning-by-doing that is a function of cumulative past output (Arrow, 1962) or cumulative production experience (Kaldor, 1962) over time. Third, growth of manufacturing output is associated with an overall increase in productivity in the economy associated with spillover effects elsewhere.

The experience of latecomers to industrialization, in the period since 1950, does not quite conform to these stylized facts, at least in terms of sequence. It would seem that, during the second half of the 20th and the first decade of the 21st century, most developing countries have moved from the first stage, in which agriculture dominates, to the third stage, in which services dominate, without necessarily going through the second stage in which industry dominates (Kuznets, 1971). China is the clear exception to this path of structural transformation. To begin with, of course, the share of the industrial sector in both output and employment does increase almost everywhere, perhaps less than in the Chenery-Kuznets worldview, but then stabilizes or even declines. However, the share of the services sector begins to rise with the fall in the share of the agricultural sector but, after a point, its share in both employment and output rises at the expense of the industrial sector. The former is not surprising as the services sector is a source of employment creation in developing countries but the latter is unexpected since it is widely believed that manufacturing is the engine of productivity growth. In conformity with this observed sequence of change, it has been argued that there may be two waves of growth in the services sector: the first wave, made up of traditional services, is when a country moves from low-income to middle-income status, while the second wave, made up of modern communication, financial and business services, is when a country moves from middle-income to high-income status (Eichengreen and Gupta, 2009).

Unfolding reality, however, is neither as uniform nor as simple as these stylized facts. Some latecomers to development, such as China, have followed the more classical pattern of structural change where the decline of agriculture is juxtaposed with the rise of manufacturing followed by an increase in the relative importance of services, while other latecomers to development, such as India, have followed the non-traditional pattern of structural change, where the decline of agriculture has been juxtaposed with some increase in industry but a much larger increase in services. Obviously, contexts in space and conjunctures in time explain some of these differences. But it is also important to note that the world has changed, particularly in the services sector, from the time that the stylized facts about structural change were formulated by the pioneers (Nayyar, 2012). Given the massive increase in the size of firms, it is more profitable to procure services, such as those in the spheres of law, accounts, transport or finance, from specialist providers rather than produce them within the firm (Coase, 1937). Indeed, telecommunications, financial or business services are now organized in a manner that strongly resembles the manufacturing sector, for scale economies and technological advance are easily incorporated to increase efficiency in providing these services. The revolution in transport, communication and information technologies has meant that hitherto non-traded services now enter into international trade. In this changed world, the services sector could also drive economic growth in terms of Kaldor's first two laws, by raising growth in GDP and in manufacturing productivity, with some possibility of spillover effects in the economy as a whole, implicit in the third law.[1]

In a study based on data for a cross-section of 57 developing countries and transition economies grouped into 12 regions, during the period 1970–2006, Ocampo, Rada and Taylor (2009) analyse the relationship between structural change and economic growth.[2] The annual growth rate of GDP per capita is juxtaposed with the changes in the shares of agriculture and industry in total GDP. The scatter plots for the period show a negatively sloped regression line for decreases in the agricultural output share and a positively sloped regression line for increases in the industrial output share for the entire sample of 12 country-groups. However, the relationship between falling agricultural shares or rising industrial shares and economic growth is clear only for the four regions in Asia that registered sustained growth, whereas the other eight regions that were slow or laggards in growth reveal a random scatter. Similarly, the fast growth regions also had rapidly rising service sector shares, but there was no apparent relationship for the lagging growth regions. It would seem that structural change is necessary but not sufficient to drive economic growth. The direction of causation does run in both directions but it is strong and positive only in countries where there are virtuous circles of cumulative causation that reflect success in development.

In this context, it is instructive to examine structural changes in the composition of output in developing countries, disaggregated by regions, as compared with industrialized countries, during the second half of the 20th century and beyond. Table 6.1 presents available evidence on these changes in the composition of output, distributed between agriculture, industry and services, for industrialized countries, the developing world and its constituent regions. It considers the period from 1970 to 2010 because complete UN national accounts statistics start from 1970, and it selects three benchmark years at intervals of two decades to limit the statistics to manageable proportions, which is both adequate and appropriate as structural changes are slow and easier to discern.

Between 1970 and 2010, in industrialized countries, the share of agriculture in GDP dropped from 5 per cent to 1.5 per cent, the share of industry declined from 38 per cent to 24 per cent, and the share of services rose from 57 per cent to 74 per cent. For developing countries taken together, between 1970 and 2010, the share of agriculture in GDP declined from 25 per cent to 10 per cent, the share of industry increased from 33 per cent to 39 per cent (of which manufacturing remained unchanged at 21 per cent), and the share of services increased from 42 per cent to 51 per cent. But there were significant differences between regions. It was Asia that witnessed structural change which was not only conducive to economic growth but also reflected progress in industrialization. In Asia, between 1970 and 2010, the share of agriculture in GDP dropped by 23 percentage points, the share of industry increased by 10 percentage points (of which manufacturing was just 2 percentage points

Table 6.1. Structural Change in the Composition of Output in Developing Countries: 1970–2010
(as a percentage of GDP)

	1970			1990			2010		
	Agriculture	Industry	Services	Agriculture	Industry	Services	Agriculture	Industry	Services
Asia	33.2	31.6 (22.5)	35.2	17.0	37.1 (23.6)	45.9	10.1	41.3 (24.6)	48.6
Africa	25.1	30.7 (13.8)	44.2	18.3	34.6 (14.9)	47.1	16.0	38.4 (10.0)	45.6
Latin America	11.6	35.6 (23.5)	52.8	9.3	35.7 (21.9)	55.0	5.7	32.6 (16.1)	61.7
Developing Countries	25.0	32.7 (21.4)	42.3	15.0	36.3 (22.0)	48.7	9.6	39.0 (21.4)	51.4
Industrialized Countries	4.9	38.1 (27.2)	57.0	2.8	31.9 (21.4)	65.3	1.5	24.1 (14.8)	74.4

Note: 'Agriculture' includes agriculture, hunting, forestry and fishing. 'Industry' includes manufacturing, mining, utilities and construction. The figures in parenthesis in the 'Industry' column are for 'Manufacturing'. The percentages have been calculated from data on GDP in current prices at market exchange rates.

Source: United Nations, UNCTADSTAT, based on UN National Accounts Statistics.

while mining, utilities and construction contributed 8 percentage points, but that was supportive of industrial production) and the share of services rose by 13 percentage points. For Latin America and the Caribbean, between 1970 and 2010, the share of agriculture in GDP declined by 6 percentage points but so did the share of industry by 3 percentage points (in which the share of manufacturing dropped by more than 7 percentage points so that mining, utilities and construction compensated for some of the decline), while the share of services increased by 9 percentage points. It is no surprise that the region witnessed a slowdown in growth and experienced some de-industrialization. Between 1970 and 2010, in Africa, the share of agriculture in GDP decreased by 9 percentage points, the share of industry increased by 8 percentage points (although the share of manufacturing decreased by 3 percentage points and mining possibly contributed much of the increase), and the share of services increased by just 1 percentage point. For a span of four decades, this structural change was, at best, modest. It did not drive economic growth and it did not reflect industrialization despite the increase in the industrial share of output.

The evidence on structural change in the composition of employment is limited but it provides ample confirmation for this story about striking disparities between regions of the developing world in terms of catch up in industrialization. Table 6.2 presents available evidence on the distribution of employment between agriculture, industry and services, for regions in the developing world, industrialized countries and the world economy, at five-year intervals from 1995 to 2010. Unfortunately, such data are not available for earlier years, for developing countries in the aggregate or for the same regional disaggregation, which could have made it comparable with the preceding table. It shows that, between 1995 and 2010, in industrialized countries, the share of agriculture in employment decreased from 5 per cent to 4 per cent, the share of industry declined from 29 per cent to 22 per cent, while the share of services increased from 66 per cent to 74 per cent. In the developing world, between 1995 and 2010, the share of agriculture in total employment dropped by 20 percentage points in East Asia, 13 percentage points each in Southeast Asia and South Asia, 10 percentage points in the Middle East and North Africa, 8 percentage points in sub-Saharan Africa, and 7 percentage points in Latin America. Over the same period, the share of industry in total employment increased by 3 percentage points each in East Asia and Southeast Asia, 7 percentage points in South Asia, 5 percentage points in the Middle East and North Africa, 2 percentage points in Latin America, but remained unchanged at the lowest level of 8 per cent in sub-Saharan Africa. It would seem that, during this period, structural change in Asia was a driver of economic growth, because it moved labour from low-productivity to high-productivity sectors, but structural change in Latin America and Africa was not

Table 6.2. Composition of Employment by Sectors in Developing Countries: 1995–2010
(in percentages)

	Agriculture				Industry				Services			
	1995	2000	2005	2010	1995	2000	2005	2010	1995	2000	2005	2010
East Asia	54.4	47.7	42.6	34.9	25.9	23.4	24.5	28.6	19.7	29.0	32.9	36.4
South-East Asia and the Pacific	55.3	49.7	45.7	42.5	15.4	16.4	18.0	18.2	29.3	33.9	36.2	39.2
South Asia	64.1	59.5	50.8	51.4	13.4	15.6	20.1	20.7	22.5	24.9	29.0	27.9
Latin America-Caribbean	23.4	20.5	18.9	16.2	20.2	21.6	22.2	22.2	56.4	58.0	58.9	61.6
Middle East	30.8*	22.4	18.3	16.9	20.3*	24.4	25.0	25.7	48.9*	53.2	56.7	57.4
North Africa		30.5	34.5	28.5		19.4	20.8	21.8		50.1	44.8	49.7
Sub-Saharan Africa	70.1	66.3	64.0	62.0	8.2	7.9	9.7	8.5	21.7	25.9	26.3	29.6
Industrialized Countries	5.1	5.5	4.2	3.7	28.7	27.3	25.0	22.4	66.1	67.3	70.8	73.8
World	44.4	40.5	36.5	34.0	21.1	20.4	21.5	22.1	34.5	39.1	41.9	43.9

Note: (*) For 1995, the figures represent aggregate shares for Middle East and North Africa combined.

Source: ILO *Global Employment Trends*, (various years).

conducive to economic growth, because it did not (McMillan and Rodrik, 2011).[3] There was an increase in the share of services in employment everywhere, which represented the difference between the decrease in the share of agriculture and the increase in the share of industry. These changes in the composition of employment were broadly consistent with changes in composition of output. But it is worth noting that the share of agriculture in employment was much higher than its share in output everywhere, whereas the share of industry in employment was much lower than its share in output everywhere.[4] The evidence on structural changes in the composition of employment reflects the considerable progress with industrialization in East Asia, Southeast Asia, South Asia as also the Middle East and North Africa, at best modest change in Latin America, and negligible progress in sub-Saharan Africa.

Some comparison with the past is worthwhile. For Asia, Africa and Latin America taken together, in 1900, the share of agriculture in total employment was 78 per cent, while the share of industry (including mining and construction) was 10 per cent, and the share of services was 12 per cent (Bairoch, 1975, p.160). There was little change in these proportions during the first half of the 20th century. In 1950, for Asia, Africa and Latin America taken together, the share of agriculture in total employment was somewhat lower at 73 per cent, the share of industry was the same at 10 per cent, while the share of services was somewhat higher at 17 per cent (Bairoch, 1975). This near absence of structural change was consistent with the slow rates of economic growth and the negligible pace of industrialization in developing countries during this period of five decades. Yet, a comparison with the distribution of employment between agriculture, industry and services in 2000 or 2010, in Table 6.2, with that in 1950, even if it is not directly comparable because it is disaggregated for regions, clearly shows that structural change in the composition of employment in developing countries during the second half of the 20th century and the first decade of the 21st century was significant everywhere, although it was enormous in Asia.

2. Industrial Production

The most visible outcome of industrialization is in output. But it is difficult to find time series evidence on industrial production in developing countries and in the world economy since 1950. And there are problems that arise from the comparability of data over time. Table 6.3 sets out the evidence that has been compiled on the share of developing countries in manufacturing value added in the world economy during the period from 1950 to 2010. It is made up of four time series: three in constant prices and one in current prices. The series at

Table 6.3. Share of Developing Countries in World Manufacturing Value Added: 1960–2010

Year	Percentage share			Year	Percentage share		
	1975 prices	1980 prices	Current prices		1980 prices	2000 prices	Current prices
1960	8.2	...	...	1986	14.8	...	16.8
1961	8.4	...	...	1987	15.3	...	16.4
1962	8.2	...	...	1988	15.1	...	17.3
1963	8.1	...	...	1989	15.0	...	18.3
1964	8.3	...	...	1990	15.3	15.9	17.5
1965	8.2	...	...	1991	15.9	16.4	17.9
1966	8.2	...	...	1992	...	17.2	18.8
1967	8.2	...	...	1993	...	18.4	20.6
1968	8.3	...	...	1994	...	18.9	20.5
1969	8.4	...	...	1995	...	19.0	21.5
1970	8.8	...	13.1	1996	...	20.0	23.6
1971	9.1	...	13.5	1997	...	20.5	25.0
1972	9.3	...	13.3	1998	...	20.6	23.7
1973	9.4	...	13.8	1999	...	20.6	23.8
1974	9.8	...	15.1	2000	...	20.9	25.6
1975	10.3	12.6	16.0	2001	...	21.7	26.6
1976	10.3	12.7	16.1	2002	...	22.4	27.0
1977	10.4	12.9	16.2	2003	...	23.4	27.4
1978	10.5	13.1	16.2	2004	...	24.0	28.5
1979	10.7	13.4	17.2	2005	...	25.0	30.8
1980	10.9	13.7	18.4	2006	...	25.8	31.3
1981	...	13.7	19.3	2007	...	27.0	33.3
1982	...	14.0	19.2	2008	...	28.3	35.8
1983	...	14.1	18.8	2009	...	30.8	39.1
1984	...	14.1	18.9	2010	...	32.1	41.4
1985	...	14.1	18.5				

Source: United Nations, UNIDO and UNCTADStat, see Appendix.

1975 constant prices provides data for the period 1960–1980. The series at 1980 constant prices provides data for the period 1975–1991. The series at 2000 constant prices provides data for the period 1990–2010. The series at current prices provides data for the period 1970–2010. Obviously, the figures from the three different series at constant prices are not strictly comparable because of index number problems. But some overlap in time between the series at 1975 and at 1980 prices, as also that between the series at 1980 and 2000 prices, makes it easier to interpret the trends. The series in current prices and market exchange rates would be difficult to interpret if presented in terms of absolute values, because of the implicit price increases and exchange rate movements. But this problem is not such a concern in considering the changing share of developing countries in the world economy because the denominator is affected as much by price increases and exchange rate movements.

In this span of fifty years, it is possible to discern three phases. Between 1960 and 1980, the share of developing countries in world manufacturing value added, at 1975 constant prices, witnessed a modest increase from about 8 per cent to almost 11 per cent, most of which occurred after 1970. Between 1980 and 1990, at 1980 constant prices, this share experienced only a slight increase from a little less than 14 per cent to a little more than 15 per cent. Between 1990 and 2010, the share of developing countries in world manufacturing value added, at 2000 constant prices, doubled from around 16 per cent to 32 per cent. In current prices, the levels were higher but the trend was almost the same, as this share increased from 13 per cent in 1970 to about 18 per cent in 1980, where it remained in 1990, but rose sharply to 41 per cent in 2010. These trends emerge with much greater clarity from Figure 6.1, which uses time series data to outline the trends in the share of developing countries in manufacturing value added in the world economy over the five decades from 1960 to 2010. The overlaps in time between the three series in constant prices and the series in current prices are also plotted in the figure. It shows that this share witnessed a modest increase during the 1970s, little change during the 1980s, followed by a rapid increase in the 1990s, which gathered momentum in the 2000s.

The picture for developing countries as a group does not reveal the significant differences between regions. Table 6.4 outlines the share of developing countries in world manufacturing value added in current prices disaggregated by regions, at five-year intervals, during the period from 1970 to 2010. It

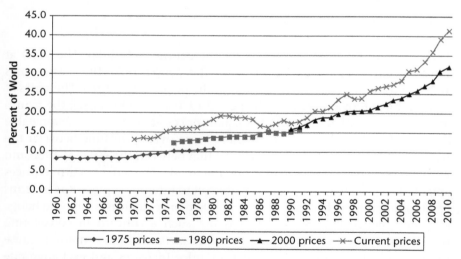

Figure 6.1. Share of Developing Countries in World Manufacturing Value Added: 1960–2010

Source: Table 6.3.

Table 6.4. Share of Asia, Africa, and Latin America in World Manufacturing Value Added: 1970–2010

(in percentages)

Year	Asia	Africa	Latin America	Developing Countries
1970	7.2	1.4	4.5	13.1
1975	8.4	1.6	6.0	16.0
1980	10.1	1.9	6.4	18.4
1985	10.7	1.6	6.2	18.5
1990	11.1	1.5	4.9	17.5
1995	14.8	1.3	5.4	21.5
2000	18.2	1.2	6.2	25.6
2005	23.7	1.4	5.7	30.8
2010	32.6	1.6	7.2	41.4

Source: United Nations, see Appendix.

shows that the trends were rather disparate between regions. The share of Africa in world manufacturing value added, but for minor fluctuations, remained almost unchanged in the range of about 1.5 per cent through the four decades. The share of Latin America in manufacturing value added in the world economy increased from 4.5 per cent in 1970 to 6.4 per cent in 1980, diminished through the lost decade to 4.9 per cent in 1990, but recovered and increased thereafter to reach 7.2 per cent in 2010. Asia provides a sharp contrast, as its share increased steadily from 7.2 per cent in 1970 to 11 per cent in 1990 and most rapidly over the next two decades to contribute almost one-third of world manufacturing value added in 2010. Indeed, it would seem that, of the increase in the share of developing countries between 1990 and 2010 as much as nine-tenths was attributable to Asia.

Even so, it is clear that there has been a dramatic transformation in the situation since 1970, as the share of developing countries in world industrial production has almost quadrupled in constant prices, from about one-twelfth to one-third, and more than trebled in current prices, from around one-eighth to two-fifths, in just forty years, which is a short span of time for so much change. In terms of simple arithmetic, this was in part attributable to the slowdown in growth of manufacturing output in industrialized countries as the golden age of capitalism came to an end in the early 1970s, and also to an acceleration in the growth of manufacturing output in developing countries beginning in the early 1970s. The latter development, which is important in the context of catch up, is analysed later in the chapter.

Some comparison with the past is instructive. The share of Asia, Africa and Latin America in world manufacturing production was about three-fourths in 1750, two-thirds in 1800 and three-fifths in 1830. At that time, in terms of the ratio of manufacturing production per capita, the level of industrialization in what are now the developing countries was comparable, even if not at par with what are now the industrialized countries. The advent of the industrial revolution in Britain led to a rapid expansion in manufacturing output from factory production. It was followed by the spread of industrialization to Western Europe and then to the United States, through the 19th century, which led to a dramatic transformation in the situation. The share of Asia, Africa and Latin America in world manufacturing production dropped sharply from 36.6 per cent in 1860 to 11 per cent in 1900 and 7.5 per cent in 1913 where it stayed until the early 1950s (Table 2.6). Indeed, as shown earlier, these regions, particularly Asia, which was as dominant then as it is now, experienced a dramatic de-industrialization during the period from 1830 to 1913. In fact the share of developing countries in world manufacturing production remained in the range of 8 per cent, roughly its 1913 level, until 1970. This share returned to its 1900 level around 1980 and its 1880 level around 1990. The situation changed rapidly thereafter. In 2010, the share of developing countries in world industrial production was higher than it was in 1860 and possible close to its level around 1850.

3. Trade Patterns

The catch up in terms of the rising share in world manufacturing output was reflected in the emergence of developing countries as important sources of manufactured exports in the world economy, which suggests that their industrial sectors also became competitive in international markets. Table 6.5 sets out value of manufactured exports from developing countries and from the world, in current prices at market exchange rates, for selected years at five-year

Table 6.5. Manufactured Exports from Developing Countries and the World: 1960–2010

(in US $billion)

Year	Developing Countries	World	Developing Countries' Percentage Share in World Total
1960	4	58	6.4
1965	6	92	6.4
1970	13	174	7.2
1975	39	473	8.3
1980	126	1049	12.0
1985	183	1138	16.0
1990	448	2498	17.9
1995	974	3739	25.8
2000	1404	4621	29.3
2005	2506	7136	33.2
2010	4163	8247	40.1

Source: United Nations, see Appendix.

Figure 6.2. Share of Developing Countries in Manufactured Exports and Manufacturing Value Added in the World Economy: 1960–2010

Note: The percentages have been calculated from data on manufactured exports and manufacturing value added in current prices at market exchange rates.
Source: United Nations, see Appendix.

intervals during the period from 1960 to 2010. Between 1960 and 1975, the share of developing countries in world exports of manufactured goods increased slowly from 6 per cent to 8 per cent. Between 1975 and 1990, this share rose from about 8 per cent to 18 per cent. Thereafter, it increased even more rapidly to 29 per cent in 2000 and 40 per cent in 2010. These changes emerge with even more clarity from Figure 6.2, which uses time series data to outline the trends in the share of developing countries in total manufactured exports in the world economy from 1960 to 2010. The three phases in this span of fifty years are clearly discernible. During the first phase, through the 1960s and the first half of the 1970s, the increase in this share was at best modest. In

Table 6.6. Manufactured Exports from Developing Countries disaggregated by Regions: 1990–2010

Year	(in US $billion)			(as a percentage of World Manufactured Exports)		
	Asia	Africa	Latin America	Asia	Africa	Latin America
1990	377	14	57	14.8	0.5	2.2
1995	812	38	124	21.3	1.0	3.2
2000	1145	37	220	24.0	0.8	4.6
2005	2128	68	312	28.2	0.9	4.1
2010	3626	115	424	35.3	1.1	4.1

Notes: The total of percentages in the last three columns for Asia, Africa and Latin America is not exactly the same as the percentage share of developing countries in the last column of Table 6.5 because of unclassified residuals.
Source: United Nations, see Appendix.

111

the second phase, from the mid-1970s to the early 1990s, this share doubled from around 10 per cent to 20 per cent. In the third phase, from the early 1990s through the 2000s, it doubled once again from about 20 per cent to 40 per cent.

It should be no surprise that this rapid expansion in manufactured exports was also distributed in an unequal manner among regions of the developing world. Table 6.6 presents data on manufactured exports from Asia, Africa and Latin America for selected years during the period from 1990 to 2010 when most changes occurred. There was a massive increase in manufactured exports from Asia, which rose from $377 billion in 1990 to $3626 billion in 2010. It makes little difference that this was in current prices and at market exchange rates, because Asia's share of world manufactured exports also rose sharply from 15 per cent in 1990 to 35 per cent in 2010. Between 1990 and 2010, manufactured exports from Latin America increased from $57 billion to $424 billion, while its share in world manufactured exports increased from 2.2 per cent to 4.1 per cent. Africa fared the worst. Between 1990 and 2010, its manufactured exports did increase in absolute terms from $14 billion to $115 billion, but its share of such exports from the world remained almost unchanged in the miniscule range of 1 per cent. Obviously, the phenomenal increase in the share of developing countries in world exports of manufactures was attributable almost entirely to Asia.

Yet it is a fact that there has been a dramatic transformation in the situation since 1975, as the share of developing countries in world manufactured exports multiplied by almost five, from one-twelfth to two-fifths, in just thirty-five years, which is once again a short span in time for such change. Obviously, manufactured exports from developing countries registered a growth that was much faster than those from industrialized countries or in the world economy. This occurrence, which is also important in the context of catch up, is analysed later in the chapter.

In this context, it is worth noting that the trends in the share of developing countries in world manufactured exports and manufacturing value added reveal strong parallels. This is confirmed by Figure 6.2, which also plots the latter, juxtaposed with the former, in the same figure. The share of developing countries in world manufacturing value added at current prices was significantly higher than in manufactured exports through the 1970s. The difference narrowed through the 1980s and the two shares were roughly similar from the late 1980s to the early 1990s. But the share of developing countries in manufactured exports exceeded their share in manufacturing value added in the world economy from the early 1990s until 2008 and the two shares moved in tandem thereafter. These similarities and differences between movements in the two shares over time are touched upon in the next section of the chapter while discussing the factors underlying the rapid growth of industrial production in, and manufactured exports from, the developing world.

Table 6.7. Changes in Composition of Merchandise Exports from Developing Countries: 1980–2010

(in percentages)

Year	Primary Products	Resource-Based Manufactures	Low-Technology Manufactures	Medium-technology manufactures	High-Technology manufactures
			Developing Countries		
1980	60.4	14.9	9.5	6.1	2.8
1990	29.0	15.5	24.7	17.3	11.9
2000	21.2	12.7	20.2	18.7	25.2
2010	18.6	15.7	16.0	21.6	24.7
			Asia		
1980	32.3	21.8	22.1	13.5	7.2
1990	13.1	13.8	33.4	20.1	17.7
2000	7.1	10.2	26.2	20.4	34.7
2010	6.7	13.6	20.1	24.0	33.6
			Africa		
1980	49.1	17.4	3.5	3.0	0.3
1990	66.9	17.8	9.7	4.7	0.7
2000	53.7	20.9	10.2	8.5	1.8
2010	54.5	20.5	7.9	11.9	1.7
			Latin America and the Caribbean		
1980	55.9	31.1	6.6	4.4	1.1
1990	51.1	23.0	10.3	12.2	2.1
2000	40.8	27.0	8.5	13.9	6.0
2010	42.6	31.1	6.1	12.8	3.8

Note: The classifications are based on Lall (2001). The columns may not add up to 100 because of an unclassified residual.
Source: Author's calculations from United Nations COMTRADE online database.

The increase in their share of world trade in manufactures was an outcome of the industrialization process in developing countries. At the same time, it is also important to examine how industrialization changed the composition of their trade. In doing so, it is necessary to make the obvious distinction between primary commodities and manufactured goods, but it is just as important to distinguish between different categories of manufactures depending upon the degree of processing and the level of technology. For this purpose, it is both appropriate and valuable to use the well-known classification, based on the natural resource-content and the technological-content of merchandise exports, developed by the late Sanjaya Lall (2001). Table 6.7 outlines the changes in the composition of exports from developing countries, also disaggregated by regions, making a distinction between primary products, resource-based manufactures, low-, medium-, and high-technology manufactures. Its focus is on the period from 1980 to 2010, when the transformation highlighted above occurred. It also presents evidence for selected benchmark years at the end of every decade to keep the data down to manageable proportions, which is adequate because structural change is slow and easier to discern.

The statistics reveal a structural transformation that confirms the impact of industrialization on trade. For developing countries taken together, between 1980 and 2010 the share of primary products in total exports dropped from more than 60 per cent to less than 20 per cent, while that of resource-based manufactures remained in the range of 15 per cent, but the share of manufactures (which were not natural-resource-based) rose from less than 20 per cent to more than 60 per cent. The changes in the composition of such manufactured exports are also important. The share of low-technology manufactures increased from 10 per cent in 1980 to 25 per cent in 1990 in the earlier stages but declined significantly thereafter, whereas the share of medium- and high-technology manufactures climbed rapidly from 9 per cent in 1980 to 46 per cent in 2010. It is clear that this transformation in the structural composition of exports from developing countries during the period from 1980 to 2010 provides a sharp contrast with the Great Specialization that surfaced during the period from 1870 to 1914 and continued until 1950. Indeed, it constitutes a reversal of the process that locked Asia, Africa and Latin America into an international division of labour with Western Europe and North America in which exports of primary commodities were exchanged for imports of manufactured goods.

It is no surprise that there were substantial differences between regions in the developing world. In Asia, the share of primary products and resource-based manufactures in total exports dropped from 54 per cent in 1980 to 20 per cent in 2010, the share of low-technology manufactures in total exports increased from 22 per cent in 1980 to 33 per cent in 1990 but decreased to 20 per cent by 2010, while the share of medium-technology and high-technology manufactures together jumped from 21 per cent in 1980 to 58 per cent in 2010 (in which the share of high-technology manufactures alone went up from 7 per cent to 34 per cent). In Latin America, between 1980 and 2010, the share of primary products and resource-based manufactures in total exports decreased from 87 per cent to 74 per cent (much of it attributable to a decrease in the former), the share of low-technology manufactures remained unchanged at around 6 per cent, while the share of medium-technology and high-technology manufactures increased from 6 per cent to 17 per cent. In Africa, the unclassified residual is large for 1980. Between 1990 and 2010, the share of primary products in total exports declined from 67 per cent to 55 per cent, the share of resource-based manufactures increased from 18 per cent to 21 per cent, while the share of low-technology and medium-technology manufactures together increased from 14 per cent to 20 per cent, but the share of high-technology manufactures was negligible. It would seem that

Table 6.8. Changes in Composition of Merchandise Imports Into Developing Countries: 1980–2010

(in percentages)

Year	Primary Products	Resource-Based Manufactures	Low-Technology Manufactures	Medium-technology manufactures	High-Technology manufactures
			Developing Countries		
1980	22.2	19.1	13.0	32.0	9.9
1990	16.8	17.5	14.1	32.8	15.6
2000	14.2	14.4	12.9	27.8	27.0
2010	17.6	18.1	9.5	26.9	23.6
			Asia		
1980	28.6	20.3	11.4	27.4	10.3
1990	15.6	16.4	14.8	32.2	17.8
2000	15.0	13.3	12.5	24.7	32.4
2010	19.7	17.9	8.0	23.7	27.5
			Africa		
1980	14.9	16.9	12.1	35.5	8.6
1990	18.9	21.7	14.7	33.6	10.0
2000	19.7	19.5	12.7	30.1	13.8
2010	16.7	21.0	12.1	35.0	12.5
			Latin America and the Caribbean		
1980	18.9	18.8	11.2	38.7	11.1
1990	20.7	20.1	9.6	35.4	12.5
2000	14.2	19.2	12.1	33.5	18.7
2010	13.2	19.3	12.9	35.7	18.0

Note: The classifications are based on Lall (2001). The columns may not add up to 100 because of an unclassified residual.
Source: Authors calculations from United Nations COMTRADE online database.

industrialization led to major changes in the structural composition of exports from Asia. But primary products and resource-based manufactures remained dominant for Latin America and Africa, although industrialization did lead to some increases in the share of other manufactures that embodied medium or high technologies in the former and low or medium technologies in the latter.

Industrialization in developing countries should also be reflected in the structure of their imports. Table 6.8 outlines the changes in the composition of imports by developing countries based on the same classification for the same period and years. For developing countries, between 1980 and 2010, the share of primary products in merchandise imports decreased from 22 per cent to 18 per cent, the share of resource-based manufactures remained unchanged in the range of 18 per cent, the share of low- and medium-technology manufactures declined from 45 per cent to 36 per cent, while the share of high-technology manufactures rose from 10 per cent to 24 per cent. These changes were consistent with the process of industrialization. Of course, there were differences between regions. In Asia, between 1980 and 2010, the share of primary products and resource-based manufactures in total imports fell from 49 per cent to 37 per cent, whereas the share of medium- and high-technology manufactures rose from 37 per cent to 51 per cent. In Latin America, between 1980 and 2010, the share of primary products and resource-based manufactures decreased from 38 per cent to 33 per cent, while the share of medium- and high-technology manufactures increased from 50 per cent to 54 per cent. In Africa, between 1980 and 2010, the share of primary products and resource-based manufactures increased from 32 per cent to 38 per cent, while the share of medium- and high-technology manufactures increased from 44 per cent to 47 per cent. It appears that the structural change in the composition of imports was broadly consistent with natural resource endowments and industrialization needs in Asia and Latin America, but it was not quite so in Africa because there was so little progress in terms of industrialization.

4. Industrialization, Openness and Intervention

There is a vast literature and much debate on industrialization in countries that were latecomers to development during the second half of the 20th century. It would mean too much of a digression to enter into a discussion about their diverse experiences and conflicting views on the subject. Given the space constraint, it is also difficult to provide a systematic, let alone complete, analysis of the underlying factors. Yet, it is essential to recognize that the degree of openness vis-à-vis the world economy and the degree of intervention by the State in the market always were, and continue to be, the critical issues in the debate about policies and strategies for industrialization.

At the beginning of the post-colonial era, it was widely accepted that developing countries must industrialize, starting with import substitution in the manufacturing sector, fostered by a supportive or leading role for the State in the process. This Development Consensus of the early 1950s was dominant until the early 1970s. It was the actual industrialization experience of economies in Asia, Africa and Latin America during the quarter century from 1950 to 1975, which led to questions.

For orthodox economics, in the neo-classical tradition, the post-mortem of failures led to diagnosis while the analysis of successes led to prescriptions. Lessons drawn from the experience of particular countries were sought to be generalized and transplanted elsewhere. The origins of such thinking can be traced to the work of Little, Scitovsky and Scott (1970), who provided an elaborate critique of the industrialization experience in selected developing countries until then, suggesting that the policy framework led to economic inefficiency and resource misallocation while the cumulative effect of these policies became an obstacle to growth.[5] The main conclusion was that industrialization policies which protected domestic industries from foreign competition and led to excessive or inappropriate State intervention in the market, were responsible for the high cost and low growth in these economies. Inward-looking policies driven by import substitution, particularly in the sphere of trade, were seen as the prime culprit. The prescription followed from the critique. More openness and less intervention would impart both efficiency and dynamism to the process. And outward-looking policies, particularly in the sphere of trade, were seen as the prime saviour. Thus, trade policies were perceived as critical in the process of industrialization and development.

It needs to be said that this approach to trade and industrialization was narrow in its focus. For it was not recognized that there is more to trade policies than the distinction between import substitution and export promotion, or inward and outward orientation, just as there is much more to industrialization than simply trade policies (Helleiner, 1992 and Nayyar, 1997). In fact, the emphasis on import substitution or export promotion, and inward or outward orientation, differed across countries and changed over time in a process of state-led industrialization. It was also not recognized that this period, when protection or promotion was provided to domestic industry, witnessed rapid industrialization in developing countries, with rates of growth in manufacturing output that revealed a sharp contrast with their past of de-industrialization during the second half of the 19th century and the first half of the 20th, when they practiced free trade. Indeed, during this period, which coincided with the golden age of capitalism, industrial growth in the developing world kept pace with that in industrialized countries.

Even so, this approach came to exercise a strong influence on thinking about industrialization. And the beginnings of a change were discernible by the late 1970s (Nayyar, 2008b). Many countries in the developing world, to be followed by transition economies a decade later, began to reshape their domestic economic policies to integrate much more with the world economy and to enlarge the role of the market vis-à-vis the State. It was, in part, a consequence of perceptions about the development experience in the preceding twenty-five years, often associated with inappropriate or excessive state intervention, which did not lead to expected outcomes in development. This was juxtaposed with the impressive economic performance of a few countries in East Asia, which was attributed to markets and openness. These success stories—Hong Kong, Singapore, South Korea and Taiwan—were portrayed as role models in development. The neo-classical critique gathered momentum through the 1980s. The policy prescriptions derived from it became increasingly influential once adopted by the World Bank, to begin with in its research agenda and subsequently in its policy menu. The process was reinforced by the reality that unfolded. The earlier success stories turned into the East Asian miracle, which spread to Malaysia, Thailand and, in the perception of some, even Indonesia. The debt crisis surfaced in Latin America, moved to sub-Saharan Africa, and ultimately caught up with South Asia. The new orthodoxy was readily accepted by economies in crisis where the IMF and the World Bank exercised enormous influence through their stabilization and adjustment programmes. The political collapse of communism reinforced the process. For the advocates of this worldview, the erstwhile centrally planned economies of Eastern Europe and the USSR represented failure, while the open market economies of East Asia epitomized success. The disillusionment with the Development Consensus was complete. And, by the early 1990s the Washington Consensus, which stressed the virtues of markets and openness to advocate generalized prescriptions across countries on the presumption that one-size-fits-all, acquired a near-hegemonic status in thinking about development.[6]

This hegemony did not last long. The belief system was somewhat shaken by the financial crises in Asia and elsewhere. Development experience during the 1990s also belied expectations. Economic growth was slower and more volatile. The orthodox prescriptions were subjected to increasing question (Amsden, Kochanowicz and Taylor, 1994, Stiglitz, 1998, and Easterly, 2001). The real dampener, however, was unfolding reality (Rodrik, 2005, Taylor 2007, and Nayyar, 2008b). Countries that were conformists and liberalizers underperformed or did not perform, whereas countries that were non-conformists without being liberalizers were the performers. Most countries in Latin America, sub-Saharan Africa and Eastern Europe adopted the reform agenda of the Washington Consensus almost in its entirety. But their performance, in terms of economic growth, industrial development and distributional outcomes, was not only much worse than other parts of the world but was also distinctly worse than their own performance in the preceding three decades. In sharp contrast, countries in Asia modified, adapted, contextualized and paced their reform agenda, to use unorthodox or heterodox policies for orthodox objectives in much the same way as the small East Asian countries had done earlier. They turned out to be star performers in terms of growth and industrialization, even if not in terms of distributional outcomes.

It is not as if the neo-classical critique of, and the neo-liberal prescription for, industrialization in developing countries was discredited by actual outcomes alone. It was subjected to question and criticism even as it was articulated and implemented, just as it was contradicted by subsequent research on the experience of latecomers to industrialization. The critics argued that it was not appropriate to draw lessons from the experience of a few small countries—Hong Kong, Singapore, South Korea and Taiwan—of which two were city-states without hinterlands, that could be generalized and transplanted elsewhere. For Hong Kong and Singapore, given the size of their domestic market, export orientation was a necessity. For South Korea and Taiwan, export promotion that supported domestic firms to compete in world markets was also a means of earning foreign exchange to support import substitution through imports of capital goods and technology. Even more important, perhaps, it was stressed that this approach was selective in its use of theory and history. For one, there was a striking asymmetry between the unqualified enthusiasm for free(r) trade, unmindful of the distinction between statics and dynamics or irrespective of time and place, and the formal exposition of the free trade argument in economic theory with its careful assumptions, proofs and exceptions.[7] For another, the characterization as success stories of economies that approximated to free trade and laissez-faire was partial, if not caricature, history for their export orientation was not the equivalent of free trade; just as the visible hand of the State was more in evidence than the invisible hand of the market.[8]

Yet, orthodoxy did not see, or chose to ignore, the fact that economic policies and development practices were not in conformity with its caricature model of markets and openness. What is more, it did not recognize that the distinction between success and failure, while important, is not exhaustive. In fact, actual outcomes in development were a complex mix which could not be categorized simply in an either-or mode. Industrialization in developing countries was characterized by success-stories in a few, muddling-through in some, and near-failure in others. It is not as if all countries could be unambiguously classified into one of these categories at all times. In fact, different classifications yield different rankings among countries (Pritchett, 1996). The development experience within countries was also an uneven mix of success and failure. Thus, prescriptive generalizations based on the presumption that one-size-fits-all, which ignored the specificities of economies in time and space, often bordered on the simplistic. Most important, perhaps, things changed over time, as countries moved from the earlier phase of learning to industrialize, through developing managerial capabilities in individuals and technological capabilities in firms, to becoming competitive in world markets. Industrialization takes time. And it was obviously not appropriate to focus on the earlier phase in isolation. It is just as important to highlight three analytical limitations of orthodoxy, which mean that it misses out on some essential dimensions of industrialization.

First, the problem is neither about means nor ends, in themselves. The real issue is the path from means to ends. The emphasis on trade liberalization, as a means of getting-prices-right, assumes that international competition will force domestic firms to become more efficient. It makes an elementary but commonplace error in the design of policies. It confuses *comparison* (of equilibrium positions) with *change* (from one equilibrium position to another). In the real world, economic policy must be concerned not merely with comparison but also with how to direct the process of change. It cannot suffice to enunciate a general principle that a reduction in protection can lead to a more cost-efficient economy, for there is nothing automatic about the process. The core issue is the transition path from the use of policy instruments to the realization of policy objectives. In this pursuit, strategic use of trade policy, industrial policy and technology policy could make the difference between success and failure.

Second, the analytical construct is narrow. Success at industrialization is not only about resource allocation and resource utilization at a micro-level. It is as much, if not more, about resource mobilization and resource creation at a macro-level. The excessive concern with resource allocation, in terms of static allocative efficiency criteria at a point in time, is misplaced, while the strong emphasis on resource utilization, in terms of competition through deregulation and openness, is important but disproportionate. This approach, which is static rather than dynamic in conception, tends to ignore inter-temporal considerations and does not quite recognize the critical importance of increasing returns, market structures, investment levels, externalities, or learning-by-doing, which are inherent in any process of industrialization.

Third, the strong emphasis on allocative efficiency is matched by a conspicuous silence on technical efficiency. It is forgotten that low levels of productivity in developing countries are attributable more to technical than to allocative inefficiency. And inter-country differences, as also inter-firm differences, are explained in large part by differences in technological and managerial capabilities at a micro-level. These capabilities determine not just efficiency in the short-run but also competitiveness in the long-term. But, given the nature of the learning process, such capabilities are both firm-specific and path-dependent (Rosenberg, 1994). Orthodoxy simply ignores this critical dimension on the supply side. In contrast, the heterodox literature places the acquisition and development of technological capabilities centre-stage in the story of success at industrialization.[9] It also shows that the presumed relationship between trade liberalization and technical efficiency is dubious in terms of both theory and evidence.[10]

Even if briefly, it is now possible to address the two questions posed earlier in the chapter. What explains the acceleration in the growth of manufacturing output in developing countries beginning in the early 1970s? What explains the phenomenal expansion in manufactured exports from developing countries beginning in the mid-1970s? Both were an integral part of the process of industrialization.

The observed outcome in terms of industrial production was attributable, in important part, to development strategies and economic policies in the post-colonial era that created the initial conditions and laid the essential foundations in countries, which were latecomers to industrialization. The import substitution-led strategies of industrialization, much maligned by orthodoxy that was concerned with comparative statics rather than economic dynamics, performed a critical role in this process of catch up (Helliener, 1992, Rodrik, 1992, and Nayyar, 1997). Of course, a complete explanation would be far more complex as it would need to recognize specificities and nuances. All the same it is clear that the role of the State in evolving policies, developing institutions and making strategic interventions, whether as a catalyst or a leader, was also central to the process (Stiglitz, 1989, Shapiro and Taylor, 1990, Bhaduri and Nayyar, 1996, Lall, 1997, and Amsden, 2001). Indeed, even among the small East Asian countries, success stories portrayed by orthodoxy as role models of markets and openness, development was more about the visible hand of the State rather than the invisible hand of the market, particularly in South Korea and Taiwan but perhaps even in Singapore (Amsden, 1989, Wade, 1990, and Chang, 1996).

Thus, industrialization was not so much about getting-prices-right as it was about getting-state-intervention-right. Indeed, it is plausible to suggest that, for a time, it might even have been about getting-prices-wrong (Amsden, 2001). It may be argued that state intervention in the form of industrial policy should recognize and exploit potential comparative advantage, but it is just as plausible to argue that instead of climbing the ladder step-by-step it could be rewarding to jump some steps in defiance of what comparative advantage might be at the time (Lin and Chang, 2009). In either case, state intervention is critical. Apart from an extensive role for governments, the use of borrowed technologies, an intense process of learning, the creation of managerial capabilities in individuals and technological capabilities in firms, the nurturing of entrepreneurs and firms in different types of enterprises, were important factors underlying the catch up in industrialization.[11] The creation of initial conditions was followed by a period of learning to industrialize so that outcomes in industrialization surfaced with a time lag. This accounts for the acceleration in growth of manufacturing output that became visible in the early 1970s. Clearly, it was not the magic of markets that produced the sudden spurt in industrialization. It came from the foundations that were laid in the preceding quarter century. In this context, it is important to note that much the same can be said about the now industrialized countries, where industrial protection and state intervention were just as important, at earlier stages of their development when they were latecomers to industrialization (Chang, 2002 and Reinert, 2007).

There were three sets of factors underlying the rapid growth in manufactured exports from developing countries that started in the mid-1970s and gathered momentum in the early 1990s, which were interconnected but sequential in time.

First, for developing countries, external markets became increasingly important in the process of industrialization. It was a litmus test for domestic firms seeking to become competitive in international markets, although exports were the end rather than the beginning of the market expansion path for such firms. But this was not so everywhere. In some countries, particularly in some sectors, transnational corporations played an important role in developing manufactured exports (Helleiner, 1973 and Nayyar, 1978). The process started with Brazil and Mexico in Latin America in the mid-1960s, where rapid export growth did not continue beyond the late 1970s. But the export expansion in manufactured goods continued, indeed gathered momentum thereafter with the East Asian success stories of Hong Kong, Singapore, South Korea, and Taiwan as these small countries became disproportionately important sources of such exports from the developing world. There was, however, a significant change, since firms from these countries manufactured for the world rather than the domestic market and relied more on large international firms as manufacturers, partners or buyers. The small Southeast Asian countries, Malaysia and Thailand followed in their footsteps, manufacturing for markets in the home countries of transnational corporations. It was not long before China and India, the mega economies of Asia, also sought access to external markets and, at this stage, their manufactured exports came from domestic firms that had been through the phase of learning to industrialize in large domestic markets. In this context, it is worth noting that export performance in China beginning 1979, in India beginning 1980 and in Brazil beginning 1964 (but only until 1980), was roughly comparable with that in Japan beginning 1960 and in South Korea beginning 1965 (Nayyar, 2010).

Second, as globalization gathered momentum in the last two decades of the 20th century, there was a progressive integration of developing countries into the world economy, particularly in the sphere of international trade. It was an outcome of the internationalization of production. This began with transnational corporations from industrialized countries engaging in offshore assembly operations under special tariff provisions, relocating production through international sub-contracting, or sourcing imports of labour-intensive manufactured goods, from a few low-wage developing countries (Helleiner, 1973, Sharpston, 1975, and Nayyar, 1978). The essential underlying factor was large differences in wages so that wage costs per unit of output in these developing countries were distinctly lower despite much lower levels of productivity. But the process was driven by the competition for markets between large international firms from industrialized countries seeking to reduce costs, in which footloose industries for assembly operations or component manufacture were relocated by transnational manufacturing firms and simple labour-intensive consumer goods such as clothing were sourced through sub-contracting by transnational buying groups, in and from selected developing countries (Nayyar, 1978). After some time, this provided opportunities for domestic firms in developing countries, where the initial conditions for industrialization had been created, to manufacture for the world market in competition or collaboration with transnational corporations.

Third, markets and globalization, reinforced by the revolution in transport and communication, led to a growing interdependence and deepening integration between countries in the world economy during the first decade of the 21st century. Such global economic integration led to an increasing relocation, which became more feasible in terms of rapid technological change and declining transport costs, of parts of production processes to developing countries with skilled labour and low wages. This, in turn, led to a massive expansion of world trade in manufactures, not only in final goods but also in intermediate goods. The phenomenon has been described as the rise of global value chains.[12] It was neither as new nor as sudden as it is sometimes made out to be, but was the culmination of a process that began two decades earlier. Given the nature of international trade statistics, however, it is obviously difficult to measure in terms of empirical evidence or quantification. Even so, it is clear that international trade flows driven by global value chains were not confined to manufactured intermediate goods but extended to manufactured final goods including consumption goods and capital goods.[13] In fact, of the three industries that are important domains for global value chains, finished goods are far more important than intermediate goods in clothing and footwear, while finished goods and intermediate goods are of almost equal importance in electronics and in automobiles and motorcycles as a proportion of world trade, imports plus exports (Sturgeon and Memodovic, 2011).[14] And it is no surprise that there has been an increasing relocation of production for these sectors in the developing world. The share of developing countries in world trade, imports plus exports, of manufactured intermediate goods was stable through the 1990s at 25.5 per cent in 1992, 27.1 per cent in 1995 and 27.5 per cent in 2001 but rose to 35.5 per cent in 2006 (Sturgeon and Memodovic, 2011, p.14). Thus, it is plausible to suggest that global value chains probably played a significant role in the rapid growth of manufactured exports in clothing, footwear, electronics, automobiles and motorcycles from developing countries during the first decade of the 21st century. This story would not be complete without recognizing that such a vertical division of labour between countries was also an important factor underlying the boom in international trade in services during the 2000s, particularly in information technology, where business-process-outsourcing, knowledge-process-outsourcing, and software development represented similar, yet different, value chains across countries, unleashed by the revolution in communications.

The share of developing countries in world manufacturing value added and manufactured exports revealed some parallels but also showed some changes in their relative importance over time. This also deserves a brief explanation. Once again, it is plausible to suggest, though impossible to prove, the following hypothesis. The share of developing countries in world manufacturing value added was higher than their share of world manufactured exports through the 1970s in their phase of learning to industrialize but this difference narrowed through the 1980s as some countries became increasingly competitive in some sectors, such as labour-intensive consumer goods. The two shares moved in tandem from the late 1980s to the early 1990s as developing countries became competitive in the world market for manufactures. The share of developing countries in manufactured exports exceeded their share in manufacturing value added in the world economy from 1992 until 2008, possibly as a consequence of their increasing international competiveness and their growing engagement with the world economy driven partly by the internationalization of production and the activities of global value chains. It is not surprising that the two shares moved in tandem once again from 2008 to 2010 in the aftermath of the financial crisis that led to an economic downturn and a persistent recession in the industrialized countries which provided the markets for manufactured exports from developing countries.

Conclusion

It is clear that there was a significant catch up in industrialization for the developing world as a whole, beginning around 1950 that gathered momentum in the early 1970s. Structural changes in the composition of output and employment, which led to a decline in the share of agriculture with an increase in the shares of industry and services, were an important factor underlying this process. There was a dramatic transformation in just four decades from 1970 to 2010. The share of developing countries in world industrial production jumped from one-twelfth to one-third in constant prices and from one-eighth to two-fifths in current prices, so that in 2010 it was close to its level in the mid-19th century. Similarly, their share in world exports of manufactures rose from one-twelfth to two-fifths. Industrialization also led to pronounced changes in the composition of their trade as the share of primary commodities and resource-based products fell while the share of manufactures (particularly medium- and high-technology goods) rose in both exports and imports. However, this industrialization was most uneven between regions. Asia led the process in terms of structural change, share in industrial production, rising manufactured exports and changing patterns of trade, while Latin America witnessed relatively little change and Africa made almost no progress. The role of the State in evolving trade and industrial policies, developing institutions and making strategic interventions, whether as a catalyst or a leader, was central to this process. The creation of initial conditions was followed by a period of learning to industrialize so that outcomes surfaced after a time lag. And it was not the magic of markets that produced the spurt in industrialization. Indeed, success was not so much about getting-prices-right as it was about getting-state-intervention-right. To begin with, for some countries it was about import substitution through protection while for others it was about export orientation through promotion. In either case, external markets became increasingly important in the process of industrialization. It was a litmus test for domestic firms seeking to become competitive in international markets. It was also an outcome of the internationalization of production that began with transnational corporations from industrialized countries, driven by competition for markets, seeking to reduce costs as manufacturers or buyers. After some time, it provided opportunities for domestic firms from developing countries, facilitated by the rise of global value chains since the late 1990s.

7

Unequal Partners and Uneven Development

It is important to recognize that aggregates for the developing world could be deceptive. In fact, evidence considered in the preceding chapter revealed that the rapid increase in the share of developing countries in world industrial production and manufactured exports was distributed in an unequal manner among their constituent regions. So was the nature and pace of structural change. It would be no surprise if this were just as uneven between countries within regions. The object of this chapter is to analyse how the overall catch up in industrialization was distributed among countries in the developing world. The rationale for such an exercise is twofold. It would identify countries that are leaders in this process and it could help understanding of the factors that made for success at industrialization. It might also suggest some lessons from the leaders for the laggards. Of course, industrialization experience is country-specific so that constraints and possibilities are never the same. Given the limited space, however, it is not feasible to analyse outcomes at country-level. Yet, it is possible to coax some stylized facts, if not generalizations, from outcomes in countries where catch up, or its beginnings, are discernible.

Section 1 analyses the economic significance of fourteen selected countries in the developing world, not only in industrialization but also in terms of their size and their engagement with the world economy, to focus on the high degree of concentration among a few. Section 2 examines the diversity among these selected countries with reference to the same attributes that reveal the concentration, to consider whether or not catch up in terms of industrialization led to the end of divergence or the beginning of convergence in incomes per capita as compared with the industrialized countries. Section 3 explores the common factors underlying success at industrialization in the selected countries and the differences that set them apart from other countries in the developing world, to highlight the lessons that can be drawn from the experience of countries that have led the process of catch up so far, for the next set of latecomers that might follow.

1. Concentration Among a Few

During the six decades from 1950 to 2010, about a dozen developing countries made impressive strides in industrialization, not only in the spheres of industrial production and manufactured exports but also in terms of structural change and economic growth, even if North America, Western Europe and Japan remained the hub of the industrialized world. This process was associated with a rapid growth in manufacturing output that was sustained through these decades. Learning to industrialize also led to the emergence of technological capabilities in domestic firms and of industrial products that were competitive in world markets. And there can be little doubt that this set of latecomers was an important part of the story about the catch up in industrial production and the rapid growth in manufactured exports.

The choice of countries that belong to this set is almost automatic, although there could be minor differences in judgment about inclusion and exclusion. In a study on late industrializers, Amsden (2001) identifies 12 countries, made up of Argentina, Brazil, Chile, and Mexico in Latin America, China, India, Indonesia, Malaysia, South Korea, Taiwan, and Thailand in Asia, and Turkey in the Middle East, described as 'The Rest', that narrowed the economic distance with 'The West' during the second half of the 20th century. In a study on developing countries in the world economy, the author (Nayyar, 2006 and 2009) identifies a slightly different set of 12 countries, made up of Argentina, Brazil, and Mexico in Latin America, China, Hong Kong, India, Indonesia, Malaysia, Singapore, South Korea, and Thailand in Asia, and South Africa in Africa. The former grouping includes Chile, Taiwan, and Turkey that the latter does not, while the latter grouping includes Hong Kong, Singapore, and South Africa that the former does not. It makes sense to include Chile, Taiwan, and Turkey, in terms of both economics and geography. But it does not make sense to exclude Africa altogether. Therefore, the inclusion of South Africa, the most industrialized economy in Africa, is clearly necessary but probably not sufficient. The two other countries in Africa that merit consideration for inclusion in this group are Egypt and Nigeria. Of these, Egypt fits the bill far more in terms of structural change, industrial production and manufactured exports, whereas Nigeria's significance lies primarily in its economic size. Hong Kong and Singapore pose a dilemma because they were such an integral part of the East Asian miracle, which received so much attention in orthodox economics, but both are city-states without a hinterland. What is more, their economic significance is limited to engagement with the world economy through international trade, particularly manufactured exports, and international investment, while their share in population, manufacturing value added, and income of the developing world is tiny or very small.[1]

Therefore, the analysis in this chapter seeks to focus on fourteen selected developing countries: Argentina, Brazil, Chile, and Mexico in Latin America; China, India, Indonesia, Malaysia, South Korea, Taiwan, Thailand, and Turkey[2] in Asia; and Egypt[3] and South Africa in Africa. This set of countries is described as 'The Next-14'. The logic underlying this description is simple enough. These countries are the most important latecomers to industrialization that have emerged during the period from 1950 to 2010, which have led the process of catch up so far, and are most likely to be among the next set of countries in the league of industrialized nations when such a study is conducted in, say, 2035. There are other countries, particularly among the erstwhile centrally-planned economies such as Poland and Vietnam, which could be in the range of consideration, and yet others that could emerge as surprises. But the Next-14 are plausible, if not obvious, choices in terms of most criteria. Of course, such a choice of countries is always subjective and a matter of judgment. In that sense, the Next-14 could also be the Nayyar-14! The discussion that follows considers their economic significance in the developing world not only with reference to industrialization, reflected in manufacturing value added and manufactured exports, but also in terms of their size, reflected in GDP and population, and their engagement with the world economy, reflected in international trade, investment and migration. This group of countries is diverse in the three dimensions of geography, history and economics. The process of catch up is also not uniform across these countries in its start or speed. Yet, their overwhelming importance in the developing world and its engagement with the world economy, which have both increased with the passage of time, is clear enough.

Table 7.1 presents evidence that has been compiled from different sources on the economic significance of the Next-14 in the developing world from 1970 to 2010. It reveals their dominance in economic size with overwhelmingly large shares of population and income. Between 1970 and 2010, their share in GDP of the developing world increased from 65 per cent to 74 per cent. This rise was continuous but for a dip in 1975 and 1980 that was attributable to the oil price hikes in 1973 and 1979, as none of these countries were significant exporters of crude oil or petroleum products. However, their share in the total population of the developing world diminished steadily from 70 per cent in 1970 to 63 per cent in 2010, despite the large and growing populations of China and India, as also Indonesia and Brazil. It is obvious that per capita income in the Next-14, taken together, increased faster than per capita income in the developing world as a whole.

These countries also dominated the engagement of developing countries with the world economy in international trade, international investment and international migration. Between 1970 and 2010, their share in total merchandise exports from developing countries rose from 36 per cent to 62 per cent,

Table 7.1. Economic Significance of the Next-14 in the Developing World: 1970–2010 (as a percentage of the total for developing countries)

	1970	1975	1980	1985	1990	1995	2000	2005	2010
GDP	64.5	59.7	56.5	59.8	67.8	71.9	71.7	71.8	73.9
Population	70.2	70.1	69.3	68.5	67.7	66.7	65.7	64.6	63.5
Exports	36.4	27.9	31.7	46.1	50.3	56.6	57.2	58.9	62.4
Imports	41.3	40.1	41.0	45.9	51.9	56.0	59.8	62.1	64.0
Manufacturing value added	75.6	74.7	73.1	71.4	75.2	77.7	85.1	85.1	85.6
Manufactured exports	62.0	58.8	58.5	61.6	62.2	64.8	67.6	71.8	75.3
FDI inward stock	n/a	n/a	24.8	27.1	34.9	45.4	46.0	49.1	45.9
FDI outward stock	n/a	n/a	91.1	84.7	72.0	52.0	31.7	34.3	41.2
Foreign exchange reserves	45.5	19.2	28.3	42.2	57.4	62.1	61.5	68.1	70.9
Remittances	n/a	n/a	49.6	50.9	49.3	47.2	49.9	51.3	52.8

Note: The Next-14 are Argentina, Brazil, Chile, China, Egypt, India, Indonesia, South Korea, Malaysia, Mexico, South Africa, Taiwan, Thailand, and Turkey.
Source: United Nations, author's calculations, see Appendix.

while their share in total merchandise imports into developing countries increased from 41 per cent to 64 per cent. The increase in both these shares was continuous but for exports in 1975 and 1980 because of the hikes in oil prices in 1973 and 1979. It is worth noting that if Hong Kong and Singapore are added to the Next-14, the share of this enlarged group in the trade of developing countries was even higher at around three-fourths.[4] Between 1980 and 2010, the share of the Next-14 in the inward stock of foreign direct investment in the developing world rose from 25 per cent to 46 per cent in 2010, although their share in the outward stock of foreign direct investment in the developing world fell from 91 per cent to 41 per cent. This suggests that their relative importance increased as countries-of-destination but decreased as countries-of-origin. The story was not quite the same for flows of foreign direct investment, as the share of the Next-14 in both average annual inflows and outflows was 47 per cent of the total for developing countries during 2006–2010.[5] It is worth noting that, in absolute terms, such outflows from these countries were more than 50 per cent of such inflows over the same period. And it is no surprise that the Next-14 accounted for more than 60 per cent of both net sales and net purchases in cross-border mergers and acquisitions on the part of developing countries during 2006–2010. It is also clear that these countries were an important source of international migration. Table 7.1 shows that the Next-14 accounted for about one-half of migrants' remittances to the developing world throughout the period from 1980 to 2010.

The dominance of the Next-14 is particularly striking, even more than for income and trade, in the sphere of industrialization. Their share of manufactured exports from the developing world increased from 62 per cent in 1970 to

75 per cent in 2010. Once again, if Hong Kong and Singapore are added, the share of the enlarged group is even more disproportionate.[6] It is plausible to suggest, even if impossible to quantify, that global value chains were among the important factors underlying the dominance of the Next-14 in manufactured exports from the developing world. World trade in manufactured goods driven by global value chains is not confined to manufactured intermediate goods since finished goods are just as important in most of these activities and distinctly more so in clothing and footwear. Even so, trade in manufactured intermediates can provide some index, if not a rough approximation, of world trade in sectors where global value chains are important channels of transmission. The Next-14 (excluding Egypt for which data are not available) accounted for 25 per cent of world trade in manufactured intermediate goods, imports plus exports, in 2006, which constituted more than 70 per cent of such trade for the developing world. If Hong Kong and Singapore are added, the share of the enlarged group in such world trade was 32 per cent, which constituted more than 90 per cent of such trade for the developing world.[7]

The dominance is even greater in the sphere of industrial production. Table 7.2 outlines the trends in the share of the Next-14 in manufacturing value added in the developing world and in the world economy during the period from 1970 to 2010. It shows that, between 1970 and 2010, the share of these countries in manufacturing value added increased from 76 per cent to 86 per cent in the developing world and from 10 per cent to 35 per cent in the world economy. Obviously, manufacturing value added in developing countries as a group increased at a much faster pace than in the world economy, which is borne out by statistics on absolute values at current prices presented in the table. Such statistics on manufacturing value added at constant prices are also available but are not presented here. Between 1990 and 2010, at constant 2000 prices, the share of the Next-14 in manufacturing value added in the developing world increased from 85 per cent to 96 per cent and in the developing world and from 14 per cent to 31 per cent in the world economy.[8] The trends are similar but the levels are different. At constant prices, the share of the Next-14 was higher in the developing world (by 5–10 percentage points) but lower in the world economy (by 2–4 percentage points), as compared with the levels at current prices, presumably because rates of inflation were lower in industrialized countries and higher in other developing countries.

Given the unequal distribution of growth in manufacturing value added among the constituent regions of the developing world, it would be instructive to examine whether this regional distribution was also unequal between these countries. Figure 7.1 outlines the trends in the share of the Next-14 in manufacturing value added in the world economy disaggregated into three country-groups based on regions. The story is similar. The share of the two African countries remained almost unchanged, at 0.6 per cent in 1970 and 0.8

Table 7.2. Manufacturing Value Added in the Next-14, Developing Countries and the World: 1970–2010

(in current prices at market exchange rates)

| Year | Manufacturing value added (US $billion) | | | Share of the Next-14 in Manufactured Value Added (percentages) | |
	The Next-14	Developing Countries	World	Developing Countries	World
1970	88	115	877	76.4	10.0
1975	194	256	1596	76.0	12.2
1980	387	515	2803	75.1	13.8
1985	398	534	2889	74.6	13.8
1986	421	563	3342	74.8	12.6
1987	473	619	3765	76.4	12.6
1988	570	732	4237	77.8	13.4
1989	634	796	4355	79.7	14.6
1990	638	810	4632	78.8	13.8
1991	675	850	4746	79.4	14.2
1992	746	931	4961	80.1	15.0
1993	832	1016	4934	81.9	16.9
1994	873	1071	5227	81.5	16.7
1995	1036	1256	5834	82.5	17.8
1996	1146	1379	5848	83.1	19.6
1997	1206	1449	5799	83.3	20.8
1998	1101	1333	5618	82.6	19.6
1999	1140	1376	5786	82.9	19.7
2000	1265	1514	5908	83.5	21.4
2001	1243	1491	5606	83.3	22.2
2002	1301	1553	5747	83.8	22.6
2003	1478	1746	6383	84.6	23.1
2004	1745	2059	7232	84.7	24.1
2005	2038	2396	7789	85.1	26.2
2006	2139	2549	8147	83.9	26.3
2007	2583	3056	9184	84.5	28.1
2008	2995	3544	9902	84.5	30.2
2009	2994	3526	9015	84.9	33.2
2010	3642	4255	10,289	85.6	35.4

Note: The Next-14 are Argentina, Brazil, Chile, China, Egypt, India, Indonesia, South Korea, Malaysia, Mexico, South Africa, Taiwan, Thailand, and Turkey. The percentages have been calculated.

Source: United Nations, author's calculations, see Appendix.

per cent in 2010. The share of the four Latin American countries increased modestly, from 3.5 per cent in 1970 to 5.4 per cent in 2010. In sharp contrast, the share of the eight Asian countries recorded a steady increase that gathered momentum in the 2000s, rising from 5.9 per cent in 1970 to 29.2 per cent in 2010. It would seem that the increase in the share of the Next-14, from 10 per cent in 1970 to 35.4 per cent in 2010, was mostly attributable to the eight Asian countries.

The preceding discussion confirms the economic significance of the Next-14, in multiple dimensions, in the developing world. The obvious determinants of such concentration are size, growth and history. In terms of size, these countries, except for Chile, Malaysia, and Taiwan, are large in population, area

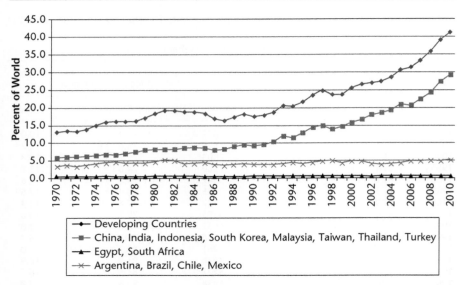

Figure 7.1. Share of the Next-14 in World Manufacturing Value Added: 1970–2010 (disaggregated into regional groups)

Note: The percentages are calculated from data on manufacturing value added in current prices and exchange rates.

Source: United Nations, author's calculations, see Appendix.

and income as compared with most countries in the developing world. In the sphere of growth, the eight Asian countries recorded high rates of economic growth, even if the step up in growth rates started at some different points in time, for South Korea and Taiwan, or Malaysia and Thailand, or China and India, as compared with most countries in the developing world. In the realm of history, about half these countries, in particular China and India, but also Argentina, Brazil, Mexico, Egypt, and South Africa have always been dominant or important in their respective regions of the developing world and have also been significant in the wider context of the world economy. Therefore it is essential to recognize that the concentration is not new. It is equally necessary to recognize that there is considerable diversity among these countries, just as there are enormous differences between them and other countries in the developing world.

2. Diversity Within the Few

The discussion in this section analyses the diversity in two steps. The first step is to consider the diversity among the Next-14 by examining the differences between them in economic size, in engagement with the world economy and in industrialization, with reference to the same attributes that revealed the concentration among them. The second step is to consider the differences between the Next-14 in terms of per capita income levels, as compared with per capita income in industrialized countries, and examine whether this gap narrowed or widened over time with the process of industrialization.

In terms of economic size, there is a concentration among subsets of the few.[9] The share of only four countries that had the largest populations among the Next-14 in 2010—China, India, Indonesia, and Brazil—in the population of the developing world was 60 per cent in 1970 (compared with 70 per cent for the fourteen) and 54 per cent in 2010 (compared with 63 per cent for the fourteen). The share of just five countries that had the highest GDP among the Next-14 in 2010—China, Brazil, India, Mexico, and South Korea—in the GDP of the developing world was 43 per cent in 1970 (compared with 65 per cent for the fourteen) and 57 per cent in 2010 (compared with 74 per cent for the fourteen). It would seem that concentration in the distribution of GDP increased while it remained the same in the distribution of population.

In terms of engagement with the world economy, once again, there is a concentration within the few.[10] The share of six countries that had the largest exports and imports among the Next-14 in 2010—China, South Korea, Mexico, India, Taiwan, and Brazil—in exports from the developing world increased from 18 per cent in 1970 (compared with 36 per cent for the fourteen) to 48 per cent in 2010 (compared with 62 per cent for the fourteen), while, in imports by the developing world, it increased from 22 per cent in 1970 (compared with 41 per cent for the fourteen) to 49 per cent in 2010 (compared with 64 per cent for the fourteen). The share of the five countries that were the largest cumulative recipients of investment from abroad in 2010 among these countries—China, Brazil, Mexico, India, and Turkey—in the inward stock of foreign direct investment in the developing world increased from 18 per cent in 1990 (compared with 25 per cent for the fourteen) to 30 per cent in 2010 (compared with 46 per cent for the fourteen). The share of the five countries that were the largest investors abroad among these countries in 2010—China, Brazil, Taiwan, South Korea, and India—decreased from 35 per cent in 1990 (compared with 91 per cent for the fourteen) to 29 per cent in 2010 (compared with 41 per cent for the fourteen). The share of the three countries that received the highest remittances among these countries in 2010—India, China, and Mexico—in remittances to the developing world increased from 22 per cent in 1980 (compared with 50 per cent for the fourteen) to 43 per cent in 2010 (compared with 53 per cent for the fourteen). Clearly, the distribution of exports, imports and remittances between the Next-14 was unequal to begin with and there was an increase in this concentration over time. But it would seem that the distribution of foreign direct investment was less uneven and its concentration diminished over time.

133

The distribution of manufactured exports between the Next-14 was always unequal. It reflected disparate levels of industrialization. Over time, however, there were significant changes in the relative importance of countries and a substantial increase in the degree of concentration. In 1970, the share of the six largest exporters of manufactures among these countries—Taiwan, India, China, Chile, South Africa, and South Korea—in total manufactured exports from developing countries was 46 per cent (as compared with 62 per cent for the fourteen), in which the top five had roughly equal shares of about 8 per cent each while South Korea had a smaller share at 5 per cent. In 1990, the share of the six largest exporters of manufactures among these countries—Taiwan, South Korea, China, Brazil, Malaysia, and Thailand in total manufactured exports from developing countries was 48 per cent (as compared with 62 per cent for the fourteen), in which Taiwan and South Korea had almost equal shares of about 14 per cent each, China was at almost 10 per cent, whereas the remaining three had much smaller shares. In 2010, the share of the six largest exporters of manufactures among these countries—China, South Korea, Taiwan, Mexico, Thailand, and Malaysia—in total manufactured exports from developing countries was 64 per cent (as compared with 75 per cent for the fourteen), in which China was by far the largest with a share of almost 36 per cent, followed by South Korea with 10 per cent, Taiwan and Mexico at about 6 per cent each, while Thailand and Malaysia shared the remainder. Between 1970 and 2010, the countries that witnessed sharp declines in their shares were India (from 8.5 per cent in 2.9 per cent) and South Africa (from 7.5 per cent to 1.1 per cent). The dramatic changes in the distribution between the Next-14, the changes in the top six and the increase in concentration, particularly in the first decade of the 21st century, suggests that global value chains were an important underlying factor even if it cannot provide a complete explanation. In 2006, China, South Korea, Taiwan, Mexico, Malaysia, and Thailand were perhaps the most engaged with global value chains in the developing world, as their share of world trade in manufactured intermediate goods, imports plus exports, was more than 19.4 per cent as compared with 24.3 per cent for the Next-14, which was 55 per cent of such trade for the developing world.[11]

In the sphere of industrial production, the degree of concentration in the Next-14 was higher than it was in the other dimensions, but the regional disaggregation suggested that it was perhaps even greater between the Next-14. Further disaggregation at the country-level provides confirmation of such concentration.[12] In 1970, the share of the five largest industrial producers among these countries—China, Argentina, Mexico, Brazil, and India—in total manufacturing valued added in developing countries was 61 per cent (compared with 76 per cent for the fourteen). In 2010, the share of the five largest industrial producers among the selected fourteen—China, Brazil,

South Korea, India, and Mexico—in total manufacturing value added in developing countries was 68 per cent (compared with 86 per cent for the fourteen). The degree of concentration among the top five did not change as they accounted for four-fifths of manufacturing value added in the Next-14. China was clearly the largest in both years. Argentina was replaced by South Korea in the top five. And the rankings changed. But there was a significant change in the relative importance of China. In 1970, manufacturing value added in Argentina, Mexico, Brazil, and India, taken together, at 31 per cent was larger than that in China at 29 per cent, as a proportion of the total for developing countries. In 2010, manufacturing value added in Brazil, South Korea, India, and Mexico, taken together, at 23 per cent was much less than that in China at 45 per cent, as a proportion of the total for developing countries.[13]

The preceding discussion has sought to focus on diversity in terms of macroeconomic aggregates across the Next-14. It has not considered differences in levels of income or stages of development. For that purpose, it is worth considering differences in GDP per capita between these countries. It is just as important to compare their levels of GDP per capita with GDP per capita in the industrialized countries, as it would reveal whether or not catch up in terms of industrialization and development has led to the end of divergence or the beginning of convergence. Chapter 4 analysed divergence and convergence in per capita incomes between the developing world and the industrialized world, during the period from 1950 to 2010, with a disaggregation by regions for Asia, Africa, and Latin America, but without a disaggregation by countries. Such an exercise, which is not feasible at a country-level as it would mean too much of a digression, is worth doing for the selected countries.

The levels of, and trends in, GDP per capita for the selected countries, in current prices and market exchange rates, are set out in Table 8.2 in the next chapter, which considers the question of divergences between countries within the developing world. For the purpose of this chapter, it is sufficient to note the following. In 1970, Argentina, Chile, Mexico, South Africa, and Turkey (in descending order ranging from $1300 to $700) had the highest GDP per capita while Indonesia, India, China, Thailand, Egypt, and South Korea (in ascending order ranging from $80 to $280) had the lowest GDP among the fourteen, with Taiwan, Brazil, and Malaysia (in descending order ranging from $400 to $330) constituting the middle. By 2010, South Korea and Taiwan had much the highest GDP per capita among the fourteen ($21,000 and $19,000 respectively), Chile, Brazil, Turkey, Argentina, Mexico, Malaysia, and South Africa (in descending order in the range $12,000 to $7000) were clustered in the middle, followed by Thailand, China, Indonesia, and Egypt (in descending order in the range $4500 to $2500), with India at the bottom (just $1300). It would seem that the five countries with the highest GDP per capita in 1970 fell behind in relative terms, two countries with a low GDP per capita in 1970 (South Korea and Taiwan) pulled away from the others by 2010, two countries in the middle in 1970 (Brazil and Malaysia) moved up the middle cluster in 2010, four countries with low GDP per capita in 1970 (Thailand, China, Indonesia, and Egypt) did some catching up, while one country (India) lagged behind.

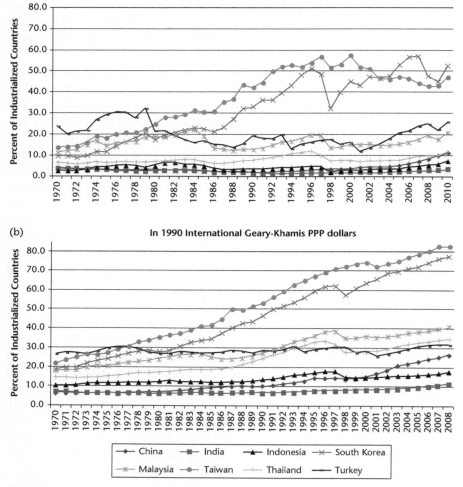

Figure 7.2. Beginnings of Convergence in GDP per capita for countries from the Next-14 in Asia: 1970–2010 (as a percentage of GDP per capita in industrialized countries)

Source: Author's calculations from United Nations, National Accounts Statistics and Maddison online database, see Appendix.

In considering catch up, it is also necessary to compare these levels of GDP per capita in the Next-14 with the levels of GDP per capita in the industrialized countries. In such a comparison, it is worth considering the trends over time using both UN national accounts statistics in current prices at market exchange rates and Maddison statistics in 1990 international (Geary-Khamis) PPP dollars.

Figure 7.2 sets out trends in GDP per capita for the eight selected Asian countries as a percentage of GDP per capita in industrialized countries at market exchange rates for the period 1970–2010 (in the top panel) and in PPP terms for the period 1970–2008 (in the bottom panel). At market exchange rates, there was a rapid convergence for South Korea and Taiwan, with a modest convergence for Malaysia in two phases and for Thailand but for a dip in the late 1990s, while China, Indonesia, and India show the beginnings of a convergence starting in the late 1990s that was most discernible for China and barely discernible for India. The picture for Turkey was mixed with convergence in the 1970s, divergence in the 1980s, followed by convergence in the 1990s and 2000s with a dip in between. In PPP terms, the trends were smoother and clearer. There was striking convergence for South Korea and Taiwan. There was clear convergence for Malaysia and Thailand. There were the beginnings of a modest convergence for China, Indonesia, and India, starting around 1990, much more for China than for India with Indonesia in the middle. The story for Turkey was mixed with short spurts of catching up. Apart from these trends over time, the notable difference between the two sets of statistics lies in the levels. As a proportion of GDP per capita in industrialized countries, the levels of GDP per capita for each of these Asian countries were much higher in PPP terms than at market exchange rates. For example, in 2010, at market exchange rates, GDP per capita in South Korea and Taiwan was about 50 per cent of GDP per capita in industrialized countries, whereas in PPP terms, this proportion was around 70 per cent in 2008; the same proportions were 20 per cent and 40 per cent respectively for Malaysia, or 10 per cent and 25 per cent respectively for China, or 3 per cent and 12 per cent respectively for India.

Figure 7.3 sets out trends in GDP per capita for the other selected countries, four in Latin American and two in Africa, as a percentage of GDP per capita in industrialized countries at market exchange rates for the period 1970–2010 (in the top panel) and in PPP terms for the period 1970–2008 (in the bottom panel). The story is very different from the Asian countries in two dimensions. First, in 1970, except for Brazil and Egypt, GDP per capita in these countries was in the range of 25 to 50 per cent of GDP per capita in industrialized countries at market exchange rates and 35 to 65 per cent of that in PPP terms, so that these countries were at much higher levels of income than their Asian counterparts. Second, there was neither convergence nor

(a)

In current prices at market exchange rates

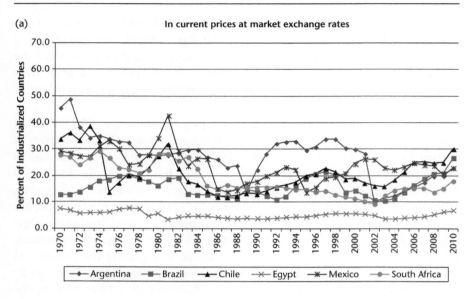

(b)

In 1990 International Geary-Khamis PPP dollars

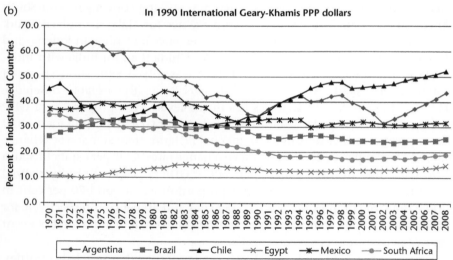

Figure 7.3. GDP per capita for countries from the Next-14 in Latin America and Africa: Divergence and Convergence: 1970–2010 (as a percentage of GDP per capita in industrialized countries)

Source: Author's calculations from United Nations, National Accounts Statistics, and Maddison online database, see Appendix.

divergence over time. At market exchange rates, GDP per capita in these countries, as a percentage of that in industrialized countries, fluctuated to diverge or converge for shorter periods, but this proportion was lower in 2010 than it was in 1970. Brazil was a possible exception where this proportion was higher in 2010 as compared with 1970 even if it happened after 2008. The story was almost the same in PPP terms. In 2008, this proportion was lower than in 1970 for these countries, except for Chile where there was some convergence starting in the early 1980s, although this proportion was just over 50 per cent in 2008 as compared with 45 per cent in 1970, and for Egypt where there was no divergence and there was a weak convergence.

It would seem that the evidence at country-level, even if limited to the Next-14, confirms the earlier conclusions about the end of divergence and beginnings of convergence at the regional-level. Asia brought an end to the divergence and saw the beginnings of a convergence, striking in some countries but modest in others. Latin America witnessed more divergence than convergence to stay roughly where it was. Africa experienced a continuing divergence. The convergence, wherever it occurred, gathered momentum during the period from 1990 to 2010, and was much more clearly discernible in PPP terms than at market exchange rates.

3. Leaders And Laggards

There can be little doubt that there is considerable diversity between the countries that were leaders in the process of catch up in industrialization, even if it was uneven over time and across space, during the second half of the 20th century and the first decade of the 21st century. Yet it is essential to focus on similarities and differences among them in terms of economic characteristics to see if there are possible clusters within the group. It is just as important to identify what they had in common underlying their success at industrialization. It would also be instructive to highlight the differences between the Next-14 and the other countries in the developing world. The discussion that follows addresses these questions to explore whether there are any lessons that can be drawn from the experience of leaders in the process of catch up so far, for the laggards who might follow as the next set of latecomers to industrialization.

The industrialization and development experience of the Next-14 suggests that there were differences in settings, drivers, emphases, transitions and models. There were different settings. Some countries were resource-rich and land-abundant (Argentina, Brazil, Chile, Mexico, South Africa, and Indonesia), other countries were resource-poor and land-scarce (China, India, South Korea, Taiwan, Thailand, and Egypt), while one was resource-rich but land-scarce (Malaysia). There were different drivers. Some countries relied on primary commodities or natural resources as the basis for manufacturing (Argentina, Brazil, Chile, South Africa, and Indonesia), while others relied on cheap labour (China, India, Malaysia, South Korea, Taiwan, Thailand, Turkey, Egypt, and, to some extent, even Mexico). There were different emphases. For some countries, external markets and external resources were critical in industrialization (Argentina, Chile, Mexico, Indonesia, Malaysia, Thailand, and Turkey), whereas for others domestic markets and domestic resources were the drivers (Brazil, China, and India), while for one or two it was external markets and domestic resources (South Korea and Taiwan). There were different transitions, reflected in patterns of structural change. Some countries moved from the extensive margin of labour absorption from the agricultural sector into the industrial sector to the intensive margin of moving labour from low to high productivity employment in the industrial sector (Malaysia, South Korea, Taiwan, and to some extent China), while most of the others did not but experienced varying transitions as the share of the agricultural sector in employment fell while that of the services sector rose but that of the industrial sector did not.

There were different models of industrialization.[14] The Latin American model relied on foreign capital, foreign technology and foreign markets, to which Brazil was the exception, while South Africa came close. Of course, this is a generalized characterization, for there were major domestic firms in Argentina, Chile, and Mexico while there were many foreign firms in Brazil. The East Asian model had three variations. There were countries where the size ranged from small to large, such as Malaysia, Thailand, and Indonesia, that relied on foreign capital, foreign technology and foreign markets. In this sense they were not very different from another variation in the city-states of Hong Kong and Singapore. There was also a third variation of this model in South Korea and Taiwan that relied on foreign markets but mobilized domestic resources and developed domestic technological capabilities instead of relying on foreign capital or foreign technology. The mega-economy model, followed by China and India, relied mostly on domestic markets, domestic resources and domestic technologies in the earlier stages of industrialization but at later stages both these countries joined the quest for external markets with a selective approach to foreign technology and foreign capital. This set of models is obviously not exhaustive. Some countries such as Brazil, Turkey, and Egypt in their pursuit of industrialization adopted a model that sought to find a blend of domestic and foreign in markets, capital and technology, which evolved over time. These industrialization models must also be situated in the wider context of their development models, each with its mix of the state and the market or openness and intervention that differed across countries and changed over time. It needs to be said that any characterization of industrialization models, or development models, is plausible in terms of stylized facts but cannot be definitive or once-and-for-all, not only because there were variations around a theme but also because there were major changes in some countries during the period under consideration.

In this manner, it is possible to disaggregate the Next-14 into smaller clusters that are neither mutually exclusive nor exhaustive. There are natural clusters in terms of geographical regions—Asia, Africa, or Latin America—for countries in the same region have many things in common. There are plausible clusters in terms of economic size determined by population and income, which range from small (Malaysia, Taiwan, and Chile) through medium (South Korea, Thailand, Turkey, Egypt, South Africa, Argentina, and Mexico) to large (China, India, Brazil, and Indonesia). There are logical clusters in terms of economic characteristics, such as the resource-rich and land-abundant (Argentina, Brazil, Chile, South Africa, and Indonesia), the resource-poor, land-scarce and labour-abundant (China, India, South Korea, Taiwan, Thailand, and Egypt), and the surplus-labour at higher wages but not resource-poor (Malaysia) or not land-scarce (Mexico and Turkey). There are possible clusters in terms of development models, which range from a strong reliance on markets and openness (Argentina, Chile, Mexico, South Africa, Malaysia, Thailand, and Indonesia), through state support with moderated openness (Brazil, Egypt, and Turkey), or strategic intervention and calibrated openness (South Korea and Taiwan), to state intervention and controlled openness (China and India).[15] The differences are more than nuances. Moderated openness was largely open economies with few restrictions in some spheres. Calibrated openness was asymmetries in openness by design manifest in strategic trade policy that was open for the export sector but restrictive for other sectors, with limits on openness to foreign capital and tight curbs on foreign brand names. Controlled openness was much more extensive, not only in trade but also with respect to foreign investment and foreign technology. These clusters in terms of geographical regions, country size, economic characteristics or development models suggest that most other countries in the developing world, except for small island economies or landlocked countries, would have something in common with one, two or a few in the Next-14, so that there are lessons to be drawn from their experience.

The clusters help to focus on what was common among these countries despite their apparent diversity even if reduced to smaller subsets. But they had more in common across subsets in factors that put them on the path to industrialization. It is possible to identify three such factors: initial conditions, enabling institutions, and the role of governments as catalysts or leaders in the process.

There were two aspects of initial conditions. The first was the existence of a physical infrastructure. The second was the spread of education in society, where primary education provided the base and higher education provided the edge. In both, a critical minimum was essential to kick-start industrialization. There were differences in levels between the Next-14, as the post-colonial era in the Latin American countries began a century earlier. However, the Asian and African countries also possessed this critical minimum in their early post-colonial era and built on it or created it soon thereafter essentially through governments. Thus, even if initial conditions were bequeathed from history, intervention could improve upon that reality without an enormous time lag, to provide a critical minimum as the basis for start-up in industrialization. But there was a relevant, even if much less critical, third dimension to initial conditions that was embedded in history, which was some sort of manufacturing experience from their past so that the origins were not the same (Amsden, 2001). For some countries, this experience was pre-capitalist, coming from artisans or handicrafts, as in China, India, Mexico, Egypt, and Turkey. For other countries, such as Indonesia, Malaysia, Taiwan, and Thailand, this experience originated in migrants, mostly from China but partly from India, while in Turkey it came from European migrants. For yet other countries, such as Argentina, Brazil, Chile, and Mexico, this experience may have started with migrant individuals from Europe but was established by foreign firms after these countries became independent so that it was not strictly colonial. But colonialism was also a source of manufacturing experience, from the British in India, Malaysia, Egypt, and China, from the Dutch in Indonesia, or from the Japanese in Manchuria (China), Korea and Taiwan. For South Africa, manufacturing experience came through a mix of migrant individuals, colonialism and foreign firms.

Similarly, for the Next-14, some institutions may have been inherited from the past but only in small part. The framework of enabling institutions to support or foster industrialization in these countries was built around the late 1950s or early 1960s. The timing was not a coincidence. It was the beginning of the post-colonial era in Asia and Africa and the rise of development planning as an ideology surfaced almost everywhere, including Latin America. In the quest for catching-up, industrialization was the common aspiration. Such institutions were put in place by proactive governments, not only in China and India but also in Argentina, Brazil, Chile, and Mexico, as well as Indonesia, Malaysia, South Korea, Taiwan, Thailand, and Turkey (Amsden, 2001), with Egypt in the same mode. It was all about industrial promotion and industrial investment whether through the use of industrial, trade and technology policy or through the establishment of planning offices, industrial boards and financial institutions. In this spectrum, development banks that provided long-term financing for investment in the industrial sector were particularly important. The object was to create production, investment and innovation capabilities in domestic firms with countries opting for different emphases on the public and the private sector (Lall, 1990). The creation and evolution of institutions was an integral part of the process of industrialization and development (Chang, 2007). Enabling institutions were not simply about secure property rights and low transaction costs as orthodoxy suggests (North, 1990). And it was obviously not about policy regimes alone. It is clear that, in the early stages, the role of the State was critical in the creation of enabling institutions that supported the process of industrialization among these latecomers, even if future transition paths turned out to be different.

In the pursuit of industrialization, the role of governments was critical almost everywhere in the developing world (Evans, 1995, Wade, 1990, and Lall, 1997), which has been discussed at some length in the preceding chapter and repetition would serve little purpose. Suffice it to say that this was even more so in the Next-14, although there were differences in nature and purpose of the role (Amsden, 2001). For countries that stressed markets and openness, it was about minimizing market failure. The emphasis was on getting-prices-right and buying the skills or technologies needed for industrialization. For countries that stressed state intervention with moderated, calibrated or controlled openness, it was about minimizing government failure. The emphasis was on getting-institutions-right and building the skills or technologies needed for industrialization. Of course, this role was not defined once-and-for-all but evolved with industrialization and development (Bhaduri and Nayyar, 1996 and Nayyar, 1997). In the earlier stages it was about creating the initial conditions by building a physical infrastructure with government investment in energy, transport and communication and in the development of human resources through education. In the later stages of industrialization there was a change in the nature and degree of this role which had three dimensions: functional, institutional and strategic. Functional intervention sought to correct for market failure, whether specific or general. Institutional intervention sought to govern the market by setting the rules of the game for players in the market, to create frameworks for regulating markets and institutions to monitor the functioning of markets. Strategic intervention sought to guide the market interlinked across sectors, not only through industrial and technology policy but also through the use of exchange rates and interest rates to attain the long-term objectives of industrialization.

Governments also fostered industrialization at the micro-level, through the nurturing of entrepreneurs in different types of business enterprises, or through the creation of managerial capabilities in individuals and technological capabilities in firms in the private sector. But that was not all. Governments also established large public sector firms for example in petroleum, steel, telecommunications, or energy, going even further into commercial banks and development banks. In the earlier stages this may have been driven by the absence of private investment in these sectors because of the lumpiness, risk, or gestation lags associated with such investments. It was not long before such firms became a strategic form of support for industrialization in the private sector. Over time, many of them evolved into competitive players in the world market and some of them have led the process of internationalization of firms from the developing world.

On the surface, it might seem that the differences between the Next-14 and the other countries in the developing world lie in their geography or their size. This could be a plausible hypothesis for the small island or the landlocked economies among the least developed countries. But it is not a plausible hypothesis for most other developing countries. The clusters among the Next-14, in terms of geographical regions, country size or economic characteristics, suggest such a wide range of attributes that most developing countries would have something in common with at least one if not a few of them. Indeed, many of the laggards in industrialization may not be very different from what the leaders in industrialization were fifty years ago.

The essential differences lie in the three common factors underlying the success of the Next-14 at industrialization: initial conditions, enabling institutions, and governments. It should be possible to create initial conditions and to build institutions. What needs to be done is obvious in the former but must be contextualized in the latter. There could, however, be a problem with governments performing their necessary role. Both democracy, which make governments accountable to people, and propriety, which prevents corruption, are desirable but not necessary for governments to perform their role in industrialization. In fact, authoritarian regimes and corrupt governments are more common than their opposites in the industrialization experience of the Next-14. However, late industrializers do need to create control mechanisms embodied in institutions that impose discipline on the economic behaviour not only of individuals and firms but also of governments (Amsden, 2001). This is the challenge.

Some scholars of industrialization (Amsden, 2001) believe that the most significant difference between the leaders and the other developing countries lies in the fact that the former had manufacturing experience while the latter did not.[16] If so, this could be a formidable constraint insofar as manufacturing experience is embedded in history, which cannot be rewritten. But the dividing line between the two sets of countries is not absolute, for manufacturing experience is a range of attributes, rather than a single binary attribute, that is difficult to measure but would always be captured better by a continuous rather than a discrete scale. Even so, it has been argued that countries without sufficient, or critical minimum, industrialization experience fell behind those that had manufacturing experience, as the developing world came to be divided into two sets of countries: those that were excluded from modern industry in the world and those that redefined its terms and learnt to industrialize (Amsden, 2001). This is an overstated hypothesis. It could, perhaps, partly explain the past. But it cannot predict the future. The reason is simple enough. Apart from the Next-14, there are many countries in the developing world that had manufacturing experience even in 1950, but possibly not enough, or did not have the initial conditions, enabling institutions and supportive governments.

It is plausible to suggest that there are other countries which could follow in the footsteps of the Next-14. In fact, Amsden (2001) notes that there are ten countries which registered the highest average annual growth rates of GDP in the manufacturing sector during the period 1950–1995, after the twelve she defined as 'The Rest': Colombia, Ecuador, Honduras, and Venezuela in Latin America; Egypt, Kenya, Nigeria, and Tunisia in Africa; and Pakistan and the Philippines in Asia. Of these, Egypt is in the Next-14, and Nigeria comes close. Pakistan is not a prospect, at least yet, for obvious reasons. But there are other countries in Asia, such as Iran and Vietnam. Thus there might be the 'Following-10' made up of Columbia, Ecuador, Honduras and Venezuela in Latin America; Kenya, Nigeria, and Tunisia in Africa; and Iran, Philippines, and Vietnam in Asia. These ten countries might follow in the footsteps of the Next-14 in the not too distant future. Even among the LDCs, there are two, Bangladesh and Tanzania, which have some potential that might enlarge the ten into a dozen.

It would seem that initial conditions, enabling institutions and supportive governments or developmental states, are essential for countries that are latecomers to industrialization. And past manufacturing experience embedded in history makes a difference. This might explain why the Next-14 did better than the others in terms of industrialization, even if there were differences between them and all of them were not a success throughout. Ultimately, however, catch up is about making a transition from being a developing country to becoming an industrialized one. The simple litmus test is whether a country is able to make a transition from imports through absorption, adaptation and diffusion to innovation, so that it advances the technology frontier in some, even a few, industries or sectors. Thus, countries that are on the path to industrialization through integration into global value chains cannot sustain the process. Unless they move up the technology ladder they would be stuck with manufacturing components or assembly operations. In this sense, South Korea and Taiwan have completed the transition. China, India, and Brazil suggest a potential. China is moving up the technology ladder, particularly in the defence sector. India is competitive in information technology and can build or launch satellites into space. Brazil has developed the Embraer aircraft and offshore oil exploration technologies. Yet none of them has arrived at the technology frontier to lead innovation in any domain.

In an analysis of technology for industrialization in developing countries, Lall (1992) made an important distinction between firm-level technological capabilities at a micro-level and national technological capabilities at a macro-level. Firms operate not on a production function but at a point so that their technical progress, building upon their own efforts, experience, and skills, is localized around that point (Atkinson and Stiglitz, 1969). Thus, evolutionary theories, which stress investment capabilities, production capabilities, and linkage capabilities, provide a far more plausible explanation of firm-level technological change, which is a continuous process of absorption, learning, and innovation (Nelson and Winter, 1982). However, technological development in firms at a micro-level is also shaped by technological capabilities in the economy at a macro-level. National technological capabilities are the outcome of a complex interaction between incentives, capabilities, and institutions. Each may suffer market failure and so require corrective intervention. Such interventions, which need careful formulation and application, are necessary for industrial success (Lall, 1990, 1991 and 1992). It becomes possible for late industrializers to complete the transition once they develop technological capabilities both at the micro-level in firms and at the macro-level in the economy.

In order to examine the implications for other latecomers in the developing world, who might follow the leaders, it is important to consider the foundations of technological capabilities and the common policy dilemmas which surface (Nayyar, 2011a). In such an exercise, the experience of some countries in the Next-14 is instructive.

The level of technological development and the capacity for innovation are often country-, sector- or context-specific. Yet, there are discernible similarities in the essential foundations. First, an emphasis on higher education and science research in the early stages of industrialization created the initial conditions. This development of human resources laid the foundations of capabilities in individuals at a micro-level. Second, import substitution in manufactured goods, or manufacturing for world markets (beyond integration into global value chains), with some special effort to establish a capital goods sector, recognized the importance of learning-by-doing. Such learning was critical in the endeavour to industrialize for it created technological capabilities in firms at a meso-level. Third, industrializing late required institutional mechanisms, which were neither mutually exclusive nor exhaustive, to support catching-up. There was an attempt to foster imitation and leapfrog on the part of domestic firms, sometimes with explicit or implicit lax systems for the protection of intellectual property rights. This was often juxtaposed with a proactive technology policy in the form of strategic interventions by the government. Economic policies in the sphere of international trade and international investment were used to promote the insertion of domestic firms into global value chains. Once domestic firms became competitive in world markets, policy regimes were modified so that the acquisition of foreign firms also became a means for the acquisition of foreign technology (Nayyar, 2008a). Such mechanisms were meant to create national technological capabilities at a macro-level.

The industrialization experience of the Next-14 suggests that each of them faced some common policy dilemmas. The most important of these was striking a balance between imports of technology and indigenous technological development. There were instances where import of technologies was followed by stagnation rather than adaptation, diffusion, and innovation at home. There were instances where indigenous technological development did not lead to widespread diffusion let alone up-gradation. In such situations, market structures and government policies did not combine to provide an environment that would encourage the absorption of imported and speed up the development of indigenous technology, or create a milieu that would be conducive to diffusion and innovation. Even so, an open regime for the import of technology is not an answer, for the discipline of the market cannot restrain the recurrence of such imports by domestic firms time after time. Such firms are much like the schoolboy who can find someone else to write the examinations for him year after year and thus never learns. Domestic technological capabilities may not emerge either because there is no incentive to learn (imports are possible) or because they are stifled (imports are better). The problem may be accentuated in sectors where technical progress is rapid and obsolescence is high. There are two other common dilemmas. For one, it is difficult to foster the culture of R&D in domestic firms. This is not automatic. It needs incentives and disincentives, embedded in industrial policy, for start-up and scale-up. For another, it is difficult to develop synergies between science and industry that transform scientific knowledge into marketable products. This is not automatic either. It needs institutional mechanisms to build bridges between the two worlds. Every latecomer to industrialization, at every stage in history, has confronted these dilemmas. Each has attempted to address the dilemmas in different ways. The countries that have succeeded in industrializing late and making the transition from importation to innovation, from know-how to know-why, have done so by resolving these dilemmas.

Conclusion

The distribution of catch up in industrialization and development was uneven not only among regions but also between countries within regions. There was a high degree of concentration among a few: Argentina, Brazil, Chile, and Mexico in Latin America; China, India, Indonesia, Malaysia, South Korea,

Taiwan, Thailand, and Turkey in Asia; and Egypt and South Africa in Africa. In fact, the economic significance of these countries, the Next-14, in the developing world was overwhelming in terms of their size, reflected in GDP and population, their engagement with the world economy, reflected in trade, investment and migration, and industrialization, reflected in manufactured exports and industrial production. The determinants of such concentration are size, growth, and history. There was also enormous diversity within the few, characterized by an unequal distribution in terms of the same attributes that revealed the concentration among them. In comparison with per capita income levels in the industrialized world, country-level evidence confirms regional differences. The eight Asian countries brought an end to divergence and saw the beginnings of convergence, while the four Latin American countries stayed roughly where they were, and the two African countries experienced a continuing divergence. There were also differences between the Next-14 in settings, drivers, emphases, transition, and models. Yet, despite their apparent diversity, it is possible to group them into clusters based on similarities in terms of geography, size, economic characteristics, and development models. They had even more in common across clusters in terms of three factors that put them on the path to industrialization: initial conditions, enabling institutions, and the role of governments as catalysts or leaders in the process. The essential differences with other countries in the developing world, apart from a history of manufacturing experience, also lie in these three common factors. But many of the laggards in industrialization may not be very different from what these leaders in industrialization were fifty years ago. Indeed, there is much that they can learn from the experience of the Next-14 in creating initial conditions, establishing enabling institutions and nurturing supportive governments. But these efforts must be contextualized. In the catch up process, there are two essential challenges for late industrializers, leaders and followers alike. It is necessary to create control mechanisms embodied in institutions that impose discipline on the economic behaviour not only of individuals and firms but also of governments. It is necessary to develop technological capabilities in firms and in the economy which can advance the technology frontier in at least a few industries or sectors.

8

Emerging Divergences:
Inequality, Exclusion, and Poverty

During the second half of the 20th century and the first decade of the 21st, economic growth in the developing world as a whole was impressive compared with the industrialized countries. It was also much faster than growth in Western Europe and North America during their Industrial Revolutions. And it was clearly far better than its own performance in the preceding eighty years. This led to a significant increase in its share of world GDP and to the end of divergence in GDP per capita even if convergence was modest and uneven. This was also associated with a catch up in industrialization which led to an increase in its share of industrial production and manufactured exports in the world economy. But these aggregates are deceptive. The distribution was unequal across its constituent regions. Indeed, there was a high degree of concentration in just fourteen countries. It is obviously essential to recognize the reality of such uneven development across space.

The object of this chapter, however, is to analyse emerging divergences that are discernible in the world economy which has witnessed considerable change over the past six decades. In doing so, it seeks to focus on how the process of catch up has influenced or shaped inequality between countries, the exclusion of geographical spaces, and the well-being of people. Section 1 analyses international inequality in terms of the wide gap between industrialized and developing countries, and the unequal income distribution between rich and poor people in the world. Section 2 considers the exclusion of countries, particularly the least developed countries, and of regions within countries, from the process of development to highlight divergences that are beginning to surface within the developing world. Section 3 asks the question whether rapid economic growth, underlying the catch up in terms of aggregate income, improved the well-being of ordinary people in the developing world, with a focus on poverty and inequality within countries.

1. International Inequality between Countries and People

There are three concepts of international inequality (Milanovic, 2005). The first is a measure of income distribution between countries, unweighted by population, which assumes that each country, irrespective of the size of its population, is made up of a representative individual and the per capita income levels in countries determine inter-country income distribution in the world. The second is a measure of income distribution between countries, weighted by population, which assumes that intra-country income distribution is perfectly equal and uses per capita income in each country weighted by its population to determine inter-country income distribution in the world. The third is a measure of income distribution between people in the world estimated from the actual incomes of individuals irrespective of the countries where they live. The most common measure for income distribution between people (or countries) is the Gini coefficient, which has a value of 100 if all the income in an economy (or all the income in the world) accrues to just one person (or just one country) and a value of zero if every person in an economy (or every country in the world) has exactly the same income.

The available evidence on world inequality in historical perspective during the period from 1820 to 2000, measured by Gini coefficients, is set out in Figure 8.1, with a separate graph for each of the three concepts of international inequality. It needs to be said that the population-unweighted and weighted estimates of inequality are derived from Maddison statistics on GDP per capita in 1990 international (Geary-Khamis) PPP dollars, while the estimates for the third concept of inequality are based on Bourguignon and Morrisson (2002) who use the Maddison statistics on GDP per capita and population but also draw upon other sources of data.

Figure 8.1.a shows that the population-unweighted international inequality between countries increased rapidly from 1820 to 1913, and once again from 1938 to 2000. Of course, this measure is not really meaningful because it ignores the population size of countries, treating large and small countries or giant economies and tiny islands at par.

Figure 8.1.b shows that the population-weighted international inequality between countries increased even more rapidly from 1820 to 1929, and once again from 1938 to 1952 but declined slowly thereafter until 2000. This measure is far better but its estimates are significantly influenced by what happens in countries with large populations. The observed trend, which suggests declining international inequality, is almost entirely attributable to the increase in per capita income in two countries, China and India, with large populations.[1] It is worth noting that their GDP per capita also increased much more in PPP terms than it did at market exchange rates. And PPP adjustment

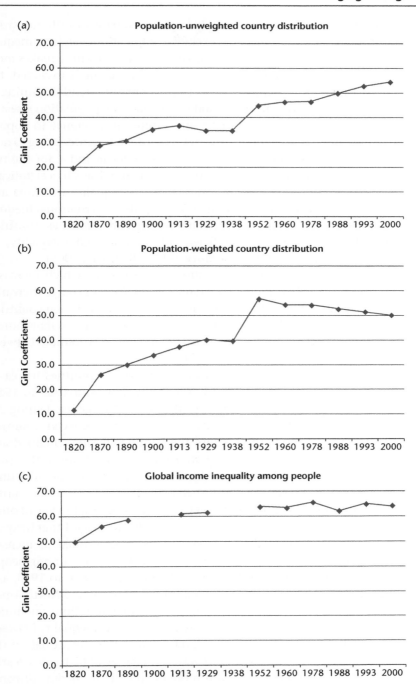

Figure 8.1. World Inequality in Historical Perspective: 1820–2000

Source: Milanovic (2005).

for China and India is disproportionately large in comparison with industrialized countries. If China and India are excluded, population-weighted inequality does not register a decline after 1980. The exclusion of China makes more difference than the exclusion of India. When China alone is excluded, the clearly decreasing trend is replaced by a clearly increasing trend beginning in the early 1980s. Obviously, in the period since 1980, the population size and rapid growth of China and India make this significant difference to population-weighted international inequality. In this context, it is interesting to note that the substitution of provinces in China and states in India, for the two largest countries in estimates of international inequality leads to a significant change in the picture. The growing inter-regional inequality in China and India has a discernible impact on population-weighted international inequality. If the provinces of China and the states of India are treated as countries, the population-weighted Gini coefficient of international inequality, so defined, reveals a significant increase since 1980 (Milanovic, 2005).

Figure 8.1.c shows that global inequality among people, which increased rapidly from 1820 to 1913, and remained roughly in the same range thereafter until 2000, was much higher than international inequality between countries. This measure is particularly important because it captures a different dimension of international inequality to focus on income distribution between people rather than countries in the world economy.

It would seem that international inequality between countries increased rapidly in the past from 1820 to 1913 and once again from 1929 to 1952. This was, in large part, a manifestation of the Great Divergence. During the second half of the 20th century, however, inequality between countries diminished slowly, if modestly, because the Gini coefficient remained at a high level of more than 50 in 2000. But, excluding China and India, such inequality between countries witnessed little change for three decades until the early 1980s and increased rapidly thereafter. Evidence on inter-country income distribution, since 2000, is not yet available. Even so, in view of other evidence considered earlier in the book, it is plausible to suggest that inequality between countries, excluding China and India, continued to increase during the first decade of the 21st century. Income inequality among people in the world also increased significantly in the past from 1820 to 1913, as a consequence of the Great Divergence when Western Europe and North America shot ahead of the rest of the world while Asia, particularly China and India, experienced a sharp economic decline. This global income inequality between people persisted at a somewhat higher level through the second half of the 20th century, when the Gini coefficient was in the range of 62 to 66. Clearly, income distribution among people was more unequal than income distribution between countries in the world economy.

The evidence presented in Chapter 4 showed that for developing countries, taken together, the divergence in their GDP per capita from that in industrialized countries stopped in the early 1970s in PPP terms and in the mid-1980s at market exchange rates, followed by the beginnings of a modest convergence, more clearly discernible in PPP terms, during the 2000s. There were, of course, significant differences between Asia, Africa and Latin America. But even average GDP per capita levels for regions do not reveal the range of dispersion. In fact there was a substantial widening of the gap between countries at the top and countries at the bottom in terms of per capita income levels. For instance, the ratio of GDP per capita in the richest 20 countries to GDP per capita in the poorest 20 countries, in constant 1995 US dollars, rose from 54:1 during 1960–1962 to 121:1 during 2000–2002 (Nayyar, 2006). It should come as no surprise that the gap between the richest and the poorest was even greater.[2] The ratio of GDP per capita in the richest country to GDP per capita in the poorest country of the world, in current prices at market exchange rates, rose from 119:1 in 1970 to 371:1 in 1990 and 916:1 in 2010.[3] The ratio of GDP per capita in the richest country to GDP per capita in the poorest country of the world, in 1990 international (Geary-Khamis PPP) dollars, increased from 38:1 in 1970 to 53:1 in 1990 and 125:1 in 2008.[4] In terms of PPP, the difference is not as high. It is only to be expected that the absolute differences between countries at the top and the bottom in income per capita, expressed as multiples, diminish as the numeraire is changed from current dollars to PPP dollars. And end points in such a wide range make the difference seem that much larger. Yet, the enormous gap is both striking and awesome.

There can be no doubt that the dimensions of international inequality were largely attributable to the gap between industrialized countries and developing countries, even if it did not widen after the 1970s and may have narrowed a little in the 2000s for the latter taken together. Table 8.1 presents available evidence on the Theil coefficient of world inequality in 1960, 1980 and 2000. This index considers only inequality between, and not inequality within countries. The inequality measure is weighted for the size of population in each country. The Theil coefficient is a measure of inequality based on information theory. If all countries in the world had exactly the same per capita income, the Theil coefficient would have a value of zero. If all income in the world accrues to just one country, the Theil coefficient would have a value of log N where N is the number of countries. The advantage of the Theil coefficient as compared with other inequality measures, such as the Gini coefficient, is that it can be decomposed. Thus it can disaggregate the contribution of inter-regional and intra-regional inequality to overall inequality between countries. It also has the useful property of being additive for the components attributable to inequality or differences between and within groups of countries.

Table 8.1. Theil Decomposition of International Inequality: 1960–2010

a. Theil Coefficient of World Inequality for all Countries			
	1960	1980	2000
Between regions	0.45 *(0.35)*	0.51 *(0.42)*	0.45 *(0.48)*
Within regions	0.07 *(0.07)*	0.05 *(0.05)*	0.08 *(0.09)*
TOTAL	0.51 *(0.42)*	0.56 *(0.48)*	0.53 *(0.56)*
b. Theil Coefficient of Developing World Inequality			
	1960	1980	2000
Between regions	0.25 *(0.17)*	0.26 *(0.17)*	0.08 *(0.12)*
Within regions	0.06 *(0.07)*	0.09 *(0.10)*	0.15 *(0.19)*
TOTAL	0.32 *(0.24)*	0.36 *(0.27)*	0.23 *(0.31)*

Note: The figures in this table are based on five-year averages for both GDP and population: 1958–1962 for 1960, 1978–1982 for 1980, and 1998–2001 for 2000. Figures in parenthesis are Theil coefficients for all countries excluding China.
Source: United Nations (2006).

The coefficients in Table 8.1 are calculated from the Maddison statistics on GDP per capita in 1990 international (Geary-Khamis PPP) dollars. It shows that throughout the period more than 85 per cent of the population-weighted inequality between countries in the world was attributable to inequality between regions. This was, in turn, entirely on account of the income gap between industrialized and developing countries. In fact, the decomposition of the Theil coefficient of international inequality, by region, for 1960, 1980, and 2000 shows that the contribution of industrialized countries to overall inequality between countries in the world was greater than what was attributable to inequality between regions.[5]

Even so, international inequality between countries in the developing world was quite significant. Table 8.1 also presents evidence on the Theil coefficient of developing world inequality. It shows that this inequality increased between 1960 and 1980, as also between 1980 and 2000 if China is excluded. Over this period, in the developing world the contribution of inter-regional inequality to total inequality between countries fell while the contribution of intra-regional inequality rose, irrespective of whether China is included or excluded. This trend in rising intra-regional inequality is reflected in the ratio of GDP per capita in the richest and poorest countries of each region.[6] The ratio of GDP per capita in the richest country to GDP per capita in the poorest country of Asia, rose from 117:1 in 1970 to 145:1 in 2010 in current prices at market exchange rates, and from 7:1 in 1970 to 23:1 in 2008 in 1990 international (Geary-Khamis PPP) dollars. In Africa, this ratio rose from 47:1 to 147:1 in current prices at market exchange rates, and from 20:1 to 88:1 in 1990 international (Geary-Khamis PPP) dollars. In Latin

America, this ratio rose from 71:1 to 93:1 in current prices at market exchange rates, and from 12:1 to 31:1 in 1990 international (Geary-Khamis PPP) dollars. The absolute income differences between the richest and the poorest country diminish significantly while the relative income gaps increase significantly as the numeraire shifts from current dollars to PPP dollars. But all the ratios suggest that intra-regional inequality was the highest and increased the most in Africa while it was the lowest and increased the least in Latin America, with Asia in the middle.

2. Exclusion of Countries and Regions

The uneven distribution of economic growth in the world is, perhaps, the most important factor underlying the persistent, or rising, inequality among countries. But the evidence considered in the preceding discussion does not capture an important dimension of the reality that also shapes outcomes. There is an exclusion of countries, as well as regions within countries, so that some geographical spaces are mostly bypassed in the process of development.

The least developed countries (LDCs) provide a most striking illustration.[7] The number of LDCs has doubled from 24 in the early 1970s to 48 in the early 2000s. Of these, 10 are small island economies and 13 are landlocked countries. In 2010, the share of LDCs in world output was less than 0.9 per cent, lower than it was in the mid-1970s. In fact, in 2010 the assets of the 20 richest people in the world were more than the combined GDP of all LDCs. This reality is daunting, even if a comparison of assets (stock) with income (flow) is inappropriate. Yet LDCs, with 833 million people in 2010, accounted for 12 per cent of world population. In current prices at market exchange rates, the average GDP per capita in LDCs in 2010 was less than one-fifth of that in developing countries and less than one-fiftieth of that in industrialized countries. Even in terms of PPP, GDP per capita in LDCs was one-fourth of that in developing countries and one-twenty-fifth of that in industrialized countries. Economic development has simply not created social opportunities for most people in LDCs.

Indeed at the end of the first decade of the 21st century social indicators of development in LDCs were much worse than the average for the developing world. Adult literacy was less than 60 per cent as compared with 80 per cent in developing countries. Life expectancy at birth was 51 years as compared with 60 years in developing countries. Infant mortality rates were 78 per 1000 births as compared with 48 per 1000 births in developing countries. Gross enrolment ratios in tertiary education were less than 6 per cent as compared with 21 per cent in developing countries. Of the total population, 38 per cent did not have access to safe drinking water as compared with 16 per cent for developing countries. The situation in LDCs is distinctly worse than the average in developing countries. It would seem that their exclusion from the process of development is an important factor underlying the international inequality between countries, not only in the world as a whole, but also within the developing world. Of course, this is a snapshot picture at a point in time. And a comparison with the situation of LDCs in 1970, for which data are not available, would almost certainly reveal progress in terms of social indicators of development during these four decades. The real question, however, is whether the economic distance between the LDCs and the developing world or industrialized countries has become narrower or wider with the passage of time.

In order to focus on income inequality between countries, so as to examine the reality in terms of convergence or divergence, Table 8.2 sets out data on GDP per capita, in current prices at market exchange rates, for the LDCs as compared with developing countries, industrialized countries and the world, at five-year intervals during the period from 1970 to 2010. For a further disaggregated comparison within the developing world, it also presents trends in GDP per capita for the Next-14 and the other developing countries that, together with the LDCs, make up the developing countries group.

It shows that GDP per capita in LDCs, as a proportion of the average for developing countries, was more than three-fifths in 1970, less than one-third in 1990 and less than one-fifth in 2010. It also shows that GDP per capita in LDCs as a percentage of the average in industrialized countries was 4.5 per cent in 1970, 1.6 per cent in 1990 and 1.7 per cent in 2010. The story was much the same with respect to other parts of the developing world. GDP per capita in LDCs, as a percentage of the average for the Next-14, dropped from 63 per cent in 1970 to 31 per cent in 1990 and 16 per cent in 2010, while, as a percentage of the average for the other developing countries, it also declined from 47 per cent in 1970 to 32 per cent in 1990 and 18 per cent in 2010. It is clear that during these four decades there was a massive divergence in per capita incomes not only between LDCs and industrialized countries but also between LDCs and the other constituents of the developing world. In fact, it is worth noting that, in 1970, average GDP per capita in LDCs was higher than GDP per capita in China, India and Indonesia. However, by 2010, GDP per capita in LDCs was less than one-sixth of that in China, less than one-fourth of that in Indonesia and about one-half of that in India.

The proportionate changes and differences highlighted above are important for the magnitudes, but the trends over time emerge far more clearly from Figure 8.2, which plots time series data on GDP per capita, in current prices at market exchange rates, for LDCs as compared with the Next-14, the other developing countries, and all developing countries, during the period from

Table 8.2. Divergence in GDP per capita between LDCs and the Developing World, Industrialized Countries and the World Economy: 1970–2010
(US dollars in current prices at current exchange rates)

	1970	1975	1980	1985	1990	1995	2000	2005	2010
Least Developed Countries	128	193	285	259	303	266	274	403	684
The Next-14	202	365	646	621	981	1464	1648	2330	4313
Other Developing Countries	275	677	1372	1125	1191	1533	1584	2460	3872
Developing Countries	*209*	*416*	*772*	*697*	*947*	*1324*	*1444*	*2081*	*3715*
Industrialized Countries	*2873*	*5387*	*9710*	*10,761*	*19,303*	*24,898*	*25,711*	*33,977*	*39,723*
World	*892*	*1579*	*2675*	*2682*	*4201*	*5247*	*5286*	*7053*	*9275*
The Next-14									
Argentina	1308	1821	2684	2904	4330	7405	7699	4736	9167
Brazil	367	998	1570	1376	2687	4751	3696	4743	10,574
Chile	970	741	2637	1505	2541	5001	4877	7254	12,052
China	114	179	317	298	360	635	957	1792	4454
Egypt	211	328	535	495	693	1110	1472	1325	2643
India	111	161	264	289	374	383	444	737	1326
Indonesia	82	248	526	569	679	1109	773	1258	2953
South Korea	284	623	1719	2432	6291	11,892	11,598	17,959	20,911
Malaysia	329	787	1838	2055	2511	4452	4006	5286	8319
Mexico	839	1786	3310	2831	3416	3400	6370	7946	9043
South Africa	796	1438	2770	1736	3044	3650	2969	5169	7206
Taiwan	400	983	2393	3291	8135	12,920	14,702	16,051	18,681
Thailand	193	353	681	743	1496	2817	1943	2644	4619
Turkey	689	1585	2097	1830	3742	3867	4189	7088	10,273

Source: United Nations, National Accounts Statistics, see Appendix.

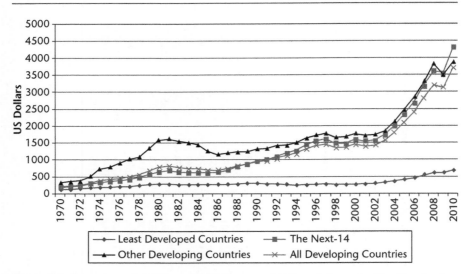

Figure 8.2. Divergence in GDP per capita between LDCs and the rest of the Developing World: 1970–2010

Source: United Nations, National Accounts Statistics, see Appendix.

1970 to 2010. It reveals that these three country-groups in the developing world were close to each other in terms of GDP per capita during the early 1970s. Soon thereafter, the other developing countries pulled away, partly but not entirely on account of the oil-exporting countries in this group that benefited from the oil price increases in 1973 and 1979. It was not long before GDP per capita in the Next-14 also began to rise and this gathered momentum from the mid-1980s. These rising trends were reflected in the average GDP per capita for all developing countries. The income gap between LDCs and the rest widened rapidly from the mid-1980s to the mid-1990s and once again at a much faster pace during the 2000s.

For LDCs, the divergence was striking. Such divergence within the developing world was new. It was a corollary of the end of divergence or beginning of convergence, with respect to industrialized countries, for some other countries in the developing world. The Next-14 provide a sharp contrast in convergence, as their GDP per capita moved close to the average for developing countries by the mid-1980s and increased faster thereafter to widen that gap in the 2000s. The real convergence for the Next-14, however, was with respect to the other developing countries. The average GDP per capita of the latter was distinctly higher than that of the former for more than three decades. But the Next-14 caught up in the early 2000s to overtake the others before the end of the decade. It would seem that there was one divergence, for the LDCs, and

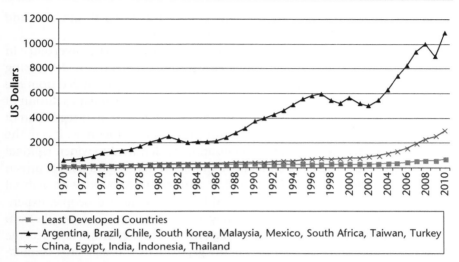

Figure 8.3. Trends in GDP per capita in LDCs as compared with the Next-14: 1970–2010 (disaggregated into two groups)

Source: United Nations, National Accounts Statistics, see Appendix.

one convergence, for the Next-14, in per capita incomes within the developing world.

A comparison between these two groups of countries might be instructive. It is important to recognize that even the Next-14 is a diverse group. In fact, as pointed out in the preceding chapter, there were significant differences among them in levels of per capita income. Indeed, in 1970, average GDP per capita in the LDCs was higher than that in three countries in the Next-14 (China, India, and Indonesia), while it was not significantly lower than that in two other countries in the Next-14 (Egypt and Thailand). Figure 8.3 outlines the trends in GDP per capita, in current prices at market exchange rates, from 1970 to 2010, for LDCs and for the Next-14 disaggregated into two groups based on GDP per capita levels in 1970: (a) China, India, Indonesia, Egypt, and Thailand, and (b) Argentina, Brazil, Chile, Malaysia, Mexico, South Africa, South Korea, Taiwan, and Turkey. It shows that the divergence in incomes per capita between LDCs and the latter set of nine countries in the Next-14 was much greater with a considerable widening of the gap over time, than it was with the former set of five countries in the Next-14 where the divergence was significantly less as it started only in the late 1990s, to gather pace in the 2000s. If the plot for average GDP per capita in all developing countries was superimposed on this graph, it would show that average GDP per capita in the latter set of nine countries among the Next-14 was slightly higher to start with but diverged progressively over time, while the average GDP per capita in the former set of five countries among the Next-14 was lower throughout and followed in parallel but did not quite converge over time.

It is, however, perfectly clear that LDCs experienced a sharp divergence in their per capita incomes when compared with other parts of the developing world, which suggests that this set of countries was largely excluded from the catch up process. It is also worth noting that there was a similar exclusion of regions within countries, particularly in countries that were an integral part of the catch up process. This is neither surprising nor altogether new. It is in the logic of markets, accentuated by liberalization, which tend to widen regional disparities because there is a cumulative causation that creates market driven virtuous or vicious circles. Regions that are better endowed with natural resources, physical infrastructure, skilled labour or educated people, experience a rapid growth. Like magnets, they attract resources and people from elsewhere. In contrast, disadvantaged regions tend to lag behind and become even more disadvantaged. Over time, the gap widens through such cumulative causation. This has happened in most countries that have experienced rapid growth to lead the catch up in output, even if it has not led to convergence in income, and the catch up in industrialization, even if it has not always led to meaningful development that improves the well-being of people.

In Brazil, regional inequalities between the northeast and the south, in particular Sao Paulo, increased significantly during the period of rapid economic growth. There is an increase in economic disparities between the north and the south in Mexico, as states in the south such as Chiapas and Oaxaca are significantly poorer while states in the north are more industrialized and developed which is partly a function of geographical proximity to the United States. In Indonesia, the economic gap between Java and the other islands is much wider. The economic disparities between coastal China in the east and the hinterland in the west are much greater than ever before. In India, the regions in the west and the south that already have a lead have left other regions in the north and the east behind. The increase in inter-regional inequality in China and India is so pronounced that, as discussed in the preceding section, if provinces in China and states in India are treated as countries, the population-weighted Gini coefficient of international inequality registers a significant increase since 1980 instead of the decrease it registers when China and India are treated as countries in measuring inter-country inequality. These examples can be multiplied across countries in the developing world where rapid economic growth has been associated with rising regional disparities. This is a potential source of social tension or political conflict.

3. Poverty and Inequality within Countries

Just as much as regions, the exclusion of people within countries from the process of development is part of the story. Economic growth in the developing world since 1950 was impressive in the aggregate, although it was uneven across countries and regions. But it should be recognized that such growth, even if it had been distributed in a more equal manner across geographical space, would not have been sufficient to ensure the inclusion of people. The essential problem was that rapid economic growth was often not transformed into meaningful development that improved the living conditions and ensured the well-being of ordinary people. In a few countries, of course, rapid growth led to such meaningful development. But in a much larger number of countries, growth did not lead to development. And a significant number of countries experienced neither growth nor development. For countries that did experience growth, the outcome was shaped by how increments in output were distributed among people and whether or not this led to an increase in incomes of the poor. It is difficult to provide systematic let alone complete evidence on both issues, income distribution and poverty levels, because data are often incomplete or simply unavailable in developing countries. There are national estimates but it is exceedingly difficult to sketch a global picture.

The incidence of poverty in the developing world c.1950 was high. There was a modest reduction in the proportion of people who lived in absolute poverty in most developing countries during the three decades from 1950 to 1980 but this reduction was nowhere near what was needed to diminish, let alone eradicate, poverty (Streeten, 1981, Stewart, 1985, and Nayyar, 2008b). It is perhaps more important to focus on the period since then, as the developing world's share in world output registered a significant increase, the divergence in per capita incomes came to an end, and the catch up on industrialization gathered momentum. Did this change the lives of poor people in developing countries? The answer to this question is critical and depends upon whether the absolute poverty in the developing world was reduced significantly during the three decades from 1980 to 2010.

It needs to be said that the measurement of poverty poses problems because there are conceptual alternatives, methodological difficulties and data constraints (Atkinson, 1987). There are three conceptual alternatives (Nayyar, 1991). The simplest is the headcount measure, which estimates the proportion of the population or the number of people below a specified poverty line defined in terms of critical minimum needs; anyone below it lives in absolute poverty. The poverty gap index comes next, which estimates the mean distance below the poverty line as a proportion of the line, so that it determines the proportion of national income that would be needed to lift everyone out of absolute poverty. There is a set of more complex measures, such as the Sen P measure, which uses the Gini coefficient to measure inequality among those below the poverty line (Sen,1976). Simply put, as the complexity of the poverty measure increases, the data constraints are more while the methodological difficulties are less. It goes without saying that international comparisons make the task more difficult (Atkinson and Bourguignon, 2001 and Deaton, 2005).

The headcount measure is the most widely used because it is the simplest to estimate and to understand. Of course, the methodological difficulties associated with it are considerable, ranging from choosing poverty lines, through finding appropriate price indices for adjusting poverty lines to inflation over time, to using sample data on household consumer expenditure or family incomes from surveys for estimates at a macro-level. Each is a source of endless debate. Such exercises, which count the poor, are either national estimates or World Bank estimates. There can be little doubt that national estimates are better and more robust in terms of their methodology and database, although even these are often much debated on points of disagreement or controversy. World Bank estimates are simply not as good in terms of their methodology or statistical foundations. Some question their method of estimation (Pogge and Reddy, 2010). Others argue that the World Bank underestimates poverty (Kaplinsky, 2005). A few even argue that the World Bank overestimates poverty (Sala-i-Martin, 2006). Of the three arguments, the first is the most convincing, the second is perfectly plausible (as the weight assigned to food and necessities in the consumption basket needs to be larger), while the third is far-fetched. However, World Bank estimates are the only possible source for inter-country comparisons over time and are used here to sketch the contours of a global picture. It must be stressed that the evidence needs to be interpreted with caution.

The latest World Bank estimates use two poverty lines, which are $1.25 per day and $2 per day in 2005 PPP (Chen and Ravallion, 2012). The first is the mean of the poverty lines in terms of consumption per capita in the poorest 15 countries of the world, whereas the second is the median poverty line for developing countries as a group. The database is provided by 850 surveys for 125 countries. The usual methodological difficulties that characterize national estimates are also present here. But the object of international comparisons introduces another difficulty insofar as national poverty lines are first converted into a common currency using PPP and then the international poverty line is converted into the national currency for measuring poverty using the same PPP. This problem is accentuated because the changed methodology of World Bank PPP estimates has led to large, sometimes inexplicable, increases in income for some countries (Chang, 2010).

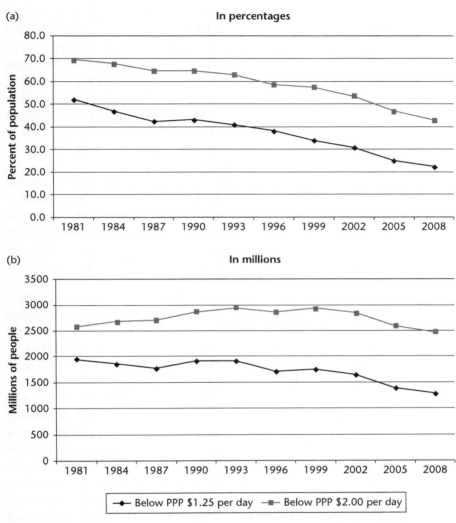

Figure 8.4. Trends in Absolute Poverty in the Developing World: 1981–2008
Source: Chen and Ravallion (2012).

Figure 8.4 outlines the trends in the percentage of the population and the number of people in the developing world, below the poverty lines of PPP $1.25 per day and PPP $2 per day, during the period from 1981 to 2008, based on these estimates of poverty at three-year intervals. Figure 8.4.a shows that there was a steady decline in the percentage of the population that lived below both the poverty lines. The proportion of people in the developing world who lived below PPP$1.25 per day dropped from more than one-half in 1981 to two-fifths in 1993 and more than one-fifth in 2008, while the proportion of people who lived below PPP$2 per day also dropped but much less from 70 per cent in 1981 to 63 per cent in 1993 and 43 per cent in 2008. It is clear that the progress was far slower in terms of reducing the number of poor people. Figure 8.4.b shows that the number of people who lived below PPP$1.25 per day remained unchanged at 1.9 billion between 1981 and 1993 although it declined to 1.3 billion in 2008, whereas the number of people who lived below PPP$2 per day was the same at about 2.5 billion in both 1991 and 2008 but was higher, close to 3 billion, throughout the 1990s. For the developing world, the number 3 billion was large, as it constituted almost three-fifths its population in 1990 and about one-half in 2000.

There is another dimension to this problem. Those who lived below the poverty line of PPP $1.25 per day were the perennial poor who were probably unable to reach the critical minimum even in terms of nutrition. Those who lived below the poverty line of PPP $2 per day were the vulnerable poor who might have been able to reach the critical minimum in terms of food and clothing plus some basic needs but not appropriate shelter or adequate health-care and education. Clearly, the population between the two poverty lines was vulnerable because any shock, such as a bad harvest, high inflation, employments cuts, or an illness in the family, could have pushed them down further into poverty. Figure 8.4.b shows clearly shows that the number of people between the two poverty lines increased significantly during the period. In fact, this number almost doubled over the period from about 650 million in 1981 to 1 billion in 1993 and 1.2 billion in 2008.

It is also worth considering the trends in poverty, in terms of absolute numbers and relative proportions, beyond aggregates for the developing world. Table 8.3 presents the same estimates, in terms of the proportion of population and the number of people below the two poverty lines, disaggregated for geographical regions in the developing world, for three selected years, 1981, 1993, and 2008, in order to keep the data within manageable proportions.[8] It shows that poverty is concentrated in three regions of the developing world: East Asia (largely China), South Asia (mostly India), and sub-Saharan Africa. In the other regions, Middle East and North Africa as well as Latin America and the Caribbean, the percentages were low and the numbers were small.

Between 1981 and 2008, the proportion of the population below the poverty line of PPP $1.25 per day declined sharply by more than 60 percentage points in East Asia, attributable mostly to China, significantly by 25 percentage points in South Asia, in India and elsewhere, and only modestly by just 4 percentage points in sub-Saharan Africa, whereas the percentages below the poverty line of PPP $2 per day declined sharply by almost 60 percentage points in East Asia, once again on account of China, modestly by 16 percentage points in South Asia and little by just 3 percentage points in sub-Saharan

Table 8.3. Proportion and Number of the Poor in the Developing World: 1981–2008
(as a percentage of population)

	Below PPP $1.25 per day			Below PPP $2 per day		
	1981	1993	2008	1981	1993	2008
East Asia and Pacific	77.2	50.7	14.3	92.4	75.8	33.2
of which China	84.0	53.7	13.1	97.8	78.6	29.8
South Asia	61.1	51.7	36.0	87.2	82.7	70.9
of which India	59.8	49.4	41.6*	86.6	81.7	75.6*
Sub-Saharan Africa	51.5	59.4	47.5	72.2	78.1	69.2
Middle East and North Africa	9.6	4.8	2.7	30.1	22.1	13.9
Latin America and the Caribbean	11.9	11.4	6.5	23.8	21.7	12.4
Eastern Europe and Central Asia	1.9	2.9	0.5	8.3	9.2	2.2
TOTAL	**52.2**	**40.9**	**22.4**	**69.6**	**63.1**	**43.0**

(in millions)

	Below PPP $1.25 per day			Below PPP $2 per day		
	1981	1993	2008	1981	1993	2008
East Asia and Pacific	1097	871	284	1313	1301	659
of which China	835	633	173	972	926	395
South Asia	568	632	571	811	1010	1125
of which India	421	444	456*	609	735	828*
Sub-Saharan Africa	205	330	386	288	434	562
Middle East and North Africa	17	12	9	52	54	44
Latin America and the Caribbean	43	53	37	87	100	71
Eastern Europe and Central Asia	8	14	2	36	43	10
TOTAL	**1938**	**1278**	**1116**	**2585**	**2942**	**2471**

Note: Figures marked with an (*) are for 2005 and not 2008. All figures for India in this table are from Chen and Ravallion (2008).

Source: Chen and Ravallion (2012).

Africa. However, progress was far less impressive in terms of reducing the number of poor people. China was the exception. Between 1981 and 2008, excluding China, the number of the poor in the developing world below PPP $1.25 per day remained unchanged at 1.1 billion, while below PPP $2 per day the number rose from 1.6 billion to 2.1 billion. In 1981, the largest number of poor people was in East Asia followed by South Asia and then sub-Saharan Africa. By 2008, this changed, as the largest number of poor people was in South Asia followed by sub-Saharan Africa and then East Asia. Yet, in absolute terms, the number of poor people in each of these regions remained large. In fact, the number of poor people remained large even in China and India, although these two countries significantly reduced the incidence of absolute poverty.

Even if the evidence presented above needs to be interpreted with caution, it is clear that the dimensions of absolute poverty in the developing world are overwhelming. During the period from 1981 to 2008, the percentage of people below the specified international poverty lines has declined steadily, more for the lower than for the higher poverty line, but these proportions remain significant. Moreover, the absolute number of people below both the poverty lines remains large; it has remained the same below the lower poverty line excluding China, just as it has remained unchanged below the higher poverty line even if China in included. In Asia, in 2008, the number of people below PPP $1.25 per day was 855 million, of whom 629 million were in India and China, while the number of people below PPP $2 per day was 1784 million, of whom 1223 million were in India and China. It is striking that poverty has persisted to this degree in Asia despite its rapid economic growth, rising share of world income, and catch up in industrialization during the period from 1980 to 2010, particularly when China and India were an integral part of that process. In sub-Saharan Africa, in 2008, the number of poor people below PPP $1.25 per day was close to 400 million, while the number of people below PPP $2 per day was more than 550 million and these numbers were roughly twice what they were in 1981. This reality is easier to understand in terms of the lost decade in the 1980s and the declining share of Africa in world income through the period, but is not quite consistent with the rapid economic growth in Africa during the 2000s.[9]

There is a triangular relationship between growth, inequality and poverty. The extent to which economic growth, for any given rate of growth, translates into poverty reduction depends upon what happens to economic inequality. If there is no change in economic inequality, increments in output or income accrue to different segments or fractile-groups of the population in exactly the same proportion as the initial income distribution. Thus, a much larger proportion of the increment in income accrues to the rich who are a relatively small proportion of the population while a much smaller proportion of the increment in income accrues to the poor who are a relatively large proportion of the population. It follows that economic growth translates into a less than proportionate poverty reduction. It is only if economic growth is associated with a reduction in economic inequality that it would translate into a more than proportionate poverty reduction; indeed, reduced inequality could also reduce poverty in the future if it stimulates growth. Of course, the reality was probably the opposite. And if higher rates of economic growth in the developing world were associated with an increase in economic inequality, the poverty reduction must have been less than proportionate. This would explain the persistence of widespread poverty in Asia, although there was a reduction in proportions below both the poverty lines, despite the unprecedented rates of economic growth witnessed during the three decades from 1980 to 2010. It would also explain the rising poverty in sub-Saharan Africa in the 2000s, despite what were unprecedented rates of economic growth.

Table 8.4. Income Distribution Changes in the Next-14: 1980–2005
(Gini Coefficients)

Country	c.1980	c.1990	c.2000	c.2005
Argentina	42.5	44.4	50.4	48.8
Brazil	57.4	60.5	58.8	56.4
Chile	53.2	55.7	55.2	51.8
China	29.5	34.0	39.0	46.9
Egypt	34.0	31.9	37.8	34.4
India	31.4	29.6	36.0	36.8
Indonesia	34.2	31.9	30.8	39.4
South Korea	38.6	34.9	37.2	32.6
Malaysia	50.6	49.1	44.3	40.3
Mexico	50.6	53.1	55.6	51.0
South Africa	49.0	63.0	60.1	69.6
Taiwan	27.7	30.9	31.2	32.2
Thailand	42.6	47.4	42.9	42.0
Turkey	52.0	46.5	46.0	44.8

Notes: See Appendix.
Source: UNU-WIDER World Income Inequality Database.

It is exceedingly difficult to find systematic or complete evidence on changes in income distribution in the developing world. The problem lies partly in statistics at the national level, which makes international comparisons over time even more difficult, particularly for country-groups or regions. Yet, it is important to sketch a picture, even if it is a rough approximation, of what happened to income inequality within countries. For this purpose, Table 8.4 puts together evidence on changes in income distribution, measured in terms of Gini coefficients, for the Next-14 during the period from 1980 to 2005.

It reveals both similarities and differences. In Argentina, Brazil, Chile, and Mexico, income inequality was high to start with in 1980 and increased further until 2000, with Gini coefficients that were at least 50, although it diminished a little in the mid-2000s. South Africa was worse as its already high inequality of incomes increased continuously and by a large proportion. China, India, and Indonesia were characterized by a low, or moderate, income inequality in 1980, which increased rapidly in China where the Gini coefficient rose from less than 30 in 1980 to 47 in 2005, close to the Latin American levels. It probably increased at a faster pace in India and Indonesia than the data suggest because the Gini coefficients for these countries relate to the distribution of consumption rather than income. Similarly, the data for Egypt and Thailand also measure consumption inequality, which is always lower than income inequality because the rich save and the poor do not, and this remained unchanged over the period, so that income inequality in Thailand was probably not much lower than it was in Latin America. Malaysia and

167

Turkey were the exceptions where the Gini coefficient that was more than 50 in 1980 declined thereafter, somewhat more in Malaysia than in Turkey. The Gini coefficient in South Korea also declined from 39 in 1980 to 33 in 2005. Taiwan was unusual insofar as its income inequality in 1980 was lower than that in China but increased in subsequent years to reach about the same level as South Korea in 2005. It would be reasonable to infer that, in most of the Next-14 which led the process of catch up, income inequality increased significantly in some countries where it was low to start with, and remained at high levels in other countries even if it decreased from higher initial levels. And, although evidence for 2010 is not available, it is most likely that income inequality increased further. Thus, the modest convergence of incomes with the outside world was associated with a divergence of incomes within these countries.

It needs to be stressed that the Next-14 were neither exceptions nor unusual in this era, as income inequality was driven up by markets and globalization everywhere. In fact, research on the subject (Cornia and Kiiski, 2001, Bourguignon and Morrisson, 2002, Milanovic, 2005, Palma, 2011, and Milanovic, 2011) suggests that, even if inequality levels differ across countries, there is a global trend of rising income inequality among people almost everywhere. In a study on income distribution in 135 countries, Palma (2011) finds that the share of the top 10 per cent in national income has risen and the share of the bottom 40 per cent in national income has fallen, while the share of the middle 50 per cent is relatively stable. In a simple metaphor, the rich have become richer and the poor have become poorer.

Although it is not possible to attribute cause-and-effect simply to coincidence in time, it is possible to think of mechanisms through which markets and globalization might have accentuated economic inequalities within countries in the developing world (Nayyar, 2006). Trade liberalization led to a growing wage inequality between skilled and unskilled workers. As a consequence of privatization and deregulation, capital gained at the expense of labour almost everywhere as profits shares rose while wages shares fell. Structural reforms, which cut tax rates and brought flexibility to labour markets, reinforced this trend. The mobility of capital and the immobility of labour changed the nature of the employment relationship and reduced the bargaining power of trade unions. The object of managing inflation was transformed into a near-obsession by the sensitivity of international financial markets, so that governments adopted deflationary macroeconomic policies that squeezed employment. Financial liberalization, which meant a rapid expansion of public as well as private debt, was associated with the emergence of a new rentier class. And the inevitable concentration in the ownership of financial assets probably contributed to a worsening of income distribution.

This era of globalization was also associated with a massive increase in economic inequality in the industrialized countries as it led to a sharp increase in the share of the top 1 per cent, as also the share of the top 0.1 per cent, of the population in national income (Atkinson and Piketty, 2007 and 2012)[10]. It would seem that a disproportionately large part of increments in income accrued to the super-rich or ultra-rich. This was not confined to the industrialized countries but extended to some developing countries for which such an exercise has also been done (Atkinson, Piketty and Saez, 2012). In India, the share of the top 1 per cent in national income rose from 4.8 per cent in 1980 to 7.4 per cent in 1990 and 10.7 per cent in 1997, while the share of the top 0.1 per cent rose from 1.4 per cent to 1.8 per cent and 4.4 per cent respectively. In Argentina, the share of the top 1 per cent in national income increased from 12.4 per cent in 1997 to 16.8 per cent in 2004, while the share of the top 0.1 per cent increased from 4.3 per cent to 7 per cent. In China, the share of the top 1 per cent in national income increased from 3.3 per cent in 1990 to 5 per cent in 2000 and 5.9 per cent in 2003, while the share of the top 0.1 per cent increased from 0.6 per cent to 1 per cent and 1.2 per cent respectively. If evidence were available for later years, say 2010, it would almost certainly confirm a further increase in the share of the super-rich or ultra-rich in national income, not only in these countries but also in other countries of the developing world that have experienced rapid growth.

Conclusion

This chapter posed three questions about emerging divergences in the world economy during the era of catch up from 1950 to 2010. The answers that emerge are clear. First, international inequality between countries and people remained at high levels. Inequality between countries diminished slowly if modestly, but if China and India are excluded it increased rapidly after 1980. Much of this was attributable to inequality between rich industrialized countries and the poor developing world although there was some increase in inequality within the latter. Inequality among people in the world, which increased sharply during the period from 1820 to 1950 as a consequence of the Great Divergence, persisted at somewhat higher levels through the second half of the 20th century. Second, the process of catch up was associated with an exclusion of countries, and regions within countries, in the developing world from the process of development. There was a massive divergence in per capita incomes between LDCs and the rest of the developing world, while there was a significant convergence in per capita incomes for the Next-14 with the rest of the developing world. But there was an exclusion of regions within the Next-14 from this convergence process. Third, rapid economic growth in the developing world, underlying the catch up in terms of aggregate income, was not always transformed into meaningful development which improved the well-being of ordinary people. During the period from 1981 to 2008, the proportion of the population below the specified international poverty lines declined steadily, more for the lower than for the higher poverty line, but these proportions remain significant. Moreover, the absolute number of people below both poverty lines remains large, while the number of people between the two poverty lines, who are vulnerable, doubled over this period. The number of poor people in 2008 was large not only in sub-Saharan Africa but also in Asia despite its rapid economic growth, rising share of world income, and catch up in industrialization. This is because economic inequality between people has been high or rising in these countries, particularly in the Next-14, that have led the catch up process. Indeed, a disproportionately large part of increments in income may have accrued to the super-rich or the ultra-rich in the population.

Epilogue

9

The Future in the Past

The objective of this book is to analyse the evolution of developing countries in the world economy situated in its wider historical context, spanning centuries, but with a focus on the period since the mid-20th century. The first part sets the stage. It examines their decline and fall during the period from 1820 to 1950. The second part is the primary focus. It analyses the extent and nature of catch up during the period from 1950 to 2010. This epilogue concludes. Section 1 outlines the contours of change in historical perspective, providing answers to the questions posed at the outset, to recapitulate the essentials of an untold story. Section 2 considers prospects, in terms of possibilities and constraints, for countries that have led this process of catch up so far and for those that might follow in their footsteps. Section 3 contemplates the future, with reference to the past, to speculate how this catch up might reshape, or be influenced by, the international context.

1. Contours of Change

In the span of world history, the distinction between industrialized and developing economies, or rich and poor countries, is relatively recent. It surfaced in the last quarter of the 19th century. In fact, one thousand years ago, Asia, Africa, and South America, taken together, accounted for more than 80 per cent of world population and world income. This was attributable in large part to Asia, where just two countries, China and India, accounted for approximately 50 per cent of world population and world income. The overwhelming significance of these three continents in the world economy continued for another five centuries until 1500. The beginnings of change are discernible from the early 16th to the late 18th century. The voyages of discovery and the colonization of the Americas were critical turning points, as the consequent mercantile expansion of trade, supported by state power and naval power, combined with social, political and institutional change in Europe, created the initial conditions for capitalist development. Even so, in the mid-18th century, the similarities between Europe and Asia were far more significant than the differences. Indeed, demography, technology and institutions were broadly comparable. The Industrial Revolution in Britain during the late 18th century, which spread to Europe over the next fifty years, exercised a profound influence on the shape of things to come. Yet, in 1820, less than 200 years ago, Asia, Africa, and South America still accounted for almost three-fourths of world population and around two-thirds of world income. The share of China and India, taken together, was 50 per cent even in 1820.

The dramatic transformation of the world economy began around 1820. Slowly but surely the geographical divides in the world turned into economic divides. The divides rapidly became a wide chasm. The economic significance of Asia, Africa, and Latin America witnessed a precipitous decline such that, by 1950, there was a pronounced asymmetry between their share of world population at two-thirds and their share of world income at about one-fourth. In sharp contrast, between 1820 and 1950, Europe, North America, and Japan increased their share in world population from one-fourth to one-third and in world income from more than one-third to almost three-fourths. The rise of 'The West' was concentrated in Western Europe and North America. The decline and fall of 'The Rest' was concentrated in Asia, much of it attributable to China and India, while Latin America was the exception as its shares in world population and income were not only symmetrical throughout but also rose over time.

The Great Divergence in per capita incomes was, nevertheless, the reality. In a short span of 130 years, from 1820 to 1950, as a percentage of GDP per capita in Western Europe and Western Offshoots, GDP per capita in Latin America dropped from three-fifths to two-fifths, in Africa from one-third to one-seventh and in Asia from one-half to one-tenth. But that was not all. Between 1830 and 1913, the share of Asia, Africa, and Latin America in world manufacturing production, attributable mostly to Asia, in particular China and India, collapsed from 60 per cent to 7.5 per cent, while the share of Europe, North America, and Japan rose from 40 per cent to 92.5 per cent, to stay at these levels until 1950. The industrialization of Western Europe and the de-industrialization of Asia during the 19th century were two sides of the same coin. It led to the Great Specialization, which meant that Western Europe, followed by the United States, specialized in and exported manufactured goods while Asia, Africa, and Latin America specialized in and exported primary commodities. The century from 1850 to 1950 witnessed a progressive integration of Asia, Africa, and Latin America into the world economy, through international trade, international investment and international migration, which created and embedded a division of labour between countries that was unequal in its consequences for development. The outcome of this process was the decline and fall of Asia and a retrogression of Africa, although in its post-colonial era Latin America fared much better except for the divergence in incomes, so that by 1950 the divide between rich industrialized countries and poor underdeveloped countries was enormous.

During the six decades from 1950 to 2010, changes in the share of developing countries in world output and in levels of per capita income relative to industrialized countries, provide a sharp contrast. In terms of Maddison PPP statistics, the share of developing countries in world output stopped its continuous decline c.1960, when it was about one-fourth, to increase rapidly after 1980, so that it was almost one-half by 2008, while the divergence in GDP per capita also came to a stop in 1980 and was followed by a modest convergence thereafter, so that as a proportion of GDP per capita in industrialized countries it was somewhat less than one-fifth in 2008. In current prices at market exchange rates, between 1970 and 2010, the share of developing countries in world GDP doubled from one-sixth to one-third, while their GDP per capita as a proportion of that in industrialized countries recorded a modest increase from one-fourteenth to one-eleventh.

Differences in GDP growth rates underlie the rising share of developing countries and the falling share of industrialized countries in world GDP. During the period 1951–1980, GDP growth rates in developing countries were somewhat higher than in industrialized countries. This performance was impressive because these three decades coincided with the golden age of capitalism when the industrialized world experienced unprecedented rapid growth. For developing countries, such growth rates provided a sharp contrast with their performance in the preceding hundred years and were also much higher than growth rates in industrialized countries at comparable stages of their development. During the period 1981–2008, GDP growth rates in developing countries were almost double those in industrialized countries. Until 1980, growth rates of GDP per capita in developing countries were lower than in industrialized countries because of high population growth rates, but this was reversed after 1980 as their GDP growth was so much higher and population growth rates slowed down. These differences underlie the end of divergence in per capita incomes c.1980 followed by the beginnings of a very modest convergence that is discernible after 1990 and more visible in the 2000s.

The engagement of developing countries with the world economy witnessed a decline during the period from 1950 to 1980, particularly when compared with the past, but revived c.1980 and grew rapidly thereafter. But this deeper engagement was a matter of choice, in sharp contrast with the compulsion of the past. Their share in world merchandise trade, exports and imports, more than doubled from less than 20 per cent in 1970 to more than 40 per cent in 2010. Similarly, their share of international trade in services registered a substantial increase to reveal their comparative advantage in exports of services. During the 1990s and 2000s, the share of developing countries in the stock and flows of inward, as also outward, foreign direct investment in the world economy increased at the expense of industrialized countries, although they were more important as countries-of-destination than as countries-of-origin. The movement of people from developing to industrialized countries emerged as a significant form of engagement despite draconian immigration laws and restrictive consular practices, with new forms of mobility such as guest workers, illegal immigrants and professional persons, driven by markets and globalization. Such international migration exercised an important influence on the world economy. It was an important factor underlying productivity increase and economic dynamism in industrialized countries. Remittances from migrants were an important source of external finance in developing countries that eased constraints on growth, although the brain drain was an obvious negative consequence but return migration could transform this into a brain gain.

There was a significant catch up in industrialization for the developing world as a whole beginning around 1950 that gathered momentum in the early 1970s. Structural changes in the composition of output and employment, which led to a decline in the share of agriculture with an increase in the shares of industry and services, were an important factor underlying this process. There was a dramatic transformation in just four decades from 1970 to 2010. The share of developing countries in world industrial production jumped from one-twelfth to one-third in constant prices and from one-eighth to two-fifths in current prices. Similarly, their share in world exports of manufactures, in current prices, rose from one-fourteenth to two-fifths.

Industrialization also led to pronounced changes in the composition of their trade as the share of primary commodities and resource-based products fell while the share of manufactures (particularly medium- and high-technology goods) rose in both exports and imports.

The role of the State in evolving trade and industrial policies, developing institutions, and making strategic interventions, whether as a catalyst or a leader, was central to this process. The creation of initial conditions was followed by a period of learning to industrialize so that outcomes surfaced after a time lag. And it was not the magic of markets that produced the spurt in industrialization. To begin with, for some countries it was about import substitution through protection while for some countries it was about export orientation through promotion. In either case, external markets became increasingly important in the process of industrialization. It was a litmus test for domestic firms seeking to become competitive in international markets. It was also an outcome of the internationalization of production that began with transnational corporations from industrialized countries driven by competition for markets seeking to reduce costs as manufacturers or buyers. After some time, it provided opportunities for domestic firms from developing countries, facilitated by the rise of global value chains since the late 1990s.

It is clear that, during the second half of the 20th century and the first decade of the 21st century, there was a substantial catch up on the part of developing countries. Some comparisons of their relative importance in the world economy at present with the past are instructive. In 2008, the share of developing countries in world GDP was close to their share around 1850, while their GDP per capita as a proportion of that in industrialized countries was about the same as in 1900. The share of developing countries in world trade, even in 1970, was the same as it was in 1913. And the significance of foreign investment for developing countries at the end of the 20th century was about the same as it was at the end of the 19th. The share of developing countries in world industrial production remained at its 1913 level until 1970 but returned to its 1880 level around 1990. In 2010, this share was higher than it was in 1860 and possibly close to its level around 1850. On the whole, it is plausible to suggest that the significance of developing countries in the world economy c.2010 is about the same as it was in 1870 or a little earlier. Given this situation in 2010, which is an outcome of the catch up process since 1950, it is also plausible to suggest that the significance of developing countries in the world economy c.2030 would be about the same as it was in 1820.

It is important to recognize that the distribution of this catch up was most uneven between the constituent regions of the developing world. The aggregates may be deceptive for they conceal almost as much as they reveal. The significant rise in share of world output and the modest convergence in per capita income for developing countries were both attributable almost entirely to Asia, as Latin America witnessed neither, while Africa experienced a declining share and a continuing divergence. The rapid expansion in their share of world trade was also attributable essentially to Asia, as Latin America barely maintained its share while Africa experienced a continuous decline, although the distribution of foreign investment was less unequal. However, the catch up in industrialization was the most uneven between regions. Asia led the process in terms of structural change, share in industrial production, rising manufactured exports, and changing patterns of trade, while Latin America witnessed relatively little change and Africa made almost no progress. Indeed, an overwhelming proportion of the increase in the share of developing countries in world manufacturing value added and manufactured exports was attributable to Asia, while the share of Latin America recorded a modest rise and the share of Africa remained unchanged.

The catch up in industrialization was uneven not only among regions but also between countries within regions. There was a high degree of concentration among a few: Argentina, Brazil, Chile, and Mexico in Latin America;

China, India, Indonesia, Malaysia, South Korea, Taiwan, Thailand, and Turkey in Asia; and Egypt and South Africa in Africa. These countries are described as the Next-14 in the context of catching up. In fact, their economic significance in the developing world is overwhelming in terms of their size, reflected in GDP and population, their engagement with the world economy, reflected in trade, investment, migration, and industrialization, reflected in manufactured exports and industrial production. The determinants of such concentration are size, growth and history. There is also enormous diversity within the few, characterized by an unequal distribution, in terms of the same attributes that revealed the concentration among them. The emerging significance of China in the Next-14 is particularly striking. Clearly, the success of these countries, which was not uniform and was characterized by specificities, must be understood in terms of their economic, social, and political contexts as also their embedded history. Yet, despite their apparent diversity, it is possible to group them into clusters based on similarities in terms of geography, size, economic characteristics, and development models. They had even more in common across clusters. Initial conditions, enabling institutions, and supportive governments were the factors that put them on the path to industrialization.

The process of catch up is associated with some persistent and some emerging divergences in the world economy. International inequality between countries and people remains at high levels. Inequality between countries is even now largely attributable to the wide gap between rich and poor nations. Inequality among people in the world, which increased sharply during the period from 1820 to 1950 as a result of the Great Divergence, persisted at somewhat higher levels through the second half of the 20th century. There is an exclusion of countries, and regions within countries, in the developing world from the process of catch up. There was a massive divergence in per capita incomes between LDCs and the rest of the developing world. And even if there was a significant convergence in per capita incomes for the Next-14 with the rest of the developing world, there was an exclusion of regions within these countries from the convergence process. Most importantly, perhaps, rapid economic growth in the developing world, underlying the catch up in terms of aggregate income, has not led to a commensurate improvement in the well-being of ordinary people. During the period 1981–2008, the proportion of the population in the developing world below the specified international poverty lines declined but these proportions remain significant. Moreover, the absolute number of people below both poverty lines of PPP \$1.25 and \$2 per day remains large, while the number of people between the two poverty lines, who are vulnerable, doubled over this period. In 2008, three-fourths of the poor in the world, below both the poverty lines, lived in Asia despite its rapid economic growth, rising share of world income, and catch up in industrialization. This is because economic inequality has been high or rising in countries, particularly the Next-14, that have led the catch up process. Hence, catch up is necessary but not sufficient to improve the living conditions of people.

2. Possibilities and Constraints

Is it, then, possible to speculate or hypothesize about the prospects of developing countries in the world economy, not simply for countries that have led the process of catch up so far but also for those that might follow in their footsteps? The past is relevant. And so is the present. But the future is not just about linear extrapolations. Yet, growth scenarios for the future are often based on an extrapolation of growth from the past. In attempting such projections, most exercises are based on simple models of capital accumulation and productivity growth combined with demographic scenarios which assume that growth rates in developing countries and industrialized countries would remain at levels observed in the recent past for some time and slow down thereafter (O'Neill et al, 2004). There are also more sophisticated exercises that use simple convergence equations to make projections about GDP and GDP per capita in PPP terms and at market exchange rates (Rowthorn, 2008).

It is no surprise that such exercises project a much higher share for developing countries in world output and a significant convergence in per capita incomes towards levels in industrialized countries by 2050, or even 2030.[1] Of course, these projections suggest broad orders of magnitude rather than precise predictions. Even so, such statistical exercises highlight the power of compound growth rates. Rates of growth do indeed matter. If GDP grows at 7 per cent per annum, national income doubles in ten years, and if it grows at 10 per cent per annum, national income doubles in seven years. Similarly, if GDP per capita grows at 5 per cent per annum, per capita income doubles in fourteen years and if it grows at 7 per cent per annum per capita income doubles in ten years. In fact, growth rates have been in this range for many Asian countries in the Next-14 for at least 25 years and for many developing countries during the 2000s. If such growth rates are sustained, their cumulative impact over time can only accelerate the catch up process. However, growth is not simply about arithmetic. Indeed, it is about more than economics. Therefore, it is necessary to consider the possibilities of, and constraints on, growth in countries that are latecomers to development.

The economic determinants of potential growth in the developing world are a source of good news. And, in principle, developing countries may be able to sustain high rates of economic growth for some time to come for the following reasons. First, their population size is large, which is a possible source of growth, and their income levels are low, which means that the possibilities of growth are greater. Second, their demographic characteristics, in particular the high proportion of young people in the population, which would mean an increase in their workforce and savings rates for some time to come, are conducive to growth, provided developing countries spread education to create capabilities among people. Third, in most developing countries, wages are significantly lower than in the world outside, which is an important source of competitiveness for some time to come. Fourth, the potential for productivity increase is considerable at earlier stages of development at the extensive margin from almost zero productivity in agriculture to some positive, even if low, productivity in manufacturing or services, followed by a transfer of such labour from low productivity employment to somewhat higher productivity employment at the intensive margin. Some countries could also move up the technology ladder.

In practice, developing countries may not be able to realize this potential for growth because of constraints that may differ across space and surface over time. It is obvious that there are specific constraints in different countries, whether leaders or laggards. Some examples are instructive. In China, the declining productivity of investment at the margin, the limit to external markets as a source of demand, and the sustainability of the political system are potential constraints. In India, the crisis in agriculture, the bottlenecks in infrastructure, and the limited spread of education in society are potential constraints. At the other end of the spectrum, in Congo or Rwanda, where the initial conditions for development have not been created, there are constraints almost everywhere that stifle the possibilities of growth. Apart from country specific constraints, there are general constraints, common to most developing countries, such as poor infrastructure, underdeveloped institutions, inadequate education, unstable politics or poor governance. In addition, there are constraints that may not be discernible but may arise from the process of growth such as economic exclusion, social conflict or environmental stress. And there are some constraints that may be exogenous to developing countries, such as worsening terms of trade, restricted market access for exports, inadequate sources of external finance or a crisis in the world economy.

The Next-14, which are leaders in the process of catch up so far, are countries characterized by considerable diversity. Yet, initial conditions, enabling institutions, and the role of governments are factors they have in common, which constitute lessons from their experience for countries that might follow. Indeed, this is the clear lesson that also emerges from the experience of all latecomers to industrialization during the period from the mid-19th to the mid-20th century. There are two aspects of initial conditions, the existence of a physical infrastructure and the spread of education in society, where a critical minimum is essential to kick-start industrialization and development. This is clearly in the realm of the feasible for latecomers. It is more difficult to establish a framework of enabling institutions. Even so, experience suggests that is perfectly possible. Some of the Next-14 may have inherited institutions from the past, but only in small part, and most such institutions were put in place by proactive governments. However, there was no standardized blueprint or design. It was an iterative process of evolution through learning by doing (Amsden, 2001 and Chang, 2007). Institutions are as much a consequence of development that enables rather than a cause that drives development. Thus, institutions must be contextualized in their economic, social, and political setting. The supportive role of governments, as catalysts or leaders, is critical in the process. Both democracy, which makes governments accountable to people, and propriety which prevents corruption, are desirable but not necessary for governments to perform their role. In fact, authoritarian regimes and corrupt governments are more common than their opposites in the industrialization experience of the Next-14. The challenge for latecomers to development is to create control mechanisms embodied in institutions that impose discipline on the economic behaviour not only of individuals and firms to minimize market failure but also of the state to minimize government failure.

The prospects of catch up on the part of developing countries in the world economy depend not only on how the Next-14 fare in times to come but also on whether this process spreads to other countries in the developing world. It is plausible to suggest that there are another ten countries in the developing world that possess many of the attributes necessary to follow in the footsteps of the Next-14: Colombia, Ecuador, Honduras, and Venezuela in Latin America; Kenya, Nigeria, and Tunisia in Africa; and Iran, Philippines, and Vietnam in Asia. And it is not far-fetched to suggest that there are two countries among the LDCs, Bangladesh and Tanzania, which have a potential in terms of some attributes. The clusters among the Next-14, in terms of geographical regions, country size or economic characteristics, reveal such a wide range of attributes that most developing countries would have something in common with at least one if not a few of them. Indeed, many of the laggards in industrialization may not be very different from what the leaders in industrialization were fifty years ago. In 1960, for example, it would have been impossible to predict that South Korea would be where it is now. In that sense, the belief that Africa is destined for underdevelopment is just not tenable.[2] Indeed, it is possible to imagine a scenario in which some African countries could be an integral part of the process of catch up in the next fifty years just as some Asian countries have been in the past fifty years.

Development is about creating production capabilities in economies and ensuring the well-being of people in countries. Initial conditions, enabling institutions, and supportive governments are necessary to kick-start industrialization, which would transform capabilities in in the spheres of production and technology. But these might not be sufficient to sustain economic growth in the long run and transform it into meaningful development if it does not improve the living conditions of people. In the pursuit of development, poverty eradication, employment creation, and inclusive growth are an imperative. For one, these are constitutive as the essential objectives of development. For another, these are instrumental as the primary means of bringing about development.[3] This is the only sustainable way forward for developing countries because it would enable them to mobilize their most abundant resource, people, for the purpose of development, and reinforce the process of growth through cumulative causation. Therefore, developing countries must endeavour to combine economic growth with human development and social progress.

This requires a creative interaction between the state and the market, beyond the predominance of the market model in the process of development. It is in part about regulating markets and in part about inclusive growth. For a similar context, but at a different time, Polanyi (1944) analysed what he characterized as the 'Great Transformation' in Europe. In doing so, he described a double-movement: the first from a pre-capitalist system to a market-driven industrialization in the 19th century; the second from the predominance of the market model to a more inclusive world in which the state played a corrective, regulatory, role. This transformation, which began in the early 20th century, was complete by the mid-20th century. But it did not last long. There was a resurgence of the market model beginning in the late 1970s. Hence, c.2010, the situation in developing countries is similar to the pre-transformation situation in Europe (Stewart, 2007). Such a Great Transformation in the developing world in the early 21st century, similar to the Great Transformation in the industrialized world in the early 20th century, could deepen and widen the catch up process.

3. Contemplating the Future

The whole is different from, if not larger than, the sum total of the parts. The process of catch up on the part of developing countries in the world economy is likely to be influenced by, just as it is likely to shape, the international context. Three questions arise. Does the recent global economic crisis have any longer term implications? What are the possible environmental consequences of the economic rise of the developing world? How would the leading industrialized countries respond or adjust to the erosion of their economic dominance and political hegemony? These are complex questions that could have important implications for how the future unfolds. But it is difficult to provide answers, let alone predict outcomes, in a world characterized by uncertainties and imponderables. In any case, such a task is beyond the scope of this book. Even so, these are touched upon briefly if only to recognize their significance.

It is clear that the financial crisis of late 2008, which turned into the Great Recession, is the deepest crisis in capitalism since the Great Depression more than 75 years ago. The difference worth noting is that developing countries, which were marginal then, are much more significant and integrated with the world economy now. On the whole, it would seem that the developing world coped better than the industrialized countries and transition economies (Nayyar, 2011). For one, the impact was less adverse. For another, the recovery was somewhat quicker. Initial conditions, policy responses and domestic demand shaped resilience and recovery. Prudence in deregulation and liberalization of financial sectors limited collateral damage. Fiscal space available to governments also made a difference. The significant increase in the share of developing countries in world output and world trade also meant that there were some external markets and resources other than in the industrialized countries. It is almost certain that robust growth in Asia provided support for this resilience. But it would be a mistake to believe that the leading developing countries, in the Next-14, can drive the process of recovery or turn into engines of growth for the world economy. They are at best complements, not substitutes, which can provide some stimulus as the old engine of growth slows down. The prospects for recovery in the world economy depend to a significant extent on the pace and nature of the recovery in the industrialized world, in particular the United States.[4] What happens to exchange rates, particularly the Euro, will also be critical. The best that is possible is to sketch alternative scenarios. Sustained recovery in the industrialized countries will revive growth, while persistent recession will slow down growth in the developing world. In either case, differences in growth rates between developing and industrialized economies will remain, so that catch up in terms of shares of output and levels of income will continue.

The environmental consequences of rapid growth in the developing world are bound to be significant.[5] The energy needs of the two mega-economies, China and India, are enormous. This is not surprising, as levels of consumption per capita are low and income elasticities of demand are high.[6] Much the same is true for large countries in the Next-14, as also for other countries that might follow in their footsteps. The negative potential is obvious as CO_2 emissions rise, which could turn into a constraint on growth. But there is also a positive spin that is possible. Growing consciousness about environmental stress and climate change may increase the availability of clean technologies for latecomers to industrialization. There could also be some shift from energy sources that use fossil fuels to those that reduce carbon emissions. Thus, the environmental constraint on growth may not turn out to be binding. Yet the problem of developing sustainable non-carbon energy sources does present a major challenge to patterns of economic growth in the long-term. History is not much help in thinking about this dilemma. The Industrial Revolution transformed production possibilities and social relations but it was based on a shift to fossil fuel energy sources.

The changes in the significance of developing countries in the world economy, which started in 1950 to gather momentum after 1980, are beginning to chip away at the economic dominance and political hegemony of the leading industrialized countries. It was reinforced for a time following the collapse of communism in USSR and Eastern Europe $c.$1990 but has been diluted in the aftermath of the financial crisis in 2008. There is an important lesson that emerges from history. Dominant powers are reluctant to cede economic or political space to newcomers. Thus, the emergence of new centres of production in economics and new centres of power in politics does have a profound effect on hegemonic powers in terms of political economy. Such processes are always slow and the present conjuncture represents an interregnum because the resurgence of Asia, particularly China, is not large enough in the context of the world economy, at least so far, to shift the hegemonic balance. But the beginnings of change with some erosion of hegemony are discernible. This is complex rather than simple as a phenomenon and will be played out over a long period of time. Both the duration and the outcome of this process are unpredictable. Even so, it is possible to contemplate, or speculate about, possible future scenarios.

It is essential to recognize that the significance of developing countries in the world would be shaped not only in the sphere of economics but also in the realm of politics. Their emerging significance in the world economy is attributable in part to their share in world population and in world income and in part to their engagement in the world economy through international trade, international investment, and international migration. In the economic sphere, their potential importance in future far exceeds their actual importance at present. In the political sphere, their importance is more discernible at the present juncture, which is attributable in part to their size in terms of population (that is young rather than old) and in part to their size in terms of geographical space. The end of the first decade of the 21st century is perhaps a turning point. It is plausible to argue, though impossible to prove, that this represents the beginnings of a profound change in the balance of economic and political power in the world.

History may not repeat itself. But it would be wise to learn from history. The early 19th century was a turning point in the world economy. It was the beginning of the end of Asia's overwhelming significance in the world economy. And it was the beginning of the rise of Europe, in particular Britain, to dominance in the world. The early 20th century was the next turning point. It was the beginning of the end of Britain's dominance. And it was the beginning of the rise of the United States to dominance in the world. The catch up and the transformation spanned half a century. The early 21st century perhaps represents a similar turning point. It could be the beginning of the end of the dominance of the United States in the world. The emergence of countries outside North America and Western Europe, particularly the powerhouse economies in Asia but also in other continents of the developing world, constitutes a striking transformation. The rise of Asia and the decline of Western Europe, in a relative rather than absolute sense, are discernible. There is an irony in this emerging situation when compared with the past of Asia and Western Europe in history.

The outcome, fifty years later, is likely to be a multipolar world in which dominance might not be so striking. Of course, in times to come, the continued rise of the Next-14, or countries that follow in their footsteps, or the developing world as a whole, is not quite predictable and far from certain. It would depend, in large part, on whether developing countries can transform themselves into inclusive societies where economic growth, human development, and social progress move in tandem. This catch up and transformation, if it materializes, could span at least half a century if not longer. Yet, the beginnings of a shift in the balance of power are discernible. And the past could be a pointer to the future.

APPENDIX

Statistical Sources and Notes

Chapter 2

Tables 2.1 to 2.5 and Figures 2.1 to 2.2
These tables and figures are based on the historical statistics compiled by Maddison on GDP and population, which have been published in several monographs or books (1995, 2001, 2003, and 2007) but have been revised from time to time. The complete statistical series that incorporates revisions is available on the Maddison Online Database (http://www.ggdc.net.MADDISON/oriindex.htm). The statistics presented in the tables and used in the figures are based on the author's calculations from this online database. GDP and GDP per capita are measured, in PPP terms, in 1990 international Geary-Khamis dollars. The composition of the country-groups is as follows. Western Europe includes Andorra, Austria, Belgium, Cyprus, Denmark, Faeroe Islands, Finland, France, Germany, Gibraltar, Greece, Greenland, Guernsey, Iceland, Ireland, Isle of Man, Italy, Jersey, Liechtenstein, Luxembourg, Malta, Monaco, Netherlands, Norway, Portugal, San Marino, Spain, Sweden, Switzerland, and the United Kingdom. Western Offshoots includes the United States, Canada, Australia, and New Zealand. Eastern Europe includes Albania, Bulgaria, Czechoslovakia, Hungary, Poland, Romania, and Yugoslavia. Former USSR includes Armenia, Azerbaijan, Belarus, Estonia, Georgia, Kazakhstan, Kyrgyzstan, Latvia, Lithuania, Moldova, Russian Federation, Tajikistan, Turkmenistan, Ukraine, and Uzbekistan. *The West* includes Western Europe, Western Offshoots, Eastern Europe, Former USSR, and Japan. *The Rest* includes Africa, Asia (except Japan), and Latin America.

Tables 2.1 and 2.3
For the years 1000, 1500, 1600 and 1700:
In the population estimates, the coverage of regions and countries is as follows. Asia excludes Japan (for which there is a separate estimate) and includes China, India, Indonesia, Iran, Iraq, and Turkey, with a residual estimate for other countries in the region. Africa includes Algeria, Egypt, Ethiopia, Libya, Madagascar, Morocco, Mozambique, Somalia, South Africa, Sudan, and Tunisia, with a residual estimate for other countries in the region. Latin America includes Brazil, Mexico, and Peru, with a residual estimate for other countries in the region. The coverage is almost complete for Western Europe (30 countries), Western Offshoots (4 countries) and Eastern Europe (7 countries). Former USSR is an estimate for the region as a whole.

In the GDP estimates, the coverage of regions and countries is as follows. Asia excludes Japan (for which there is a separate estimate) and includes China, India, Indonesia, Korea, Iran, Iraq, and Turkey, with a residual estimate for other countries in the region. Africa includes Egypt and Morocco with a residual estimate for other countries in the region. Latin America includes Brazil and Mexico with a residual estimate for other countries in the region. Eastern Europe and former USSR are simply estimates for the regions as a whole. But the coverage is complete for Western Europe (30 countries) and Western Offshoots (4 countries).

For the year 1820: The coverage for Western Europe, Western Offshoots, Eastern Europe, former USSR and Japan is the same as in the earlier years. But it is far better for the other three regions as compared with the earlier years. In population estimates, there are 55 countries in Asia, 11 countries in Africa, and 44 countries in Latin America, with residual estimates for other countries in the regions. In GDP estimates, there are 47 countries in Asia, 6 countries in Africa and 26 countries in Latin America, with residual estimates for other countries in the regions.

Table 2.2

For both population and GDP estimates in this table, the coverage, in terms of the number of countries in each of the regions, in 1870 and 1913 is almost the same as in 1820 (specified above). For Asia, Africa and Latin America, it was smaller in 1900 and 1940, but larger in 1950.

Table 2.6

The estimates of manufacturing production in this table are based on physical output estimates for different sectors, averaged over a period of three or five years, weighted by the contribution of each sector in a particular country to obtain an aggregate index for countries and country-groups using industrial output in the United Kingdom in 1900 as the base of 100.

Table 2.7

This table is based on an unpublished paper, 'International Trade Statistics 1900–1960', prepared by the Statistical Office of the United Nations in May 1962. It is available from the United Nations Statistics Division website unstats.un.org. The statistics on the value of exports from, and imports into, Asia, Africa, and Latin America in this table, include the following country-groups or regions: Latin America Dollar Area, Latin America Non-Dollar Area, Burma, Ceylon, India, Pakistan, Middle East, Other Countries, Other Middle East, Mainland China, Indonesia, Cambodia, Laos, Vietnam, and Other Far East. The coverage of the developing world is obviously not complete but it does provide a reasonable approximation. The value of total exports from countries and regions included in the table was $18,902 million in 1953. International trade statistics published by the United Nations, which are complete, report that the value of total exports from developing countries in 1953 was $23,345 million.

Chapter 4

Tables 4.1 to 4.2 and Figures 4.1 to 4.3

These tables and figures are based on the historical statistics available from the Maddison Online Database (http://www.ggdc.net.MADDISON/oriindex.htm). The statistics presented in the tables and used in the figures are based on the author's calculations from this online database. GDP and GDP per capita are measured, in PPP terms, in 1990 international Geary-Khamis dollars. The group of developing countries is made up of Africa, Asia excluding Japan, and Latin America including the Caribbean. The group of industrialized countries is made up of: (a) Western Europe (Andorra, Austria, Belgium, Cyprus, Denmark, Faeroe Islands, Finland, France, Germany, Gibraltar, Greece, Greenland, Guernsey, Iceland, Ireland, Isle of Man, Italy, Jersey, Liechtenstein, Luxembourg, Malta, Monaco, Netherlands, Norway, Portugal, San Marino, Spain, Sweden, Switzerland, and the United Kingdom); (b) North America (Canada and the United States); (c) Oceania (Australia and New Zealand); and (d) Japan. Eastern Europe and former USSR is made of the erstwhile centrally planned economies and present transition economies of Europe (Albania, Bulgaria, Czechoslovakia (now the Czech Republic and Slovakia), Hungary, Poland, Romania, Yugoslavia (now Bosnia and Herzegovina, Croatia, Macedonia, Montenegro, Serbia and Slovenia), and the countries of the former USSR (Armenia, Azerbaijan, Belarus, Estonia, Georgia, Kazakhstan, Kyrgyzstan, Latvia, Lithuania, Moldova, Russian Federation, Tajikistan, Turkmenistan, Ukraine, and Uzbekistan). The group of 'Developing Countries' constituted by Africa, Asia and Latin America in these tables and figures corresponds exactly to the country-group described as 'The Rest' in Chapter 2. However, the group of countries termed 'The West' in Chapter 2 is not used any further. Instead, it is disaggregated into two groups: (i) the group of 'Industrialized Countries', in these tables and figures, as also in the rest of the book, which is constituted by North America, Western Europe, Japan and Oceania; and (ii) the group 'Eastern Europe and former USSR', which is constituted by the erstwhile centrally-planned economies and the present transition economies of Europe.

Tables 4.4 to 4.5 and Figures 4.4 to 4.6

These tables and figures are based on United Nations National Accounts Statistics as reported in UNCTAD Stat. Developing Countries are made up of Africa, Asia excluding Japan, and Latin America including the Caribbean. Industrialized Countries are made up of North America, Western Europe, Japan, and Oceania. Eastern Europe and former USSR is made up of the erstwhile centrally-planned economies and present transition economies in Europe. The data on GDP and GDP per capita are in US dollars in current prices and at market exchange rates. The statistics presented in the tables and used in the figures are based on the author's calculations.

Tables 4.6 and 4.7

The Maddison data on GDP and GDP per capita in 1990 international Geary-Khamis PPP dollars are obtained from the Maddison Online database. The United Nations data on GDP and GDP per capita in 1990 US dollars are obtained from UN National

Accounts Main Aggregates Database, Statistics Division, with population statistics from World Population Prospects, The 2008 Revision, Population Division, Department of Economic and Social Affairs, New York. The Maddison data and UN data on GDP and GDP per capita are not strictly comparable. The statistics in these tables cover 129 countries, of which 21 are industrialized countries (the original OECD member countries) and 108 developing countries. The average annual growth rates for each of the periods in the table are computed as geometric means of the annual growth rates in the respective periods.

Table 4.8
The United Nations data on GDP and GDP per capita in 1990 US dollars and 2005 US dollars are both obtained from the same sources as for Tables 4.6 and 4.7 above. The statistics on GDP and GDP per capita starting 2008 are in 2005 US dollars. The average annual growth rates, for the period 2001–2008, for both the 1990 and 2005 dollars series in the table are computed as geometric means of the annual growth rates. These two sets of figures are almost the same so that the two series are comparable. The growth rates for 2008, 2009, 2010 and 2011 are annual growth rates in each year over the preceding year.

Chapter 5

Table 5.6
The figures for sales and purchases in cross-border mergers and acquisitions in this table are calculated on a net basis as follows. *Sales* are sales of companies in the host country to foreign transnational firms *minus* sales of foreign affiliates in the host country. *Purchases* are purchases of companies abroad by domestic transnational firms *minus* sales of foreign affiliates of domestic transnational firms abroad. The data cover only those transactions that involve an acquisition of an equity share of more than 10 per cent. The data refer to net sales by the country or region of the acquired company, and net purchases by the country or region of the ultimate acquiring company.

Chapter 6

Tables 6.3 to 6.4 and Figure 6.1
These tables and the figure are based on United Nations statistical sources. For data on manufacturing value added at constant prices: (a) 1960 to 1980 at 1975 prices, UNIDO (1981); (b) 1975 to 1991 at 1980 prices, from UNIDO *International Yearbook of Industrial Statistics, 1995* and *1997*; and (c) 1990 to 2010 at 2000 prices, UNIDO Secretariat, Vienna. For data on manufacturing value added at current prices, during the period from 1970 to 2010, United Nations, from UNCTADStat, based on UN National Accounts Statistics. The percentages in the table and the figure at constant prices for each of the three series have been calculated from data on respective US dollar values in 1975, 1980 and 2000 prices. For the series in current prices, the percentages have been calculated from US dollar values at current prices and current exchange rates. Similarly, in Table 6.4, with disaggregated figures on manufacturing value added in Asia, Africa

and Latin America, the percentages have been calculated from US dollar values in current prices at market exchange rates.

Tables 6.5 to 6.6 and Figure 6.2

For data on the value of manufactured exports, in US dollars at current prices and exchange rates: (a) for the period from 1960 to 1999, United Nations, *Yearbooks of International Trade Statistics*, various annual issues; and (b) for the period from 2000 to 2010, United Nations, UNCTAD Stat. In this table, manufactured goods are defined as the sum of SITC 5 (chemicals), SITC 6 (manufactured goods), SITC 7 (machinery and transport equipment) and SITC 8 (miscellaneous manufactured articles), the value of exports for which are obtained from the UN *Yearbooks of International Trade Statistics*. This is the most complete definition of manufactured goods. The more common definition of manufactured goods is SITC 5 to 8 less 68 (non-ferrous metals). It is not used here because, for the period from 1950 to 1980, international trade statistics provide this disaggregation at country-level but not for country-groups or regions. In UNCTAD Stat, however, manufactured goods are defined as SITC 5 to 8 less 68 (non-ferrous metals) and 667 (pearls, precious and semi-precious stones). SITC 68 has been added to the statistics on manufactured exports obtained from UNCTAD. The values of exports in SITC 667 are very small, almost negligible, in relation to the values of total manufactured exports. This makes the two data sets almost perfectly comparable. The percentages reported in the tables and used in the figure have been calculated from US dollar values in current prices at current exchange rates. In Figure 6.2, the plot for the share of developing countries in world manufacturing value added, at current prices, is reproduced from Figure 6.1.

Chapter 7

Table 7.1

This table has been compiled from statistics published by the United Nations. For data on population, World Population Prospects, Population Division, Department of Economic and Social Affairs, New York. The percentage share of the Next-14 in the total has been computed from the absolute figures in millions. For the other rows in the table, the percentages have been calculated from the sum of dollar values for the Next-14 and the total for developing countries. For data on GDP, and on manufacturing value added, in current prices at current exchange rates, United Nations National Accounts Statistics as reported in UNCTAD Stat. The data on exports and imports, also in current prices and at current exchange rates, are obtained from UNCTAD Stat. For data on manufactured exports, defined as SITC 5 + 6 + 7 + 8, from United Nations, *Yearbooks of International Trade Statistics* for the period 1970–1995 and UNCTAD Stat for the period 2000–2010. For data on the inward and outward stock of foreign direct investment, UNCTAD FDI online database. For data on remittances, in current prices and at current exchange rates, UNCTAD Stat based on IMF, *Balance of Payments Statistics*, World Bank, *Migration and Remittances*, Economist Intelligence Unit, *Country Data*, and national sources. The data on foreign exchange reserves are obtained from IMF, *International Financial Statistics*.

Table 7.2 and Figure 7.1
This table and figure are based on the author's calculations from United Nations National Accounts Statistics as reported in UNCTAD Stat.

Figures 7.2 and 7.3
For data on GDP per capita in current prices and at market exchange rates, United Nations National Accounts Statistics as reported in UNCTAD Stat. For data on GDP per capita, in 1990 international Geary-Khamis PPP dollars, Maddison online database. The percentages have been calculated from data on GDP per capita in each of the selected countries as a proportion of the weighted average GDP per capita in industrialized countries.

Chapter 8

Table 8.2 and Figures 8.2 to 8.3
The table and the figures are based on United Nations National Accounts Statistics as reported in UNCTAD Stat. The figures on GDP per capita, in US dollars in current prices at market exchange rates, for 'The Next-14' (as also the disaggregation of the fourteen into two groups in Figure 8.3), and the 'Other Developing Countries' have been calculated as averages from data on GDP and population. The figures used for 2010, the most recent year, are what was reported at the time the table was compiled but these continue to change for some time as national accounts estimates are revised.

Table 8.4
The headings for columns in this table are *c.*1980, 1990, 2000 and 2005 because data on Gini coefficients in the specified years are not necessarily available for all countries, so that the figures are for the closest possible year. In the column *c.*1980, the figure on Malaysia is for 1979, on Brazil, Egypt, and Taiwan for 1981, on India and Turkey for 1983 and on Mexico for 1984. In the column *c.*1990, the figure on Turkey is for 1987, on Malaysia and Mexico for 1989, and on Egypt for 1991. In the column *c.*2000, the figure on South Africa is for 1997, on South Korea for 1998, on India and Indonesia for 1999, on Brazil for 2001, and on Turkey for 2002. In the column *c.*2005, the figure on Thailand is for 2002, on China, Egypt, India, and Malaysia for 2004, on Chile, South Korea and Turkey for 2006, and on South Africa for 2008. In the case of Egypt, the reported Gini *c.*1980 is for rural areas alone. The Gini coefficients in the table are based on nationally representative household surveys, except for Argentina where the sample is for the 28 largest cities. The Gini coefficients for Argentina, Brazil, Chile, China, Malaysia, Mexico, South Africa, South Korea, Taiwan, and Turkey are based on the per capita disposable income, while the Gini coefficients for Egypt, India, Indonesia, and Thailand are based on per capita expenditure.

Endnotes

Chapter 2

1. Maddison adopts the Geary-Khamis approach, which is appropriate for comparisons across a large number of countries over long periods of time. The method is 'multilateral' rather than 'binary' and it assigns a weight to countries corresponding to the size of their GDP, which makes comparisons transitive and imparts other desirable properties. This approach was also adopted by Kravis, Heston and Summers (1978). The Maddison exercise uses 1990 as the benchmark year to provide the inter-spatial and inter-temporal anchor for GDP estimates. Thus, the numeraire is termed '1990 international Geary-Khamis dollars'. For a more detailed discussion, see Maddison (2003).

2. Western Europe and Western Offshoots in the Maddison estimates do not include Eastern Europe and Japan, which are included in the Bairoch estimates for what he describes as 'Developed Economies'. The Maddison estimates are separate for Latin America, Africa, and Asia, whereas the Bairoch estimates group the three continents together. It is possible to address the latter difference. Calculations based on the data in Table 2.4 show that GDP per capita in Latin America, Africa, and Asia, taken together, as a percentage of GDP per capita in Western Europe and Western Offshoots, taken together, fell from 47.3 in 1820, to 26.7 in 1870, 20.1 in 1900, 17.9 in 1913, 16.4 in 1940 and 13.6 in 1950.

3. These figures include most but not all countries in the regions, because trade statistics were not complete in terms of reporting and coverage, particularly for Africa, during the first half of the 20th century. The same series records that the value of total exports from these countries was $18,902 million in 1953. International trade statistics published by the United Nations, which are complete report that the value of total exports from developing countries in 1953 was $23, 345 million. Thus, it is reasonable to infer that the data in Table 2.7 provide a good approximation.

4. This percentage has been calculated from data on the value of merchandise exports in US $million in current prices at current exchange rates, in 1870, for a sample of 42 countries, reported in Maddison (1995, pp.234–5). The sample includes 7 countries from Latin America, 6 from Asia, 4 from Africa, 13 from Western Europe, 4 from Western Offshoots, 4 from Southern Europe, and 4 from Eastern Europe.

5. It has been estimated by Maddison (1989) that, at 1980 prices, in 1900, the stock of foreign capital in Asia, Africa and Latin America was $108.3 billion (p.30), while the GDP of 15 selected countries in Asia and Latin America was $338.8 billion (p.113).

Chapter 3

1. There is little doubt that when Europe was just starting out on its voyages of discovery, the Chinese already knew the coasts of India, Arabia and East Africa, so that their maritime knowledge was far more advanced. Morris (2010) reports that, in 1405, when Admiral Zheng He sailed from Nanjing for what is now Sri Lanka, he had 27,000 sailors, including 180 doctors and pharmacists, three hundred ships, tankers carrying drinking water, elaborate signalling devices, magnetic compasses, and enough information about the Indian Ocean to fill a twenty-one-foot-long sea chart. In sharp contrast, when Christopher Columbus sailed from Cadiz in 1492, he had just 90 men in three ships, no freshwater tankers, no real doctors and no sea charts, while the hull of his biggest ship displaced only one-thirtieth the water as compared with Admiral Zheng's biggest ship.
2. The European slave trade had little impact on the economies of Arab ruled States because the Islamic slave trade continued in parallel during this era.
3. This comparison emerges with clarity from a lucid passage in Findlay and O'Rourke (2007, p.355): 'The Ottoman, Safavid and Mughal Empires, as well as that of the Manchu Qing dynasty of China, were not mere tyrannies expressing the will of a single despot but complex exercises in multiethnic state building far more intricate than that of the Hapsburgs. All four were formidable military machines, sustained by productive agrarian economies, and leavened by considerable commerce both internal and external, which were impervious to Western intrusion until the eighteenth century.'
4. For a discussion on economic development in Latin America during the period 1820–1950, which provides a systematic analysis of the underlying factors, see Bertola and Ocampo (2012).
5. For a lucid discussion on why culture simply cannot provide an explanation for underdevelopment even in the contemporary world, see Chang (2007a).

Chapter 4

1. It is worth noting that the group of 'Developing Countries' in Table 4.1, constituted by Africa, Asia, and Latin America, corresponds exactly to the country-group described as 'The Rest' in Table 2.2. However, the country-group described as 'The West' in Table 2.2 is not used any further but is disaggregated into two groups. The group of 'Industrialized Countries' in Table 4.1, as also in the rest of the book, is constituted by North America, Western Europe, Japan, and Oceania, which corresponds to Western Europe, Western Offshoots, and Japan in Table 2.2. 'Eastern Europe and former USSR' are the same set of countries in Tables 2.2 and 4.1.
2. It is essential to note that, for 1950, the figures on GDP per capita ratios in Table 4.2 are not the same as the corresponding figures in Table 2.4. The reason is that the denominator in the two tables is different. In Table 4.2, the denominator is GDP per capita in Industrialized Countries, made up of North America, Western Europe, Japan, and Oceania. In Table 2.4, the denominator is GDP per capita in Western Europe and Western Offshoots, which includes North America and Oceania but

not Japan. For a study on catch up that seeks to focus on the second half of the 20th century and beyond, it is both necessary and appropriate to include Japan among industrialized countries.

3. In principle, this could be a problem for the Maddison estimates used in Chapter 2. In practice, it is not, for three reasons. First, the Geary-Khamis approach adopted by Maddison is a more sophisticated exercise in international comparisons based on PPP, because it assigns a weight to countries corresponding to the size of their GDP. Second, a 'multilateral' rather than 'binary' method of obtaining results makes comparisons transitive and imparts other desirable properties. Third, in any case, for the period before 1950, the possible distortions mentioned in the text should be minimal. For a more detailed discussion, see Maddison (2003, pp.227–30). In this context, it is important to note that there are almost no other estimates for the period before 1950, and what little exists is partial or incomplete. And, for the period after 1950, international comparisons are also made in this chapter using data on GDP and GDP per capita from national accounts statistics at market prices and market exchange rates.

4. For an analysis of why the impact of the financial crisis and the Great Recession on the developing world as a whole was less adverse and their recovery was faster, see Nayyar (2011).

Chapter 5

1. There is a vast literature on this subject of trade and industrialization. See, for example, Helleiner (1992) and Nayyar (1997). For an analysis of changes in thinking about openness, industrialization and development which translated into turning points for policy regimes in the developing world during the second half of the 20th century, see Nayyar (2008b).

2. The proportions for the early 20th century cited here are reproduced from Chapter 2, while the proportions for the early 21st century cited in this paragraph are calculated from the UNCTAD foreign direct investment online database. It must be said that these figures on the geographical distribution and sectoral composition need to be interpreted with caution because the coverage is not complete and world totals are extrapolated on the basis of information for 80–100 countries that are estimated to account for about four-fifths of total stocks and flows in the world economy. But the figures do provide broad orders of magnitude.

3. The implications and consequences of international migration for economic development are analysed, at some length, elsewhere by the author (Nayyar, 2002 and 2008). The discussion that follows draws upon this earlier work.

4. Interestingly enough, this represented the opposite of migration from the home country to the colonies earlier in history, albeit on a smaller scale, as the British migrated to India and the Caribbean, the French to Algeria and Vietnam, and the Dutch to Indonesia and Surinam.

5. Malaysia has for a long time relied on workers from Indonesia for its agriculture and plantations. During the 1990s and 2000s, Hong Kong, the Republic of Korea, Singapore, and Taiwan have also emerged as destinations for migrant workers.

6. The evidence cited in this paragraph is based on time series graphs of remittances as a percentage of GDP, net aid inflows, and inward flows of foreign direct investment, for developing countries, from sources noted in this chapter. These graphs are not reproduced here because of the constraint on space.

7. This proposition may appear paradoxical at first sight because, in an accounting sense, it follows from the national income accounting identity that there would be a corresponding increase in savings. But it is gross national saving rather than gross domestic saving that would rise and the economy would be able to realize an excess of investment over the latter.

Chapter 6

1. For an extensive discussion on the services sector in the wider context of structural change and economic development in countries that are latecomers to industrialization, with particular reference to the Indian experience, see Nayyar (2012).

2. These 57 countries are classified into 12 country-groups: East Asia, Southeast Asia, China, South Asia, semi-industrialized countries mostly from Latin America but including South Africa and Turkey, the smaller Andean countries, Central America and the Caribbean, 'representative' and 'other' countries in sub-Saharan Africa, the Middle East and North Africa, Eastern Europe, and former USSR represented by Russia and Ukraine. The authors examine the relationship between annual growth rates of GDP per capita and structural changes in the composition of output on employment, at this level of disaggregation, during the last three decades of the 20th century, making a distinction between country-groups that experienced sustained growth (essentially Asia), slow growth (semi-industrialized countries, Central America and the Caribbean, Middle East and North Africa, Eastern Europe) and stagnant growth (Andean countries, Africa, and former USSR).

3. McMillan and Rodrik (2011) extend this further to argue that, during the period 1990–2005, in some Latin American and sub-Saharan African countries, structural change was growth-reducing because the large share of primary products in exports limited the scope for productivity-enhancing structural change.

4. In this context, it is important to recognize that employment growth is possible, in a sector or in the economy as a whole, only if the growth in output per capita is higher than productivity growth.

5. It was based on a set of studies that analysed the industrialization experience in seven countries. This critique was followed up and developed further in studies by Krueger (1978) and Bhagwati (1978).

6. Williamson (1994) was perhaps the first to use the term 'Washington Consensus' to describe this set of policies, which were advocated by the World Bank and the IMF. These institutions were based in Washington DC. And such policies were prescribed as conditions in their lending to developing countries.

7. In an essay on the debate about trade and industrialization, this proposition was set out most succinctly by Diaz-Alejandro (1975, p.96): 'In the trade and development literature, there has existed for a long time, going back at least to John Stuart

Mill, a striking difference between the rigour of formal proofs on the static advantages of free trade, typically involving careful assumptions and caveats, and the impetuous enthusiasm with which most of the professional mainstream advocates free or freer trade policies, on both static and dynamic grounds, for all times and places.' See also, Krugman (1987) and Nayyar (1996).

8. In the literature on the development experience of the four tigers—Hong Kong, Singapore, South Korea, and Taiwan—Lee (1981) was among the first to emphasize this limitation. It has come to be recognized far more widely with the subsequent work of Amsden (1989), Wade (1990) and Chang (1996), which provided systematic evidence based on careful research that contradicted the neo-classical interpretation of the East Asian miracle.

9. See, for example, Pack and Westphal (1986), Lall (1987), Dahlman, Ross-Larson and Westphal (1987), Amsden (1989), Lall (1990), and Bell and Pavitt (1993).

10. In an essay that analyses the relationship between trade policy and technical efficiency, Rodrik (1992, p.172) reaches the following conclusion. 'If truth in advertising were to apply to policy advice, each prescription for trade liberalization would be accompanied by a disclaimer: Warning! Trade liberalization cannot be shown to enhance technical efficiency; nor has it been historically demonstrated to do so.'

11. For a complete and convincing exposition of this argument, see Amsden (2001). In earlier work, Lall (1987 and 1990) developed similar, related, ideas. See also, Chang (2002).

12. There is a growing literature on this subject. See, for example, Feenstra (1998), Humphrey and Schmitz (2002), Greffi, Humphrey and Sturgeon (2005). See also, Lall (2000) and Kaplinsky (2005).

13. It is estimated that the share of manufactured intermediate goods in world imports of manufactures declined from 71 per cent in 1962 to 52 per cent in 1993 and stabilized around that level until the early 2000s to increase a little thereafter. The share of final goods, consumption goods plus capital goods, in world imports of manufactures registered a corresponding increase (Sturgeon and Memedovic, 2011).

14. Between 1988 and 2006, the share of intermediate goods in total trade (imports plus exports) decreased from 39 per cent to 28 per cent in clothing and footwear but increased from 43 per cent to 55 per cent in electronics and from 43 per cent to 47 per cent in automobiles and motorcycles (Sturgeon and Memedovic, 2011, p.23).

Chapter 7

1. In 2010, for example, as a proportion of the total for developing countries, the share of Hong Kong in population was 0.15 per cent and in manufacturing value added 0.1 per cent, although it accounted for 1.1 per cent of GDP. These proportions were even lower in 1970. In 2010, the corresponding share of Singapore in population was 0.1 per cent, although its share in manufacturing value added and GDP of the developing world was about 1 per cent. These proportions were

distinctly lower in 1970. The percentages cited in this note are calculated from the same sources as for Table 7.1.

2. Some regional classifications include Turkey in the Middle East and North Africa, which is made up of countries in West Asia and North Africa. But the classification used in this study makes a distinction between just three regions in the developing world: Asia, Africa, and Latin America including the Caribbean. United Nations statistics use the same classification, which includes Turkey in Asia. Therefore, in this book, Turkey is classified as a part of Asia, which is reasonable even in terms of geography as Turkey lies at the intersection of Asia and Europe.

3. Some regional classifications include Egypt in the Middle East and North Africa. However, given the regional classification used in this study, explained in the preceding note, Egypt is classified as part of Africa. In terms of the geography of continents that make up the developing world, it is in Africa just as Turkey is in Asia.

4. As a proportion of the total for developing countries, between 1970 and 2010, the share of Hong Kong and Singapore, taken together, rose from 6.8 per cent to 11.8 per cent in exports and from 8.8 per cent to 12.4 per cent in imports (calculated from the same sources as in Table 7.1). Thus, over this period, the share of the Next-14 plus the two city-states in exports from developing countries decreased from 77 per cent to 74 per cent, while their share of imports into developing countries increased from 50 per cent to 76 per cent.

5. These percentages have been calculated from the UNCTAD online database on foreign direct investment. For the selected countries, during 2006–2010, foreign direct investment inflows were $261 billion per annum whereas outflows were $135 billion per annum. The percentages on cross-border mergers and acquisitions, net sales and net purchases, cited later in the paragraph are calculated from the UNCTAD M&A online database.

6. The share of Hong Kong and Singapore, taken together, in manufactured exports from developing countries dropped from 22.9 per cent in 1970 to 14.8 per cent in 2010 (calculated from the same sources as in Table 7.1), essentially because exports of manufactured goods from other countries in the developing world emerged and registered a rapid expansion in this period. Even so, it is worth noting that the share of the Next-14 plus the two city-states in manufactured exports from developing countries was overwhelmingly large at 85 per cent in 1970 and 90 per cent in 2010.

7. The figures on world trade in manufactured intermediate goods, in 2006, cited in this paragraph, are calculated from Sturgeon and Memodovic (2011, p.16). In the same year, the share of industrialized countries (North America, Western Europe, Japan and Oceania) in manufactured intermediate goods world trade was 56 per cent while that of Eastern Europe and the CIS was 6 per cent. The share of Hong Kong and Singapore alone was 7 per cent. There is an unreported residual as this source provides statistics on the top fifty countries in such trade.

8. These percentages have been calculated from the same sources that have been cited for Table 6.3.

9. The percentages relating to shares of subsets of countries, among the Next-14, in population and GDP of developing countries, cited in this paragraph, have been calculated from the same sources that have been used in Table 7.1.

10. The percentages relating to the shares of subsets of countries, within the Next-14, in exports, imports, foreign direct investment and remittances from or to the developing world, cited in this paragraph, have been calculated from the same sources that have been used in Table 7.1.

11. The shares of each of these six countries in world trade (imports plus exports) in manufactured intermediate goods in 2006 were: China (8.5 per cent), South Korea (3 per cent), Taiwan (2.6 per cent), Mexico (2.4 per cent), Malaysia (2.7 per cent), and Thailand (1.2 per cent). It is worth noting that India and Brazil were not far behind with shares of 1.2 per cent and 1 per cent respectively, but this was not sufficient to help them preserve their place among the leading exporters of manufactured goods from the developing world. The country-shares cited here are from Sturgeon and Memodovic (2011, p.16).

12. The percentages on the share of the top five countries in total manufacturing value added in developing countries, cited in this paragraph, are calculated from the same source that has been used in Table 7.2.

13. It is worth reporting the shares of the top five countries in total manufacturing value added in developing countries. In 1970, the shares were: China (29.3 per cent), Argentina (9.7 per cent), Mexico (7.9 per cent), Brazil (7.5 per cent), and India (7 per cent). In 2010, the shares were: China (45.2 per cent), Brazil (6.6 per cent), South Korea (6.6 per cent), India (5.3 per cent), and Mexico (4.2 per cent). There were, of course, changes in the relative importance of these countries over time. China's share declined from 29.3 per cent in 1970 to 17.9 per cent in 1990, recovered in the 1990s to reach 31.9 per cent in 2000 and increased very rapidly in the decade that followed. This suggests that industrial growth was faster in the other selected countries until 1990. However, industrial growth in China caught up in the mid-1990s and was much faster than in the other countries during the 2000s. Between 1970 and 2010, Argentina witnessed the sharpest decline in its share from 9.7 per cent to 1.6 per cent. The share of Taiwan rose from 1.4 per cent in 1970 to 6.3 per cent in 1990 but dropped to 2.7 per cent in 2010. Similarly, the share of Turkey rose from 4 per cent in 1970 to 6.8 per cent in 1990 but dropped to 2.7 per cent in 2010. The shares of South Africa, Chile, and Egypt witnessed an almost continuous decline, while the shares of Indonesia, Thailand, and Malaysia recorded a steady increase.

14. There is an extensive literature on the industrialization experience of the Next-14. It would mean too much of a digression to enter into a discussion of these diverse experiences here. Indeed, given the space constraint, it is exceedingly difficult to cite even the important references. Therefore, this note provides a few selected references to the literature on the subject. For a systematic analysis of the Latin American experience, see Bertola and Ocampo (2012). On East Asia, see Wade (1990) and Chang (2004). Some references to the literature on country-experiences are as follows: Argentina (Diaz-Alejandro, 1970), Brazil (Fishlow, 1972, and Baer, 1995), Mexico (Ros, 1994), India (Nayyar, 1994b), Indonesia

(Hill, 1996 and Booth, 1998), Malaysia (Jomo, 1993 and Rasiah, 1995), Thailand (Lall, 1998), Taiwan (Ranis, 1992), and South Korea (Amsden, 1989 and Chang, 1996) See also Amsden (2007).

15. Amsden (2001) makes a distinction between three sets of countries among the 12 that she describes as 'The Rest': those with national ownership (China, India, South Korea, and Taiwan), those with foreign participation (Argentina, Chile, Mexico, Indonesia, Malaysia, and Thailand) and those that adopted a mixed path (Brazil and Turkey).

16. This proposition is perhaps the foundation of the hypothesis on late industrializers developed by Amsden (2001). She argues that it is manufacturing experience that separates the twelve countries—Argentina, Brazil, Chile, Mexico, Turkey, China, India, Indonesia, South Korea, Taiwan, and Thailand—that she describes as 'The Rest' from the other countries in the developing world that she describes as 'The Remainder'. The difference between those who moved ahead and those who fell behind was manufacturing experience c.1950. She goes further to suggest that the type of manufacturing experience shaped the differences among 'The Rest'.

Chapter 8

1. For a systematic analysis of this issue, including supporting evidence, see Milanovic (2005). The discussion that follows in this paragraph draws upon it.

2. The ratios reported in this paragraph have been calculated from UN national accounts statistics for GDP per capita in current prices at current exchange rates, and from the Maddison online database for GDP per capita in 1990 international Geary-Khamis PPP dollars.

3. In 1970, 1990 and 2010, respectively, the richest countries were Bermuda, Switzerland, and Luxembourg, while the poorest countries were Laos, Vietnam, and Somalia.

4. In 1970, 1990 and 2010, the poorest countries were Malawi, Chad, and Zaire, respectively, while Switzerland was the richest in 1970 and the United States the richest in the other two years.

5. The contribution of industrialized countries to overall inequality between regions in the world, in terms of the Theil coefficient, was 0.61 in 1960, 0.67 in 1980 and 0.69 in 2000, whereas the Theil coefficient of world inequality between regions was 0.45 in 1960, 0.51 in 1980 and 0.45 in 2000 (United Nations, 2006, Annex Table A.1, p.151). In this analysis, the industrialized (developed) countries include North America, Western Europe, Japan, and Oceania. The developing world is made up of the following regions: Latin America, Africa, West Asia, East and South Asia (China, India, Indonesia, Philippines, Republic of Korea, Taiwan, Thailand, Bangladesh, Hong Kong, Malaysia, Myanmar, Nepal, Pakistan, Singapore, and Sri Lanka) and Rest of Asia. Eastern Europe and former USSR are separate regions.

6. The ratios for each of the regions reported in this paragraph are calculated from the same sources cited in note 2 above.

7. The statistics on LDCs cited in this paragraph are essentially obtained from UNCTAD (2011). Some are from earlier annual issues of the UNCTAD Report on

Least Developed Countries. The Forbes list of 'The World Billionaires' reports that, in 2010, the net worth of the top 20 billionaires in the world was $634 billion. In 2010, the total GDP of all LDCs was $614 billion. In PPP terms, the ratio of GDP per capita in LDCs to that in developing countries and industrialized countries is calculated from World Bank *World Development Indicators*.

8. This table includes Eastern Europe and Central Asia in the developing world because that is the World Bank classification, although it is not in conformity with the regional classification used throughout the book in which the three regions are Asia, Africa, and Latin America including the Caribbean. However, the percentages and the numbers of the poor in Eastern Europe and Central Asia are small, almost negligible, in relation to the magnitudes for the developing world as a whole.

9. For an analysis of the economic performance of Africa during the 2000s, in terms of rapid growth and good governance, see Noman, Botchwey, Stein and Stiglitz (2012).

10. In the United States, for instance, the share of the top 1 per cent in national income increased from 8.2 per cent in 1980 to 13 per cent in 1990, 16.5 per cent in 2000 and 18 per cent in 2006, while the share of the top 0.1 per cent rose from 2.2 per cent in 1980 to 4.9 per cent in 1990, 7.1 per cent in 2000 and 8 per cent in 2006. In the United Kingdom, the share of the top 1 per cent in national income rose from 6.7 per cent in 1981 to 9.8 per cent in 1990, 12.7 per cent in 2000 and 14.3 per cent in 2005, while the share of the top 0.1 per cent rose from 1.5 per cent in 1981 to 3.1 per cent in 1995 and 5.2 per cent in 2005 (Atkinson, Piketty and Saez, 2012).

Chapter 9

1. Most such projections are for a small subset of countries. The frequently cited Goldman Sachs study (O'Neill et al, 2004) attempted to project GDP and GDP per capita for Brazil, Russia, India, and China (BRICs) in 2050. The more sophisticated Rowthorn (2008) exercise relates to China and India. There are now many variations around this theme. For a discussion on this literature, see Nayyar (2010).

2. For a convincing exposition of this argument, see Chang (2010). There is also research and evidence to suggest that the economic performance of Africa during the 2000s provides reason for hope and not despair (Noman, Botchwey, Stein and Stiglitz, 2012). In this context, it is worth noting that, during the period 1951–1980, GDP growth rates in Africa were at par with GDP growth rates in industrialized countries, which were high in the golden age of capitalism, and not significantly lower than GDP growth rates in Asia and Latin America (Table 4.6). Similarly, during the period 2001–2008, GDP growth rates in Africa at more than 5 per cent per annum, were lower than in Asia but higher than in Latin America and almost three times the average GDP growth rates in industrialized countries (Table 4.7).

3. This argument is similar to Amartya Sen's conception of development as freedom. Sen (1999) argues that development is about expanding real freedoms that people

enjoy for their well being, social opportunities, and political rights. Such freedoms are not just constitutive as the primary ends of development. Such freedoms are also instrumental as the principal means of attaining development.

4. The argument outlined in this paragraph draws upon earlier work of the author. For an analysis of the impact of the financial crisis and the Great Recession on developing countries, in the wider context of the world economy, see Nayyar (2011). See also Ocampo (2011). For an analysis of the causes and consequences of the financial crisis in industrialized countries, see Taylor (2010).

5. There is a vast literature on this subject and it would mean too much of a digression to enter into a discussion here. This problem is accentuated because of complex issues and contending views. See, for example, Stern (2007), Foley (2009), Heal (2009), Khor (2010), and United Nations (2011).

6. For some discussion and evidence on this issue, see Rowthorn (2008).

References

Abramovitz, Moses (1986). 'Catching Up, Forging Ahead and Falling Behind', *Journal of Economic History*, 46: 385–406.

Acemoglu, Daron, Simon Johnson, and James Robinson (2005). 'The Rise of Europe: Atlantic Trade, Institutional Change and Economic Growth', *American Economic Review*, 95: 546–79.

Acemoglu, Daron and James Robinson (2012). *Why Nations Fail: The Origins of Power, Prosperity and Poverty*, New York: Crown Business, Random House.

Allen, Robert C. (2009). *The British Industrial Revolution in Global Perspective*, Cambridge: Cambridge University Press.

Amsden, Alice H. (1989). *Asia's Next Giant: South Korea and Late Industrialization*, New York: Oxford University Press.

Amsden, Alice H. (2001). *The Rise of the Rest: Challenges to the West from Late Industrializing Economies*, New York: Oxford University Press.

Amsden, Alice H. (2007). *Escape from Empire: The Developing World's Journey through Heaven and Hell*, Cambridge, Mass: The MIT Press.

Amsden, Alice H., J. Kochanowicz, and Lance Taylor (eds) (1994). *The Market Meets its Match: Restructuring the Economies of Eastern Europe*, Cambridge, Mass: Harvard University Press.

Arrow, Kenneth J. (1962). 'The Economic Implications of Learning by Doing', *Review of Economic Studies*, 29: 155–73.

Atkinson, A.B. (1987). 'On the Measurement of Poverty'. *Econometrica*, 55: 749–764.

Atkinson, A.B. and François Bourguignon (2001). 'Poverty and Inclusion from a World Perspective', in Joseph E. Stiglitz and Pierre-Alain Muet (eds) *Governance, Equity and Global Markets*, Oxford: Oxford University Press.

Atkinson, A.B. and T. Piketty (2007). *Top Incomes over the Twentieth Century: A Contrast between Continental European and English-Speaking Countries*, Oxford: Oxford University Press.

Atkinson, A.B. and T. Piketty (eds) (2012). *Top Incomes: A Global Perspective*, Oxford: Oxford University Press.

Atkinson, A.B., T. Piketty, and E. Saez (2012). 'Top Incomes in the Long Run of History' in A.B. Atkinson and T. Piketty (eds) *Top Incomes: A Global Perspective*, Oxford: Oxford University Press.

Atkinson, A.B. and Joseph E. Stiglitz (1969). 'A New View of Technological Change', *Economic Journal*, 79: 573–8.

Baer, Werner (1995). *The Brazilian Economy: Growth and Development*, Westport: Praeger Publishers.

Bairoch, Paul (1975). *The Economic Development of the Third World since 1900*, London: Methuen.

Bairoch, Paul (1981). 'The Main Trends in National Income Disparities since the Industrial Revolution', in P. Bairoch and M. Levy-Laboyer (eds) *Disparities in Economic Development since the Industrial Revolution*, Basingstoke: Macmillan.

Bairoch, Paul (1982). 'International Industrialization Levels from 1750 to 1980', *Journal of European Economic History*, 11: 269–333.

Bairoch, Paul (1983). 'A Comparison of Levels of GDP per capita in Developed and Developing Countries: 1700–1980', *Journal of Economic History*, 43: 27–41.

Bairoch, Paul (1993). *Economics and World History: Myths and Paradoxes*, Chicago: Chicago University Press.

Bairoch, Paul and Richard Kozul-Wright (1996). 'Globalization Myths: Some Historical Reflections on Integration, Industrialization and Growth in the World Economy', *UNCTAD Discussion Paper 13*, Geneva: United Nations.

Baran, Paul A. (1957). *The Political Economy of Growth*, New York: Monthly Review Press.

Baumol, W.J. (1967). 'Macroeconomics of Unbalanced Growth: The Anatomy of Urban Crisis', *American Economic Review*, 57: 415–26.

Baumol, W.J. (1986). 'Productivity Growth, Convergence and Welfare: What the Long-Run Data Show', *American Economic Review*, 76: 1072–1085.

Bell, M. and K. Pavitt (1993). 'Accumulating Technological Capability in Developing Countries', *Proceedings of the World Bank Annual Conference on Development Economics*, 1992: 257–81.

Bértola, Luis and José Antonio Ocampo (2012). *The Economic Development of Latin America since Independence*, Oxford: Oxford University Press.

Bhaduri, Amit and Deepak Nayyar (1996). *The Intelligent Person's Guide to Liberalization*, New Delhi: Penguin Books.

Bhagwati, Jagdish (1978). *Foreign Trade Regimes and Economic Development: Anatomy and Consequences of Exchange Control*, Cambridge, Mass: Ballinger.

Blanchard, Olivier (2011). *Macroeconomics*, New York: Prentice Hall.

Booth, A. (1998). *The Indonesian Economy in the Nineteenth and Twentieth Centuries: A History of Missed Opportunities*, New York: St. Martin's Press.

Brenner, Robert (1985). 'Agrarian Class Structure and Economic Development in Pre-Industrial Europe', in T.H. Aston and C.H.E. Philpin (eds) *The Brenner Debate: Agrarian Class Structure and Economic Development in Pre-Industrial Europe*, Cambridge: Cambridge University Press.

Brenner, Robert (1993). *Merchants and Revolution: Commercial Change, Political Conflict and London's Overseas Traders, 1550–1653*, Cambridge: Cambridge University Press.

Bourguignon, François and Christian Morrisson (2002). 'The Size Distribution of Income among World Citizens: 1820–1992', *American Economic Review*, 92: 727–44.

Chang, Ha-Joon (1996). *The Political Economy of Industrial Policy*, London: Macmillan.

Chang, Ha-Joon (2002). *Kicking Away the Ladder: Development Strategy in Historical Perspective*, London: Anthem Press.

Chang, Ha-Joon (2004). 'East Asian Industrialization', in H.J. Chang (ed.) *Rethinking Development Economics*, London: Anthem Press.

References

Chang, Ha-Joon (ed.) (2007). *Institutional Change and Economic Development*, Tokyo: UNU Press and London: Anthem Press.

Chang, Ha-Joon (2007a). *Bad Samaritans: Rich Nations, Poor Policies and the Threat to the Developing World*, London: Random House.

Chang, Ha-Joon (2010). *23 Things They Don't Tell You About Capitalism*, New York: Bloomsbury Press.

Chen, Shaohua and Martin Ravallion (2008). 'The Developing World is Poorer Than We Thought, But No Less Successful in the Fight against Poverty', *Policy Research Working Paper 4703*, Washington DC: The World Bank.

Chen, Shaohua and Martin Ravallion (2012). 'More Relatively-Poor People in a Less Absolutely-Poor World', *Policy Research Working Paper 6114*, Washington DC: The World Bank.

Chenery, Hollis B. (1960). 'Patterns of Industrial Growth', *American Economic Review*, 50: 624–54.

Chenery, Hollis B. and A. Strout (1966). 'Foreign Assistance and Economic Development', *American Economic Review*, 56: 679–733.

Clark, Colin (1940). *The Conditions of Economic Progress*, London: Macmillan.

Clark, Gregory (2007). *A Farewell to Alms: A Brief Economic History of the World*, Princeton: Princeton University Press.

Clark, Gregory (2009). 'Review of Angus Maddison, Contours of the World Economy: 1–2030 AD', *Journal of Economic History*, 69: 1156–61.

Clemens, Michael A. and Jeffrey G. Williamson (2002). 'Close Jaguar Open Dragon: Comparing Tariffs in Latin America and Asia before World War II', *NBER Working Paper Number w9401*, Cambridge, Mass: National Bureau of Economic Research.

Coase, R.H. (1937). 'The Nature of the Firm', *Economica*, 4: 386–405.

Cornia, Giovanni Andrea and Sampsa Kiiski (2001). 'Trends in Income Distribution in the post-World War II period: Evidence and Interpretation', WIDER Discussion Paper 89, Helsinki: UNU-WIDER.

Dahlman, Carl, B. Ross-Larson, and Larry Westphal (1987). 'Managing Technological Development: Lessons from Newly Industrializing Countries', *World Development*, 15: 759–75.

Deaton, Angus (2005). 'Measuring Poverty in a Growing World (or Measuring Growth in a Poor World)', *Review of Economics and Statistics*, 87: 353–78.

De Long, Bradford (1988). 'Productivity Growth, Convergence and Welfare: Comment', *American Economic Review*, 78: 1138–54.

Diamond, Jared (1997). *Guns, Germs and Steel: The Fate of Human Societies*, New York: W.W. Norton.

Diaz-Alejandro, Carlos F. (1970). *Essays on the Economic History of the Argentine Republic*, New Haven: Yale University Press.

Diaz-Alejandro, Carlos F. (1975). 'Trade Policies and Economic Development', in P.B. Kenen (ed.) *International Trade and Finance: Frontiers for Research*, Cambridge: Cambridge University Press.

Dunning, John H. (1983). 'Changes in the Level Structure of International Production', in Mark Casson (ed.) *The Growth of International Business*, London: Allen and Unwin.

Easterly, William (2001). *The Elusive Quest for Growth*, Cambridge, Mass: The MIT Press.

Eichengreen, Barry and P. Gupta (2009). 'The Two Waves of Services Sector Growth', *NBER Working Paper Series,* WP Number 14968, Cambridge, Mass: National Bureau of Economic Research.

Evans, Peter (1995). *Embedded Autonomy: States and Industrial Transformation,* Princeton: Princeton University Press.

Feenstra, R. (1998). 'Integration of Trade and Disintegration of Production in the Global Economy', *Journal of Economic Perspectives,* 12: 31–50.

Findlay, Ronald (1976). 'Relative Backwardness, Direct Foreign Investment and the Transfer of Technology: A Simple Dynamic Model', *Quarterly Journal of Economics,* 92: 1–16.

Findlay, Ronald and Kevin H. O'Rourke (2007). *Power and Plenty: Trade, War and the World Economy in the Second Millennium,* Princeton: Princeton University Press.

Fisher, A.G.B (1935). *The Clash of Progress and Security,* London: Macmillan.

Fishlow, Albert (1972). 'Origins and Consequences of Import Substitution in Brazil', in L.E. Di Marco (ed.) *International Economics and Development: Essays in Honour of Raul Prebisch,* New York: Academic Press.

Foley, Duncan (2009). 'Economic Fundamentals of Global Warming', in J.M. Harris and N.R. Goodwin (eds) *Twenty-First Century Macroeconomics: Responding to the Climate Challenge,* Cheltenham: Edward Elgar.

Foreman-Peck, James (1983). *A History of the World Economy: International Economic Relations since 1850,* Brighton: Wheatsheaf Books.

Frank, Andre Gunder (1971). *Capitalism and Underdevelopment in Latin America,* Harmondsworth: Penguin Books.

Frank, Andre Gunder (1998). *Re-Orient: Global Economy in the Asian Age,* Berkeley: University of California Press.

Furtado, Celso (1970). *Economic Development in Latin America,* Cambridge: Cambridge University Press.

Gereffi, G., J. Humphrey and Timothy Sturgeon (2005). 'The Governance of Global Value Chains', *Review of International Political Economy,* 12: 78–104.

Gerschenkron, Alexander (1962). *Economic Backwardness in Historical Perspective,* Cambridge, Mass: Harvard University Press.

Gomulka, Stanislaw (1970). 'Extensions of the Golden Rule of Research of Phelps', *Review of Economic Studies,* 37: 73–93.

Heal, Geoffrey (2009). 'The Economics of Climate Change: A Post-Stern Perspective', *Climate Change,* 96: 275–97.

Helleiner, Gerald K. (1973). 'Manufactured Exports from Less Developed Countries and Multinational Firms', *Economic Journal,* 83: 21–47.

Helleiner, Gerald K. (ed.) (1992). *Trade Policy, Industrialization and Development,* Oxford: Clarendon Press.

Hill, Christopher (1966). *The Century of Revolution: 1603–1714,* New York: W.W. Norton.

Hill, H. (1996). *The Indonesian Economy Since 1966,* Cambridge: Cambridge University Press.

Hirschman, Albert O. (1958). *The Strategy of Economic Development,* New Haven: Yale University Press.

References

Hobsbawm, Eric (1987). *The Age of Empire*, London: Weidenfeld and Nicolson.

Hobson, John M. (2004). *The Eastern Origins of Western Civilization*, Cambridge: Cambridge University Press.

Humphrey, J. and Hubert Schmitz (2002). 'How Does Insertion in Global Value Chains Affect Upgrading in Industrial Clusters', *Regional Studies*, 36: 1017–27.

Hymer, Stephen (1972). 'The Multinational Corporation and the Law of Uneven Development', in J. Bhagwati (ed.) *Economics and World Order from the 1970s to the 1990s*. London: Macmillan.

ILO (1936). *World Statistics of Aliens: A Comparative Study of Census Returns 1910–1920–1930*, Studies and Reports, Series O (Migration), Geneva: International Labour Office.

Jomo, K.S. (1993). *Industrializing Malaysia: Policy, Performance, Prospects*, London: Routledge.

Kaldor, Nicholas (1962). 'Comment on Economic Implications of Learning by Doing', *Review of Economic Studies*, 29: 246–50.

Kaldor, Nicholas (1966). *Causes of Slow Rate of Growth in the United Kingdom*, Cambridge: Cambridge University Press.

Kaplinsky, Raphael (2005). *Globalization, Poverty and Inequality*, Cambridge: Polity Press.

Khor, Martin (2010). 'The Equitable Sharing of Atmospheric and Development Space', *Research Paper 33*, Geneva: South Centre.

Kindleberger, Charles P. (1996). *World Economic Primacy: 1500–1990*, New York: Oxford University Press.

Kravis, I.B., A. Heston, and R. Summers (1982). *World Product and Income*, Baltimore: The Johns Hopkins University Press.

Krueger, A.O. (1978). *Foreign Trade Regimes and Economic Development: Liberalization Attempts and Consequences*, New York: National Bureau of Economic Research.

Krugman, Paul (1987). 'Is Free Trade Passé?', *Journal of Economic Perspectives*, 1: 131–44.

Kuznets, Simon (1966). *Modern Economic Growth: Rate, Structure and Spread*, New Haven: Yale University Press.

Kuznets, Simon (1971). *Economic Growth of Nations*, Cambridge, Mass: Harvard University Press.

Lall, Sanjaya (1987). *Learning to Industrialize: The Acquisition of Technological Capability in India*, Basingstoke: Macmillan.

Lall, Sanjaya (1990). *Building Industrial Competitiveness in Developing Countries*, Paris: OECD Development Centre.

Lall, Sanjaya (1991). 'Explaining Industrial Success in the Developing World', in V.N. Balasubramanyam and S. Lall (eds) *Current Issues in Development Economics*, London: Macmillan.

Lall, Sanjaya (1992). 'Technological Capabilities and Industrialization', *World Development*, 20: 165–86.

Lall, Sanjaya (1997). 'Imperfect Markets and Fallible Governments: The Role of the state in Industrial Development', in Deepak Nayyar (ed.) *Trade and Industrialization*, Delhi: Oxford University Press.

Lall, Sanjaya (1998). 'Thailand's Manufacturing Competitiveness: An Overview', in J. Witte and S. Koeberle (eds) *Competitiveness and Sustainable Economic Recovery in Thailand*, Bangkok: National Economic and Social Development Board.

Lall, Sanjaya (2000). 'The Technological Structure and Performance of Developing Country Exports', *Oxford Development Studies*, 28: 337–69.

Lall, Sanjaya (2001). *Competitiveness, Technology and Skills*, Cheltenham: Edward Elgar.

Landes, David S. (1969). *The Unbound Prometheus: Technological Change and Industrial Development in Western Europe since 1750 to the Present*, Cambridge: Cambridge University Press.

Landes, David S. (1999). *The Wealth and Poverty of Nations: Why Some are so Rich and Some so Poor*, New York: W.W. Norton.

Lee, Eddy (ed.) (1981). *Export-Led Industrialization and Development*, Geneva: ILO.

Lewis, W. Arthur (1954). 'Economic Development with Unlimited Supplies of Labour', *The Manchester School*, 22: 139–91.

Lewis, W. Arthur (1978). *The Evolution of the International Economic Order*, Princeton: Princeton University Press.

Lin, Justin and Ha-Joon Chang (2009). 'Should Industrial Policy in Developing Countries Conform to Comparative Advantage or Defy It?', *Development Policy Review*, 27: 483–502.

Little, I.M.D., T. Scitovsky, and M. Scott (1970). *Industry and Trade in Some Developing Countries: A Comparative Study*, London: Oxford University Press.

Lucas, Robert E. (2000). 'Some Macroeconomics for the 21st Century', *Journal of Economic Perspectives*, 14: 159–68.

Maddison, Angus (1983). 'A Comparison of Levels of GDP per capita in Developed and Developing Countries, 1700–1980', *Journal of Economic History*, 43: 27–41.

Maddison, Angus (1989). *The World Economy in the Twentieth Century*, Paris: OECD Development Centre.

Maddison, Angus (1995). *Monitoring the World Economy: 1820–1992*, Paris: OECD Development Centre.

Maddison, Angus (2001). *The World Economy: A Millennial Perspective*, Paris: OECD Development Centre.

Maddison, Angus (2003). *The World Economy: Historical Statistics*, Paris: OECD.

Maddison, Angus (2007). *Contours of the World Economy, 1–2030 AD: Essays in Macroeconomic History*, Oxford: Oxford University Press.

Marglin, Stephen and Juliet Schor (eds) (1990). *The Golden Age of Capitalism*, Oxford: Clarendon Press.

Massey, D. (1988). 'Economic Development and International Migration in Comparative Perspective', *Population and Development Review*, 14: 383–413.

McMillan, Margaret and Dani Rodrik (2011). 'Globalization, Structural Change and Productivity Growth', in M. Bacchetta and M. Jansen (eds) *Making Globalization Socially Sustainable*, Geneva: ILO-WTO.

Milanovic, Branko (2005). *Worlds Apart: Measuring International and Global Inequality*, Princeton: Princeton University Press.

Milanovic, Branko (2011). *The Haves and the Have-Nots: A Brief and Idiosyncratic History of Global Inequality*, New York: Basic Books.

Morris, Ian (2010). *Why The West Rules—For Now: The Patterns of History and What They Reveal About the Future*, New York: Farrar, Straus and Giraux, Picador.

Nayyar, Deepak (1978). 'Transnational Corporations and Manufactured Exports from Poor Countries', *Economic Journal*, 88: 59–84.

Nayyar, Deepak (1988). 'Political Economy of International Trade in Servises', *Cambridge Journal of Economics*, 12: 279–98.

Nayyar, Deepak (1994). *Migration, Remittances and Capital Flows: The Indian Experience*, Delhi: Oxford University Press.

Nayyar, Deepak (1994a). 'International Labour Movements, Trade Flows and Migration Transitions', *Asia and Pacific Migration Journal*, 3: 31–48.

Nayyar, Deepak (ed.) (1994b). *Industrial Growth and Stagnation: The Debate in India*, Delhi: Oxford University Press.

Nayyar, Deepak (1996). 'Free Trade: Why, When and For Whom?', *Banca Nazionale del Lavoro Quarterly Review*, 49: 333–50.

Nayyar, Deepak (1997). 'Themes in Trade and Industrialization', in Deepak Nayyar (ed.) *Trade and Industrialization*, Delhi: Oxford University Press.

Nayyar, Deepak (1998). 'International Trade and Factor Mobility: Economic Theory and Political Reality', in Deepak Nayyar (ed.) *Economics as Ideology and Experience*, London: Frank Cass.

Nayyar, Deepak (2002). Cross-Border Movements of People, in Deepak Nayyar (ed.) *Governing Globalization: Issues and Institutions*, Oxford: Oxford University Press.

Nayyar, Deepak (2003). 'Globalization and Development Strategies', in John Toye (ed.) *Trade and Development: Directions for the Twenty-first Century*, Cheltenham: Edward Elgar.

Nayyar, Deepak (2006). 'Globalization, History and Development: A Tale of Two Centuries', *Cambridge Journal of Economics*, 30: 137–59.

Nayyar, Deepak (2008). 'International Migration and Economic Development', in Narcis Serra and Joseph E. Stiglitz (eds) *The Washington Consensus Reconsidered: Towards a New Global Governance*, Oxford: Oxford University Press.

Nayyar, Deepak (2008a). The Internationalization of Firms from India: Investment, Mergers and Acquisitions, *Oxford Development Studies*, 36: 111–31.

Nayyar, Deepak (2008b). Learning to Unlearn from Development, *Oxford Development Studies*, 36: 259–80.

Nayyar, Deepak (2009). 'Developing Countries in the World Economy: The Future in the Past?', WIDER Annual Lecture 12, Helsinki: UNU-WIDER.

Nayyar, Deepak (2010). 'China, India, Brazil and South Africa in the World Economy: Engines of Growth?', in Amelia U. Santos-Paulino and Guanghua Wan (eds) *Southern Engines of Global Growth*, Oxford: Oxford University Press.

Nayyar, Deepak (2011). 'The Financial Crisis, the Great Recession and the Developing World', *Global Policy*, 2: 20–32.

Nayyar, Deepak (2011a). 'Economic Growth and Technological Capabilities in Emerging Economies', *Innovation and Development*, 1: 245–58.

Nayyar, Gaurav (2012). *The Service Sector in India's Economic Development*, New York: Cambridge University Press.

Nayyar, Rohini (1991). *Rural Poverty in India: An Analysis of Inter-State Differences*, Delhi: Oxford University Press.

Nelson, Richard and E.S. Phelps (1966). 'Investment in Humans, Technological Diffusion and Economic Growth', *American Economic Review,* 56: 69–75.

Nelson, Richard and S.J. Winter (1982). *An Evolutionary Theory of Economic Change,* Cambridge: Cambridge University Press.

Noman, Akbar, Kwesi Botchwey, Howard Stein, and Joseph E. Stiglitz, (2012). *Good Growth and Governance in Africa: Rethinking Development Strategies,* Oxford: Oxford University Press.

North, Douglass C. (1990). *Institutions, Institutional Change and Economic Performance,* Cambridge: Cambridge University Press.

Ocampo, José Antonio (2011). 'Global Economic Prospects and the Developing World', *Global Policy,* 2: 10–19.

Ocampo, José Antonio and Joseph E. Stiglitz (eds) (2008). *Capital Market Liberalization and Development,* Oxford: Oxford University Press.

Ocampo, José Antonio, Codrina Rada, and Lance Taylor (2009). *Economic Structure, Policy and Growth in Developing Countries,* New York: Columbia University Press.

Okhawa, K. and Henry Rosovsky (1973). *Japanese Economic Growth: Trend Acceleration in the Twentieth Century,* Stanford: Stanford University Press.

O'Neill, J., S. Lawson, D. Wilson, et al. (2004). *Growth and Development: The Path to 2050,* London: Goldman Sachs.

O'Rourke, Kevin and Jeffrey G. Williamson (1999). *Globalization and History: The Evolution of a Nineteenth Century Atlantic Economy,* Cambridge, Mass: The MIT Press.

Pack, H. and L. Westphal (1986). 'Industrial Strategy and Technological Change: Theory and Reality, *World Development,* 12: 87–128.

Palma, J. Gabriel (2011). 'Homogeneous Middles vs. Heterogeneous Tails, and the End of the Inverted-U: It's All About the Share of the Rich', *Development and Change,* 42: 87–153.

Parthasarathi, Prasannan (2011). *Why Europe Grew Rich and Asia Did Not: Global Economic Divergence, 1600–1850,* Cambridge: Cambridge University Press.

Perlin, Frank (1983). 'Proto-Industrialization and Pre-Colonial South Asia', *Past and Present,* 98: 30–95.

Pogge, Thomas and Sanjay Reddy (2010). 'How Not to Count the Poor', in Joseph E. Stiglitz, Sudhir Anand, and Paul Segal (eds) *Debates in the Measurement of Poverty,* Oxford: Oxford University Press.

Polanyi, Karl (1944). *The Great Transformation: The Political and Economic Origins of Our Times,* Boston: Beacon Press.

Pomeranz, Kenneth (2000). *The Great Divergence: China, Europe and the Making of the Modern World Economy,* Princeton: Princeton University Press.

Pritchett, Lant (1996). Measuring Outward Orientation in LDCs: Can it Be Done?, *Journal of Development Economics,* 49: 307–35.

Pritchett, Lant (1997). 'Divergence, Big Time', *Journal of Economic Perspectives,* 11: 3–17.

Ranis, Gustav (ed.) (1992). *Taiwan: From Developing to Mature Economy,* Boulder: Westview Press.

Rasiah, R. (1995). *Foreign Capital and Industrialization in Malaysia,* London: Macmillan.

Reinert, Erik S. (2007). *How Rich Countries Got Rich and Why Poor Countries Stay Poor,* New York: Carroll and Graf.

Robertson, D.H. (1938). 'The Future of International Trade', *Economic Journal*, 48: 1–14.

Rodrik, Dani (1992). Closing the Productivity Gap: Does Trade Liberalization really Help? In G.K. Helleiner (ed.) *Trade Policy, Liberalization and Development*, Oxford: Clarendon Press.

Rodrik, Dani (1997). *Has Globalization Gone Too Far?* Washington DC: Institute for International Economics.

Rodrik, Dani (2005). 'Rethinking Growth Strategies', WIDER Annual Lecture 8, Helsinki: UNU-WIDER.

Ros, Jamie (1994). 'Mexico's Trade and Industrialization Experience since 1960', in G.K. Helleiner (ed.) *Trade Policy and Industrialization in Turbulent Times*, New York: Routledge.

Rosenberg, N. (1994). *Exploring the Black Box: Technology, Economics, and History*, Cambridge: Cambridge University Press.

Rowthorn, Robert E. (2008). 'The Renaissance of China and India', in Philip Arestis and John Eatwell (eds) *Issues in Economic Development and Globalization: Essays in Honour of Ajit Singh*, London: Palgrave.

Rowthorn, Robert E. and John R. Wells (1987). *De-Industrialization and Foreign Trade*, Cambridge: Cambridge University Press.

Said, Edward (1978). *Orientalism*, New York: Random House.

Sala-i-Martin, X. (2006). 'The World Distribution of Income', *Quarterly Journal of Economics*, 121: 351–97.

Schumpeter, Joseph A. (1942). 'The Creative Response in Economic History', *Journal of Economic History*, 7: 149–59.

Sen, Amartya (1976). 'Poverty: An Ordinal Approach to Measurement', *Econometrica*, 44: 219–31.

Sen, Amartya (1999). *Development as Freedom*, New York: Alfred E. Knopf.

Shapiro, Helen and Lance Taylor (1990). 'The State and Industrial Strategy', *World Development*, 18: 861–78.

Sharpston, M. (1975). 'International Subcontracting', *Oxford Economic Papers*, 27: 94–135.

Solimano, Andrés (ed.) (2008). *The International Mobility of Talent: Types, Causes and Development Impact*, Oxford: Oxford University Press.

Solow, Robert M. (1956). 'A Contribution to the Theory of Economic Growth', *Quarterly Journal of Economics*, 70: 65–94.

Stalker, P. (1994). *The Work of Strangers: A Survey of International Labour Migration*, Geneva: International Labour Office.

Stern, Nicholas (2007). *The Economics of Climate Change*, Cambridge: Cambridge University Press.

Stewart, Frances (1985). *Planning to Meet Basic Needs*, London: Macmillan.

Stewart, Frances (2007). 'Do We Need a 'New Great Transformation? Is One Likely?', in George Mavrotas and Anthony Shorrocks (eds) *Advancing Development: Core Themes in Global Economics*, Basingstoke: Palgrave Macmillan.

Stiglitz, Joseph E. (1989). 'On the Economic Role of the State', in A. Heertje (ed.) *The Economic Role of the State*, Oxford: Basil Blackwell.

Stiglitz, Joseph E. (1998). 'More Instruments and Broader Goals: Moving Toward the Post-Washington Consensus', WIDER Annual Lecture 2, Helsinki: UNU-WIDER.

Streeten, Paul (1981). *First Things First: Meeting Basic Needs in Developing Countries*, Oxford: Oxford University Press.

Sturgeon, Timothy J. and Olga Memodovic (2011). 'Mapping Global Value Chains: Intermediate Goods and Structural Change in the World Economy', *Development Policy and Strategic Research Branch Working Paper 05/2010*, UNIDO, Vienna.

Taylor, Lance (1994). 'Gap Models', *Journal of Development Economics*, 45: 17–34.

Taylor, Lance (2007). 'Development Questions for 25 Years', in George Mavrotas and Anthony Shorrocks (eds) *Advancing Development: Core Themes in Global Economics*, Basingstoke: Palgrave Macmillan.

Taylor, Lance (2010). *Maynard's Revenge: the Collapse of Free Market Macroeconomics*, Cambridge, Mass: Harvard University Press.

Tinker, H. (1974). *A New System of Slavery: The Export of Indian Labour Overseas: 1830–1920*, Oxford: Oxford University Press.

UNCTAD (1994). *World Investment Report 1994*, Geneva: United Nations.

UNCTAD (2006). *World Investment Report: FDI from Developing Countries and Transition Economies: Implications for Development*, New York and Geneva: United Nations.

UNCTAD (2011). *The Least Developed Countries 2011 Report*, New York and Geneva: United Nations.

UNIDO (1981). *World Industry in 1980*, New York: United Nations.

United Nations (2006). *Diverging Growth and Development, World Economic and Social Survey 2006*, New York: United Nations.

United Nations (2011). *The Great Green Technological Transformation, World Economic and Social Survey 2011*, New York: United Nations.

Veblen, Thorstein (1915). *Imperial Germany and the Industrial Revolution*, London: Macmillan.

Wade, Robert (1990). *Governing the Market: Economic Theory and the Role of Government in East Asian Industrialization*, Princeton: Princeton University Press.

Williamson, Jeffrey G. (1996). 'Globalization, Convergence and History', *Journal of Economic History*, 56: 277–306.

Williamson, Jeffrey G. (2002). 'Winners and Losers over Two Centuries of Globalization', WIDER Annual Lecture 6, Helsinki: UNU-WIDER.

Williamson, John (1994). *The Political Economy of Policy Reform*, Washington DC: Institute of International Economics.

Index

J. ALLEN BOONE began his career as a journalist, then became a pioneer in the Hollywood motion picture industry. Later he was asked to tutor and take charge of Strongheart, the movie dog, an experience recorded in KINSHIP WITH ALL LIFE which opened up a new career for him. He was appointed commissioner of the new board of animal regulation in Los Angeles, and made human-animal relationships his lifework. J. Allen Boone was a Hollywood figure of importance, a lecturer, writer and friend of thousands.

Jacket photo Standard Oil Co. (N.J.)

Kourken Photo, Pasadena

THE LANGUAGE OF SILENCE

With warm humor and well-seasoned experience, J. Allen Boone reenters the wonderful world of unspoken communication between humans and animals. The author was an explorer into the realm of the unexpected. He felt that most people underestimate the mental and spiritual qualities possessed by animals, and thereby miss seeing the oneness and wholeness of life.

THE LANGUAGE OF SILENCE salutes the Divinity within all living creatures. In his encounter with "Just Joe," his monkey-companion, Boone struggles to become the pupil, with "Just Joe" the teacher—a teacher whose wisdom is not measured in words, but in his ability to vibrate with life's unity.

These thoughtful tales demonstrate how the author spoke silently with all forms of life and how he grew to understand their silent replies. Boone never looked *down* on animals as "lesser creatures"; rather, he looked across at them as companions in the grand adventure of life. His cultivated mental affinity with nature allowed him to see that everything that lives has something of value to share with us—whenever we are ready for the experience.

THE
LANGUAGE OF
SILENCE

J. ALLEN BOONE

Edited by Paul and Blanche Leonard

1817

HARPER & ROW, PUBLISHERS

New York Evanston and London

FIRST EDITION

LIBRARY OF CONGRESS CATALOG CARD NUMBER: 72-126035

CONTENTS

A TRIBUTE TO J. ALLEN BOONE

by Paul and Blanche Leonard

His name was J. Allen Boone. It was not until the time he "changed his world," as the Japanese put it, that we learned that Allen was a direct descendant of Daniel Boone.

Allen never lived more than a stone's throw from Hollywood Boulevard during the thirty years that we knew him. Yet Allen was as far from the modern manias of the film capital's commercial output as an eagle is from a mole. He was a saint of Hollywood, an Assisi in the land of the Silver Screen.

Allen, though fully aware of the "animality" that lurks in mortals, lost no time moralizing about it. He was too busy admiring the natural nobility, the physical prowess, and excellent qualities he so keenly saw in animals.

In a previous and very successful book, *Kinship with All Life* (Harper & Row, 1956), Allen tells of his remarkable relationships with animals—especially Strongheart, the million dollar movie dog. These memorable tales are not mere animal stories, but demonstrations of his deep metaphysical belief in the Oneness of all life. With a dog for a friend, he made discovery in human-animal relationships his lifework.

As author and lecturer, Allen never tired in conveying his great but simple message: that man can achieve a relationship with all living things far beyond that usually accepted or expected. Allen had cultivated a mental affinity with nature. He never looked *down* on animals as "lesser creatures"; rather, he looked *across* at them as companions in the grand adventure of life. He had a cosmic sense which enabled him to soar above all man-made distinctions between humans and animals.

Allen was an explorer into the realm of the unexpected. From his ever-revered Rhode Island mother, he received his basic encouragement for the adventure of exploring. His first job away from home was that of a reporter—and, there is no doubt he was outstanding. When only twenty, he was already an authority on, and writing intimately about, "The 400"—the fabulous Newport society of that period. He worked on Boston, New York, and Philadelphia newspapers, and for syndicates. As a Washington correspondent, he not only told *what* happened, but tried to tell *how* and *why* it happened. He went through every kind of newspaper work from ordinary reporting to interviewing the very famous. His feature story on Caruso is a classic. Caruso was an abstraction, magnificent but far away. Most persons felt that to watch this opera star was similar to watching a beautiful but distant celestial star. But Allen wrote a story which revealed the man.

He knew Houdini and the other great magicians of that day. Once Houdini was privately showing him some of his tricks. After a little while, it became boring. So Allen asked, "Why don't you show me how you do it?" Houdini did so, and the demonstration was truly fascinating. Later the famous magician tried this on audiences, and it was most popular. Allen said: "People want to know 'how it works.' They want to be let in on the secret, to borrow it, and use it themselves." Allen was a backstage character. The footlights, as such, held no charm for him. He was forever looking for the wheels behind the wizardry. He forever asked himself: "What makes it tick?" His was surely the scientific spirit.

Newspaper work led Allen to writing publicity for the burgeoning motion picture industry, then centered in New York. When the Robertson-Cole Company, a leader in the field, moved to Hollywood, Allen went with them as production superviser and became a pioneer in the new film city. Robertson-Cole went on to become the gigantic RKO enterprise.

Allen was the producer of the first costume picture ever made. It was *Kismet*, starring Otis Skinner, and was a sensation at the time. In that glamorous early period of Hollywood, he worked with some of the celebrated stars of the day: Pauline Frederick, Dustin Farnum, Lew Cody, Bessie Love, and Sessue Hayakawa. Allen was very close friends with Douglas Fairbanks, Sr., and his wife Mary Pickford. The three of them did much traveling together. On one trip, Fairbanks and Allen went around the world. He commented: "With Douglas, it was always a continuous adventure. I never knew what would happen within the next twenty minutes. He was as great off the screen as on. He had that same adventurous, spontaneous, dynamic quality everyone loved in his films."

Once during a motion picture location trip into the African jungles with Fairbanks, Allen refused to carry weapons. He

believed that all the jungle creatures he met, despite their
bad reputations, would be friendly if his thoughts about them
were friendly.

Allen admired the American Indian and his ability to get
along with any creature on earth. It was his belief that the
mental atmosphere the Indian exudes is like an invisible
handshake of goodwill toward other creatures.

In Africa, the head of a Dutch exporting firm said to Allen:
"Until I read your book *Kinship with All Life*, I never knew
why the wild life attacks white people, but seldom attacks
the natives." Allen responded, "The natives have a mental
rapport with the animals. With those who know it and practice it, there is an interrelating oneness between the man and
the creature. I have to be right myself mentally to experience
it."

Allen's animal books are unusual. Most other animal books
are objective. They tell about the training of the animal,
about what man does *toward* or *to* the animal. But Allen
wrote about the "Law of Reciprocation," meaning that the
thoughts that emanate from man come back like a boomer-
ang. He believed that animals are sensitive to the thoughts of
humans about them. He was convinced that man must grasp
the Law of Reciprocation before he can improve the world.
This subtle Law is difficult for civilized man to grasp, but
easily understood in primitive cultures. In one instance, a
jungle native explained it to Allen as: "What goes out mentally and vocally, comes back to one and at one." This communication between Allen and the native was accomplished
by sign language and "intuition," or the silent speech which
is possible between men and animals.

He realized that many people ridiculed the stories about
his having communicated with creatures other than humans.
But they did so only because they had not learned the truth

that all living creatures reflect the same Universal Intelligence and can communicate with each other when they make contact on the same level.

In the early Hollywood days, two persons changed Allen's life—Jane Murfin, a famous playwright (*Smilin' Through*; *Lilac Time*), and Larry Trimble, a topnotch animal trainer. Together Miss Murfin and Trimble had formed a company and searched until they found—in Germany—the greatest dog available. He was Strongheart, a 125-pound German shepherd, a combat dog. Strongheart had worked in World War I and was the greatest blue-ribbon winner in Germany. With great love and patience, Trimble untrained him from his combat habits—unthinking obedience, viciousness on command—and encouraged Strongheart to do his own thinking. The dog became a sensation in the movies. He was the first dog movie star—pioneer to later canine stars like Rin Tin Tin and Lassie.

There was a litigation, however, and Trimble went to New York. Jane Murfin also had to leave for New York suddenly, to see about one of her plays on Broadway. In the studio cafe one day, Miss Murfin mentioned to Allen the problem of what to do with Strongheart. Without thinking, he answered, "I guess I could put him up and feed him." Miss Murfin, delighted with his offer, took him up on it before he could back out. Allen had no idea what this would entail or the adventures he was to experience.

"I had never had even a two-dollar dog," he would recall, "and here I was baby-sitter to a million-dollar dog! It proved to be not so much what I could do for him, but what he could do for me. That dog took me over as if he were my mother. I learned things from him I have been sharing ever since. It has revolutionized relationships—my own, and through my books, that of others all over the world. The year Stongheart xii A Tribute To J. Allen Boone

and I were together was filled with the most subtle and exalting mental adventures."

Speaking out of his vast professional experience in the theater, he once said: "With a few exceptions, I have never known a human actor or actress who could compete successfully with a dog in front of a motion picture camera or a theater audience. You can have the greatest cast of human actors, but put a dog on the stage and he'll wreck their performance. Why? Because something in us turns toward that which is genuine, like a flower turns toward the light. A dog never gives less than one hundred per cent of himself. Can you imagine humans doing this? If they would, a transformation would come over the entire world. A dog is popular all over the world for this reason. He gives of himself; he establishes right inner relations."

"Yesterday I gave a lecture to a group of psychologists," he continued, "and I surprised them with this idea of two-way thought traffic. Man usually speaks down to the lower animals, saying to them: 'Here I am up here with a big brain, and down there you are with a little brain. What can you send up to me?' I have learned that there is one infinite Intelligence moving through all life. Philosophers with four legs, six legs, or no legs at all, can give to me and share with me. All forms of life with which man comes in contact are eligible for this communication in a grand Oneness of the universe. The communications I have had with such forms of life have surpassed all the interviews I ever had with the so-called 'great' in the world."

Allen reminded people of things they already knew but had forgotten to remember. Upon hearing him speak on a certain occasion, the head of a university said, "Suddenly I knew that, as a practicing Christian, I wasn't practicing what I was supposed to know." It's the idea of an all-including compassion that most persons of all faiths have overlooked. One is reminded of Albert Schweitzer, with his Reverence for Life philosophy.

J. Allen Boone was a dynamic man. We never knew anyone who could reform so much, yet with never any sense of preaching or "finger wagging." In the years we knew him, as his hair grew whiter, we found him still learning from everything—up to the very "end." He was constantly sharing the best in him, the best he knew, with others.

His credo: "Everything that lives, even a common domestic housefly, has something of value to share with you—whenever you are ready for the experience."

THE LANGUAGE OF SILENCE

CHAPTER ONE

"JUST JOE"

He was one of the finest, as well as the most amusing experts
I ever met, in knowing how to live rhythmically and raptur-
ously, in whatever it was that he happened to be doing. With
his sparkling energy, his imagination, and his sense of fun,
and particularly his ability for "putting on a good show," both
for himself and for others, he was a continuous delight. All his
ancestors in the earth scene had been monkeys, and so, of
course, he was bouncing around in the form of one, too. When
I first met him, he was supposed to be crazy and killingly
dangerous, although I was completely unaware of it at the
time.

It all began aboard a schooner yacht, anchored in the harbor of Newport, Rhode Island, one that was being used more
as a houseboat than as a cruiser. The owner, an old friend of
mine, was a well-known retired yachting captain. His wife
and two of her women relatives were living aboard the
schooner with him that particular summer. Since I had a
continuing invitation from the captain to spend as much time

with them as possible, I did so. I greatly enjoyed not only their company, but also the animated harbor scenes, the swimming and sunbathing, and the many other values having to do with that kind of relaxed salty living.

On one occasion, after some necessary absence of several weeks, I returned to the yacht. There was no response to my shouts as I rowed near the boat, so I concluded everyone had gone ashore. Then, to my astonishment, I saw a monkey. He was sitting at the extreme end of the bowsprit. From out of his wrinkled little face he was squinting at me with unmistakable suspicion and fear. I wondered how he happened to be on the yacht. There was a collar around his neck, and dangling from it was what looked like a broken chain, which only added to the mystery.

As I climbed the yacht's ladder to the deck, the monkey hurried in from the bowsprit, then speedily climbed the foremost rigging to the crosstrees, as only he could have done. Then he moved hand-over-hand along a stout wire brace, with his body swinging rhythmically in various directions. He reached the crosstrees of the mainmast, where he had an unobstructed view of the deck below, and especially of me. It was plainly evident that serious trouble of some kind had taken place on the yacht before I arrived. The deck was littered with broken things. Every chair had been knocked over, one completely wrecked. And what had evidently been a little house for the monkey, was upside down and damaged.

Completely baffled by it all, I straightened up one of the chairs and sat down in it, then began aiming my questioning attention at that monkey above me, just as he was aiming his down at me. Visually, as well as mentally, we were each giving the other a thorough going-over as suspects, and I had the feeling that he was topping me in all phases of it. Then suddenly, and most unexpectedly, he leaped through the air to a long, loose rope that was hanging down from the upper rigging. At varying speeds, he began swinging back and forth like an eccentric pendulum that had no regard for conventional movements.

Watching that performance above me was as thrillingly exciting as it was educational. I was witnessing the superlative, in movement, in rhythm, in timing. Everything that monkey did on the swinging rope was as unpredictable as it was impressive. Not for even a split second did he come out of his exquisite bodily movements. Watching him was far more than casual conventional interest on my part, for at the time this happened I had, as an amateur, been winning all sorts of honors in acrobatics and gymnastics, both as a solo performer and as a member of a tumbling trio. So, every least thing that that monkey was doing in his performance had a very special appeal in my direction.

As that monkey squinted down at me, during one of his brief pauses, I began an equally intense squinting up at him. Not only that, but I started talking vocally to him too, quite as though he had been another human being that I had suddenly come to admire and respect. I explained who I was, and how I happened to be on the yacht. I told him of my keen interest in gymnastics and acrobatics, particularly thanking him for some of the new things he had just shown me in spring-offs, self-propelled flights through the air, precision timing, body-swingings, and flexible, gentle landings. After a pause, I asked him if he would please show me some more stunts.

As my last vocal sound went upward, the monkey leaped back onto the crosstrees again, and went into an even more spectacular exhibition. The little producer and star of the show walked tighrope fashion, with perfect balancing, along the wire brace between the two masts. Then, as a fitting climax, he jumped to the long, dangling rope that he had used for swinging purposes, and slid rapidly to the deck, not far from where I was, and sat down. As he looked wistfully and pathetically in my direction, I slowly extended my hand and invited him to come and join me. Within seconds he was nestling in my lap, quite as though such things had been going on between us for a long time.

As I gently stroked his body, to which he responded with a kind of purring satisfaction of his own, I told him in considerable detail what a truly great artist he was in perfected rhythmical action, and what a privilege it had been to watch and learn from him. He kept his eyes focused on every movement of my lips. I knew that he understood me; knew, too, that he and I were establishing silent, good correspondence between us. I was also aware that we were beginning to harmonize our seemingly unrelatable twoness into an understanding togetherness and oneness, and doing so from our innermost essences, to our outermost emanations.

In the midst of our sharing delight there were strange and startling noises behind me. Turning, I saw the yacht's launch approaching. Standing in the bow, and doing the steering, was the captain's wife. Just to her left was a policeman. He had a rifle in his hands and was ready to go into instant action. Standing close behind them were the other two women that lived on the yacht. All five were in a state of dramatic excitement.

The captain's wife was shouting explosive words in my direction that I couldn't understand, but that monkey did. As a result, he leaped fearfully from my lap, raced up the mainmast rigging on the far side, and hid himself behind a roll of sail on the crosstrees.

The launch came alongside. One by one the occupants came cautiously aboard, each apprehensively watching the roll of sail above them, from behind which the little monkey was peeking down with fear and trembling. The three women began talking loudly and almost incoherently at me, at the same time, with all sorts of vehement hand gestures to stress what they were saying. Out of it I gradually managed to get the following. The monkey, already named Just Joe, had been given to the captain by an old seagoing friend. It was a new experience for the captain. He was delighted. So was Just Joe. They became instant and almost inseparable friends.

A short time after this, the captain was called away from Newport for a few weeks on important business. Regretfully, he had to leave Just Joe behind on the yacht. The day following the captain's departure, according to the three women, Just Joe became insane and not only tried to kill them, but to wreck everything that he could on the yacht. During a brief interlude in "the monkey savagery," the women had managed to sneak out of the main cabin, into which they had locked themselves for protection, get into the launch, and head shoreward for police help. It was while they were on this mission that I innocently rowed into the dramatic situation.

At the end of a turbulent discussion as to what was best to do under the circumstances, the shooting of Just Joe by the policeman was temporarily called off. But there was a major proviso in our vocal agreement: I was to take the monkey ashore with me, providing it could be done. I was to assume full responsibility for him until the captain returned and could decide what to do with his "crazy pet." The three women and the policeman agreed to leave the yacht immediately. They were to remain completely out of sight until the monkey and I got ashore, or at least had an opportunity to make the attempt.

When the launch finally disappeared behind some anchored boats at the end of the harbor, I called to Just Joe to come down, assuring him that he had nothing to fear as all was well below. He didn't have to be told that, for with his far-seeing outer vision and his alerted intuitive awareness, he knew what was actually going on. But being a monkey, he had to be extremely cautious, whatever the occasion. For some minutes he remained hidden behind the roll of sail at the crosstrees, staring in the direction that the launch had taken. Then satisfied that the troublemakers were completely out of the situation, he came down the rigging, hurried across the deck, and leaped up into my lap again.

For quite some time Just Joe and I remained totally relaxed in that chair, rocking with the gentle rolling of the yacht. As we did so, I knew, and I know that he did too, that our hearts were echoing back and forth, in a mutuality of interest . . . of respect . . . of understanding . . . and of love. Through the revelation of direct experience I was being gently but effectively shown that life, in all its aspects, is an inseparable togetherness. Is a perfect oneness in knowing . . . in being . . . in doing . . . and in sharing, even with such animated items as a supposedly "normal human" and a supposedly "crazy monkey."

Then with Just Joe still nestling contentedly in my arms, I climbed down the yacht's ladder and got into my own boat, slowly and gently explaining to him everything that I did and why I was doing it. I placed him in the stern seat, where he could keep one eye on me, and the other on the harbor traffic. Then with our echoing heartbeats, and participating insight and outsight, I rowed us ashore.

CHAPTER TWO

MONKEYWISE

In spite of the many bad indictments that the women aboard the yacht in Newport Harbor had fastened on little Just Joe the monkey, he was a perfect little gentleman in all particulars throughout the entire time that we lived together. After that dramatically eventful day, we established our headquarters in a large fenced-in yard back of the house where I lived. There he had plenty of space and freedom in which to do whatever he pleased, whenever he pleased, and just as it pleased him to do so. There was one exception—when I had to be away, it was necessary, because of his liking for adventure, to chain him temporarily to the little house, where he did his sleeping and meditating.

Nothing ever dimmed, at least for long, that monkey's enthusiam for being alive, nor the joy, fun, and satisfaction he was able to get out of each moment, as it came ticking into his experience, nor his curiosity in wanting to know the reason and purpose for everything that he squinted at. Unless he was requested not to do so, he usually tried to take com-

pletely apart every puzzling object that he could. In those
efforts he would minutely examine the thing, not only with
his eyes, hands, and feet, but also with his nose, ears, and
teeth. Then having reduced whatever it happened to be to
bits, he would examine each bit visually, mentally, and smell-
ingly, and finally toss it aside as utterly meaningless in his
experience. It wasn't that he was "mischievous and destructive" in those actions. It was simply his particular method for
doing his own research work in an exceedingly puzzling
world, especially for a monkey.

Just Joe was filled to overflowing with spontaneity and
showmanship, and knew how to make each moment yield
some kind of a dividend in sharable satisfaction. So life with
Just Joe was completely free from sameness and dullness.
That monkey had mastered the art of avoiding boredom, not
only for himself, but for anyone or anything that happened
to be watching him. Whether moving along the ground in his
unique waddle, or climbing seemingly impossible things, or
doing spectacular leaps through the air, Just Joe was always
a fascinating as well as thrilling symphony in motion.

It was relatively easy to understand and then companion
with the visible part of Just Joe, even though I knew so little
about monkeys. My difficulty, at least in the beginning of our
adventure, was how to identify rightly, and then companion
with the invisible part of him—with his unseen individuality,
his thinking, his feelings, his hopes, and with the many other
things that were constantly bubbling within him, and demanding outer expression and sharing.

I didn't have to be told that there was vastly more to that
monkey as a living entity than either my human intellect or
physical senses could possibly identify. That fact was easily
apparent in almost everything that I watched him do. My
need, as Just Joe and I began discovering each other, was

mentally to penetrate his outer appearance and actions, then discover what it really was that was motivating him about in such a rhythmical and delightful manner, and then try to blend my own total best with his total best in a mutuality of understanding.

The more that I tried to establish the right inner, as well as outer, interrelations with Just Joe, the more of an enigma he became. His visible behavior patterns were relatively easy to understand and then cooperate with, but his invisible behavior patterns seemed hidden in an unsolvable mystery. With all my careful observations, intellectual analysis, and minutely sifted conclusions, I found myself mentally wandering in and out of blind alleys, so to speak, and apparently getting nowhere at all, except back to where I had started from.

Then, to my private embarrassment, I discovered what was wrong. It was I. I was actually blocking my own way by what I thought I knew as "an educated human" but wasn't able to demonstrate in a testing time. What I needed, it became unmistakably clear, was to set my human intellect completely aside. Also my pride in species. Then I would seek what I needed to know about Just Joe from Just Joe himself. So following that intuitive whispering, I made a radical change in my efforts. In all humility and sincerity, I appointed that little monkey my private tutor, and then let him go to work on me in an educational way.

During this effort to become monkeywise, under the direction of Just Joe, a curriculum began developing that was as unique and delightful as it was bettering and expanding for me as a human. However, it demanded many disciplines, such as a genuine willingness to be taught by a monkey . . . the courage to follow facts wherever they led . . . the constant practice of humility and patience . . . flexible intuition, with its accompanying inhearing and inseeing . . . the need for keeping my intellectual tailfeathers lowered . . . and childlike expectancy, receptivity, and appreciation.

What made that monkey tutoring so effective was the simple fact that one is always more convinced and helped by what he sees actually demonstrated than by what he merely listens to or reads. All that Just Joe had to do in order to get one of his lessons across to me was to be his own genuine self, and then let the magic of the universe flow through him. Having had to listen to so many carbon-copy opinions, with accompanying visible or invisible finger-waggings, from members of my own species as to just how all the rest of us must think and live, it was refreshing to gather in needed wisdom through the persuasiveness of a silent, fine example. Even the instructing example of "only a monkey" with a bad reputation.

Attaining the receptive capacity for being Just Joe's pupil was by no means easy in the beginning of the experience. For one thing, I was too far out in the generally unfamiliar. For another, I was handicapped by all sorts of humanly generated illusions as well as educated and encouraged stupidities having to do with life in general and monkeys in particular. Then once again my efforts became completely blocked, and once again I had to learn that I was intellectually getting in my own way. In all genuineness I had made that monkey my tutor, and really wanted to be taught by him. And yet, without being aware of the paradoxical effort, I had been trying to do all the thinking for both of us. And our monkey-human educational curriculum just wouldn't work in that manner.

At this point I had to learn another needed lesson in the science and art of being in right relations. With all my respect and liking for Just Joe, and with my deep admiration for his skill in knowing how to think himself around in such a rhythmical and interesting manner, I was practicing a serious fault in most of my contacts with him. That was the customary human pattern of mentally looking down my nose at him as "an inferior expression of life." From that downslanting viewpoint I, being a human, was incomparably high up in the humanly arranged scale of living values, while he, being a monkey, was far, far below me as "a lesser creature," and so to be treated as such.

That downward-slanting mental attitude of mine, from my self-elevated ego-perch, had of necessity to be changed. And what I did to help remedy the situation was to set up an invisible bridge between myself and Just Joe. A mental bridge, for two-way rather than one-way thought traffic. A bridge that had to be kept high, as well as perfectly horizontal, in order to make silent communication between us possible and effective. The more that I gave strict attention to my part in this, the more the many illusions, supposedly separating us from each other as rational fellow beings, began evaporating. And the more that happened, the easier it became for that monkey and me to share ourselves in the universal harmony and rhythm of "We-Us-and-Our."

Aside from being a continuously delightful companion, Just Joe was also an adventurer, an explorer, a philosopher, an entertainer, and an animated poem, all wrapped up in "one package." He was also a specialist in demonstrating how many more ways there are for getting genuine satisfaction out of everyday living than those practiced by most of the members of the human species. I shall always be indebted to that little fellow for the many bettering and broadening values he shared with me in this direction, and most particularly for what he privately showed me about expanding my thinking beyond intellectual boundaries, and then sharing in the consciousness of a monkey.

Day after day I would carefully study the lovely and lovable qualities that Just Joe released from his rhythmical withinness into his rhythmical withoutness—qualities that were as pure and as fine in their outmost emanations as they were in their innermost essences. The more proficient I became in identifying the character tone of that monkey and its vibrating relationship to my own character tone, the more clearly a great and eternal fact began dawning over the horizon of my awareness. This: that in reality, there were no separating barriers between one living thing and another. That innately, Just Joe, I, and every living thing that we could identify were needed individual parts, or expressions in the forever functioning of the inseparable oneness of all life. And this, it was also silently stressed, is true regardless of all surface appearances and seemings to the contrary.

CHAPTER THREE

THE LOST LINKAGE

The ground-and-lofty education that I was receiving under the tutoring of Just Joe the monkey was almost continuous, for as long as that little fellow was visible, regardless of what he was or even wasn't doing, school was in session and I was being well taught. The fresh wisdom and knowledge that I acquired from him was as practical and usable in my everyday living as it had been entertaining and amusing in the way he managed to get it across to me. And thus under the guidance of that monkey I was being shown all sorts of new ways in which to look at life . . . to think about life . . . and to enjoy life.

Being a monkey, my little instructor was, of course, entirely without academic sanction. And no association of teachers, it is safe to assume, would have approved of him as a member. But things like that didn't bother Just Joe in the least. They couldn't have . . . not with his independence . . . his imagination . . . his joy . . . his sense of fun . . . and the manner in which he always poured out his reflected best . . . his keen ability in knowing how to let his intuitive awareness not only silently speak for him, but also silently teach and preach for him wherever he happened to be.

Just Joe never had to be taught that being in the earth scene, especially for a monkey, is an exceedingly challenging experience. He had to be exceedingly alert and cautious most of the time, or else! But he seemed to like it that way, as it afforded him plenty of opportunities to practice what he thought he inwardly knew and could outwardly do. Sparked by the desire to understand the real meaning and purpose back of all encountered phenomena, Just Joe was always on some kind of a frontier, thereby experiencing the puzzling, the confusing, and much of the time the frightening. But in spite of all that, he was always trying to go the happy, fun-filled, and sharing way. And such educational pace-setting was most helpful, especially for a human that was trying to escape into larger areas of knowing and being.

It wasn't the least bit difficult when I first met Just Joe to know that he was burdened with a serious and baffling problem. It was apparent in his eyes and wrinkled little face. It was also feelable in the mental atmosphere that he was diffusing. Just Joe was starving. Not for food, but for understanding, appreciation, and love. For someone, or something, that he could really believe in and trust. For opportunities to flow out and share his best, and thereby come into a greater awareness and cooperation with all life.

Then it was that the intuitive whisper came to give Just Joe the greater opportunity he needed, by having him become my teacher and go to work on me in an educational way for our mutual good. It was one of the wisest things I ever did, as the results subsequently proved. My part as pupil and learner in this most unconventional arrangement was first to become properly humble, attentive, and receptive, then carefully to watch every least thing that my little teacher did. While doing so, I had to give alerted attention to every impression that came into my knowing, or awareness, from out of my not-knowing. In those gently-arriving impressions would always be the answer or answers to whatever it was that I particularly needed to know at the time.

The widely practiced method in conventional human education, wherein the teacher endeavors to force upon his pupils certain standardized theories and practices that were first forced upon him, had no place in the postgraduate course that I was taking under the direction of that monkey. It couldn't have had. Not with Just Joe's sparkling aliveness . . . his genuineness . . . his originality . . . and his total bounce. And particularly not with his artistry in knowing how to share so abundantly his joy and love whenever given the opportunity to do so.

The fresh wisdom and knowledge that my little instructor shared with me required neither vocal sounds, chalk marks on a blackboard, or the least bit of finger-wagging. Just Joe always taught, and most effectively so, through the persuasiveness of his silent, fine example—always flowing out with his best and all in every least thing that he did, regardless of whether anyone was watching him or not. And that provided the ultimate in teaching as well as in educational pace-setting. Often, in the midst of that monkey tutoring, I would recall for new pondering purposes the famous statement made many centuries ago by Pliny the Elder that "Man is the only one who knows nothing and can learn nothing without being taught."

What Just Joe and I particularly liked doing was getting into an old-fashioned rocking chair, with just the right rhythm to it, and then rocking ourselves out into all sorts of mental adventures and discoveries. To get the most satisfying results, we always rode the old chair in a slow, gentle rhythm, with occasional variations to blend with our changing thinking and feeling. In those mental-physical oscillations, my little monkey associate and I would first totally relax. Then, as a most important requisite, we got our heartbeats to echoing back and forth in the right tonality, and then in harmony and rhythm with the universal heartbeat. And that would always give us the participating balance we each needed, inwardly as well as outwardly.

These rocking-chair journeys took us out of the limiting egos that claim to separate us into monkeys and men. I would often get into the old chair without Just Joe being in the room. The moment I did so, he would instantly quit whatever he happened to be doing, wherever he happened to be, come racing into the room as fast as he could, leap up into my lap, and relax for another one of our rhythmical expeditions. How that monkey knew, without being in the room, that I had seated myself in the rocking chair greatly puzzled me at first. Gradually I began discovering his "secret." He had never been educated, or otherwise lured away, from using his natural, innate, intuitive faculties—from hearing with his "inner ear" and seeing with his "inner eye." Or did he, through his bones and marrow, sensitized to the slightest rhythm, catch the vibrations of the rocking chair as it reverberated through the house—imperceptible to the human faculties? Our "educated" faculties have been alienated from the kinetic source of all vibrations—or the vibrant and vibratory source of all movement. All life is in motion—the universe dances to unheard-of melodies in the symphony of life.

The monkey was pulsing with the impersonal all-pervasive vibrations of life, unobstructed by the human conceit of a separatist intelligence that blocks the free flow. Ever since Adam, symbol of the myth of separation, a false ego has made man stand apart from the universality of all creation—making distances—creating divisions—by naming, measuring, and judging all around him. In this hypnotic grip of self-deception the human considers himself superior to the animal world and other living things, when actually he has fallen below the level, even of *normal* sense perception.

Those who have the humility of a child may find again the key to reverence for, and kinship with, all life.

It is a known fact that our children, primitive peoples (nature's children), and animals are all more alive to nature's rhythm, are more sensitive to environment and environmental disturbances, than are civilized adults. Is it because civilized adults have had their basic faculties educated away or partially paralyzed? Children and animals are more alert to disturbances simply because they are more in tune with the basic harmony of the universe. Children and animals, therefore, are the real pros when it comes to living in tune with the universal, and that tune is played on the scale of Love— a love for all living things—the unifying principle.

Surely, fractured modern man, overcivilized, overmechanized, overeducated, yes, oversexed, and chronically frustrated, can go to what he considers the lesser forms of life to learn the higher lessons of living harmoniously.

"Except ye become as little children, ye shall not enter into the kingdom of heaven." "Suffer little children to come unto me: for of such is the kingdom of heaven"—of *harmony*.

In those rocking-chair adventures of ours, Just Joe and I would rock, and intuitively listen. Rock, and inwardly hear and see. Rock, and specifically know what each of us needed to know, both as individuals and as a twosome. Thus would the edges of my thinking touch the edges of that monkey's thinking. And that, in turn, would make silent, helpful correspondence between us possible. The more that he and I perfected ourselves in that unspoken speaking, the easier it became for us to get beyond our monkey and human definitions and boundaries, and then start experiencing each other, as individual states of consciousness, as vibrant ideas of the Mind of the universe. Our "inner spaces" had touched, synchronized by the universal Mind.

As Just Joe and I continued to share our totalities in this manner, thereby not only discovering more of the wonders of each other but also expanding our frontiers of awareness in all sorts of other directions, the more a great fundamental fact began to unfold. Briefly stated, it was this: that in strict reality, neither my monkey pal nor I was operating with a private and independent mind of his own. On the contrary, each of us, in our current earth-riding episode, was being guided by cosmic Wisdom. We had come through, in a measure—through the haze and daze, as well as the distortions and confusions caused by centuries of stupidly wrong guessing and miseducation about the real meaning and purpose of life.

In this manner, too, did Just Joe the monkey and I begin to find, and then reestablish the lost link between us—the linkage which ever holds all life together, in inseparable kinship and oneness. This link may have many connotations. One that comes to mind from my experience with Just Joe is the binding element of mutual appreciation. How we need that in the human experience! Appreciation is the sunlight of love that makes relationships grow and bear fruit. It is the sunlight that can awaken the seed of greatness in another. And it must be admitted that only great individuals can have great relationships. The future of society, if there is a future, will have to be built upon great friendships—friendships between men and men, women and women, men and women, adults and children, of civilized man with the so-called uncivilized, of the privileged with the underprivileged and the underprivileged with the privileged.

It will be seen in the light of evolution as a spiritual adventure, the ascent of man from the simple animal stage to the complex, with its infinite possibilities. "Privilege" is to be less and less a matter of economic or social status, and more and more a matter of self-evolution in upgrading the *inner* resources—those inalienable gifts that are the true and vital concern of the "inalienable rights." The young are already beginning, not only to see, but to live this evolutionary realism. Flocks of young people from "privileged" homes are busy working with the "underprivileged" and their children —in a mutual give and take. Some have renounced the status quo of social and economic standards. altogether, in their fearless march toward the Whole Man.

CHAPTER FOUR

THOUGHT BAYONETS

One thing greatly puzzled me in the beginning of my adventure with Just Joe the monkey. What was it, really, that started all the trouble on the yacht in Newport Harbor that melodramatic morning? While the captain was aboard, Just Joe had been a perfect little gentleman in all particulars. Then, following the captain's departure, the monkey had gone "killingly insane," according to the captain's wife and her two women relatives. When I arrived on the yacht, during the time the women were ashore seeking police help, Just Joe was again a perfect little gentleman, and such would he remain throughout the entire time that we lived together.

My suspicion was that there had been much more to the episode on the yacht than the three women had reported either to the police or to me. But I couldn't seem to sniff it out mentally. The women vehemently insisted that Just Joe was entirely to blame, that the monkey had been both insane and vicious when first brought aboard the yacht, but that the captain had not been sufficiently alert to detect this. Conse-

quently, they said, when the monkey got the desired opportunity, he had tried not only to kill them, but to wreck everything that he could on the yacht. The police report confirmed
this.

But I wasn't satisfied. Could it be, I wondered, that Just
Joe's violent behavior was a natural reaction to something
very wrong that had first been done to him and was being
kept secret? And how, I asked myself again and again without getting any satisfying answer, is it possible for such "mad-
ness and badness" so suddenly to appear in a monkey, and
then just as suddenly to disappear? Could it be, I even inquired of myself, that Just Joe is a kind of simian "Dr. Jekyll
and Mr. Hyde," and is accustomed to making such extraordinary changes in character and actions whenever he feels in
the mood to do so?

What I really needed in order to solve the intriguing mystery was Just Joe's version as to what it was that set all that
human-monkey trouble in motion. And incredible as it may
appear to those unfamiliar with such intercommunicating
between human and nonhuman forms of life, I got the facts
that I needed from Just Joe himself—not all at once, but
during a series of most unconventional interviews that I had
with him as he and I rode our old rocking-chair together in
balancing understanding and sharing. This was an action in
which that monkey and I were able to establish unspoken
speaking between us through the greatest of all languages—
the universal language of pure hearts. We were moving and
rocking, in tune, at once moving and rocking together.

During the interviews Just Joe would sit relaxed in my lap,
looking up into my face with an expression that always in-
dicated his keen alertness and interest, mentally as well as
visually. Then I would begin asking him questions, usually
without making vocal noises in my throat. The questions were

never aimed mentally downward at him as "a monkey," in the conventional and limiting meaning of that term, but always sent high and horizontally across to him as a rational fellow being. Having asked the question, I would then listen, as politely as possible, with all of me. And then, providing that I was properly childlike and receptive, I would always inwardly hear, like a gentle but distinct whisper, the answer that I needed.

The silent but effective correspondence that went on between Just Joe and myself, during those intimate sessions, was never the functioning of "a superior human brain in my skull" with "an inferior monkey brain in his skull." Just Joe and I, in that rather uncommon experience of ours, were individual inlets and outlets for the everywhere-present and everywhere-operating Mind of the universe—like rays of light and warmth in their relationship to the sun.

The more practiced I became in finding how to establish the right kind of two-way thought traffic with that monkey as a fellow state of consciousness, the easier it became for us to move along together in a mutuality of knowing ... of being ... of doing ... and of sharing. The easier it also became to speak silently to that monkey so that he could instantly understand me, and for him to speak silently to me so that I could instantly understand him. He and I were accomplishing, through the lovely and invaluable language of echoing heartbeats, a language that is ever moving from out of the silence, through the silence, and into the silence. But a language, I also had to learn, that can be spoken and heard only by those whose hearts are sufficiently pure for such cosmic intercommunicating.

The information that Just Joe silently shared with me during our interviews as to what had really started all the trouble on the yacht was so completely contrary to what the captain's wife and her two women relatives had reported that it demanded immediate investigation and verification. This I set in tactful as well as unsuspected motion during subsequent visits to the yacht. As part of my "detective work" I purposely said almost nothing at all about Just Joe, from my point of view, but gave the women plenty of opportunities to talk fully and freely about him. This they did with enthusiasm and competitivelike enmity, still regarding the little monkey as "a viciously bad and killingly dangerous nuisance."

As I carefully listened to what the three women said about Just Joe, with their condemning attitudes, I also gave close attention to what each of them was mentally saying about herself back of the vocal sounds. Then gradually, as I watched and listened to their totalities in this manner, and then sifted and analyzed the results, I came into possession of the corroborating facts that I was seeking. Now I knew that the version Just Joe had silently shared with me about the trouble on the yacht was the correct one—that the three women, and not he, were entirely responsible for it all.

What I was really experiencing in that special "detective work" of mine aboard the yacht was a penetrating look-see from a monkey's angle into the secret operation of undeclared mental warfare—a malicious and ruthless operation for mentally damaging and killing others . . . one that the members of the human species have been carrying on for centuries, not only against their own kind, but against nearly all other living things. . . a guerrillalike warfare that, while savage and deadly in its intentions and purposes, is usually carefully camouflaged behind "socially-correct" outer behavior patterns.

Just Joe had suddenly found himself the point of attack for one of those vicious undeclared mental wars. The women aboard the yacht were his enemy—three women who, while careful not to display it in their words and other actions, because of the captain, were constantly attacking the little monkey mentally, with their ugly and destructive ill will.

And here is the hidden plot of it all. When Just Joe was first presented to the captain by his seagoing friend, there was an immediate echoing back-and-forth between them of pure-toned heartbeats. A mutual overflowing of admiration, of respect, and of love. A blending of their total best. They invisibly shook hands with each other, so to speak, like the gentlemen they were, and became understanding friends, well illustrating the long-stated truism that right relations are possible outwardly only when they have first been made so inwardly.

The attitudes of the three women on the yacht were completely different. They loathed monkeys in general, and Just Joe in particular. They didn't want him on the yacht under any circumstances, but there was nothing they could do about it, as the captain's word was law, and he wanted the monkey aboard. Thus completely blocked outwardly, the women started their guerrillalike mental war against Just Joe —doing so by first putting sharp bayonets on their thoughts, and then jabbing and slashing the little fellow with those invisible weapons. Just Joe, who was highly sensitive to the vicious and cruel mental attacks, and who knew from whence they were coming and why, in self-protection became more and more unfriendly toward the three women.

Shortly after the captain's sudden departure that dramatically eventful morning, the invisible warfare between the three women and the little monkey broke out into the open and became visible. It began when one of the women was sweeping the deck. A very short distance away, Just Joe was sitting on top of his little house, but chained to it, watching her with wariness and suspicion. The woman, feeling free now that the captain was absent, began to lash out vocally and viciously at Just Joe, letting him have it with every uncomplimentary thing that she could think of.

Before she could finish all that she had in mind to say, Just Joe went into sudden action with a common and usually effective skill. Taking a deep breath, he spat at the woman, hitting her on the chin. Embarrassed and furious, the woman swung at him with the broom that she had in her hands. Just Joe wrenched the broom away from her and threw it aside. Then he leaped on one of her arms, and before hitting the deck again, had ripped off part of her dress. In frantic terror, and screaming with alarm, the woman ran back into the main cabin.

Some minutes later the three women emerged in their kind of objective battle formation. They began throwing all kinds of things at Just Joe, hoping thereby to damage him sufficiently "to teach him the lesson that he needed." The little fellow managed to avoid each object flung in his direction. Then, as best as he could, he began picking up each object and flinging it back at the women. In the midst of all this, Just Joe's chain broke under the jerking pressures that it was getting, and he was on the loose. The women raced back into the main cabin and closed all entrances. Just Joe rushed after them and tried to wrench off the cabin door. Failing to accomplish this, and by way of easing his resentment at what the women had done to him mentally and otherwise, Just Joe tried to wreck everything that he could on the deck.

Finally exhausted by his strenuous efforts, Just Joe had to quit. Then he went slowly out to the end of the bowsprit, which was as far away as he could get horizontally from the trouble scene. That gave the women the opportunity they needed for getting into the yacht's launch and hurrying ashore for police help. And it was at that point, too, that I rowed into the extraordinary adventure.

CHAPTER FIVE

NAKED BANANAS

The captain eventually returned to Newport, reclaimed his pet, and they moved to a distant city. This meant, of course, that I had to part with Just Joe. I knew at once how much I would miss that little monkey, who had taught me so many lessons about life and the secret of intercommunication between life's creatures, on whatever level of experience.

A few years after my social and educational experience with Just Joe, I was sent to Washington, D.C. as a special correspondent for a large newspaper syndicate. I arrived there with high enthusiasm and hope, but with a handicap that I wasn't aware of. I had been brought up in Rhode Island traditions, one of which was: when a man looks you straight in the eye and tells you something as fact you can believe him, and act accordingly.

Now I found myself in the wining and dining manipulations of official, political, social, lobbying Washington. There I interviewed all sorts of public people about all sorts of things, reporting what they told me to many thousands of newspaper readers.

The more I carried on my interviewing work in the Washington scene, the more I became aware, to my dismay, that certain important people had acquired the habit of juggling facts and falsehoods. The deception was usually so well camouflaged and so cleverly and subtly put across as to make the double-talk a kind of diabolical art. Ordinarily, once one got wise to this, one would listen to such a mixture of fact and fancy and then shrug it off with a mental yawn of boredom or disbelief. But I was making newspaper copy of this double-talk of professional politicians, and the kickbacks from my editors, as well as readers, was causing me much concern.

How does one really distinguish between fibs and facts during an important interview? I knew that there existed a solution to my problem, and that I would either have to find that solution, or probably be recalled as a Washington correspondent.

No matter how hard I tried with my various intellectual approaches, I couldn't find a demonstrable answer, and the situation was growing steadily worse. Then, in a manner as unconventional and delightful as it was amusing and revealing, I came into possession of "the magic secret."

A vivid memory picture came scooting across time and space from Newport, Rhode Island. The only performer in it was my pal and private tutor, little Just Joe the monkey. He was sitting solemnly on the ground, going through the ceremony of slowly and cautiously stripping the outer covering from a banana, as I had watched him do countless numbers of times.

Just Joe's neat technique for dealing with a banana, from the instant he got his hands on it until there was no more to be eaten, was as studious, as rhythmical, and as precise as it was effective in its results—one, too, that was always filled with valuable implications and suggestions for human borrowing purposes. For instance, I would appear in the large yard in Newport, where Just Joe and I spent so much time, with a banana hidden on me, but pretending that I didn't have one. Then, as part of this effort, I would make believe that I was very busy with certain important things that had to be attended to but which didn't concern him in the least. Never once did I fool him. He always identified my thoughts and purposes as accurately as though I were visibly enacting them.

Suddenly, without the least outer indication of what I was about to do, I would swing around from my "important business" and throw the banana at him. Sometimes its flight would be fast and straight. In other efforts it would curve to the right or left. Occasionally, it would go lofting and twisting above his head. But no matter what the banana's speed or curves happened to be, he never failed to make the catch. This often required extraordinary leaps into the air, as well as perfect timing of his reactive mind and little hands. Then he would instantly sit down on the ground, and with an eager expression on his wrinkled little face, would wait for me to say something complimentary about the manner in which he had come into possession of the flying fruit.

Following this, the more important part of the ceremony would take place. Clutching the banana with his feet, as well as his hands, Just Joe would begin turning it around and around in all directions. He inspected and appraised it as he did so—not only with his hands, his feet, and his eyes, but also with his nose, his ears, and his teeth, as the ultimate in cautiousness. Slowly and rhythmically, he would strip off the banana's outer covering, carefully squinting and sniffing at each part before tossing it aside. Having reduced the banana to its stark nakedness, he would give that part of the fruit an even more intimate going-over. And then, if thoroughly satisfied, he would begin eating it, with frequent swift glances in different directions for possible unsocial interruptions.

Now I had my clue. I realized at once that here was the answer to my burning question. Now I knew what to do with those diplomats and politicians in Washington. The image of little Joe sitting there peeling that banana had in it all the wisdom and action I needed for identifying who was or was not telling the exact truth during newspaper interviews. I knew that Just Joe had used on me that very technique the first time we ever met on that yacht in Newport Harbor. I came to realize that Just Joe was always using the same banana-denuding and evaluating technique on all humans he ever met. As as expert in such matters, he knew that both specimens—bananas and humans—had to be completely nakedized, for his own protection, and so he always did so both neatly and effectively.

To get the key to the men-monkey-and-mind triangle it is important to understand:

(1) that animals do operate with different mental processes than men;

(2) that men, the higher embracing the lower, can voluntarily include the wave length of the "minds" in the animal world;

(3) that both are aspects of the one Universal Mind; and

(4) that therein lies both the variety and the unity of mental activity from the lowest creatures, via monkeys, to men.

Little Just Joe was in explicit possession of what can be called "the reactive mind." He could not consciously remember even so simple a fact that only the inside of the banana was edible and that the skin was unfit for food. He had to go through the whole sensory process each time he came face-to-face with a banana. The advantage in this was that Just Joe's senses were kept utterly alert. The human in his reliance upon memory and reasoning leaves behind his reactive mind and tucks it away in the unconscious and allows his senses to become dull and his basic naturalness atrophied.

For all practical purposes, one marketable banana is much like another. Not so with humans. On the surface, and more so underneath, they retain vast varieties in personality. The conclusion is that a good reporter will keep his senses and the channels of his perception as keen and open when he meets a politician to interview as Just Joe did face-to-face with a new banana.

It is the pitfall of our species to let reliance on memory and "reasonableness" become fossilized into pet patterns that replace original and creative thinking. Men and women with patternized minds are forever busy and forever frustrated in trying to fit everyone they meet into these prefabricated patterns of the non-creative mind. This is, of course, fatal to the whole realm of relationships that could be so spontaneous, beautiful, fruitful, and satisfying for all of us.

CHAPTER SIX

TRANSPARENCIES

The endeavor to borrow and then practice the denuding and evaluating technique that Just Joe the monkey had so success-fully used on humans as well as on bananas set an assortment of adventures in motion that were as unpredictable as they were intimately revealing. The adventures began when I decided to try out that monkey method on myself. I stripped my own self mentally naked—reduced me to my bare es-sences. Then I took an honest and appraising squint at what was going on deep down in my thinking and character that motivated my vocal sounds as well as other channels of ex-pression. This enabled me to know more about myself, all the way through—a right preparation before going to work on others in the same manner.

One day, as I continued with this strictly *private* detective work that had to do with my unseen individuality and what went on therein, I was gently reminded, "from out of no-where," of a most important and needed bit of wisdom. It was tucked inside nine words that I had read many times before but had forgotten to remember. For my own greater good they now came back to me: "Blessed are the empty, for they shall be filled."

At this point it became abundantly clear to me why I was so far behind Just Joe the monkey in being able to identify accurately what others were invisibly up to, back of their outer appearances, vocal sounds, and other actions. I wasn't sufficiently empty. Was too full of myself. Was overstuffed with my own beliefs, supposings, and opinions. Consequently, there wasn't sufficient room within me for much of anything else to get in. And it had to get inside first, like a seed, before it could expand me into greater understanding . . . certainty . . . experience . . . and usefulness.

To remedy this, I formulated three disciplines for myself. The first: try to keep myself as empty as possible, so there would always be plenty of room for fresh wisdom and knowledge to flow in. The second: try to function more with the childlike attitude, with its integrated genuineness . . . its humility . . . its willingness to be taught by everything . . . its natural receptivity . . . and its enthusiasm for sharing. And the third: to listen more attentively to intuitive whisperings, with their accompanying unfoldments, as that little monkey had so instinctively and expertly done throughout the time that he and I had lived together.

Thus for my greater good and expansion, and with a delightful blending of whimsy and reality flavoring it, did I start along the unique educational trail of seeking to become somewhat less of a human, and somewhat more of a human. It was "monkey business" at its topmost levels. It also afforded exceptional opportunities for mentally rising above human densities, with their pet illusions and chronic confusions. Then I experienced the fun and satisfaction of finding the real meaning and purpose in each encountered component of life—even when that component happened to be a monkey who wasn't physically present at the time. But it was an effort that demanded the strictest secrecy and discipline at the time because of the surrounding "squinting eyes and bending bows."

As part of the adventurous quest, I always tried to keep my concept of Just Joe completely outside and above all conventional human opinions having to do with monkeys. I tried to think of him only in his best qualities, as an individual and unlimited state of consciousness, rather than as a very limited biological item inside of a little furry skin casing. The more I did this, even though we seemed to be separated by time and space, the more aware I became of our inseparability as mental fellow beings in the forever kinship and oneness of all life, presided over by the one Mind. I became more aware, too, that regardless of all human opinions and seemings to the contrary, Just Joe and I were illimitable ideas, needed in the eternally functioning plan and divine purpose.

When Just Joe and I lived together in Newport, experiencing the delight of beginning to discover each other in our totalities, my thinking about him, as well as my experience with him, had been mostly objective. But quite some time afterward, in Washington, I began to know him more subjectively. I was finding a more realistic way to identify with him mentally and spiritually, beyond obstructing physicality. The more I succeeded in this, the more Just Joe began disappearing from my consciousness as "a monkey" in the restricting biological meaning of that term, and the more he began appearing there in his real nature, as an idea—a cooperating idea.

From that more inclusive and realistic point of recognition it became increasingly easier to understand how it was that that monkey always seemed to know whatever he needed to

know, whenever he needed to know it. It was survival consciousness. This he had without the least bit of education,
without needing to read "how-to" books about it. The "secret" of it—as I had somewhat sniffed-out before—was as
simple as it was profound and effective. Just Joe had not been
dependent upon a private, independent, and separate mind
of his own to tell him what to do and when and how to do
it. He functioned as a reflection, or expression, of the Mind
of the universe. He did this as naturally and as easily as
breathing. He was in full possession of "the reactive mind,"
something we analytically-minded humans have left behind,
to our private and collective hurt. It is difficult for most humans to understand this "reactive mind." It is lost along the
intellectually fogged-up earth levels, except to those with
eyes to see and hearts to understand.

The common practice of most humans is to separate, judge,
and evaluate—from an ego position—then deal with one another almost entirely in externals. They are busy trying to
create impressions—by outwardly displayed personality
effects, by vocal sounds, by visual sights. "How much have
they got?" is an ever-recurring question. Not so, however,
with Just Joe the monkey. Being the smart little philosopher
that he was, he always insisted, as a preliminary and protec-
tive action, upon finding out just what was going on behind
the scenes . . . what was invisibly motivating all phases from
behind the fronting that the observed human was putting on
for the occasion. Joe always managed to acquire this intimate
information through his effective detective work, in mentally
sniffing-out supposedly well-concealed motives and purposes. With those inner facts at his disposal, he could best
react to the situation outwardly.

Just Joe, I was now coming more clearly to understand, had
always depended upon his inborn, natural and wisdom-

reflecting intuition for whatever he needed to know and do. He had listened as best he could to the gentle inner whisperings of the universal Mind. He watched humans inwardly as well as outwardly, at one and the same time.

The more that I pondered those interesting and revealing facts the more obvious it became why it was that Just Joe had had to use his denuding skill on humans as well as on bananas. It was to distinguish between the good and the bad in each specimen, for his own protection. With a banana, he carefully and studiously peeled off the outer covering to know what the hidden fruit was like. With a human he mentally, and with more studious care, peeled off all the latter's outer personality effects to see what he was really like on the inside. Then with those inner facts at his disposal, he knew how best to react in all cases.

Without ever having been taught anything about it, Just Joe, I now recalled with new interest, had always moved in harmony and rhythm with a powerful universal law. It is a law that most humans have forgotten to remember, to their great disadvantage, especially in their contacts with other living things. It is a law that has been well translated into these words: Inner causes of necessity produce outer effects, and these effects must of necessity declare the exact nature, reason, and purpose of those inner causes. Unless they do, the effects are phoney, which is not difficult to detect with the inner eye.

Just Joe had always been a keen observer, as well as practitioner, of the potent and far-reaching rule of cause-and-effect. He had applied this rule instinctively in every visual, mental, and physical contact that he made. He always mentally squinted through every observed outer effect and deep into its inner causes, and he did this most intensely.

The various dualistic humans who happened to come

within his range of awareness—those who were often pretending to be one kind of person on the outside, but actually were the opposite on the inside, and that, for personally gainful reasons—were stripped to their cores, like Just Joe's bananas.

As I reached this point in my inner listening and hearing, there was a profound silence for some minutes. Then suddenly, as a fitting climax to the occasion, some precious wisdom came gently gliding back again into my memory, wisdom that had a most significant bearing on what I had been rethinking about little Just Joe and his amazing skill in evaluating humans in their totalities. It was wisdom that had been uttered centuries ago by the far-visioning philosopher Plotinus. And what that rare one pulled out of the generally unfamiliar at the time, for sharing purposes, was this: "In the intellectual world everything is transparent, and all the essences see one another and interpenetrate one another in the most intimate depths of their natures."

CHAPTER SEVEN

DEEP SEE-GOING

It was at that point that I decided to make a radical change in my newspaper reporting methods. I would borrow the denuding and evaluating techniques that Just Joe had used so successfully and begin using it on my celebrities.

Most newspaper reporting follows a more-or-less common pattern, pivoting around the objective rather than the subjective. It is a writing mold geared to the superficial and sensational. While interviewing, the reporter's interest is generally concentrated on the outer act that the celebrity is putting on for the occasion. The average reporter, with a trained nose for news, is like a bird dog. He is alert for anything that will appeal to the crowd-minded and imitators, stir up their feelings and imaginations, and then astonish and shock them.

Up to the time of my Washington assignment, most of my newspaper work had been along that line of surface stuff that is supposed to sell papers. But now, in Washington, with a dawning sense of responsibility toward my readers, considering the political significance of my interviews, I was compelled to become more subjective in what I was looking at, listening to, and then writing about. This meant to listen with the inner ear as well as the outer ear, to listen *through*, which is to Listen 100 per cent. It meant to listen to the thought quality in the voice of the one who was speaking. In this way, I was keyed to discovering the character of the man I was facing as reporter. It was Disraeli, British statesman, who said: "There is no index to character so sure as the voice."

Listening 100 per cent was the "chief fundamental" of the inspired "Adult Re-education" work via voice training, the work of Emma Dunn, as set forth in her book *Thought Quality in the Voice*, appearing first as a series in *The Christian Science Monitor*. Her many years of teaching the rules of verbal inspiration—showing that inspiration has its rules—was to benefit many public lecturers and to influence untold numbers of students both in the United States and Great Britain. While not on lecture tours, she was playing mother parts to Gary Cooper, Lew Ayres (Dr. Kildare series, with Lionel Barrymore), and many other parts in Hollywood, where both of us had finally settled. I had first met her, in line of duty, when interviewing her for a Kansas City paper as the outstanding star of the David Belasco Theatre, on tour. So deeply was I impressed by the utter sincerity of the woman in her, and the utter artistry of her performances (playing Ase at the age of eighteen to Richard Mansfield's *Peer Gynt*), that I gave her the title of "Duse of America." We remained lifelong friends.

Listening 100 per cent also implies "listening" with the eyes, to watch for facial expressions which sometimes contradict what the voice says out loud. It means to become discerning to the way in which a person moves—to get a feel for the rhythm of another human being. Of course, all this was natural to Just Joe, but it seems that humans, with their sensibilities dulled and the "portals of their perception" clogged with secondary fractured and unrelated bits of misinformation (thanks largely to our contemporary educational system), have to be retrained or know how to retrain themselves, to find out what's going on behind the scenes. The youth of today seem to understand all this when they talk about "good vibrations" and "bad vibrations."

During the time that Just Joe and I lived together in Newport, various kinds of people came to call. The instant one of them arrived for the first time, my little associate would always quit whatever he happened to be doing and focus his entire attention on the "suspect." For "suspect" the visitor definitely was to the monkey until he had been cleared by monkey "intelligence." Within seconds, and often with no more than a sweeping glance, Just Joe would have mentally added and subtracted the "suspect" into a correct total. Then, having processed the visitor, and with continuing alerted caution, he was poised for what he knew was apt to follow.

What was it that so swiftly took place in him, in a kind of animal computer process of the "reactive mind"? What sort of information did Just Joe the monkey feed into his inbuilt computer to get such amazingly correct answers about the totality of any specific human—information that served as a basis of unerring, unequivocal, and uncompromising reactions? I was puzzled. Why was it that we humans, as a whole, with all our boasted superiority and strut, were not more proficient in matters of this kind for our own greater good?

At first, the more that I explored and pondered Just Joe's "intelligence," along with the remarkable things that I had watched him accomplish with it, the more of an enigma he became. What all along puzzled me was how it ever came to be, in the "plan of things," that a supposedly inferior form of life like that monkey was so far ahead of me, a supposedly vastly superior form of life in so many important things having to do with our everyday living. And most particularly, how was it that Just Joe had acquired such far-beyond-human ability in knowing how to move his body about as he did, with such superlative coordination, agility, speed, harmony, rhythm, fun, satisfaction, and sharable delight?

Obviously, there was much more that I needed to learn about monkeys in general, and Just Joe in particular. But how to go about it in a practical rather than theoretical way? Just Joe, with his ability to teach through the persuasiveness of his silent, fine example was no longer physically present. And there was no one among the members of my own species that I dare consult about such an unconventional situation. Then suddenly, from out of the proverbial blue, a plan suggested itself. I decided to take all intellectual clamps off my thinking. With the memory of Just Joe leading the way, and my intuitive faculties wide open to receive, I would carefully listen to what was inwardly whispered to me, and then follow that whispering, regardless of where it led.

Although I set the plan in immediate motion, I didn't get far with it, except into more bewildering uncertainties. I wondered what was causing the obstruction. Then, as had happened once before in a similar predicament, I began to find out. It was I again! No one else, nothing else. I had forgotten to take the intellectual clamps sufficiently off my habitual thinking. As a result, I was intellectually groping about in the wilderness of the suppositional, the delusive, and the unreal. I had been trying to gather in fresh and needed wisdom, by way of expanding my awareness, with an already made-up human mind—caught in its own intellectualizations and rationalizations. As a result, I had fogged-up the entire situation for myself.

At this point in the exploratory adventure, I was abruptly knocked off my self-elevated ego perch, hitting the bottom of my state of awareness with a thud that still reverberates in consciousness. It was as dramatic as it was bewildering. It was also, I subsequently came to find, one of the best things that ever happened to me. For having thus been reduced to a "lowly and meek" state of mind, in the cosmic significance of those two wonderful terms, I found myself in a position where I had to begin thinking and living anew. I had reached the bottom of the valley. Now I had myself definitely heading toward "the mount of vision" where one can begin to see creation as the Creator sees it.

The more I succeeded in expanding my outlook and actions, and my experience, in the direction of "the mount of vision," the more I found myself moving through a fascinating as well as most illuminating and revealing paradox. Only as one humbly descends with all of himself into the valley of humility can he possibly ascend, with all of himself—through "the mist that went up from the earth"—to "the mount of vision." Here we can find the enduring harmony, peace, joy, and satisfaction that we have long been seeking in vain, by striving for effects rather than by searching for causes. We are living too much on the fringe of ourselves, floundering about, fractured and frustrated, in mere superficialities, instead of being at home *inside* first.

I had begun, at last, to lay hold of this precious gift of man, the creative imagination—rooted in a redemption of the senses. This is something the computer will never have. It implies a deeper sense of awareness and appreciation, tangibly companioned by deeper *breathing*, which is synonymous with deeper *thinking*, and analogous to a state of inspiration (*in-spirare*, L. to be in breath.) I had succeeded, to some extent, in cleansing the channels of the perception. It was William Blake, the great English mystic poet and artist, who had written: "If the portals of the perceptions were cleansed, everything would appear as it really is—infinite."

CHAPTER EIGHT

SECRET OPERATION

Of the countless numbers of various kinds of people that I interviewed, not only in Washington but subsequently all over the world, not one of them even remotely suspected that he was being monkey-processed. He was being stripped mentally naked, for inner as well as outer evaluating purposes, and for more accurate reporting. Nor were any of them ever aware, as they talked fully, freely, and usually flatteringly about themselves, that they were unconsciously parading back and forth in front of me, in a state of complete mental nudity—like an animated but completely stripped banana.

With all their intellectual equipment, their opportunities for observation and experience, and their pride and satisfaction both in and with themselves, practically every one of those many hundreds of interviewed people had failed to discover a most important fact about himself. Their thinking and feelings, as well as their motives and purposes, were actually as much on display, and more so, than anything they were doing, or could do, to outer appearances.

The more diligently I used Just Joe's banana technique, the easier it became mentally to strip off the usually cleverly-managed personality effects and wrappings of the one being interviewed. Then I noted what was inwardly causing his outwardly expressed vocal sounds and other modes of expression. This made it easy to add and substract him into his correct total. Then I could write about him as such, rather than in mere fragments of a displayed personality. All of this continuously illustrated, with all sorts of surprising revelations, the wisdom-warning sounded long ago by "the great Galilean" when he said: "There is nothing covered, that shall not be revealed, nor hid, that shall not be known."

It wasn't necessary to depend upon any intellectual efforts of my own in order to make in-depth interviewing with the banana technique the success it became. What I had to do was to set my human intellect aside and substitute for it the right inner and outer monkey attitude. From that point of vantage, and with all of me as wide open to receive as possible, I would intuitively watch and listen. Then, providing that I was sufficiently attentive and receptive, the withinness of the one being watched and interviewed for publication would begin silently to emerge and reveal itself. This was done through every vocal sound, every physical gesture, and everything else that he did, or omitted to do.

The more that I got into the continuously revealing adventure, with my monkey-borrowed banana technique, the better acquainted I became with an important but much-overlooked language—that of unspoken speaking. This is a language that the wise ancients were highly effective in using, not only with one another but with all other living things, too—a language which, in its purity and soundlessness, contains the utmost in expression . . . loveliness . . .

eloquence ... scope ... potency ... and results. It is a language that is as easy to speak, as well as to hear, across great distances as it is in intimate closeness. But it is a language, too, that can cause incalculable damage whenever it is spoken from an impure heart.

This unspoken language I found most important to watch carefully in subsequent contacts that I made with various minds of animals, birds, snakes, insects, and other nonhuman forms of life. Every one of those nonhuman fellows, I came to discover, began hearing my unspoken speaking, and especially what I was silently saying about them, the instant that we made visual contact with one another. Then having accurately heard what I was inwardly saying about them, each, in its own particular way, had reacted accordingly. Until I had learned better, this caused me to blame them for the things I myself had mentally started and was keeping in motion.

Just Joe's banana technique became ever more helpful as it gently but effectively revealed to me the inner facts I needed to know. As the one being interviewed and I faced each other for the reporting ritual, I would outwardly set in motion the customary ebb and flow of questions and answers. During this, I would listen carefully to everything that was vocally aimed in my direction. But as I did so, and without the least sag in my outer attention, I would mentally strip off his outer personality effects, like the outer skin of a banana. Then I would take an evaluating look at what was invisibly motivating his visible actions and their accompanying vocal sounds.

As my outer observation followed the visible performance of the one being interviewed, so my inner observation gave careful heed to what was going on in the supposedly invisible part of him. The banana technique would be in full operation. Then the total facts about him would silently, but most realistically, announce themselves—in the various details of his biological appearance ... in the clothes he had on and the way he was wearing them ... in his choice of words and how he spoke them ... in his easily perceptible ego vibrations ... in the mental atmosphere he was diffusing through everything that he thought, said, and did. And so the degree in which his interest and actions were either flowing out and along with life, or turned deliberately inward for self-satisfaction and personal gain, was laid bare before me.

This intimate identification at one and the same time of the unseen as well as seen individuality of the person being interviewed could be successfully done, however, only when my "inner ear" was really open to hear, and my "inner eye" really open to see. Then, providing that the rest of me was properly attuned and receptive, wisdom-filled impressions would begin to arrive in my awareness, like gentle but distinct whispers. And in those impressions would be whatever I needed to know, for correct interpreting purposes, about the one being interviewed. Never once were any of those inner whispers wrong. They couldn't have been. They were part of "the forgotten language"—that language which the Mind of the universe is ever speaking through all life, for the greater good of all living creatures, all the time.

Whenever I became sufficiently childlike and receptive in the true meaning of those cosmic terms, I always found myself in rapport with the omnipresent and omniactive Mind of the universe. Then it would become easily possible to hear silently whatever I needed to know about the person, situation, or whatever else it was that required my reporting attention. And those silent communications always appeared to be as boundless in their scope, their value, their meaning, and their purpose as was their eternal Source. It was individual, trustable counseling that was indescribably beyond all sen-

sory methods, as well as beyond all such negations as chance
. . . uncertainty . . . insufficiency . . . and failure.

What I was actually experiencing in this unusual adventure were the belated results of the important lessons that Just Joe had been trying to teach me silently throughout the time that we lived together. These lessons pivoted around the generally overlooked fact that regardless of our forms of species identification, the unseen individuality of each one of us living items is as much on public display as our seen individuality. We are all unavoidably moving about, mentally naked, in a universe of mental nudists. It is a situation in which nothing about one's inner self can be really hidden from vigilant observation. This is what that little monkey pal and tutor of mine had been such an expert in knowing, demonstrating, and teaching.

CHAPTER NINE

MASQUERADE

At the end of my assigned time as a special correspondent in Washington, I had the fortunate experience of being turned loose as a roving reporter. I was free to go anywhere I pleased in the world, and to write about anything I pleased—providing, of course, that what I typed into newspaper copy was satisfying to my editors. This, of course, made a reporting experience that was exciting, fascinating, and unpredictable. Almost anything could happen and usually did. And what sparked and provided most of the helpful significance was the monkey-banana technique that I used not only on the people who talked to me for publication, but also on things and events. I stripped them all down to their bare essences for total observation, evaluating, and reporting.

The more this roving reporter adventure expanded, and the more practiced I became in identifying people in their unseen, as well as seen individualities, the more I came to find myself an intimate observer. I could slip "behind the scenes," so to speak, of the greatest show on earth—humanity unmasked. It is the most extraordinary and, at times, incredible show throughout the entire planetary system. It is the unrehearsed show that is being put on day and night, in all parts of the world, by the members of the human species. It is an endless parade of private as well as public exhibitions —drama, farce, burlesque, tragedy, and more—the very stuff evolution is made of. It is an unceasing and flamboyant spectacle in which just about everything that the human mind can imagine, and human bodies can do, becomes part of the production—the onward march of time on the upward path of timeless ideas.

When one watches a performance from out front, within the walls of a theater, one outwardly sees "realities" in words and actions. But inwardly observed, he knows that what he is visually following and listening to with the outer ear is all carefully planned and rehearsed. It is make-believe staged for his benefit and for possible profit. Drama is pretendings that have been deliberately set to words and acts, charged with emotion, to capture and hold his attention, to stir up his imagination and feelings to peak proportions. The plan is to win his attention, his admiration, and applause for this make-believe, and thereby also help ticket sales at the box office. The spectator who views this same performance from behind the scenes, from the wings, experiences a different view. It may be the exact reverse. He sees the manipulations, the tricks, and the many clever devices that are being used to make all that pretending "out front" seem genuine and sincere. That much greater becomes one's appreciation for the mere handful of actors and actresses of genius that appear like stars in the theatrical heavens of any given age.

Most of the world-show that I was professionally watching in my roving reporting was in the nature of a vast public masquerade—a masquerade with unlimited theatrical flavorings and displays that I was carefully noting "from behind the scenes," as well as "from out front." In these masquerad-ings each observed performer was using every skill at his command to attract all possible attention to himself, both for ego satisfaction and for some kind of personal gain. After all, favorable publicity is big business. The one being inter-viewed was often trying to operate successfully with one kind of behavior patterns on the outside, for approving pub-lic attention, and contradictory behavior patterns on the in-side, for "strictly private" reasons.

I met quite an assortment of those public and private mas-queraders in the various countries that I visited. Nearly all of them were listed as "important" and "influential" in their particular areas. Many had a place in *Who's Who*. My inter-views with them were, as a rule, formally arranged for me, and then just as formally carried out. But as our vocal sounds went into the customary interaction for such occasions, I would invisibly go to work with my monkey-borrowed ba-nana technique. Not everyone that I interviewed via the banana technique was participating in the public mas-querade for personal acclaim and private gain; but frankly speaking, most were. It was an easily observable phenome-non almost everywhere I went—a manner of human behavior that was deeply set in a prefabricated success formula: First, acquire all possible external cleverness, a bagful of tricks; then smartly, ruthlessly if necessary, grab all that can be pried loose, and amass it; then, holding on to the accumula-tion of some form of matter against all other greedy grabbers of things, try to corner the market; set up some sort of monopoly to milk the public. This contemporary curse, these deadening dynamics of the rat race are in accord with the obsolete notion, rejected by a growing portion of our youth, that it is more important to make a good living than to live a good life—for oneself and for the sake of others. The wise men of all ages have considered this antiquated chase after externalities, this modernism built upon a sound profit motive degenerated into a sick profiteering motive, as a waste of time and energy. As the writer of Ecclesiastes so succinctly put it: "All is vanity and vexation of spirit"—in the realm of getting and spending, of hold-up and hoarding. When all is said and done, "You can't take it with you." I am equally certain that the *qualities* we train for, possess and express, such as sincerity and generosity, we can take with us—when we change our worlds.

From my point of observation, the cleverly arranged disguises that those public masqueraders were using, in their competitive efforts to outdazzle and outdo one another by way of acquiring all possible wealth, fame, and influence for themselves, was educational as well as challenging. Educational were the intimately revealing studies into human artifice and cunning. And challenging it surely was to have to decide, just how to handle, or not to handle, such disrobed facts in newspaper copy. Each of those interviewed public masqueraders was operating almost entirely in externals. Their values were outer ones, the kind that they could identify and exploit with their physical senses. To them the physical and material were the important things in life. All the rest, they believed, was for "impractical dreamers."

Although reporting about important people, places, and events was the primary demand upon me by my editors, my favorite method for acquiring unusual and appealing newspaper copy was quite unorthodox. Without any set plans, I would quietly slip away from wherever I happened to be, in whatever country it was, and then go wherever the intuitive winds blew me, either near or far. Then whenever my inner and outer eye would identify some particular person as a promising one to talk with for publication, I would always do so. In not one of those instances did I know who the person was, or anything else about him. I simply went with my inner seeing, and its accompanying whisper—and the successful results always followed as a natural consequence.

Having come into mutually visible contact with the stranger, I would inwardly, as well as outwardly, bow my sincere respect and goodwill in his direction. To this mental approach there would always be a gracious response in one way or another. Then I would usually ease us into conversation by asking a question about some nearby object that I knew he could explain. This, in turn, would set up an invisible bridge between us for two-way thought traffic. Our hearts and understanding would be in tune and in time not only with each other, but also in harmony and rhythm with life itself. And out of this would always come exceptionally fine material for sharing purposes via newsprint.

Since most individuals are evaluated by the customary standard wherein wealth and fame, regardless of how acquired, are usually considered the real signs of achievement and worth, all the strangers that I met and interviewed in this manner were "nobodies at all"—not worth that kind of attention and effort. None of them had ever been considered important enough before to have anything written about him for publication. Nor did any of them have any tangible possessions that would have been the least bit envied by conventional-minded observers.

A delightful and thought-provoking paradox always went skipping along with this phenomenon. Of the many hundreds of people in different countries that I first watched in action and then depth-interviewed, the most successful ones—that is, those who were demonstrating genuine happiness, joy, satisfaction, and peace of mind—were those "nobodies with nothing." Not the "famous ones with everything." And by an unforgettable turn in the paradox, the most satisfying material for the editor and the reader alike, that I managed to acquire throughout my entire reporting career, came not from widely publicized personalities that I talked with professionally, but from those simple, humble, most refreshing "nobodies."

The fresh wisdom and knowledge that those "nobodies" shared with me seldom came from anything that any of them had heard, read, or been taught, but from within their own individual selves. From listening to the intuitive whisperings of the infinite Mind of the universe, and then acting accordingly, they had found themselves. From the natural radiations of their own distinct but unseen individuality they had something genuine to share. From a pure heart each was sending forth his song of himself as simply and naturally as he was breathing—as birds do their song and as flowers send forth their fragrance. There are vibrations as perceptibly felt in their gentle impact as they are easy to interpret rightly after the impact has been made.

To meet with an understanding heart one of those "nobodies with nothing" was always like coming in contact with a fresh, salty sea breeze—experiencing the exhilarating and bettering effects of it. Through pioneering efforts in their own individual states of consciousness, each had discovered for himself how to maintain a maximum of happiness, fun, and satisfaction while riding the earth's merry-go-round about the sun. And they had learned to establish the right inner as well as outer interrelations with the other earth-riding passengers they met—regardless of forms, species identifications, or reputations.

Their "secret" for such rare accomplishments was as simple as it was profound and far-reaching. Each of them loved living, and loved everything living that he met, while casting the gentle radiance of his own sweet significance upon things without life.

CHAPTER TEN

TOPSY-TURVY WORLD

During my global reporting I had to encounter a human world that was prodigiously on the loose . . . a world rushing frantically through dramatic changes that were often as difficult to keep up with as they were difficult to interpret adequately into newspaper copy. It was a period of dense mental fog and accompanying low visibility in which the general atmosphere was saturated with selfishness . . . insincerity . . . dishonesty . . . disillusionment . . . and despair. It was a period when, as seldom before, in nearly all public activities defectives were performing for other fascinated defectives, and being highly paid and honored for it. It was a time, too, that was vibrating to the clashes and crashes caused by an ever-widening breakdown in morals, ethics, good taste, and gracious manners.

Along with numberless other professional observers, my editors were greatly disturbed by the downward-skidding trend in local, national, and world conditions. To them almost everything was not only in a deplorable and alarming state, but was rapidly worsening. So as part of my reporting assignment I was requested to interview as many different kinds of people as possible, and find out not only what they thought was to blame for the generally bad world conditions, but how best to correct them. The private opinion of my editors, but subject to change if they could be convinced, was that modern civilization was not only decadent, but speeding toward a total eclipse.

Almost every one of the many hundreds of persons in different countries that I subsequently interviewed about the disturbing human behavior had ready answers and remedies for all of it. By an amusing as well as a revealing coincidence, each of them placed the blame on some particular personality that he didn't like at all or on some particular group that he didn't belong to or like either. Then having indicted the other fellow or fellows for their local, national, or world misconduct, the interviewee would generally go into guerrilla-like action against them, with hate-filled, damaging thoughts and words.

The zeal for placing the blame for whatever was wrong in the human scene on the other fellow was exceedingly popular almost everywhere. As a particular person talked for publication, he first pruned the behavior patterns of the one being criticized. Then the speaker would make him over into his own image and likeness, and, if possible, control the person's thinking as well as other actions. And always there was the proud implication that the one being interviewed was far better qualified to live the life of the one he was condemning, than the latter was himself.

I was not in entire agreement with the pessimistic opinions of most of the people that I interviewed. My own feelings were that regardless of all viewpoints and seemings to the contrary, an understanding, friendly, and cooperating world was both possible and practical—not only between all kinds of humans, but between humans and all other living things, not in some vague future, but in the immediate here and now. Just how this was to happen was not quite clear at the time, for I was having to meet a common challenge—navigating myself through the confusions and contradictions of centuries of wrong guessing about the real meaning and purpose of life, and how each of us fits into its cosmic plan.

Then, within a short space of time, I had two unforgettable interviews that provided rare and illuminating breakthroughs in my reporting quest. One took place on top of a lonely mountain in the Orient, the other in a jungle. Neither of the individuals had ever before talked to anyone for publication. As a matter of fact, neither of them was the least bit aware that he was being thus processed when I went to work on him. Conventionally evaluated, each was not supposed to know much of anything, about anything, that was really worth listening to and then passing along, especially in printed words.

The man on top of the mountain was sitting cross-legged on the ground when I unexpectedly walked into his presence. The palms of his hands were together just below his chin. His closed eyes opened as he heard me. I had interrupted him in his meditations. His smile and gracious bow were a welcome and a blessing in one movement. He invited me to join him on the ground. I did so. As he was able to speak my variety of vocal language, our thinking and words began flowing back and forth in a refreshing mutuality of interest and understanding. His intimate knowledge of world conditions was amazing, and so was the gentle, penetrating wisdom. He was an exceptional find.

For some time we talked analytically about the serious sag in moral and ethical human behavior throughout the world, and of its damaging consequences.

Then I asked him if he thought it would ever be possible

for the members of the human species throughout the world to get out of their disorders, confusion, strife, destruction, misery, and the rapid deterioration of human relationships. He smiled and nodded reassuringly. He had no doubt of it. "How?" I asked. I recalled, as I did so, how almost everyone else had recommended drastic action against some particular person or group for whom he had a carefully cultivated enmity.

He closed his eyes and for some minutes kept the lids down. When he opened them again he looked across at me, and said in his gentle, soft-spoken manner: "There is only one way in which it can be done, and that is by individual purification and refinement. As each of us improves himself, he helps the world just that much. As he neglects to improve himself, he holds the world back just that much."

That observation will long reverberate in galleries of my memory. And while that humble and almost naked little fellow was never aware of it, his wisdom-filled words reached many thousands of people all over the world—through the printed word, radio, and person-to-person sharing. That little "nobody with nothing," but richly equipped with a pure heart and its corresponding clear vision, had set an incalculable amount of good in motion by simply "letting his light shine."

The second of these unconventional interviews was with a philosopher of the jungle. I had been wandering about in an African jungle, curious, fascinated. Suddenly, a native and I turned the same bend on the same trail, from opposite directions. All outer movements in each of us instantly stopped. Before I could think what to do next, he smiled. I smiled back. We started finding and sharing ourselves in remarkable degree. From that time on, for as long as I was in that part of the jungle, he and I were almost inseparable.

My newly acquired friend had lived in the jungle for over forty years. During this time he had mastered, to a superlative degree, the science and art of right relations. As a result, he could instantly establish silent good correspondence with every living thing he met. To him every form of life that he encountered was both an admired and good neighbor, even those classified as "exceedingly dangerous and deadly." And as far as I was able to observe, they were all treating him as an admired and good neighbor, too.

My friend's skill in knowing how to get along happily with wild animals, birds, snakes, insects, and kindred fellows was so intriguing that I began to find out, whenever possible, what he did to make such extraordinary relationship results so mutually successful. It wasn't easy at first, owing to the fact that neither of us could understand the other's national language. So what we had to depend on was an improvised sign language, and alerted inner listening, hearing, seeing, and understanding.

Gradually, through outer observation and intuitive listening, and with no intellectual theories or opinions permitted to get in the way and fog up needed unfoldings, I managed to discover his "magic secret." When he and a wild animal, for instance, came into visual contact with each other for the first time, they would both instantly stop and become as motionless as statues. Then they looked across at each other with almost expressionless faces. For the conventional observer it would be a dramatic and shivery experience—one in which he would wonder which of them would do the most deadly damage to the other.

But neither bodily damage nor any killing would result from that unexpected meeting between those two supposedly implacable enemies. Instead, it would be the beginning of a swift balance in inner as well as outer interrelations.

How did they reestablish the fraternal linkage between them? As the odd tableau between them started, that untaught but exceedingly wise little jungle man would instantly go into his invisible but most effective action. With his thinking filled with genuine admiration, respect, and love for the wild animal, he would identify it with its best qualities. Then in the same rhythmical action he would blend his own best qualities with the animal's.

In this manner those two seemingly unrelatable jungle dwellers would successfully bridge across to each other. Through the universal language of echoing pure heartbeats they would thus establish silent and mutually helpful correspondence between them. Then as man and animal carefully listened to the inner whisperings of the Mind of the universe, they would each intuitively know what best to do about whatever needed to be done. Both as distinct individuals and as a two-legged and four-legged twosome, they would enter the path of peace and survival.

CHAPTER ELEVEN

DRUMBEATS

Three special interests always accompanied me, roaming the world as a reporter looking for the unusual to write about. The first: to explore, with a friendly curiosity, the inner significance and purpose of all encountered phenomena, whether person, place, or thing. The second: to find out all that I could about "the lost linkage" that innately holds all life together in kinship and oneness. And the third: to listen to drumbeats.

Why I was so interested in listening to drums that I often went far out of my way to do so puzzled me at first. I always found inspiration in the exhilarating things those sounds did to me all the way through. No other instruments were needed upon those occasions, as far as I was concerned—just a single drum, or an assortment of them. There was one exception: whenever I was privileged to "sit in the lap of Mother Earth" with some of my American Indian friends, I would also listen to exquisitely lovely sound poetry produced by a flute and drum.

Although I was unable to explain the mystery of it, I could

always sense a fascinating and revealing language spoken through every drumbeat that I heard. It is language filled with important tonal symbols, and their meanings are the most primitive. Whenever any kinds of drummings were to take place, I always tried to be there. Then, figuratively speaking, I would sit at the feet of the performers as attentive as possible.

Each drummer I listened to expressed values in living that were bubbling deep within himself and demanding outer expression for sharing. Each of them was thumping his feelings through his instrument, in the universal language of drumbeat. Here is an ancient method of communicating that vibrates with the basic rhythm of all languages, that of pure sound. It is a language impossible to understand unless one's intellect is turned off and his intuitive faculties, his instincts, and his primitive feelings are turned full-on.

Many of the drums that I listened to with facinated interest were sounded across to me in various parts of the United States. In American Indian territory the drum has always played an important ceremonial part in group activities. I also listened to their rhythmic beat in many European, African, and Oriental countries. I heard drumbeats on faraway and almost deserted mountains, in jungles, and on lovely, fragrant South Sea Islands. I heard the vibrant pulsebeat in many places where people were experiencing perfect coordination through the joy-filled rhythms of the beating of drums.

The drums used during those various occasions were made of all kinds of materials, and were just about as diversified in size and design as they were in decorative effects. At one end of the assortment were drums that had been made from tree trunks and were a dozen feet or more in length. The tribal drums required at least a dozen men to lift and then aim them in the desired direction. They were always beaten with padded clubs in order to produce the loudest possible booming effects. At the other end of the assortment were all sorts of small drums, some of them made from tiny shells and so delicate that they had to be gently tapped by a fingertip. Between these two extreme groupings were all sorts of various-sized drums. Some of them were soft-spoken drums for inspirational purposes, and others were loud-speaking drums for emotional and physical stimulation, for warnings, and for warfare.

Sometimes the drummer would straddle his drum, like "Riding a cockhorse to Banbury Cross." From that vantage point he would start his drum saying things for him that he couldn't possibly have expressed in either vocal or written language. More often, though, the drummer would hold his instrument affectionately under one of his arms, or in one of his hands, or hitched to his body, or slanted toward him on the ground. Then he would translate his intimate thinking and feelings into all kinds of sound vibrations—by thumping the drum either with the palms of his hands, his fists, his fingertips, or by the use of one or two sticks.

Most of the medium-size drums that I listened to were being used at various kinds of social, ceremonial, and other more-or-less formal occasions. In nearly all instances the drums were being thumped for one primary purpose. It was to speak rhythmically and emotionally to everyone present, thereby encouraging them to mingle and share themselves. Most of the smaller drums that I occasionally heard were being tapped by lone pilgrims on the sacred way in Eastern countries. Each pilgrim was sitting on the ground, in complete solitude, at the time. And as he prayed or chanted or just quietly meditated, he finger-tapped his tiny drum with a gentle beat and rhythm. He was doing so in the effort to express or underscore more adequately his deep spiritual longings.

Quite unforgettable, because of their size, their uniqueness, and the purposes for which they were being used, were the big drums that had been made from tree trunks. Each one of those drums had been designed to have a deep, powerful, far-reaching, and even frightening voice. The voice of the drums was usually boomed forth for one or the other of two important purposes: that of communicating code messages to far-distant listeners, or to warn away all trouble-makers in the neighborhood, be they humans, animals, or anything else— like demons or evil spirits.

The more that I listened, inwardly as well as outwardly, to those various drum voices, the more apparent it became how boundless the scope of language really is, and how utterly impossible it is to limit language to vocal sounds, written words, or physical gestures. Through the simple but highly informative eloquence of those various drumbeats I was constantly being reminded of a much-overlooked fact: language is any means whatsoever by which infinite Intelligence speaks to receptive hearts and minds, thereby causing more of the as yet unknown to become known and provable.

The perfect climax to my wide experience of listening to drum voices took place on the famous and fabulous island of Bali. Along with a few specially invited guests, I was sitting on the ground in the soft, fragrant atmosphere of a sacred grove. A full moon was shining overhead. The occasion was a special performance by one of the island's famous gamelan orchestras. It was a large group of exceedingly skilled musicians. Unlike most orchestras, however, the instruments used by the Balinese were almost entirely percussion ones, consisting of drums, cymbals, gongs, metal kettles, bells, and many other objects that I could not identify, all producing the most uncommon and fascinating sounds when struck.

The orchestra had no leader. None of the performers required scores. And there had been no rehearsals for this special performance. It was all a natural, spontaneous expression. It flowed rhythmically from their individual withinness into their collective withoutness. For rich and stimulating tonal qualities, for exotic and refined rhythms, and for most unpredictable beginnings and endings, it far surpassed anything that I had ever heard before or could have imagined. No least phase of it was governed by the Western law of harmony. The Balinese performers were completely unhampered in their melodic withinness and its outward melodious expression. The impact of those rare and exquisite sounds transformed all of us listeners into new dimensions of being.

In the midst of this delectable occasion I became aware, as never before, of the interesting correlation that always exists between a drummer and his drum. It is a correlation in which the drum becomes the rhythmical and interpretive, the ritual voice of the one doing the drumming. And out of this dedicated performance by the Balinese musicians were flowing hauntingly lovely and rare tonal values and rhythms.

The intimate affiliation between each of the Balinese musicians and his particular percussion instrument, became revealingly clear to me. It was a perfectly blended symbolical action between them, one in which the heartbeat of the performer and the soundbeat of his instrument vibrated together in blended articulation, in the boundless harmonies and rhythms of universal togetherness. It became more readily understandable why it is that down through the centuries, and in every country of the world, the drum has been such a much-loved and popular instrument.

Those Balinese experts were realistically demonstrating in every least percussion sound they made that drums are not merely instruments for percussion purposes. They are tonal symbols of struggles . . . of failures . . . of losses . . . loves . . . and of sorrows. They are rhythmic symbols of accomplishment . . . of success . . . of satisfaction . . . and of joy. And symbols of many, many other things they are—throbbing deep within the individual heart. They are ever asking expression beyond spoken and written words, quite on the border of the kinetic, of movement itself, the basic faculty of man and his earliest means of expression. Could there be a transmission of rhythmic vibration more intimate and direct —unless it be the rhythm between an Indian rider and his horse to the rhythmic beat of the horse's hoofs?

What added such fine flavoring to the rare music by the Balinese was the fine impact that their individual characters and purposes were having, through their music, on everyone that happened to be listening. It was irresistible. It was also the basic secret for their phenomenal success. Before going into orchestral action I managed to discover that each of the musicians first attuned himself to himself as a living instrument. Then he would blend that living tone of his with the living tones of his melodious and rhythmical associates. And then each of them would fill every instrument sound that he made with the pure, divine sounds that he was distinctly hearing within himself.

Thus with his particular instrument to do the talking for him each of the Balinese virtuosos would thump the exquisitely lovely and meaningful things that were thumping deep within him, demanding to be shared in rhythmical expression. And usually accompanying this, I also came to find, was a longing on the part of each one of them to get his heartbeat, as well as the soundbeat of his instrument, in tune and in time with the universal heartbeat. This enabled the Balinese musicians more effectively to become contributing parts in the celestial symphony of the universe.

CHAPTER TWELVE

JUNGLE CLEARING

During my world-roving reporting experience it occasionally became necessary, for my own peace of mind, to escape from "modern civilization." I simply had to get away from having to listen to the members of my own species talk about themselves for publication. My customary plan for those refreshers was to slip away quietly from wherever I happened to be. I would intuitively find some inviting and quiet place where I could totally relax. Then I listened to the Voice of the Silence as it gently spoke its enriching wisdom through everything. This put me in tune to moving out of myself and the contemporary intellectual scene and into unity with the cosmic harmony and the rhythm of the universe.

Those temporary escapes provided the needed opportunities for carefully pondering the things that I had been observing and that had been thrust upon my consciousness. We all need time off: for sifting values from nonvalues. For correcting faulty observations and conclusions. For regaining an inner as well as an outer balance. This inward journeying is indispensable for acquiring more demonstrable angles on what life is all about, the why and wherefore of living, and what one should be doing about it.

One of the most unforgettable of those retreat experiences took place in a clearing in an Eastern jungle. For some time I had been footing-along a wiggling trail, wondering where it was going and what would happen to it and me when we got there. I arrived at the clearing. The scenic arrangement of the place, with its exotic colorings, its pungent fragrance, and its cathedral-like silence, was enchanting. It was a fairly large place, encircled by living walls of dense vegetation. Trees of many varieties had intertwined their branches overhead, clasping uplifted hands to create a beautiful green ceiling through which the sun's rays were penetrating with constantly changing color effects.

It was a perfect place in which to relax . . . to watch . . . to breathe deeply . . . to listen . . . and to be silently taught. So I walked in and took possession of the place. Or at least I thought I had taken possession. I spied a tree with just the right slant to it, sat down on the ground, and leaned comfortably back against it. For quite some time my only conscious activity was inbreathing the fragrant atmosphere, enjoying the quiet, and outbreathing my gratitude.

In the midst of this felicity there came an unexpected interruption. From one of the trees at the other side of the clearing a fairly large monkey dropped to the ground. He looked swiftly and cautiously first to the left and then to the right. With continuing caution he waddled rhythmically to the middle of the clearing. Then paused. Then sat himself down with all the solemnity of a supreme court justice. And then began scrutinizing me from out of his much-wrinkled face. Outwardly, I remained as motionless as the tree against which I was leaning. Inwardly, however, I went into a special alert, with all of my intuitive faculties as full on as possible, to try and understand just what was happening.

That monkey-squinting in my direction continued for some minutes, with neither of us making the least outer movement. It was a perfect tableau in still life. I knew at least something of his intent, as I had been through similar experiences many times before with that pal and tutor of mine, little Just Joe. I was being monkey-processed, and thoroughly so. That wild monkey was using the banana technique on me. Was reducing me to my bare essences. Was stripping me mentally naked, so that he could find out in all details what was going on back of my outer appearances. But why? I wondered.

Outwardly and conventionally observed, we were just "a wild monkey" and "a tame human," sitting in a jungle clearing and staring across at each other, with no least indication as to the reason for it or what either of us might do next. Inwardly, however, I knew from experiences with other monkeys that an important ceremony was taking place between us. In this ceremony the edges of my thinking were touching the edges of his thinking, and we were contacting each other as fellow states-of-consciousness rather than as mere physical forms. We were meeting and getting to know each other in our unseen individualities—that is, in our thinking, feelings, characters, motives, and purposes. Silently, I threw into the balance my total best.

It became easily apparent that the heartbeat of that wild monkey, and my own heartbeat, were not only echoing back and forth, but also beginning to move in harmony and rhythm with the universal heartbeat. Without the least outer action being necessary by either of us, we were blending ourselves in a perfect mutuality of interest . . . of respect . . . of confidence . . . and of understanding. This I could feel all the way through me, and so, I knew, could he. We had invisibly shaken hands as gentlemen, so all was well with us.

Suddenly, the monkey stopped scrutinizing me. He began looking slowly around in various directions, from ground levels to tree tops. The clearing, I surmised, was a popular gathering place for wild monkeys. In that case, the monkey was a scout, and I was an intruder upon monkey territory. He had come there to investigate me thoroughly on behalf of the other monkeys that might be hiding in the neighborhood. He was to report back to his tribe. On the basis of his report, they would know how to react to my presence.

That my intuition was correct was soon to be vividly illustrated. That monkey across from me was a special scout with the gifts of a detective. As such he had given my inner as well as my outer behavior patterns a thorough going-over, from the point of view of a monkey and his fellows. Apparently, his investigation of me had yielded facts of a favorable nature. My genuine admiration, respect, and liking for all kinds of monkeys had paid off in kind. He had placed his invisible stamp of approval on me. I believe he felt certain the monkeys he was scouting for had nothing to fear from my presence in the clearing. So, next, he silently "passed the word along" to the other wild monkeys in the neighborhood, telling them to come on in as they had nothing to fear from me.

Within the next few minutes the clearing became alive with monkeys. Never before had I ever witnessed a spectacle like it. Nor such an assortment of monkeys. There were big ones and little ones. Old monkeys, middle-aged ones, and babies that had to be carried. Groups of them, as well as aloners. Some of them were chattering loudly, others completely silent. They came dropping down from the trees—it was raining monkeys! They came leaping, walking, galloping, waddling, bounding, and skidding-in along the ground levels.

Some even appeared to pop out from nowhere by special magic of their own.

Then another never-to-be-forgotten thing happened in the general excitement of it all. As the wild monkeys came hurrying into the clearing in the widely varying ways and equally different speeds, not one of them felt it necessary to give me more than a brief glance, so completely free were they from suspicion and fear. Their glances radiated confidence, understanding, and friendliness, even in their momentary contacts. They showed their individual, as well as collective, willingness to have me, a human, remain in the clearing as part of the occasion. It was a gesture that both humbled and exalted me. They had accepted me as one of themselves.

Having arrived in the clearing from their various hiding places in the surrounding jungle, the assortment of highly animated, keenly imaginative monkeys then proceeded with the much-delayed "business of the day." That "business" was first to turn their individual totalities full on, and then to establish the perfect response in knowing and doing by simply letting the creative force of the universe flow harmoniously and rhythmically through them in fun-filled and sharing togetherness.

CHAPTER THIRTEEN

DISTANT COLLISIONS

When it comes to the art of expressing, at one and the same time, harmony and rhythm, joy and fun, entertainment and education, monkeys, for my vote, are tops! I never tire of watching them, as well as of learning fresh living values from them, regardless of whether they happen to be imprisoned in a cage or enjoying freedom of expression in a jungle. Relatively few of the many human entertainers I have known could really educate and expand others as they did. And few of the human educators that I have watched in action were able to flavor their educating with real entertainment. But almost every monkey that I observed throughout the world was a fluid expert in blending entertainment and education.

The large assortment of wild monkeys that I so unexpectedly met in the jungle clearing was no exceptions to this. Each was an entertainer and educator in one package. The speed, agility, coordination, cooperation, and precision with which they moved themselves about was almost unbelievable. Not once as they went past, over, under, and around one another, at those excessively high speeds, was there a single collison—not even a casual sideswipe. It was perfection in individual and group timing, and in self-steering.

In the exciting and delightful entertainment that those monkeys put on there was not the least trace of either sameness or dullness. It was a natural, spontaneous outflow of sharable feelings and actions. Each monkey seemed to be keenly aware that he was alive all over. Each one appeared to get maximum satisfaction out of every experience as he flung his entire aliveness into it. They were all realistic expressions of Plato's saying that "Beauty of style and harmony and grace and good rhythm depend upon simplicity." And fortunately for those wild monkeys, none of them had been educated away from that great fact.

When I had first walked into the loveliness and stillness of that jungle clearing, its impact was so appealing that I instantly turned it into a cathedral for meditating purposes. Then into my sanctuary came all those wild monkeys, who proceeded to turn it into a circus arena. But they were more than welcome to do so, for the circus they put on for me far surpassed in real entertainment values anything that I had ever witnessed before. It was so extraordinary, as well as invigorating and refreshing, that it elevated me into a kind of sublime daze as I wondered how such things could possibly happen outside of a fairy story.

That those wild monkeys were willing for me, a human, to remain there in the clearing and watch their play-and-have-fun time was an honor I can never forget. The more I gave thought to this, even in the midst of the exciting performance, the more understandable it became why they were doing so. Those monkeys and I had established subjective recognition between us by mentally bridging across to one another through all sorts of mental barriers. We had balanced both inner and outer interrelations as fellow beings of life. To my sense, our heartbeats were echoing back and forth in perfect attunement.

The performance those monkeys put on continued hour after hour, without an interruption or the least sag in the thrilling, amusing, and unpredictable things they did. But it was vastly more than a lot of monkeys having their kind of a pleasurable time together. It was an enchanting pageant! The superlative-plus in showmanship! It was also a rare exhibition of animated poems ... of essays ... of sermons ... and of other compositions. A demonstration, too, in which all those monkeys were letting the cosmic energy and rhythm flow fully and freely through them, both for their individual and collective delight.

In the midst of that monkey frolicking and sharing there was a most dramatic anticlimax. With startling abruptness, every monkey quit whatever he happened to be doing, then swiftly looked in the same southerly direction. And then, motivated by obvious fear and panic, they went stampeding out of the clearing in a northerly direction. It was such an unexpected and extraordinary phenomenon that it knocked me for the proverbial loop, leaving me stunned and bewildered.

What had caused the sudden exodus I couldn't remotely imagine. I decided to remain where I was, with my back against the friendly tree, and see what was going to happen next. As part of this, I made myself totally alert, the way animals do. Then I began listening with all of me, the way that animals do, too. But try as I did, I couldn't mentally sniff out what had caused that sensational monkey exodus. The silence in the clearing was profound. And pervading the general atmosphere was a tense but indefinable something that was steadily spelling t-r-o-u-b-l-e!

Three puzzling hours went ticking by. Then into the clearing from the south came five men walking in single file. The first two were carrying rifles, the other three were attendants. They were as surprised to find me there as I was to see them. We introduced ourselves. The two men with the rifles were wealthy American "sportsmen." They were making a tour of the world, shooting various kinds of wild animals to have them stuffed and sent to their homes for exhibition purposes. Their reason for coming to the clearing was "to bag some fine specimens of monkeys," which, they had been told, could usually be found there. But luck had been against them, as they hadn't seen a single monkey to take a shot at, and there were none in the clearing.

I kept silent about the unconventional experience that I had had with all those wild monkeys, preferring to listen to the hunters talk about themselves and carefully noting what each of them was mentally saying back of his vocal sounds and physical gestures. In the midst of this a most illuminating fact was revealed. At the precise moment those two hunters had picked up their rifles and headed for the clearing, three hours' walking distance away, every monkey in the clearing had fled from the place.

It was a perfect demonstration by every one of those wild monkeys in accurately hearing with "the inner ear" as well as accurately seeing with "the inner eye." And doing so as easily as breathing. Space seemed no obstacle. It was a memorable monkey-taught lesson, too, in the simple, natural functioning of pure intuition . . . of effortless awareness . . . of correct foresight . . . and of how best to react to such intimate disclosures. And particularly interesting is the realization that the episode had taken place in the lives of an assortment of wild monkeys that had never been educated, in the conventional meaning of that term, nor had they ever experienced life outside of a jungle.

The disclosure of what invisibly must have taken place

between the hunters and all those wild monkeys in the clearing, when they were so far apart, gave me much to think about. Long after the hunters had started on their return journey, keenly disappointed in not finding any monkeys to shoot and have stuffed, I pondered this problem in transmission of thoughts and intents to kill. It was a vivid reminder of what takes place, either for better or for worse, when there is a clash of mental forces moving in opposite directions—no matter what the earth-riding form of the thought carriers. Species identification and the distance separating physical bodies was no block to an alerted sense of survival—the genius of the reactive mind.

The essential drama between the two hunters and all the wild monkeys that had been entertaining me, I managed to unravel as follows: the instant that the two hunters began readying themselves for their hoped-for monkey killings, they began generating a mental atmosphere toward monkeys that was sinister, cruel, murderous, deadly. They were thinking themselves into a hunting mood full of destruction for "lower forms of life."

Then the two hunters picked up their rifles and headed for the distant clearing where all those wild monkeys and I were having such a delightful time—the monkeys sharing their acrobatic sense of fun, I keenly appreciative. Without being the least bit aware of the invisible forces they were setting in motion, the hunters began projecting a discordant mental atmosphere incalculably far ahead of themselves. These states of thought were as ugly and bad-intentioned as they were destructive. Cold-blooded monkey murder was rumbling in their minds and hearts at every step they took. And the reverberations of those rumblings were vibrating far out in all directions, for every kind of an alerted inner feeling to receive—somewhat as a radio receiving set tunes in on audio air waves.

Could it be that the reverberations of the ground the cruel men were treading during their murderous mission, or the oscillation of the air they were breathing or speaking into, carried their deadly thought-quality on tele-kinetic or tele-audio waves strong enough to be picked up by the monkey's built-in monitor, or radar warning system, pro-survival equipment installed by Mother Nature as an integral part of the reactive monkey mind? Did the monkeys possess a sort of survival computer sensitive enough to pick up and process vibrations of the ground and the air that sent along antisurvival messages? Could it be those messages of an animal magnetic nature travel on electromagnetic wave bands between telepathy and ordinary sense perceptions—in other words, supersensory perceptions? Who dares limit or circumscribe the infinite media of the one universal Mind?

The inevitable happened! The deadly thinking the two hunters were somehow projecting far ahead of their physical bodies crashed into the joy-filled vibrations of all those monkeys in the clearing. And while the crash was seemingly "only mental," its impact was terrific to witness outwardly. It was a major collision, even though invisible to the material senses. It was the equivalent to an explosion—an explosion in the awareness of each one of those monkeys. Two irreconcilable forces had met head-on: the antisurvival force of the hunters, and the prosurvival force of the monkeys. Every one of those monkeys knew intuitively what had caused the terrific clash and what was to follow from a killing purpose.

As I walked out of the clearing late that afternoon, still pondering what I had witnessed in long-distance mental or vibratory collisions between those two hunters and all those wild monkeys, my intellectual tailfeathers were at an all-time low, and there was much less of a human strut in me. I had been taught an invaluable lesson having to do with the potency, the sweep, and the influence of individually projected thinking, riding on invisible vibrations, be they telekinetic, sonic, electromagnetic, animal magnetic, or whatever. How utterly impossible it is, I realized, to escape the reactions to the thoughts that one consciously or unconsciously sets in motion—even in the direction of nonhuman forms of life. That precious and far-reaching lesson was taught me, I shall never forget, not by educated, learned, and superior humans, but by an assortment of utterly uneducated and "inferior" wild monkeys in a jungle clearing.

CHAPTER FOURTEEN

THE UNITIVE WAY

Meeting men and women in different parts of the world who were proficient in knowing how to get along understandingly, happily, and cooperatively not only with wild animals but also poisonous snakes, stinging insects, and other generally hated and feared living things, was always educational, expanding, and thrilling. Nearly all of those rare individuals were "just nobodies," but delightfully and refreshingly so— "nobodies" that liked companioning with "wild life" because of the sharing of happiness and satisfaction they got out of it. Each was participating in the same superlative achievement —that of knowing how to establish the right inner as well as outer interrelations, with every living thing they met, especially those humanly classified as "dangerous and deadly." They knew how to think horizontally across to whatever it happened to be, and then along with it, as a rational and cooperating fellow being.

As I watched those different "tame humans" and the various kinds of "wild animal" or "wild snake" associates in action, I would carefully note what each was outwardly doing, not only as an individual but as his part in the twosome. I became as totally receptive as possible, and then through the use of my "inner ear" and "inner eye" tried to identify what each of them was like and how they were functioning—in the unseen individuality—in the intimacy of thoughts, motives, feelings, character, and purposes. In those unseen individualities of theirs would always be hidden away the correct interpretation for everything they were doing, or failing to do, in their easily observable withoutness.

In not one of those human-nonhuman relationship balancings that I watched had there been the slightest use of "the strong-arm method"—a popular or prevalent method for "handling animals" wherein the animal is "trained" into certain standardized behavior patterns by threats, fear, and various kinds of applied force. This blocks the animal's behavior patterns to a great extent. It disrupts or destroys natural spontaneity of expression. It hinders the animal's innate desire to understand, to be understood, to share its best, and to be appreciated. It usually accomplishes the trainer's purpose of so enslaving the animal's reactive mentality that it always moves in complete obedience to the vanity and domination urges of its "lord and master."

The "animal handling" by those delightful "just nobodies" was completely contrary to all generally practiced training methods. To those originals in human forms, the most effective way to establish total right relations with other living things, regardless of their forms, species identification, or even reputation, is first to start doing so mentally and feelingly, at the highest possible levels. They succeeded in establishing a mutuality of genuine respect, interest, understanding, goodwill, and cooperation. They let the good seed of recognition flower into rhythmical and reciprocating action. And from that blending of rhythms of hearts and minds were flowing truly amazing results in shared knowing, being, and doing.

Each of the observed participants, in those uncustomary relationship balancings, had found the cosmic link which innately holds all life together in kinship and oneness. As a result, the heartbeat of each of those humans was in tune and in time with the heartbeat of the wild animal—the snake, or whatever else the creature he was companioning with. Appreciation and love was their "magic secret" for getting along happily and well with all other living things. None of the animals had ever wandered, or been educated away from the great fact that life, in its real meaning and functioning, is an all-including and boundless totality, an inseparable oneness, a complete participation and sharing. And with that fact motivating and steering all, each was constantly looking for the divine and eternal in every other living thing. With each contributing its best and trying to move in harmony and rhythm with the best within, outer unity and mutual satisfaction were established.

In a world where the mass control and manipulation of human thinking was at such peak proportions, it was reassuring here and there to find men and women who had the initiative and courage to be themselves. They were men and women whose interest and compassion included every living thing they could identify. *Rather than depend upon others to do their thinking and living for them, each of those unique ones was following his inner, intuitive guidance in every least thing that he did.* When each was confronted by the common challenge of either being like all the others or going it alone, each had chosen to go it alone. And in a crowded "aloneness" each was experiencing the satisfaction and rewarding results that always come from that kind of pioneering—"far from the madding crowd," but never in want of heart companions.

Having left the broad highway of the superficial-minded, the multitudes of lock-stepping imitators of common consent, each of those unspoiled originals was blazing a unitive trail through the wilderness of his own state of consciousness— seeking that point in awareness where "all things work together for good." In those trailings and seekings, each had had to become not only a lone explorer for a season but also a lone experimentalist and discoverer every thought and step of the way. It was rarefied adventure for each one of them, far out in the generally unfamiliar where seeking becomes experience . . . experience becomes knowing . . . knowing becomes being . . . and being becomes certainty in its part in Being—in the Wholeness of Being.

Intuitively blazing those individual initiative trails hadn't been easy for any of them. It demanded unusual dedication, inner discipline, unwavering courage and vision, mental flexibility. A thorough integration of heart, thinking, character, motives, and purposes are requisites in mental-spiritual pioneering. In those unitive trailings most of them had come to discover that what appeared to be objective, or "out there," in his experience was really taking place entirely within his own individual self. Everything significant began within the boundaries of his own intuitive thinking . . . his own feelings and mentation . . . his own state of awareness—where he, and he alone, was at his own thought controls. He chose to be his own decider about everything—in central control unfolding from within. Exploring out from that basis, each was more and more learning how to move in harmonious and rhythmical interaction with all life.

The more successful I became in penetrating into the invisible motivating causes back of the visible actions of those rare men and women, the easier it became to understand why they were all such experts in knowing how to balance inner and outer relations with everything they met, especially with all forms of "wild life." Their common method was as elemental and simple as it was practical and resultful. Each of them was consistently living the best that he could, at each tick of the clock; each then radiated that best to whatever happened to be holding the attention. Always the best came back from whatever it happened to be. The interaction vividly illustrated how every living thing, regardless of its form, species identification, or level on the evolutionary scene instinctively turns toward that which is genuine—like flowers turn to the light. Perhaps behind it all stands the dynamics of growth—of spiritual progress.

As each of those pioneers moved along his own unitive trail, he was placing his emphasis for living more on the mental-spiritual than on the physical-material. He was acquiring the wisdom and knowledge that he needed from his own intuition, rather than from outer hearsay and booksay. (In-tuition literally means being taught from within.) He was more interested in what he could put into life, as his part of it, than in what he could take out of life for his own personal profit. So each of them was more and more leaving the limiting personal for the expansive impersonal, the selfish for the unselfish, and the egocentric for the universal. But it was a way of life, they were all having to learn, that had to be acquired through individual effort and experience, and could not be found for them by any other person.

Another unforgettable fact about those rare individuals was that each of them had so expanded his sense of being that he regarded the entire universe as his "home." And every living thing that he contacted in his home immediately became an interesting and respected relative. But love, to them, was not a conventional human emotion or sentiment. Love, they believed, is the universal, divine Intelligence and Energy that, flowing out in its boundlessness, makes, motivates, and manages all that really is—linking all things with all things, in harmonious interrelations. Love became the unifying Principle whose dynamics are sharing.

Each of those delightful authentics had learned the same basic lesson in mastering self and the selfless skill of knowing how to establish rational and satisfying togetherness with whatever it was they happened to meet. They had learned how to tune in with the divinity in all living things—for they began to see all living things within the encompassing divinity of Love.

Love seeks and finds the mutual good in all relationships. And that lesson always pivoted around the time-honored "word to the wise"—that to experience life at its genuine best and fullest, one must love, without reservations, at his best and fullest. Each learned that to stop loving in any direction is, to that degree, to shut off the flow of infinite Life and thereby to stop living to a degree. And so each of them, as best he could, was letting the law of infinite Love flow through everything that he inwardly thought and felt, as well as what he outwardly did.

Thus was each of those humble virtuosos of life an accomplished expert in the science and art of right relations. They were accomplishing extraordinary, and at times impossible seeming results. With their integrated inner world, their pure heartbeats, and their childlike spontaneity in living and loving, they were all happily operating far out beyond intellectual and orthodox routines. They were living in expanded and satisfying states of consciousness. Thus it had become possible for each of them to discover more of the real meaning of life and love. Thereby each experienced how all things belong together as rational complementary and cooperating fellow beings in the kinship and oneness of all life.

CHAPTER FIFTEEN

LANGUAGE AND SPEECH

One night during my reportorial wanderings I was sitting alone in the bow of an anchored boat far down the river Nile in Egypt. A full moon was creating the superlative in gorgeous color effects. The soft, fragrant atmosphere was filled with mystery and charm. It was an enchanting place to be in and to be part of. I had returned that afternoon from an extended trip into the surrounding desert where there had been exceptional opportunities for watching rational relationship balancings between Egyptian drivers and their philosophical companions—camels, horses, and donkeys. They were unforgettable phenomena in which humans and animals had successfully bridged-across to one another intuitively, rhythmically, and spiritually.

The bow of that boat was a perfect place for horizontalizing one's feet, that is, thoroughly relaxing: to look, to listen, and to learn. So I proceeded to do just that. The more receptive I became to what was really happening all about me, the more I found myself an audience—an audience to the most magnificent symphony in color and movement that I had ever witnessed. Here was a symphony that was showing forth almost indescribable magnitudes in design, beauty, and meaning. My sensory and supersensory perceptions were moving gently but effectively through everything observable, atuned to the reciprocating rhythms of the universe.

The more I penetrated into the significance of the color symphony that was taking place all about me, the more I began recalling other unforgettable symphonies that I had been audience to in different parts of the world. They were symphonies that required neither instruments nor conductors for the fascinating results they produced ... symphonies consisting of interblending enriching thoughts, and their resultant reciprocating outer actions ... symphonies that were in perfect attunement, with the real meaning, purpose, and flow of life. They were soundless symphonies in shared being that had been produced by various individual humans and their particular artists-associates in the animal forms—a bird, a snake, an insect.

As I reviewed the fascinating symphonies in shared being between "tame humans" and "wild life" that I had been privileged to audit, I saw that all of those odd humans had used the same method in achieving their extraordinary results—in symphonic *atunement.* The instant that one of them, for the first time, met a wild animal somewhere out in the open, he would become totally motionless. So would the animal. Then the human went into effective invisible action. He did this by mentally sending his genuine admiration, respect, and goodwill across to the animal. And echoing back from the animal there invariably came its best in thinking and feelings. It was like an invisible handshake between two gentlemen—a soul-shake.

This automatically started a right balance in inner interrelations between them. A corresponding balance took place in their outer interrelations for their mutual expansion. Thus that "tame human" and "wild animal" established a unison of understanding and good purpose within as well as without. Then, in that interblending togetherness, they could move happily into the symphonic rhythms of sharing themselves in their totalities atuned to a universal key.

The "tame human" and "wild animal" got to know each other in their unseen as well as seen individualities. An awareness for the possibilities of sharing and a desire to share made it easy for them to blend themselves as a twosome, suspended in a fluid mutuality of understanding, of fun, and the fullest possible satisfaction. Thus two seemingly unrelatable entities attune themselves, their media, the cadence of pure heartbeats. A joy-filled reciprocity of fragrant consorting on supersensory levels can rise from the cosmic harmony and rhythm that lie ever at the heart of all that really is. Thereby both human and animal can contribute their best living tones in "the symphony of infinite response."

As I continued pondering those facts and their far-reaching implications, the Egyptian silence became even more intense and impressive. I began getting gentle inner reminders to the effect that only in aloneness and stillness can one learn the important things about life, about oneself. What one really needs to know is revealed in the silence that, contrary to general belief, is not a blank, but the most realistic, beautiful, and informative of all voices. It is a voice as omnipotent and omnipresent as it is intimately omniactive—a voice that is always uttering the ultimate in wisdom, knowledge, loving-kindness, and helpfulness—a voice, however, that is usually interrupted by human speaking. Vocal sounds or chatter have a way of blocking its flow. It is a voice, too, I had to learn, that can be heard only with an attentive inner ear and the childlike attention and receptivity of a pure heart.

There is no sound as eloquent as complete silence—like the "silence between a man and a maid, for which music alone has the words."

The more I was able mentally to receive and contain what was really going on all about me as I sat in the bow of that Nile river boat, the easier it became to identify a vast and significant meaning that was moving through that constantly changing Egyptian color symphony. Briefly summarized, it was a tangible, realistic expression of an exquisitely lovely, a flawlessly-managed universe. I had the reassurance that permeating and governing everything, everywhere, was an infinite and perfect divine Cause—the presence, the intelligence, the substance, and the energy of all that IS, or can be. Every least thing that I could identify in the surrounding Egyptian stillness and loveliness was an integral and needed part in the forever harmonious flow of the inseparable oneness of all life. Is not this a touch of Cosmic Consciousness? Can one ask for more?

Then, from out of the eloquent silence of that Egyptian loveliness, there came another gentle, revealing reminder. This had to do with "that wondrous long ago," when, according to the ancient records, everything that lived, did so in perfect understanding and cooperation with everything else. It was a period in which "the whole earth was of one language, and one speech." Could it be that long before "vanity sounds" were introduced as self-centered media that divide rather than unify, "one language" served as medium of communication, so basic and direct, it was understood by all living things? If that is so, this same universal language still lives on, deep underneath the dusty debris of the dead letter, the fallen and standing "towers of Babel" of mass miseducation, and of corrupted and commercialized mass media, fracturing society, and creating world wide discord and universal despair.

The silent language and speech that those ancients used with all other expressions of life, I was now coming to learn in the bow of that Egyptian boat, was so simple and natural that it didn't have to be taught to anyone or anything, any more than did their breathing. They seem to have intuitively known, and had never wandered away from the fact, that what was really doing all the thinking and communicating in each one of them was the everywhere-functioning Mind of the universe—the divine consciousness, or omniactive intelligence.

How may modern man, frustrated from lack of meaningful communication, floundering in a dead sea of the dead letter, adrift in an ocean of conflicting words, regain again the simple medium of direct intercommunion? Is it enough to say that what the ancients were aware of is the universal Mind?

How to relate to the universal Mind is the supreme problem in media. It is constantly to listen inwardly, or subjectively. Then only can each hear, know, do, and experience—each true to his inner being. The Egyptian silence whispered that everything that lived in that wondrous long ago did so with a pure, a dedicated, and a universal heartbeat.

The pure in heart, those genuine originals, true to themselves, have no difficulty whatever, in communicating with one another. They know the way; they *understand media.* They also know that calm and intelligent communications, from one well-integrated nervous system to another, are the invisible yet living and reliable building blocks. Bridges across, and solid relationships that are enriching, enduring, and satisfying, are built upon good communications.

It can be said that relationships crystallize along strong lines of communications, like nerve fibers along which a growing body is unfolded. Positive relationships are built on positive communications. Negative relationships or hostilities, develop along lines of negative communications.

When positive communications are forced out of a free and spontaneous flow into constricting channels, are exposed to the static of internal frictions, or are interfered with by disruptive outside influences, they may turn into negative communications. In such a case, relationships begin to disintegrate—even good relations of long standing. As this happens, people find they "get on each other's nerves," as we say in psychosomatic language.

As I pondered these deep things that trouble contemporary life, relaxed in that boat on the Nile, a fascinating correlation began unfolding itself between those ancient experts in the science and art of right relationships and the present-day demonstrators of it. By contrast, the lack of demonstration in right communications and right relationships is appallingly evident in the modern setting that has the symptoms of a disintegrating civilization.

The relationship experts look out upon life as a divinely attuned and all-including totality, an inseparable kinship and oneness. Nothing can be excluded. In interactions of boundless scope, everything has constantly to contribute its total best in order to move in harmony with everything else. Those ancients and moderns include everything they can identify in their interest . . . respect . . . love . . . loyalty . . . and cooperation.

A new day began dawning over the bow of the boat. An enchanting occasion had come to an end. I was filled with humble as well as profound gratitude—for all the fresh wisdom and knowledge that had been shared with me from out of that lovely Egyptian night and the eloquent Egyptian still-ness. I felt nourished from receptivity to the eternal and divine. I had clearly and understandingly heard the Voice of Existence as it silently spoke its universal language—in the perfect cadences of endless and reciprocal being.

CHAPTER SIXTEEN

AMERICAN INDIANS

American Indians were among the most colorful and unforgettable works of living art with whom I crossed trails. Not one of them was the least bit like the Indians one usually sees so grossly distorted in the entertainment media. On the contrary, they were exceptionally fine specimens, not only physically but also mentally and spiritually. What gave them special distinction was the fact that not one of them that I talked with had permitted himself to be either soiled or spoiled by the behavior patterns of the whitemen with whom he came in contact, nor by the ugly and viciously bad things that whitemen had done to the Indians down through the years in the name of "an advancing civilization."

Millions of people throughout the world have been highly excited and thrilled by watching American Indians in melodramatic action in motion pictures, television, and other entertainment outlets. But relatively few of them, it is safe to assume, ever learned what the real American Indian is really like, or discovered the superb values in thinking, in character, and in living that the Indian has to share in such abundance. What those entertainment viewers were mostly witnessing, as well as mentally inhaling, in those Indian-flavored productions were overemotionalized and overdramatized distortions.

Another reason for the failure of the average whiteman correctly to evaluate and appreciate the American Indian, pivots around a common paradox—that of the inability of most whitemen really to see an American Indian, even while looking at one with their eyes wide open. In other words, the whiteman is unable mentally to penetrate beyond the Indian's silent and shielding outer personality, recognizing his interesting unseen individuality, and so getting to know him in his totality. The whiteman has missed discovering the Indian's amazing know-how for establishing inner and outer interrelations with earth and sky and all that is between.

Yes, the real American Indian can share splendid living values in abundance. However, for years I accepted what others had said or written about him without the least effort to weigh their conclusions on my own thought scales. I had been conventionally footing-it along with the crowd-minded as just another animated carbon copy. Then came opportunities to meet Indians in their own sections of the country, to watch them in their significant individual as well as group actions. Particularly, I learned to listen to them tick mentally and spiritually back of the things they were outwardly doing, or even not doing. Thus I acquired silently taught lessons that were important to practice in my own earth-riding experience.

Whenever an Indian and I met for the first time, an invisible ceremony always took place, a ceremony that had a most important bearing on all our contacts with each other. It would begin with the Indian standing as tall, as stately, and as motionless as possible. Then from an almost expressionless face he would squint across at me. But I always knew what was going on, back of that outer fronting and squinting. With his highly sensitive intuitive faculties full-on, he was adding-and-subtracting me into my correct total. And never once did I know any of them to make a mistake in their inner as well as outer appraisal.

As a particular Indian started appraising me in this manner, I would also go to work on him. I did so by mentally stripping him down to his bare essences, with the help of my monkey-borrowed banana technique. Then I carefully noted what he was like in his unseen as well as seen individuality. This duo-action always helped us to get to know each other all the way through—that is, in our thinking, feelings, characters, motives, and purposes, as well as in what each of us had on visible display. Then as our inwardness began blending in understanding and respect, our outwardness would do so too. And thus would we start moving along together in our totalities.

The Indian has a penetrating ability to know how to identify correctly the cause or causes back of all observed phenomena. To get along intelligently and well with a real American Indian, I gradually came to find that first of all one had to have a right balance in inner interrelations. And the foundation for this is always posited on the Indian's silent but insistent question: "Is your heart pure, White Brother?" If the pure heart is lacking, that ends the situation as far as the Indian is concerned. But if the heartbeat of the whiteman is genuinely pure in its tone, it instantly starts blending with the pure heart tone of the Indian. Then all becomes harmonious with him in whatever he thinks, says, or otherwise does.

I carefully observed every least detail of what my Indian friend did, when he and I were together, whether he happened to be astride a horse . . . walking along a trail and trying not to harm the earth when he stepped upon it . . . or just sitting motionless and silent, in listening-and-hearing meditation. I would also try to identify the tone and significance of that which was motivating him about spiritually and mentally. This was always expanding, educational, and refreshingly different.

The more I studied with friendly curiousity the inner as well as outer behavior patterns of my various Indian friends, the more understandable it became why they were all so proficient in knowing how to blend their total best with the universal life force all about them, then move in harmony and rhythm with it. I saw why, too, they were all so skilled in carrying on effective, silent, rational correspondence with animals, birds, snakes, insects, and other nonhuman "younger brothers." One of the primary reasons for those splendid results was the fact that each was living up to his individual obligation of being a contributing member in the brotherhood of mutual usefulness.

None of those Indian friends regarded their admirable and demonstrated living values as having originated within themselves, but as reflected manifestations from what they reverently spoke of as "The Big Holy." And to them "The Big Holy" was the universal Cause . . . the Substance . . . the Intelligence . . . the Understanding . . . and the action of all that really is. So to keep in rhythm with the cosmic Plan and Purpose, each of those Indian friends was diligently looking for expressions of "The Big Holy" in every encountered living thing. They usually spoke of this individual searching as "the great mystery"—through which, they believed, all have to go in order to learn individually that all life is one, and all living things brothers and sisters.

Trying to persuade my Indian friends to tell me just what

it was that they invisibly did in order to establish rational correspondence as well as outer cooperation, not only with nonhuman forms of life, but even with things growing out of the earth, was always difficult. It was not because they were indifferent or ungracious, but because they preferred to let their demonstrated results speak for them. Most of my Indian friends were of the opinion that talking, unless wisely and frugally done, causes one's power to leak away, reducing him to being just another unnecessary noise. That is why although each of them was alert and active mentally, he was outwardly traveling "the silent way." It seems that most whitemen talk as much as they can; most Indians as little as they can.

Whenever one of my Indian friends and I talked together, we usually did so slowly and cautiously, using only a few nouns, and filling in all the rest with brief hand gestures in the Indian's picturesque sign language. Their favorite method for acquiring fresh wisdom and knowledge, and especially immediately needed information, was not to seek it vocally from some other Indian, or even from printed words. On the contrary, each individually went into the silence, with his silence, and then let the silence whisper to him whatever it was that he specifically needed to know. As far as I was able to find out, the silence had never once failed to cooperate with them in this manner.

One way to get expanded into a larger awareness of knowing and being is to "sit in the lap of Mother Earth" humbly with an Indian friend, look off into scenic loveliness and far distances, and listen for the good counsel from the silence as it gently speaks to each of us in the infinite language of all life. This language is eloquent in its boundless expression and helpful in the fresh and needed facts that are always supplied. It is a language that was never difficult for my Indian friends and me to hear and understand, providing that we were "of one mind" and listening "as one mind."

Whatever success I had in those valuable Indian-shared occasions came mostly from borrowing the Indian's effective technique in matters of this kind—that of first setting aside one's outer senses, then becoming as totally still and receptive as possible, then carefully listening to the gentle inner whisperings of infinite Intelligence as it speaks its precious wiseness from out of the surrounding eloquent silence. Thus would the Indian friend and I blend our inhearing and inseeing into a sharing knowing—experiencing together the unity and serenity of the divine Is-ness, Now-ness, and Here-ness.

CHAPTER SEVENTEEN

HEARTBEATS AND HOOFBEATS

As your thinking goes stepping along the surface of these printed pages, I would like to wave a special magic wand, mutter the right conjurations, and bring into our mutual visibility some of the exceptionally fine riders and their horses, that I met in different parts of the world. Then having introduced them to you, let them put on a special show in horsemanship for us. It would be an unforgettable experience. We would see demonstrated what almost unbelievable feats humans and horses can accomplish whenever heartbeats and hoofbeats are in tune and in time.

The horseman that I have selected to open our "magic show" is a Bedouin chief from the Arabian desert. He has long been distinguished for the exceptionally fine Arabian horses and camels that he breeds. As the chief makes his formal appearance in our "show," he is riding one of his famous horses. The picturequeness of the chief himself, the loveliness of his horse, and their coordination in thinking as well as in rhythmical and unpredictable movements sets the pace for all that follows in entertainment and education.

The second rider to be introduced is a colorful American Indian chief from the wide-open spaces of the West. He is astride an exceptionally intelligent and lively horse, moving at its topmost speed. Following them—and each rider is given a special introduction—is a charro from Mexico on his favorite horse. Then a gaucho from the Argentine. Then, one by one, some distinguished exhibitors of show horses from England, France, Italy, Japan, and the United States. Then a skilled steeplechase rider and his blue-ribbon horse from Ireland. And finally enters a hat-slanted, bow-legged, rough-riding cowboy from Texas.

In order to achieve its real purpose our "magic show" must be observed and evaluated both subjectively and objectively. In the objective, or outer phases of it, we would witness the ultimate-plus in what riders and horses can do when heartbeats and hoofbeats are echoing back and forth. This makes it possible for rider and horse to balance themselves in understanding . . . in respect . . . in love . . . in joy . . . and in fun. The climax is shared outer accomplishments in a superb performance of "horse-man ship."

To make the subjective part of our experience effective, we need to go into a most unconventional act—that of interviewing each rider and horse after watching them in action. This can be done vocally with the human, but silently only with the horse. Also, we need to keep in the forefront of thought that the greatest and most effective of all languages is the silent universal language of the heart. It is a language that every living thing, regardless of its form or species identification, is innately equipped with for communication. It is a language, as all the experts in it have long pointed out, that can be spoken, heard, and understood only by the pure in heart, never by those whose hearts are impure and whose minds are mixed up.

Watching the Bedouin chief and his exceptionally fine horse perform, you might wonder—had you ever before seen such unusual horsemanship? But as we depth-interviewed each of them afterward, thereby identifying the invisible causes and links back of their visible coordinated actions, we might come into possession of their "success secret." Then we would clearly know that what we had been witnessing was a perfect balancing in inner as well as outer interrelations between a man and a horse. The chief and his four-legged associate were sharing themselves in the unheard music of motion—their common key, the indissoluble connection that ever exists between all living things.

Admiring that Arabian horse for expressing such exceptional loveliness . . . refinement . . . graciousness . . . initiative . . . and skill, in every least thing that it did, we would be in contact with a horse that had constantly been encouraged and helped to fulfill itself. That is why the purebred Arabian horse, like the one we were watching, is so greatly admired, respected, and loved throughout the world.

We would also come to find that the Bedouin chief was treating his horse as a rational and cooperating fellow being —as a state of being, or consciousness, rather than as a limited biological item on four legs and conventionally tagged as "a horse." The creature was a companion, through synchronized rhythm, and a much-appreciated and admired partner in an important enterprise. The horse had as much to share as the man in their united efforts to blend their total best.

But what would probably elevate your eyebrows to hit a peak would be the discovery that the Bedouin chief, with deep humility and reverence, treated his horse as "a muluq!"

—as "an angel!" Furthermore, whenever the chief prayed or meditated, he did so with one of his Arabian horses or camels nearby. This enabled the animals to become blessed and blessing companions, in their tribulations as well as in their joys.

As the American Indian chief came dashing in for his part in our "magic show," he too would be mounted on an unusually intelligent as well as highly animated horse. Then once again we would witness the seemingly impossible in horsemanship. And what would flavor the thrills with amazement and bewilderment would be the fact that the chief was riding his horse without saddle or blanket, nor did he need a bridle and reins to maneuver the horse with. How he managed to stay aboard that "naked horse" with such relaxed ease as they performed their spectacular feats was another mystery in human-horse relations.

As we interviewed the Indian chief and his horse afterward, using vocal and sign language with the former and the silent but effective universal language of the heart with the latter, we would gather in many important facts as well as facts worth borrowing—all about the science and art of right relations. During this we would find that the foundation for their success in rhythmical togetherness was the fact that the Indian chief from the American desert, like the Bedouin chief from the Arabian desert, had removed all possible limitations from his horse—mental, physical, and even spiritual limitations. The American Indian was likewise sharing life with his horse as a rational, understanding, cooperating, and much-respected associate—life in motion at its most exciting. We would also discover that the Indian chief was finding great satisfaction in spending time with his horse not only as a companion and playfellow, but also as "a lodge brother." That the horse, like himself, was a member in good standing of "the brotherhood of mutual usefulness." It is a "brother-hood" in which the best thoughts, motives, and actions of each of them is kept in continuous and wise outflow, a "brotherhood," too, in which rhythmic feelings were echoing back and forth between the chief and his horse—to blend in harmonious vibrations in everything that they did together.

The chief and his horse had fused their seemingly separated "twoness" into a complementary "oneness." They were in perfect inner and outer equilibrium. They were harmonizing upon the theme of their togetherness, using their best inner tones and chords. And thus we find man and horse established for themselves a perfect balance in participating interaction . . . in reciprocal being . . . in venturesome doing . . . in precision . . . in ease of movement . . . and in the fullest possible sharing and daring.

As our "magic show" continues, we again witness the superlative and unforgettable in horsemanship by the other specially selected riders from different countries. Each horseman is wearing picturesque riding clothes and is mounted on an exceptionally fine horse. Each of them, horses as well as riders, is sparkling with vitality as well as the desire and daring to accomplish the seemingly impossible in everything that is done together. And joyfully overflowing into every least action of theirs is the fun of the shared expression of movement . . . of change . . . of thrills . . . and unbounded delight.

As we vocally interview each rider and silently interview each horse after their performances, we come upon many more illuminating facts having to do with the science and art of right relations. One of the important truths to come out of this is the fact that each of those two-leggers and four-leggers is doing his best to live in accord with the golden rule. Each is actually "doing unto the other" as he would like the other to "do unto him." They all seem to know innately, in their contacts with one another, that the golden rule always is the acid test of thought, of feelings, as well as of actions.

This practicing of the golden rule between the rider and his horse we might come to discover, in turn makes it possible for each rider and horse to carry on silent, rational correspondence or instant intercommunication with each other. They establish between them an invisible bridge for two-way thought traffic of the reactive mind. They find, know, and experience the best in each other. And out of that flowers their rhythmical togetherness in heartbeats and hoofbeats. Thus open wide for each rider and horse the floodgates of possibilities in coordination and cooperation, in unification through perfected communications. This is the Ruling Design, the Divine Plan of Central Unification ever moving through all phases of the kinship and oneness of all life.

And on that note of unfenced, coordinated and sharing togetherness our "magic show" ends.

CHAPTER EIGHTEEN

BOMBER DOG

The ability of animals, and especially dogs, to identify the motives and purposes in human thinking, even across long distances, has long provided me with fascinating but embarrassing phenomena to watch and then ponder. Fascinating, in finding out what experts animals are in instant, subjective recognition. And embarrassing, in being thus shown how far behind animals most of the members of the human species are in intuitive sensing, hearing, and seeing—in arriving at immediate and correct knowing without having to depend upon outer faculties or go through the laborious processes of reason and education flavored by guessing.

The more privileged I was to have animals, birds, snakes, insects, and other nonhuman fellows silently instruct me in the things I needed to know, for my greater good and expansion, the more aware I became of the enriching values that every living thing has to share whenever one is ready for such an experience. But qualifying for this demands a balancing of inner as well as outer interrelations with whatever it happens to be. Then one needs to move mentally back and forth with the creature over the invisible routes of hearts and minds wherein only the best is set and kept in motion. Thus one not only experiences the harmony and rhythm of genuine to-getherness, but also expands the limitations and frontiers of his awareness.

In this way, too, it became possible to establish mutually helpful correspondence with my nonhuman associate—not by vocal sounds or physical gestures, but by sharable intuitive awareness. But establishing silent good talk in this manner demands a strict discipline, especially mentally.

Dogs are expert readers of human hearts, minds, and char-acters, without ever being taught the valuable skill. I had this experience with all dog owners: I would be sitting in a room with a dog associate asleep on the floor. Suddenly, the dog would get to its feet, go into an intense alert, with its eyes, nose, and cupped ears aimed at the entrance of the room, plainly indicating that he had mentally heard something, either good or bad, that was moving in our direction, and was readying himself for its arrival. Then, sooner or later, the invisibly identified person would visibly arrive, and in his behavior patterns would be exactly like what the dog had mentally heard and seen ahead of time.

I marveled at the precision and accuracy with which indi-vidual dogs could identify what was going on in individual human thinking, and corresponding outer actions, even across great distances. As the dog mentally "sniffed out" of the seemingly invisible whatever it needed to know about the distant personality that was holding its attention, I would mentally "sniff out" along with him, so to speak, to find out, if possible, how dogs happen to be so accomplished in this area. One of the "sniffed-out" discoveries was this: none of the dogs that I watched in those long-distant mind-reading accomplishments was handicapped by an educated and pat-ternized intellect. Each was living in unspoiled receptivity from a basis of natural, intuitive unfoldment.

I also discovered that each of those accomplished "ordi-nary" dogs was operating from a much higher level of being than is ordinarily thought possible. None of those interesting four-leggers was functioning with a private and independent mind of his own. All were reflecting the universal Intelli-gence as naturally and easily as they were their breathing. They were expressing the divine Consciousness which ever includes, permeates, animates, and directs the entire uni-verse, like individual rays of light and warmth express the sun. But this is rather difficult to grasp and understand unless one has mentally penetrated, at least to some degree, "the mist that went up from the earth."

A dramatically unforgettable illustration of the ability of a dog inwardly as well as accurately to hear and see across great distances took place during the last world war. A pilot, who had been captain of an American bombing group based in England for bombing Germany, shared this with me.

The captain's closest friend in the bombing group was a fellow navigator. Shortly after the American fliers arrived in England for the first time, the captain's navigating friend acquired a little tramp of a dog. The mutt had been doing much lonely wandering about in a country where everyone and everything was experiencing great difficulties. The little dog was starving—not alone for food, but for understanding, love, and opportunities to express and share himself. His hopes were abundantly fulfilled. He was adopted by the navigator, named Bomber Dog, and made mascot of the American flying group. The only bombings the little fellow ever participated in was in bombing everyone with his en-thusiasm and affection.

The navigator and Bomber Dog became inseparable pals, except when the former had to be away on his flying assignments. At the predawn gathering in the briefing hut where orders for the day's bombings would be given, Bomber Dog would always be in attendance, lending his moral support and enthusiasm to the occasion. When the session came to an end, Bomber Dog would hurry to the long runway where he would watch each plane take off with its heavy load of bombs. Then, when the last plane was no longer in the sky, he would sadly return to the barracks and just hang around until the fliers returned.

One afternoon Bomber Dog was standing in front of the briefing hut, waiting for the fliers and especially his pal, as usual. But the little mascot was looking and acting like a different dog. His sparkle and bounce were entirely gone; he was dejected and disheartened. The first plane came in and the fliers entered the hut to report the results of their mission. But the one the dog was specially looking for was not among them. Another squadron landed, but his pal was not among them either. Then it was reported that the navigator's plane had been hit by enemy fire, blown apart, and that everyone had been killed.

For the next ten days Bomber Dog stood in front of the briefing hut, intensely watching the sky in the direction of Germany. There was a melancholy downbeat in his expression and actions. He wouldn't eat any food. None of the fliers could cheer him up or even hold his attention beyond a brief glance. The captain followed all details of the little dog's actions with studied interest, sensing that Bomber Dog was in contact with something important in the seemingly invisible that neither he nor any of the other fliers was able to identify.

Then one morning when stormy weather made flying impossible, Bomber Dog appeared in the barracks and not only resumed eating, but also played and had fun with the fliers. All was well again. The following day he was in another dismal mood, refusing to eat or having anything to do with anyone. Those unpredictable changes in moods and actions went on and on, with no one able to understand the reason for the unusual behavior. Often while in deep sleep the little dog would suddenly get to its feet, as though struck by something, and with terror in its face go into another black mood. As the puzzling phenomena continued, the captain, as much as he could, carefully watched and made notes of all phases of it.

Toward the end of the sixth month Bomber Dog went into his most melancholy mood, hiding himself under the barracks and shaking with misery. A few days later the little four-legged mystery suddenly appeared again in the barracks where all the men were. He was almost exploding with excitement and happiness, barking as loudly as he could at all of them, trying to tell them something of the greatest importance that none of them could understand.

Having shared the "big news" with the fliers in the best way he could, Bomber Dog turned around and raced out of the barracks. Then, as fast as his legs could carry him, he speeded to the main entrance of the bomber base some distance away. And there the little fellow stood, just inside the gateway—barking, trembling, and almost wagging his tail off. An army truck drove in, stopping for the customary inspection. Sitting in the front seat, with the driver, and grateful to be alive and back again, was the supposedly dead navigator —Bomber Dog's pal.

After the excitement had somewhat quieted down among the men at the bomber base, the captain and his navigator friend, along with Bomber Dog as a most important part of the occasion, began comparing notes. Out of it came these facts: the navigator's plane had been hit and destroyed by enemy fire, but unknown to all observers, he had managed to parachute safely to the ground. He found himself in particularly dangerous enemy territory, escape from which seemed utterly impossible. As this happened, Bomber Dog, alertly waiting for him all those many miles away in England, intuitively and accurately identified the facts. Then he went into the first of his corresponding reactions to what was happening to his pal in Germany.

Some days after landing, the navigator made contact with underground workers who provided him with a temporary safe hiding place. As this happened in Germany, Bomber Dog, in England, inwardly heard the good news, came out of his discouraged and dismal mood, began eating again, as well as playing and having fun with the fliers in the barracks. Then began the difficult effort of trying to smuggle the navigator through enemy territory. As week followed week in the seemingly impossible effort, every forward or blocked action was instantly and correctly identified by the navigator's knowing, worried, and faithful little dog pal at the American bomber base in England.

The time came when the Allied forces that were advancing through France and Belgium began bringing their lines closer to Germany. As that happened, Bomber Dog began going through his most puzzling series of moods and actions. At least they were puzzling until it was subsequently learned that every mood and outer action of that intuitively far-seeing little dog was a corresponding reaction to what was happening to his navigator pal as the latter was being sneaked through enemy territory against such great odds.

After all those many weeks of extraordinary changes in inner and outer behavior, Bomber Dog came out of the blackest of them and reached his highest peak in excitement and joy. That was the day when the navigator finally arrived within the American lines and plans were made for flying him back to the American bomber base in England—back to where his understanding and faithful little dog pal was eagerly awaiting him so that they could resume sharing life together again.

CHAPTER NINETEEN

TRADE RATS

My dinner host at the Hollywood restaurant was a well-known publisher, author, and old friend then living on a picturesque estate in the mountains of Southern California that overlooked wide stretches of desert. Just as we finished ordering our food, my friend said that he had a very serious problem that he specially wanted to discuss with me—one that had been "knocking me dizzy" for some time. With his brilliant wit, which he liked to set in motion from behind a serious face, his words could have meant almost anything, or nothing at all. So with this in mind, I asked him what kind of a problem could possibly baffle him, with all that he was supposed to know, and all that his press agent was saying about him, expecting him in return to let loose his concealed joke.

"Trade rats!" he vocally flung across at me with genuine annoyance and disgust.

Then followed a bitter denunciation of trade rats, with a lengthy review of what they had been doing on his mountain estate to make life miserable for everyone. He added that while they kept killing "the things," others always sooner or later moved in, resuming the species' odd habit of carrying away valuable articles. Nothing of carryable size, belonging to him, his family, or their guests, was safe. It was, of course, a most unusual topic to discuss during dinner, but I accepted it in a spirit of new adventure.

"From what you have just told me," said I in the most impressive judicial manner I could assume, "you are not getting anywhere with your problem for obvious reasons. To begin with, you are dealing with the situation objectively, instead of subjectively. You've been concentrating your efforts on effects, in place of causes, stressing the outer and physical rather than the inner and mental. Consequently, you are intellectually upside-down, as well as inside-out! You are all fogged up by what you don't know. So naturally it's impossible for you to make anything work sensibly or successfully, either for the trade rats or yourself!"

I paused, but there being no response from my host, facially or vocally, continued. "You seem to have forgotten to remember in your trade rat dilemma," said I, "that consciousness is primary—that everything that appears to exist, as far as you are concerned, is a concept within yourself . . . a concept that you have knowingly or unknowingly formed and are experiencing within your own thinking, your own individual consciousness, your own range of awareness, your specific environment. It is here where you, and you alone, are constantly bettering or worsening each concept of yours, whether you choose to call it a trade rat, a human being, or something else."

I paused again. My friend's physical body was still across from me, but where he had gone to mentally, and what he was doing there, was anyone's guess.

I resumed talking. "So there you are at your own thought controls," said I, "and what do you do? You believe trade rats to be all the terrible things that you've said about them, and have been seeing your own beliefs fulfilled, or objectified. You expect trade rats to enter your home and carry away valuable things, and they accommodate you in that particular, too. So why should you squawk or be confused or baffled! You have simply been experiencing the operation of the law of expectation-and-fulfillment in action, completely overlooking the scientific fact that nothing can be corrected in your experience, whatever its nature, outside your own mentality.

For some minutes neither of us spoke. We had to catch up on our food intake. In addition, my friend seemed to be floundering about in a mental daze. Finally, he wanted to know how I had arrived at such a slant on things, especially in reference to trade rats.

"Some of it," I replied, "was acquired from human hearsay and booksay. But most of it came from regaining, at least to some extent, the mind of a learner and the heart of a child. As humbly and receptively as possible, I let everything that I met teach me, especially animals, birds, snakes, and insects, and even things growing out of the ground."

Each of those creatures, those nonhuman teachers of mine, I stressed to my friend, was an expert in knowing that "thoughts are things." They could always identify my "thought things" before I was able to express them in visible, or outer action. Every one of those four-legged, six-legged, or no-legged instructors of mine felt the impact of my thinking the instant we met. If my thoughts were flavored with genuine respect and goodwill, the equivalent would always come reechoing back from whatever it happened to be. But if there were bad elements in those "thought things" of mine, our thinking would clash, and I would usually be in for some kind of conflict and trouble.

My friend began staring ceilingward, stroking his chin as he did so, plainly indicating that he was whirling around in a mixture of interest, wonder, perplexity, and hooting questions.

Encouraged, I continued. "Trade rats," said I, "are unusually intelligent little fellows and belong to a most effective 'trade union.' Now, let's assume that a number of those unionized trade rats are coming up your mountain, and there ahead of them as they turn a bend in the road, is your beautiful home. The head trade rat, who happens to be in the area for the first time, wants to know who lives in the house. The other trade rats tell him that you do. He wants to know if you are for or against them. The other trade rats let him know that you are not only against them, but murderously so.

"All right, then, fellows," the head trade rat orders, "let's go in there when they're all asleep and pack out with everything that we can carry or drag away!"

My friend laughed for the first time that evening, and on that note the occasion ended, as he had to hurry away to keep another engagement.

Late that night, sitting in my garden, I began recalling experiences that I myself had had with trade rats in different Western homes where I was a guest. Most outstanding were experiences in which, while sitting alone in a room, as motionless as the chair I was in, I would watch a trade rat in action, without in the least interrupting his plans. Those observations became increasingly interesting as I more and more began finding out about the inner and outer behavior patterns of the trade rat . . . especially its cleanliness and neatness . . . its keen intuition . . . its sparkling vitality . . . the intelligent way in which it thinks itself about . . . its rhythmical variations in movement . . . its sense of comedy . . . and especially the manner in which it "does business" with humans, who are asleep at the time.

As the trade rat made his appearance, he would have a twig or bit of something else in his mouth that he had found out of doors. Having given me a brief inspection and so evaluating me, the little fellow would start moving about swiftly in different rooms, until he came upon some bright, appealing, but not too heavy object. Then he would "close the deal" by leaving what he had been carrying in his mouth. Next I would see him carrying or dragging the object away to wherever his hideaway happened to be. A hideaway that was also his storehouse for jewelry, knives, forks, spoons and other items with the required glint and glitter to them that he had acquired through his various "trade deals."

Some months after my publishing friend and I had had our discussion about his serious and baffling trade rat problem, we again met for dinner and talk. This time his mood was entirely different. He was like an excited and happy little boy eager to share his news. His trade rat problem had been completely solved. Then he told the facts. Returning to his mountain home following our previous meeting, he and his family, as well as the help, went into what he termed "an emergency session." This consisted of a frank analysis of the kind of thinking that each of them had been doing about the trade rats on the place. They evaluated their individual and collective thinking. They searched their thoughts concerning the law of compensation and of action-and-reaction. They concluded that one unavoidably gets back what he has sent forth in the exact measure of the sending.

At the end of their huddle the publisher, his family, and the help decided upon an experiment, new for them. They would all stop the viciously bad thinking they had been doing about the trade rats and try never again to harm them, mentally or physically. Instead, they would look for only the best in them and expect only the best from them. Thus did they establish the law of universal love in their hearts and minds and set it vibrating in the direction of the trade rats. Then, to their fascinated delight, the magic rebound happened. Echoing back from the trade rats came their invisible as well as visible best. As a result, every trade rat disappeared, and permanently so, from the publisher's lovely mountain estate. The seemingly impossible had happened! And what had brought it all about, they discovered, was simply a change in concepts.

Most of the fellow humans with whom I have discussed trade rats loathed and hated them with a carefully cultivated intensity. And not only that, they were killing or hiring killers for the trade rats that came into their experience. But in nearly all observed instances, they did not achieve the lasting success they desired. Consequently, a struggle ensued in which each side tried to outwit the other. But neither side seemed to be winning much of anything except more trouble.

Here and there, however, in different parts of the West, I came upon rare individual men and women who had found an effective but most unconventional way for solving their trade rat problems. Their framework for this was set in the conviction that all life is one, with a boundless variety of manifestations. Hence, no one can possibly get anywhere at all in the science and art of right relations until he has the law of universal love functioning in his heart. Next comes the diligent practice of this law with every living thing one meets. This enables one to establish a mutuality in understanding, in respect, and in cooperation with whatever it happens to be, even a trade rat.

That, briefly stated, was their "success secret." Those human originals, I managed to discover, were simply sending their total best across to the trade rats, and the latter were echoing back with their total best. But what those two-leggers and four-leggers were really doing, back of that uncustomary phenomenon, was silently speaking to one another in the infinite language of Life and Love. This is the one language, I was gradually coming to find out, that every living thing is innately equipped to hear, to understand and correspondingly to speak. This enables the nonhuman as well as the human to cooperate in the removal of limitations, and thereby each assumes more realistically his part in the symphony of universal responsiveness.

CHAPTER TWENTY

SEAGULLS

Seagulls are experts in living the rhythm and harmony and loveliness of the Infinite in motion. I like their aerial qualities and the graceful manner in which they blend those qualities with enthusiasm, joy, and fun. And I particularly respect them for their skills of navigation in the air, regardless of whether they happen to be in headwinds, tailwinds, side-winds, or no wind at all. I like going to one of the beaches in Southern California, either early in the morning or late in the afternoon, when seagulls are at their best. I let them teach me things that are important to know about the science and art of rising above the earth levels into higher, broader, and more satisfying awareness.

For quite a period of time on various oceans of the world, as well as along the coastlines of different countries, I had been taking special postgraduate courses in the higher education, under the tutelage of seagulls. Not once, in all that time, can I recall a dull or unprofitable occasion. What those winged instructors taught me, through the persuasive eloquence of their silent, fine examples, was always an enriching blend of entertainment and education . . . of fun and wisdom . . . and of surprise and delight. And this was so regardless of whether I was being taught by a single seagull on the beach or flocks of them in the air.

Whenever a seagull was in sight (and it made no difference what it was doing or not doing), school was in session and I was being taught, and well taught, too—if I happened to be inwardly, as well as outwardly, ready for the experience. So, you see, it was up to me whether anything of real value happened between us. All that my seagull tutor had to do at our "class time" was just be his own delightful and unpredictable self. My part, as student, was always to become totally still, like something the tide had washed in. I learned to watch outwardly, and listen inwardly, with all of me wide open.

My social and educational experiences with seagulls began on a beach at Newport, Rhode Island, where I was a small boy with a salt wave ever splashing in my face and the throb of the ocean ever in my heart. At one end of the beach, on a point of land jutting out into the Atlantic Ocean, was a farm where my family and I spend the summers. Motivated by a friendly curiosity, plus a love for adventure, I spent most of my time discovering for myself the meaning and purpose back of everything that I looked at, and how to react to it. The beach was the setting of favorite adventures. There, under the promptings of my mother, I was encouraged to go exploring wherever I desired. Then I returned and shared with her what I had discovered. My mother was unusually liberal in this regard, making only one condition—that I would always return to report to her what I had experienced. Here were the seeds sown for my career as reporter. Surely, a mother is not only the strongest of educators, but can be a strong influence in determining one's career.

It was during those youthful adventures that I came to know seagulls as much-admired relatives. I remember distinctly standing on the beach at low tide one time, eating a large homemade doughnut. I was busy puzzling out what made ocean breakers. Suddenly a seagull landed nearby and gave me, or rather the doughnut, his interested attention. I offered him a piece of it. He walked closer and accepted it with gulping delight. Then, in mutual satisfaction, we finished eating the remainder of the doughnut together. When the seagull eventually flew away, it carried along with it a number of my affectionate pats on its head.

What makes seagulls so fascinating is their lovely appearance, their rhythmical movements on land, at sea, and in the air, and the valuable lessons they silently teach wherever they happen to be. With my Rhode Island background and flavoring, I also admire them for their independence—for the manner in which they do what they please, when they please, and just as it pleases them to do so. In comparison, the humans and the various animals that I knew on the farm seem dull and limited. They couldn't, for instance, if they felt in the mood to do so, suddenly quit what they were doing, like seagulls, dart joyfully skyward, and have all sorts of exciting and satisfying fun together.

One of my long-standing regrets is that I have not been able to demonstrate a way whereby I could spread something equivalent to wings, and then accompany seagulls in their flights. The neat manner in which they take off from the ground, their enchanting movements in flight, and their gentle landings afterward, always fill me with a mixture of admiration and envy. But while my physical body must remain on the land during those flight occasions, I can always go along with the seagulls in my imagination. And whenever I do so, with sufficient alertness and receptivity, it never fails to be a bettering and expanding experience.

The most effective way to be taught by seagulls, I came to find, was first to relax my physical body on the beach, then pretend I was a junior gull that needed plenty of instructing. This would get me above the foggy and swirling levels of the intellect, with its varieties of carbon-copy undemonstrable opinions having to do with how everyone else should think and act. In this way it would become possible mentally to companion with the seagulls in the harmony and rhythm of the universal heartbeat. It would also give me a clearer understanding of the kinship of all life, wherein all life is inseparably one.

During my educational experiences under the tutelage of seagulls I would often be reminded of a fascinating and illuminating story about the great Italian painter, sculptor, architect, and engineer—Leonardo da Vinci. According to the story, Leonardo frequently went into the Tuscan fields, carrying a cage filled with birds. Reaching the best place for observation purposes, he would set the birds free. Then with his extraordinary vision, and equally extraordinary receptivity, he would carefully study what each bird did in its glad upward winging. At the close of the day Leonardo would start home to resume work on his famous drawings and designs with the words, "They shall have wings!"

It is a well-known fact that this many-sided genius, perhaps the first modern man, spent many hours on top of Tuscan hills to study the flight of birds. He was probably the first man to analyze the dynamics of flight, or aerodynamics. All that Leonardo needed to perfect the first airplane was motor power. One wonders how much of Leonardo's greatness rests with his powers of observation, with his patient study and keen ability of the laws of nature, as paraded before our eyes daily in such humble creatures as seagulls and birds of every kind.

Seagulls, like sailors, cannot possibly be made in calm weather. Both require lots of experience in all kinds of weather, especially the turbulent kind. This gives both seagulls and sailors the salty flavoring they need. It also helps perfect the skills they require in having to meet their common challenge of shifting winds. The tougher and rougher the weather becomes, the more do the seagulls like getting up into it. This provides them with exciting fun-filled opportunities for practicing what they know about ocean and air navigation.

Whether in "airs from heaven, or blasts from hell," as Shakespeare phrased it, seagulls in flight are always superlative objects to watch, study, and then carefully ponder. And this is particularly so when those "blasts from hell" keep all shipping in the harbors, most humans under some kind of shelter, but lure the seagulls into it for sharing adventure and fun. Then as the observer continues to watch the thrilling phenomena, he becomes filled with bafflling wonderment as to how it is possible for seagulls to do amazing precision flying under such conditions.

Another fact about seagulls that has long fascinated me is that throughout the years that I have been watching them in flight, in various parts of the world, I have never witnessed a collision between them—not even in their most sensational stunt flying in gales of wind. Nor have I ever seen a seagull even accidentally brush the wingtip of another seagull in their fast, close-together, and in-and-out flying. There is always precision accuracy in thinking, in timing, in navigating, and in speed management. This gave me much to ponder seriously, especially when I compared it with the shocking and almost incredible accident and death rate among humans as they attempt to steer themselves about in automobiles, airplanes, and boats.

As I became more receptive to the values that those seagulls were silently sharing with me, I began to discover why they were all such superlative experts in navigation. They had never been taught, nor had they read any "how-to-do-it" books. The mystery of it all was as elemental and simple as it was profound.

Not a single seagull ever operates with a private and independent mind of its own. Each is moving in harmony and rhythm with the one infinite Intelligence, with the all-embracing cosmic Cause. Each is a fluid inlet-and-outlet for all-pervading divine Consciousness. Not one of them needs any other instructing, guidance, or help in its spectacular feats of aerial flight.

CHAPTER TWENTY-ONE

THE LOVE COMPASS

Early one evening as I stopped at the home of a friend to leave a book, I walked into a fascinating adventure. My friend is a professional authority and consultant on human behavior patterns. As I handed him the book, he asked me to come in and join some of his professional friends who were having "an emergency discussion on a critical public situation." My entrance and introduction briefly interrupted a highly animated debate on the shockingly bad and worsening trends in what people were thinking and doing. As I sat down in the only remaining chair in the room, the debate was resumed again with no one pulling any punches either mentally or vocally.

Because of the involved professional terms that were being used, the rapidity with which words were being flung back and forth, and the frequent interruptions in the middle of sentences, it became extremely difficult for me to keep up with them. As time went ticking along, the verbiage became heavier and heavier. So did the general atmosphere. And so did I. It finally reached such a density that I began trying to think of some tactful way by means of which I could get out into the night air again.

Just then an abrupt silence broke out in the room while most of those present lighted some form of tobacco for inhaling purposes. The man sitting to my right, and not at all in tune with the gravity of the occasion, asked the others if they had heard about the cat that a few days before had walked its way from San Francisco back to its former home in the Los Angeles area. What that started will always be a much-cherished memory.

The cat home-coming episode had been stirring up unusual public interest at the time. A woman living in the Los Angeles area who had a number of cats, gave one of them to a visiting woman friend. The latter took the cat with her to her home in San Francisco. Not at all approving of the new arrangement, and with typical catlike independence and initiative, the little four-legger slipped out of the San Francisco house and footed its way back to its former home in Los Angeles.

The conversation in the room had suddenly switched from what had to be done professionally to improve current human misbehavior, to the land-navigating accomplishment of a cat possessed with an amazing homing instinct. I couldn't resist becoming a part of the discussion, as they were now focusing their attention on one of my favorite subjects. By way of qualifying myself, I told them that for a number of years I had been a member of the Board of Animal Regulation for the city of Los Angeles. I had long been much interested in the remarkable manner in which cats, dogs, and other animals make long-distant land journeyings under their own navigation.

Most of the land-navigating animals that I managed to obtain records of had been left far beyond the boundaries of

California. Their owners had moved permanently to Southern California. Weeks or months later their left-behind pets had joined them—on their own. These animals had successfully navigated themselves across those many miles of unfamiliar territory. With unfailing instinct they had found where their former human associates were living—in a city, on a mountain, in the desert, or somewhere along the Pacific coastline.

One of the most astonishing illustrations of four-legged land navigating had to do with a lovely, intelligent, and unusually affectionate sheepdog named Sally that lived with an elderly couple on a farm in Southern Arkansas. Sally liked mothering everything, even humans. She mothered all who would permit her to do so. She and the elderly couple were almost inseparable. Then, in order to take an extended rest from their strenuous farm life, the man and his wife decided to go to a small health retreat hidden away in the mountains of Southern California and far off all the main highways. Regretfully, Sally had to be left behind on the farm.

Early one morning, three months later, as the couple were sunning themselves on the front porch of their cottage, a gaunt dog came slowly limping down the trail toward them. Its sides were torn. Its feet were bleeding. It was swaying with exhaustion. But its tail was gently wagging. The couple stared in breathless, incredible amazement. It was Sally. Their devoted Sally! She had footed herself all the way from the farm in Southern Arkansas to the hidden-away retreat in the mountains of Southern California. Sally had accomplished her mission—that of finding her much-loved "Paw" and "Maw" so that she could resume taking care of them again.

While the story about Sally fascinated those professional diagnosticians of the human scene, it left them in a bewildered daze, intellectually speaking. They just couldn't figure the thing out. In the midst of their individual and collective mental whirlings I asked them how they thought, as professional observers, it was possible for Sally to navigate herself so successfully across all those many hundreds of miles of country, and then, with unerring precision, find that hidden health retreat in the Southern California mountains. I pointed out that she didn't require roadmaps or a compass, nor did she stop at gas stations along the way to ask the right directions.

There was a sanctuary-like silence in the room for some moments. Then one of them spoke, doing so with all the solemnity of a supreme court justice that was handing down a final and irrevocable decision. Said he: "It's an instinct that certain lower forms of life seem to have and apparently know how to use upon occasions like this one." When I asked him just what he meant by the term "instinct," he looked surprised. Then he began talking in professional generalities and disappeared, so to speak, in an intellectual fog.

As a sudden change in strategy, and for whatever fun and findings might come out of it, I asked how many of them rode horses. Almost everyone present did. Then I inquired how many of them had ever been lost while riding their horses in unfamiliar territory. They had all been through that experience many times. "What do you do in situations like that?" I then tossed across to them. "Loosen the reins!" said a few. "Give the horse its head!" said the others. "What happens then?" I asked as naïvely and innocently as possible. They answered like a rehearsed chorus: "Why, then, the horse takes you home!"

Unsuspectedly, they had walked into my invisible trap. Having them in there, and in a spirit of inner fun but outer seriousness, I let this one go in their direction. "Gentlemen," said I, "and remember please, I am asking you as professional observers and diagnosticians, how is it that you with your 'superior brains' are unable to find your way home when lost on your horse, while your horse with its 'inferior brain' is able to take you safely home every time?"

The astonished and bewildered expressions on their faces was fascinating to watch. They had been toppled off their self-elevated ego perches and didn't quite know how to react. Perhaps it was a realistic reminder to all those savants present that only as one descends with all of himself can he really ascend to that altitude of being where he begins experiencing the universal wisdom wherewith life equips all its manifestations in the name of survival.

It was as though a fresh, salty seabreeze had blown through the room, sweeping away self-centeredness and professional struttings. The old combat urge, to top everyone else in vocalized opinions, was audibly deflated. A more invigorating and satisfying atmosphere prevailed. As a result, everyone present suddenly became "as a little child," and, as such, began experiencing the fun, the joy, and the superlative adventure of exploring the unfamiliar togetherness.

As the evening went rolling along, my host and his professional associates began recalling truly remarkable things that they had watched various kinds of animals do. But now, with a more childlike and intuitive approach, they had come into possession of three important but forgotten facts. The first: that they had been thinking of animals as dumb, inferior, and relatively unimportant formations, and that, consequently, they had been experiencing the results of that kind of negative thinking. The second: that all life is far greater than any of the forms that it appears to assume. And the third: that every living thing reflects an intelligence that the human intellect cannot index nor adequately explain.

And yet, certain reasonable propositions do present themselves and certain conclusions might be drawn.

What is the force that draws the lost or abandoned animal? It feels an impelling attraction to seek again the company whose dominant atmosphere is love, protection, companionship. Love, then, is the supreme attractive force. The humans who possess this capacity to love their pets must have within them a sort of love-magnet, a particular magnetic pole of affection. This may act unconsciously, like a sender of love radiations. The animal, in turn, eager to pick up these love-radiations, may have a built-in receiver set, as part of its reactive mind, that can be tuned in, directionally, to the source of the radiation.

Here, then, we have a magnetic pole and a compass as a minimal directional steering unit.

Another proposition is that there exist wave bands for transmitting primitive survival emotions, wave bands between the light waves utilized for physical vision and the air waves utilized in the transmission of the electromagnetic impulses translated back and forth to create televisional images on the television screen of the home receiving set.

Perhaps, again, the love-hungry animal is equipped with instinctual, reactive, prosurvival radarlike scanning devices that can pick up the direction from which the strongest love impulses are flowing toward it.

Hate being the direct opposite of love, a destructive and antisurvival force, it stands to reason that the animal radar system works also as an effective warning system. These prosurvival radar and communications systems, wherewith nature equips even her lowliest creatures, may range from telekinetic warnings picked up by miniature seismographs of extreme sensitivity that record the slightest tremors of the ground struck by enemy feet. These warning systems and media of communication are, no doubt, tied into certain sections of the animal's nervous system and may be related to electromagnetic fields.

Some of these built-in devices may scan disturbances in the ether, just above ordinary sound waves, and a possible rarefaction and extension of the sound waves. As Hamlet stated: "But this is wondrous strange! There are more things in heaven and earth, Horatio, Than are dreamt of in your philosophy."

It may well be that our media-conscious age and its most advanced communication scientists, biologists, and neurologists, together with the fascinated explorers of the lush fields of extrasensory perception, have before them fertile territories for scientific investigation. Positive findings in these critical areas may turn out to be most helpful in the planetary survival task for engineering the impending breakthrough from a materially scientific to a spiritually scientific basis of operations. Otherwise, the age seems headed toward the ultimate destructiveness of worldwide atomic fission.

It was almost dawn when our adventure came to an end. As it did so, we were all sharing a common conviction—the great importance of "becoming as a little child." For then and then only does "the miracle" happen, and everything becomes "an open window" through which one may see and experience the Infinite One.

CHAPTER TWENTY-TWO

GOPHER CORRESPONDENCE

For those who don't know much about them, let it be briefly stated: a gopher is about nine inches long, broadheaded, and mostly brown-furred. Generally classified, he is a homely rodent, plus a lot of other uncomplimentary things that humans have long been hanging on them. But in spite of this low rating, he is an exceptionally wise and impressive little fellow. Life for the gopher has never been a bed of roses. Almost everywhere that he goes, humans are eager to trap, poison, or otherwise destroy him. And if some human doesn't end the gopher's career, then any hawk, coyote, snake, or fox that happens to be in the neighborhood will happily do so for eating purposes. So the gopher, of necessity, has to operate with unusual ability and agility.

With his powerful foreclaws, developed for underground tunneling, his sharp incisory teeth, and the manner in which he knows how to use them, the gopher is fascinating to watch in action. At least if one is not the owner of the garden or orchard in which the little fellow is expertly at work snapping off flowers, vegetables, young trees, and other growing things. Then, unless one's feelings are under unusual control, a person is apt to explode into undiluted savagery—for when it comes to wrecking gardens and orchards, the gopher is in a class all by himself.

How best to solve gopher problems effectively and permanently has long been both a headache and a challenge for countless numbers of people. The methods used for "getting rid of the nuisances" has included just about every known kind of killing process. But usually, after the killings, other gophers sooner or later move in to take the places of those destroyed. And so it has gone on and on, with neither side ever seeming to win a lasting victory.

It is rarely recognized that individual human thinking always plays an important part in human-gopher contacts. Three memorable episodes proved this to me.

The first had to do with a wealthy and prominent woman in Southern California who for many years has bristled with the firm conviction that what she thinks and says about anything is the final word on the subject, and that anyone who disagrees with her is definitely deficient in good breeding and intelligence.

While she was strolling through the formal garden of her large house one afternoon, the woman discovered a gopher at work on one of her rare plantings. Furiously angry, she began throwing everything that she could get her hands on at the little fellow. The latter ducked each flung object with perfect timing and rhythmical ease, then disappeared down a nearby hole which shortly before he had come out of. Hurrying to her greenhouse, the woman returned with a can of "guaranteed instant death poison" for all kinds of rodents. This she dumped down the gopher hole with all the muderous hatred that she could send along with it.

Early the next morning the woman hurried out into her

garden to learn the effects of her poisoning efforts. Putting on her elaborately designed gold-rimmed glasses, she lowered her face as close to the gopher hole as possible for an intimate look-see. Almost instantly there was a horrified scream and the woman fell over on her side, her face covered with blood. The gopher had bitten her in the nose with his long, sharp incisory teeth. The bite was so serious that she had to be rushed to an emergency hospital. As the ambulance took her away, the gopher calmly emerged from his hole and resumed work on the rare plantings in the garden.

Through some special detective work on my part, I managed to unravel the invisible facts. Being a wise little fellow, the gopher had refused to have anything to do with the poison that had been dumped down the hole. Early the next morning he intuitively heard an important fact—that his would-be killer was physically moving toward his hole. As part of his strategy in the conflict of interests, the gopher alerted himself for action just inside the entrance to the hole. Then, when the woman's face came close enough in her hoping-for-the-worst inspection, he let her have it! And how!

The second episode had to do with another prominent woman whose beautiful home has a large flower garden on one side and a particularly fine vegetable garden on the other. While she was inspecting the latter one morning, she found that a gopher had not only dug its future home under a trellis of special cucumber vines, but had done considerable damage to the vines. Instead of going into some form of outer destruction against her uninvited guest, she went into inner action. This she did by first becoming as calm and introspective as possible. Then she checked on the extent she had been living up to her cosmic obligation of always trying to identify the greatest wisdom and good in every living thing, even in a vine-wrecking gopher.

The reason for this was the woman's conviction that her

gopher problem had to be solved inwardly rather than outwardly, because the entire phenomenon was taking place
inside her own thinking and nowhere else. It was happening
exclusively within the boundaries of her own state of consciousness. Consequently, all phases of the situation had to be
worked out subjectively, owing to the fact that the objective,
whatever its seeming appearance and actions, is always
within the subjective and is always composed of the individual observer's own thoughts.

As the woman, with alerted intuitive listening and hearing,
continued with her subjective exploring, a fact with tremen-
dous meaning and scope began gently unfolding in her
awareness. Briefly stated, it was this: she, the gopher, the
cucumber vines, and everything else that she could identify
were innately all of the same eternal substance, all reflections
of the same infinite Source of life, all expressions of the same
infinite Mind, the same all-including Intelligence. They were
therefore all important and needed factors in the perfect
operation of the divine Plan and Purpose.

Then it dawned upon the woman that the particular gopher ruining her cucumber vines was not the real cause for
her disturbing situation. The fault was entirely her own. She
had been doing bad thinking about gophers, particularly
with plans of what she expected to do to gophers if any of
them ever got into her gardens. She had, in the conventional
human manner, been flinging detrimental thought-things at
all gophers whenever they came to mind, and the thought-
things, as they have a way of doing, had come boomeranging
back again in her vegetable garden.

At this point, the golden rule was solidly set at the entrance
to the woman's thinking, feeling, and outer actions—especially in reference to gophers in general and the one in her
vegetable garden in particular. She was now aware, as never

before, that her gopher problem was entirely a mental picture of her own—a mental picture that she had formulated in her withinness and was projecting into her withoutness. She saw that as she bettered her own mind picture of the gopher in the garden, the so-called outer results had to correspond, as they were aspects of one and the same thing.

There followed a balance of understanding and cooperation between them, although neither could see the other at the time. It was a harmonizing of invisible as well as visible action between those two seemingly unrelatable forms of life. It was a perfect illustration, too, of the ancient truism that when one's heartbeat is in tune and in time with the universal heartbeat, everything that he meets will want to cooperate with him and be his friend. The proof of this was that the gopher stopped destroying the cucumber vines, gave up his newly dug home under them, and then moved off the place. Gophers never again came into her gardens.

The third of these episodes has to do with the owner of a large estate whose special hobby is raising rare plants, flowers, and trees for exhibition purposes. He, too, had a gopher problem—one that had long been causing him trouble, anguish, and emotional explosions. In his efforts to get rid of "the damaging nuisances," he had applied all sorts of destructive methods with enthusiasm and high expectancy, only to find that after each of the killings, other gophers had arrived to resume wrecking the various kinds of valuable growing things in his gardens.

Then one day this perturbed estate owner happened to read a book that I had written called *Kinship with All Life*, in which, among other things, I told how a large army of ants had invaded my house during a weekend that I was out of town. And how, as an experiment in the unusual, I had mentally broadcast an appeal to the ants, as "a gentleman to gentlemen," for their consideration and help in the situation. Then how, as a result of the appeal, every ant had gone marching out of my house. Unforgettably, this illustrated how effective such qualities as intelligence, respect, and understanding can really function, even between such living items as a human and an army of ants that had invaded his house.

My experience with the ants left that estate owner dazed but fascinated. What particularly intrigued him was that as a result of my seemingly silly action, all the ants had left my house, and permanently so. Then, in a spirit of childlike adventure, but in the strictest secrecy, he decided to see if he could work out a "gentlemen's agreement" with the gophers on his estate. So he sat down at his desk and wrote a letter to them, patterned after the appeal that I had made to the ants in my house. Late that night, after the members of his family had gone to bed, and in a continuing childlike spirit of adventure, curiosity, and faith, he sneaked out of his house and pushed the letter down the nearest gopher hole.

The following morning this experimenter in the seemingly outlandish went searching all over his estate to see what if any reactions there had been to his letter to the gophers. To his fascinated amazement, he couldn't find a fresh gopher track anywhere. The investigation continued daily for a number of weeks, but not the least evidence of gophers could he find, either above or below ground. Then he was convinced that the gophers had realistically understood his "gentlemen's appeal" to them and had reacted accordingly, like the "little gentlemen" they really were.

CHAPTER TWENTY-THREE

L'ENVOI

*It is the man who is the missionary. It is not his words. His character
is his message. In the heart of Africa, among the great Lakes, I have
come upon black men and women who remembered the only white
man they ever saw before—David Livingstone; and as you cross his
footsteps in that dark continent, men's faces light up as they speak
of the kind doctor who passed there years ago. They could not understand him; but they could feel the love that beat in his heart.*

—Henry Drummond, *The Greatest Thing in the World*

The most skilled experts in the science and art of right relations that I was privileged to watch in action were basically
using the same method that David Livingstone did in his
famous journey across Africa. The love that beat in their
hearts was as pure and fine in its essences as it was in its
all-including emanations. When one has the right heartbeat
—when the right motives and purposes are ticking deep
within him—then everything that he meets, feeling the
genuineness and worth of those emanations, will react accordingly and want to be his friend.

Many of those delightful human authentics that I came to know were experiencing comradeship and sharing and happifying adventure with "dangerous and deadly" forms of wild life that most people would have agreed should have been instantly killed, or locked up inside of a safe cage. But none of them were using any of the conventional outer techniques for "animal handling." On the contrary, they were all acting in a simple, natural way, much after the manner of unspoiled, and so unpatternized children.

Each of these rare humans was getting maximum satisfaction out of his everyday living by being genuinely interested in every living thing that he met, and always genuinely loving whatever it happened to be, but without ever being a trader in love. They would aim their total best at whatever happened to be holding their attention and interest. Echoing back from the latter would always come its total best in harmonious living tones and chords. That was the "magic secret." Through those totally expressed and sharing love actions, each of those "tame humans" and "wild nonhumans" would interblend themselves into a twosome. Then they started helping each other, to find more of the perfect beyond the imperfect . . . more of the absolute beyond the relative . . . and more of the infinite beyond the finite.

What each of those simple, modest, and highly accomplished virtuosos in the science and art of right relations seemed instinctively to know, and had never been educated away from, was that "we are all made of the same stuff eternity is made of," as Shakespeare so aptly phrased it. And with that awareness, each of them, as best he could, was constantly looking for "that stuff"—divinity, in every living thing that he met. Then identifying a measure of the eternal grandeur, in whatever it happened to be, each of them would first mentally bow his admiration and respect, then diligently try to blend his indwelling divinity with theirs, for their mutual fun, happiness, good, and expansion.

This would enable those seemingly unrelatable humans and nonhumans to know each other in their unseen as well as seen individualities—that is, in their totalities. Then as pals and partners in a common enterprise, they would let the cosmic power and influence of Love flow through every least thing that they thought or otherwise did. Thus would they establish perfect mutualities, with their particular animal, snake, or human associate, in understanding . . . in respect . . . in individualized expression . . . and in sharing accomplishment. And so with their heartbeats echoing back and forth in this manner would each of those human-nonhuman twosomes not only find themselves in total harmony and rhythm with each other, but also in rhythm with the universal heartbeat that ever pervades as well as sustains the kinship and oneness of all life—wherein all is well, always.